A Life of
William Inge

A LIFE OF WILLIAM INGE

The Strains of Triumph

RALPH F. VOSS

UNIVERSITY PRESS OF KANSAS

© 1989 by the University Press of Kansas

Published by the University Press of Kansas (Lawrence, Kansas
66045), which was organized by the Kansas Board of Regents and is
operated and funded by Emporia State University, Fort Hays State
University, Kansas State University, Pittsburg State University,
the University of Kansas, and Wichita State University

Library of Congress Cataloging-in-Publication Data

Voss, Ralph F.
  A life of William Inge.
  Bibliography: p.
  Includes index.
  1. Inge, William—Biography. 2. Dramatists, American
—20th century—Biography. I. Title.
PS3517.N265Z95   1989   812'.54 [B]   88-33902
ISBN 0-7006-0384-0 (alk. paper)

British Library Cataloguing in Publication Data is available.

Printed in the United States of America
10 9 8 7 6 5 4 3 2 1

The paper used in this publication meets the
minimum requirements of the American National
Standard for Permanence of Paper for Printed
Library Materials Z39.48-1984.

To

CARL W. CHRISTENSEN

1942–1983

If we are lucky in life, we meet a few people—very few—who become such good friends that without meaning to, they truly help to shape and influence the quality of our own lives. Carl was such a friend.

Success is counted sweetest
By those who ne'er succeed.
To comprehend a nectar
Requires sorest need.

Not one of all the purple Host
Who took the Flag today
Can tell the definition
So clear of Victory

As he defeated—dying—
On whose forbidden ear
The distant strains of triumph
Burst agonized and clear!

—*Emily Dickinson*

OLD MAN (*His back to the audience,*
  speaking to himself and anyone
  who cares to listen): I look
  forward to the games all year long.
  Last October I bought my season
  ticket to the Student Activity
  Program and have attended all the
  events during the year. I
  happened upon this little knoll a
  few years ago when I was out on
  one of my walks, and I saw what a
  splendid view it offers of the
  stadium, so I've been coming here,
  where I enjoy being a solitary
  spectator. You see, I'm rather a
  childish old man, and I get so
  excited watching the games that
  I'm embarrassed for others to see
  me, particularly my students, who
  surely would think I had taken
  leave of my senses if they saw me
  jumping up and down and pounding
  the air with my fists. (*He gives*
  a little chuckle) So I gave my
  ticket to the cleaning woman. And
  it pleased me to do that, for I
  can't afford to pay her much and
  she loves the games, too. *Everyone*
  loves the games. Although not
  everyone cares to contend in them.
  I never did care to. I was studious
  even as a child. And I was frail.

I was always getting a nosebleed. So
I made myself content to watch and
not participate. I suppose all people
are divided into two groups, those
who participate and those who watch
and observe. Sometimes, in my more
melancholy moments, I wonder if I have
lived life at all, if my life has not
been, rather, a period of observation
on earth, watching others live,
studying the way they live and
commenting on their success or failure
in the process. Being very moved by
them at times, but still detached so
that my envy of their success is
fleeting, and my sadness at their
failure passes when I sit down at a
good meal or take a glass of sherry.
Once I was in love, and it terrified
me. She was so beautiful, so tender,
so fine that I trembled in her mere
proximity. The reality of her seemed
too much for me to bear, and I fled.
I could not accept the responsibility
of loving her. (*He sighs*) Alas!
Sometimes I am very lonely, of course.
I go to bed, some nights, despondent,
but I always awake feeling free. But
I must admit, I always hurry to my
office to become involved in my
research as quickly as possible, for if
I remain idle very long, I sometimes
become very depressed.
(*A rousing cheer comes from the stadium*)

—Professor Benoit, in
The Strains of Triumph

Contents

Preface

In May, 1955, just as I was finishing the sixth grade in Lyons, Kansas, there was a good deal of local excitement because movie stars William Holden, Kim Novak, and Rosalind Russell were in the area, making the movie *Picnic*. Scenes were being shot at places I knew: the beach at Sterling Lake, the big grain elevators at Hutchinson, even a small white frame house by Kansas Highway 96 in Nickerson. I had not heard of William Inge then, but I was as avid a moviegoer as my parents would allow, and the proximity of such excitement was thrilling. About a year later, the much-awaited film came to the Star Theater on the west side of the courthouse square, and for a few days, manager John Neely enjoyed a packed house for each showing, a phenomenon quite rare in those days when television was beginning to close movie theaters in Kansas villages. I saw *Picnic* twice, and I left the theater humming "Moonglow" both times. The song could be heard daily on the radio; like the film, it was a hit. Still, I had not heard of William Inge—and I was not one in those days to read film credits.

A few years later, a senior in high school, I was in my dad's car, parked at the Sky-Vue Drive-In Theater in Plainville, Kansas. I happened to notice that the screenplay for the film I was about to see, *Splendor in the Grass*, was by William Inge. Then, in the opening scene, the location and the time—southeastern Kansas, 1929—appeared briefly on the screen. Here was something unexpected: a movie set in Kansas. *Splendor in the Grass* even *looked* as if it had been filmed in Kansas. I liked the film, and I was surprised to learn, a short while later, that William Inge was best known as a playwright and that he had written *Picnic*. More than that: he was *from* Kansas. He had also written *Come Back, Little Sheba* (I remembered seeing Shirley Booth in the preview for the film version—and that she had won an Academy

Award) and *Bus Stop* (I had seen Marilyn Monroe and Don Murray in the film at the Fox Theater in Lyons). He had also written *The Dark at the Top of the Stairs* (I had seen the film version at the Moore Theater in Plainville, and I was proud to tell friends that one of its stars, Shirley Knight, was from Lyons, where I had once lived). Like most Americans who have ever heard of William Inge, I learned that he was a playwright after I had seen the film versions of his popular plays. I was proud to know he was a Kansan.

A few years later still, in graduate school, I made my first decision to write about William Inge and his work. That was in 1967, and over the next twenty years, I found myself studying and writing about him many times. As must surely be evident, I still like his work, and I am still proud that William Inge was a Kansan. But that does not mean that the value of his life's work is purely a matter of regional pride: William Inge would have been a significant writer regardless of geography. That he was a midwesterner, a Kansan, gives his best-known work a certain character, a fidelity of detail, that contributes to but does not wholly constitute its significance.

In writing this biographical study, I have tried to create a plausible reconstruction of Inge's life, based primarily upon his writing itself (both published and unpublished) and bolstered by such other sources as interviews, articles, clippings, letters, memoirs, and so on, as have been available. I do not claim that the account that follows is always the absolute, documentable truth: John Connolly, Inge's secretary and friend for many years, told me that Inge was "the most private person in the world," and after many years of study, I have no reason to doubt Connolly. I do not wish to imply that in my research I have left no stone unturned, followed every suggestion, and double-checked every piece of information in two or more unrelated sources, because I have not. But over time, a definite pattern of Inge's life emerged, and it is that pattern that I convey here.

As John Connolly and several others have suggested, a part of the pattern of Inge's life is secrecy. Regarding his homosexuality, Inge was particularly quiet among his associates. Many who came to know details about this part of Inge's life also chose, like him, to remain quiet about it. They took their knowledge to their own graves, or they maintained selective silence when being interviewed. Most people who knew Inge considered him decent and gentle and shy, and several of them obviously thought he should be allowed to keep most of his embarrassments secret. It was an attitude I found easy to respect, for I believe the essential story of William Inge's life can be productively and honestly told primarily from his own writing, and told with a high degree of accuracy. Thus, while I do not claim that what follows is *the* life of William Inge, I am confident that as *a* life of William Inge, it is highly truthful.

Upon finishing a work such as this, I hardly know where to begin acknowledging the encouragement and assistance of so many people, institutions, and programs that helped to make it possible. My debts are many, and my gratitude is great. I can only begin and hope, in my stumbling way, to do some justice in return for all the help I have been so privileged to enjoy.

First of all, I wish gratefully to acknowledge a summer stipend from the National Endowment for the Humanities (FT-23261–83) and a travel grant from the University of Alabama Research Grants Committee (Project 1183-Voss), which together enabled me to travel to the William Inge Collection at Independence Community College in Independence, Kansas, and to stay there long enough to examine its contents thoroughly. Without these, I never would have been able to give the Inge Collection the necessary prolonged study that it deserves and that a work of this sort demands.

Special mention must be made here regarding the facilities, holdings, and staffs of several libraries and special collections of materials. This book simply could never have been done were it not for the Inge Collection; the Kansas Collection at the Kenneth Spencer Research Library at the University of Kansas in Lawrence, Kansas; the Harry Ransom Humanities Research Center at the University of Texas in Austin, Texas; the Billy Rose Theatre Collection at the New York City Public Library at Lincoln Center; and the Amelia Gayle Gorgas Library at the University of Alabama in Tuscaloosa, Alabama. I found all with whom I worked at these facilities highly competent, cooperative, and friendly. I name but a few here, and thus I must apologize to many whose names escaped the distracted mind of a visiting scholar. At the Inge Collection: Del Singleton, director; Melissa Ruberson; and Yvonne Martinez. Special thanks go to William ("Bill") Pfannenstiel and Karen Van Kirk, who were responsible for cataloging the Inge Collection and thus often saved me precious time. I am also grateful to the Inge Collection and the officials of Independence Community College (I.C.C.) for granting me permission to use most of the photographs in this book. At the Kansas Collection, I wish to thank Sheryl K. Williams, Jean S. Skipp, and the staff; at the Harry Ransom Humanities Research Center, director Decherd Turner, Cathy Henderson, and the staff; at the Billy Rose Collection, Dorothy L.

Swerdlove and the staff; at the Gorgas Library, William ("Will") Henderson, head of the Reference Department.

All members of the administration, faculty, and staff of Independence Community College have my lasting gratitude for their support, their help, and their hospitality over the last few years. To name all of them would be impossible, but specific mention must be made of two: Margaret Goheen, a former chair of the Drama Department at I.C.C. and the ongoing codirector of the Annual William Inge Festival and Conference; and her codirector, Jo Ann C. ("Jody") McDowell, president of I.C.C. Margaret and Jody have tirelessly, imaginatively, and meticulously organized each annual event, and their efforts continue to make it a truly extraordinary celebration of which William Inge could not help but be proud. It was at Inge Festivals that I was privileged to meet and talk with such playwrights as Robert Anderson, William Gibson, and Jerome Lawrence, all of whom were friends of Inge's at key times during his life. These gatherings have also brought to Independence such performers as Barbara Baxley, Eileen Heckart, Shirley Knight, and Martha Scott—all of whom knew Inge and appeared in versions of his work. At Inge Festivals, I have also enjoyed conversations with members of the Inge family and of the community and have shared perceptions with other scholars with whom I have presented papers in the conference portion of the festival. I and many others shall always be grateful to Margaret Goheen and Jo Ann C. McDowell who, with the cooperation of their I.C.C. colleagues and community members, have built the annual festival from top to bottom, from pursuing funding to finding rides for participants.

Others, formerly of I.C.C., must also be acknowledged. My thanks go to Tom Snyder, one of the initiators of the Inge Collection; and to Paul Fry, who first showed me Michael Wood's remarkable slide-and-sound show, *William Inge: From Penn Avenue to Broadway*, one hot August afternoon when school was not in session. Both Michael Wood and Independence attorney Tim Emert have been major contributors to this book, for their long hours of taped interviews with numerous individuals who knew Inge were already awaiting my eager ears when I arrived at the Inge Collection. Wood, now associate director for media production at Wichita State University, conducted his interviews to use for *Penn Avenue to Broadway*. Emert conducted his to use as part of the events surrounding the dedication of the Inge Theater and the later opening of the Inge Collection. Michael and Tim also gave freely of their time and knowledge on many additional occasions as I worked on this book.

Helene Inge Connell deserves mention here because she gave me full cooperation and support until 1982, when she entered into an exclusive arrangement to assist an authorized biographer. After that, she continued to be helpful and supportive in ways that she could. To my knowledge, Helene's commitment has resulted in my not being able to see only one important source, a diary Inge kept for a time during his California years. However, individuals who have seen the diary and who have also read the relevant sections of this book tell me that seeing the diary would have made no essential difference in what I say here. Although I found all members of the Inge family whom I had occasion to speak with both friendly and courteous, I especially wish to thank the playwright's nephew Luther C. Inge for his interest and his cooperation about details.

Special thanks also go to Bridget Aschenberg of International Creative Management, Inc., the agency for William Inge's professional estate, for granting permission to quote liberally from certain of Inge's unpublished writings.

A mere alphabetical listing of names of those who, over the years, gave me information, confirmed information, pointed me toward yet more information, or helped in countless other ways does little justice to the gratitude I feel. Call this, then, not a list, but a roll call of collaborators, great and small, famous and obscure. My humble thanks to all: Robert Anderson, Thomas Fox Averill, Barbara Baxley, Paul Bigelow, Carolyn and John Bird, Edwin T. Bowden, Jackson R. Bryer, Elma Byrne, John and Margaret Clement, John Connolly, Marion Coulson, Mary Davidson, Mark Dawson, Gene DeGruson, Robert Kent Donovan, Clifford D. Edwards, Utica Garrison, William Gibson, Maxine Hairston, Kate Hopkins, Therese Jones, Hee Kang, Carol McGinnis Kay, Michael L. Keene, Jo Ann Kirchmaier, Shirley Knight, Jane Lange, Jerome Lawrence, Lyle Leverich, John MacNicholas, Arthur F. McClure, Maurine McElroy, Mark Minton, William L. Nance, Robert Quinn Rhode, Robert Russell, Pamela Schlemmer, Fred Sheldon, Wilda M. Smith, Nora and Stella Steinberger, Marilyn Sudlow, Dan Sullivan, William R. Thompson, George Wedge, John Weigel, Thomas Whitbread, and Fred Wilhelm.

I am grateful to Professor Claudia Johnson, chair of the English Department at the University of Alabama, for her long-term encouragement and support. In fact, support at "home base" has been most gratifying. Assistant Dean Robert Garner of the College of Arts and Sciences found a modest travel grant which helped me to begin research at the University of Kansas. Colleagues Robert Halli, John ("Pat") Hermann, and Elizabeth Meese gave me invaluable advice about applications for grants. The university supported me during a sabbatical in which I was able to organize and begin writing this book in earnest. To all my colleagues and friends at Alabama, my thanks for their "How's it going?" and "Hang in there!" spirit.

Finally, my heartfelt thanks belong to a few people whose judgment, patience, steady reliability, and support I shall never forget. Chief among these is Yvonne Willingham, now retired, of the University Press of Kansas. All aspiring authors should have the luxury of working with someone like Yvonne. My thanks also go to the following individuals who read all of this book in manuscript form and contributed mightily toward its improvement: John Weigel and Professors Thomas P. Adler of Purdue University, Jackson R. Bryer of the University of Maryland, and Gene DeGruson of Pittsburg State University. Angela Bramlett has now helped me with the preparation of two book manuscripts, and her remarkable efficiency and good will have never flagged. Four others have been a constant source of support, comfort, and love: my wife, Karen, and our three sons, John, Walker, and Collin.

I first began research on the life and work of William Inge more than twenty years ago, and it has been nearly six years since I decided to write this book. Undoubtedly, there are more individuals, institutions, and programs I am indebted to. My failure to mention them here is my shortcoming, not theirs. And any value this book has must be shared with all the above mentioned (and unmentioned). Any faults it has are entirely my own.

Tuscaloosa, Alabama   New Year's Day, 1988

Part One • Kansas: Origins

1 • Independence

Founded in southeastern Kansas near the confluence of the Elk and Verdigris rivers in 1869, Independence today is a town of about eleven thousand people, the county seat of Montgomery County. Bordering on Oklahoma, Montgomery County is an area rich in agriculture, oil, and natural gas. Its gently rolling hills, wood-bordered streams, and patchwork fields of cattle pasture, alfalfa and milo—all interspersed with oil wells—defy the easterner's stereotype of Kansas as a huge, flat wheat field. U.S. Highways 75 and 160 intersect in the business district of Independence; together they become Main Street in the western half of the community. No Interstate highways are nearby.

Independence is a town of clean tree-lined streets, some 37 churches, more than 170 retail firms, 5 financial institutions, 5 light manufacturing companies, and 2 industrial parks. Its 4 public elementary schools feed students into one public junior high and one public high school. Independence Community College, a two-year institution, lies a mile or so south of town on the west side of Tenth Street. The college basketball team, the Pirates, won the National Junior College Athletic Association championship in 1977 and again in 1978. The college theater is named the William Inge Theater, after the person who is not necessarily the most famous or the most popular former resident of Independence.

Thirteen miles southwest of town, just off U.S. 75, is a farmstead replica called "The Little House on the Prairie." Laura Ingalls Wilder once lived on this site before moving to Minnesota and eventually writing the book by that name. Independence was also at one time the home of Alf Landon, later a Kansas governor who ran as the sacrificial Republican candidate for president against Franklin D. Roosevelt in 1936. Another Kansas governor,

L. U. Humphrey, once lived in Independence, as did the explorer and author Martin Johnson, the actress Vivian Vance (who, thanks to syndicated reruns, is still well remembered as Ethel Mertz on television's "I Love Lucy" during the 1950s), and the oil magnate Harry Sinclair (who is less well remembered for his role in the Teapot Dome oil scandal during Warren G. Harding's presidency in the 1920s). Able, the first monkey the United States sent into outer space, was born at the Ralph Mitchell Zoo here in Riverside Park. The first organized night game in the history of baseball was played between Western Association opponents Independence and Muskogee under the lights at Riverside Park Stadium in 1930, just a few weeks after William Inge graduated from the local high school. About twenty years later, during the last days of minor-league baseball in Independence, the Yankee slugger Mickey Mantle, most of whose hits coincided with Inge's in New York, began his professional playing career at Riverside Park.

North of its intersection with U.S. 160 in the business district, U.S. 75 is known as Pennsylvania Avenue, Penn Avenue for short. On Penn Avenue is Memorial Hall, the long-time community center whose two-thousand-seat auditorium through the years has hosted such visitors as Will Rogers, John Philip Sousa, Billy Sunday, Gene Autry, Fred Waring, Pat Boone, and the Oak Ridge Boys. At Memorial Hall each October, Independence crowns its Queen of Neewollah (Halloween spelled backward) as part of an autumn celebration that had once been abandoned but was revived after *Picnic*, Inge's second successful Broadway play.[1]

Farther north from Memorial Hall on Penn Avenue's east side is Mount Hope Cemetery, its southern entrance dominated by two mausoleums made of native stone. A hundred yards or so behind the mausoleums, in one of the oldest parts of the cemetery, is a large stone marker with a single family name: Inge. Arrayed near this marker are the smaller stones of family members. Largest of these, though still quite modest in comparison to stones in nearby plots, is that marking the grave of William Motter Inge, 1913–1973. A single additional word on the stone catches the eye of a visitor: Playwright.

MAUDE SARAH Gibson Inge probably would have been very proud if, on May 3, 1913, someone had told her that her son William, born that day, was to become a famous and award-winning playwright. Her own mother, Harriet Booth, was said to have been a relative of the famous Booth family of actors, a relationship Maude apparently could neither prove nor deny; still, at forty-two, with the oldest of her three living children already sixteen years old and her

youngest nearly six, she perhaps needed no further encouragement to consider her newborn son something special. Maude was a shade more than
two years older than her husband, Luther Clayton Inge. She had been
born to Brian Malcolm Gibson and Harriet Booth Gibson on October 12,
1871, in Hamilton County, Missouri. The Gibsons later moved to Garden
City, an optimistically named community in semiarid western Kansas, where
Brian Gibson was to become a harness dealer and Maude was to meet
Luther.

Luther had been born to William Hanson Inge and Lucy Jane Vandever
Inge on November 22, 1873, on an Allen County farm near the Neosho
River in southeastern Kansas. The elder Inge was inclined more toward
trade than toward farming, however; so he moved his family to Garden City,
where he became the proprietor of a dry-goods store. Young Luther showed
little real interest in the operating details of his father's business; he was more
impressed with the traveling salesmen who stopped at the store and with
the cowboys and ranch hands who were working in the area's growing beef
industry. Garden City was only about fifty miles west of Dodge City, Kansas'
most famous cow town, which was only a decade or so removed from its
most notorious era. The railroad from the East and the cattle drives from
Texas had brought together commerce and cowboys in a Wild West Kansas
setting, initially a somewhat tumultuous mixture. But eventually a stable
and civilized society developed in the area—just right for shopkeepers but
a bit too routine and unromantic for a young man of Luther Clayton Inge's
spirit.[2]

Details of Luther and Maude's meeting and courtship are lost to time.
Perhaps she, nearing twenty-five—perceived to be an advanced age for an
"eligible" woman at the time—saw him as a good catch, an heir to the mercantile class, however unwilling. Perhaps he, at about twenty-three, thought
he was bowing to the inevitable, by settling down and getting on with whatever business life held for him. Neither was unattractive; he was a tall man
with a ready smile, an outgoing personality, and an eye for the ladies—all
qualities that would serve him both well and ill later in his long career as
a traveling dry-goods salesman. She was short, slightly plump, and neat in
appearance, and she spoke with a pleasant voice that did not betray the
neurasthenic nature she was later to show. In all likelihood, there was for
Luther a sexual urgency in their courtship that Maude would not yield to
without matrimony; certainly, that is suggested in some of their younger
son's most autobiographical work (especially in *The Dark at the Top of the
Stairs*). In any case, they were wed on April 5, 1896, in El Dorado, Kansas,

and then went to live in Syracuse, a town even farther west than Garden City, near the Colorado line, where Luther's father had acquired another dry-goods store. Luther then apparently attempted to become a shopkeeper. At Syracuse, their first daughter, Lucy Helen, was born on January 9, 1897, nine months and four days after their wedding. Shortly thereafter, they moved back to Garden City, where Luther continued to work in the family dry-goods business. At Garden City, the couple's first son, Luther Clayton, Jr., was born on March 22, 1899.[3]

Despite his growing family and what must have been reasonable prospects for success in his father's business, Luther, Sr., was restless. He wanted to be outside more, to be on the move, and shopkeeping would not permit that. Becoming a cowboy was not a wise option for a family man at the turn of the century: the pay was low, and living quarters for his family would not be provided by ranchers. Other opportunities were not available. William Hanson Inge, aware that not only Luther but also another son, Oliver, were restless and unhappy, apparently decided that it was the western-Kansas location, not the dry-goods shopkeeping business, that was troubling them. He therefore sold the stores, and the extended family—including Luther, Maude, and their children—moved to Independence on July 4, 1899. Shortly thereafter he opened a dry-goods store in Independence, and both Luther and Oliver resumed working for him there.[4]

Maude could hardly have been very pleased about this move. They already had two children, and Luther, Sr., did not want to settle into the relatively secure, stable life they could share in Garden City. Moreover, he was taking her away from her family's home, and she had no relatives in Independence. In all probability, these were the beginnings of the obvious tensions their son would one day portray between the parents, Rubin and Cora Flood, in *The Dark at the Top of the Stairs*. These obvious tensions were to grow during the years after the move to Independence, but it is likely that they had their inception before that move, in the less obvious but most basic of marital relationships.

If William Inge's 1971 novel, *My Son Is a Splendid Driver*, can be seen as a largely factual memoir thinly garbed as fiction—as there is ample reason to believe—then a difference in sexual attitudes plagued the relationship of Luther and Maude Inge from the very beginning of their marriage.[5] As protagonist Joey Hansen (Inge has taken as his fictional last name a variant spelling of his paternal grandfather's middle name), Inge writes: "I can only guess that their sexual union seemed loveless and carnal to Mother, and so she came to feel degraded by my father's animal desires." He goes on to say:

I heard her tell, much later in my life, how she fled from him the day after they were married—the morning after their first intercourse. She was so frightened and repelled by what had happened in their marriage bed that she returned to her parents and begged them to let her stay. But Grandma urged her back to her duty as a wife, counseling her that "Men's ways are not always seemly to a delicate woman. You've got to give in to things you may not like, Bess. That's part of being married." (*Driver*, pp. 66–67)

Bess in *Driver* is Maude Sarah Inge, to whose memory the novel is dedicated. In this novel, Bess Hansen finds it impossible to admit that she might enjoy sexual union with her husband; she also finds it impossible to forgive her husband for philandering, something she began to suspect him of shortly after he began working as a traveling dry-goods salesman. Like Rubin Flood in *Stairs* and Brian Hansen in *Driver*, Luther Clayton Inge was, shortly after the move back to Independence, a traveling salesman who found occasional female companionship on the road. Like Cora Flood and Bess Hansen in the same two works, Maude Sarah Inge was inhibited by her husband's sexuality even while she wanted him to find nontraveling work that would make his sexual allegiance more likely.

For Luther, the opportunity to leave his father's store to travel and sell dry goods for the Wheeler and Motter Dry Goods Company of St. Louis must have seemed a deliverance of sorts. He knew the dry-goods business, and he knew people; he understood the attitudes of the shopkeepers he greeted in little towns in southeastern Kansas and northeastern Oklahoma. The money was at least adequate for his family's needs, and best of all, he was free to move about, to escape the confines and day-to-day responsibilities of the household, where he was perfectly willing to let Maude establish control. He was usually home on weekends, but not on week nights, and occasionally he took long swings that kept him away for a month. Although Maude could count absence and infidelity against Luther, he could not be faulted as a provider or as a stern or forbidding father to the children. When he was home, he was gentle with them and more tolerant than Maude. The distance between him and his children was caused more by physical absence than by emotional attitude.[6]

Well established in a marriage that was maintained largely for the children and for the conventions of the time, Luther and Maude Inge had their third child, Irene Madeline, on March 30, 1901. This child, however, died on June 8, 1904, barely three years old. The loss of little Irene left Maude despondent; she became ever more protective and indulgent of Lucy and Luther Boy, as she called her son to distinguish his name from his father's. The children were her guard against loneliness and her proof to the external world that her marriage was successful. Moreover, the children needed her love, protection, and guidance.[7] Their house at 504 North Ninth Street was at least filled with the consistent love Maude and her children bore for each other, if not the consistent love of Maude and Luther, Sr.

Still, there were times when Maude's apprehensions gave way to what she saw as marital duty or when Luther and Maude found their way to each other in consolation against whatever misgivings they felt. And probably to their at least mild surprise, when Lucy was ten and Luther Boy was eight, they had another daughter—Helene Grace, born on July 31, 1907. This daughter, now the sole survivor of Luther and Maude's family, was not to be their final child, but for some time it seemed that she was; Helene was nearly six years old when William was born in the house at 504 North Ninth Street.[8] Named for his paternal grandfather and one of his father's employers, young William Motter was christened "Billy," a diminutive he would never completely escape until he left Independence many years later.[9]

WHEN BILLY was a year old, Luther moved the family to the large house at 514 North Fourth Street, where Billy would grow to young manhood and where he would set his first play, *Farther off from Heaven* (later *The Dark at the Top of the Stairs*). The house was large enough so that the children would not have to share rooms; it was also in a somewhat nicer, better-kept part of town. Maude wasted no time settling into the new home and establishing her dominion there, with Billy as a focal point.

For Maude, Billy's birth was very important: here was a new and helpless infant to love and protect in ways that Lucy, Luther Boy, and even Helene no longer needed. Billy ensured that several more years of Maude's family devotion would be needed before, her children grown and gone, she would be left with only Luther and whatever regrets she felt. Maude had held her previous children close to her as a kind of compensation, but Billy she was to hold closest of all. Moreover, the other children, even Helene, joined Maude in doting over Billy. He was the classic "baby of the family" as well as "momma's boy," positions of early privilege that would later play their parts in bringing him pain. "Well, mother . . . loved her children," Helene recollected many years later; "she hung on to us just as long as she could."

As the last born, Billy was also the last child for Maude to hang onto, a grip that seemed to hold in some ways even long after her death.

Maude had a nervous but strong personality that stamped all four of her children in one way or another, but particularly the two younger ones. Helene, continuing her recollection, called her mother "quite a talker." "I didn't learn to talk really until I got away from home. . . . Mother was always talking, and I had to remain quiet, because children were seen and not heard in those days."[10] In fact, Helene was very shy as a young girl and later as a young woman. That shyness is the dominant element in the personality of her stage representation as Reenie Flood in *The Dark at the Top of the Stairs*. "My mother was a highstrung little woman," writes William Inge (as Joey Hansen) in *My Son Is a Splendid Driver;* "at home we were accustomed to my father's absence and to the nervous matriarchy that my mother brought us up in" (pp. 5-6). That "nervous matriarchy" apparently included an exaggerated fear of harm for her brood, which manifested itself in near-constant caution. "Mother had a cautioning for every move we made in life, for every function we performed," says Inge in *Driver* (p. 42).

Given such fears, Maude indeed must have been nearly beside herself one evening when Billy, then three or four years old, was playing on the stairs. Maude and Helene were nearby, but neither noticed when he placed his head in a square hole formed by a step and the configuration of the wooden banister. When she saw him, Maude told him to get his head out of there—but he couldn't. Suddenly, what had seemed like a cute trick had become a serious business. "We were panic-stricken," remembers Helene. Everything they tried in order to help Billy failed, doubtless to his increasing cries. Eventually, they got a saw from the garage and sawed the bottom of the banister in two where it joined into a vertical rail, thus enabling Billy at last to get his head out.[11]

Such mishaps must have reinforced Maude's fears for her children, magnifying her sense that it was the children who were her greatest treasures, not to be lost in any sense if she could help it. But by the time of the stairway incident, Lucy and Luther Boy were already young adults, soon to strike out on their own. Lucy was a very attractive young woman, long pampered as the firstborn to Maude and Luther and the firstborn grandchild on both sides. Inge writes in *Driver* that Treva (the fictional name he gives Lucy) was "favored like a princess" (p. 12). She preferred expensive clothes and enjoyed shopping at Montaldo's, an exclusive store where she later took a job. Men noticed Lucy, and she was seldom without a date, even after she had become

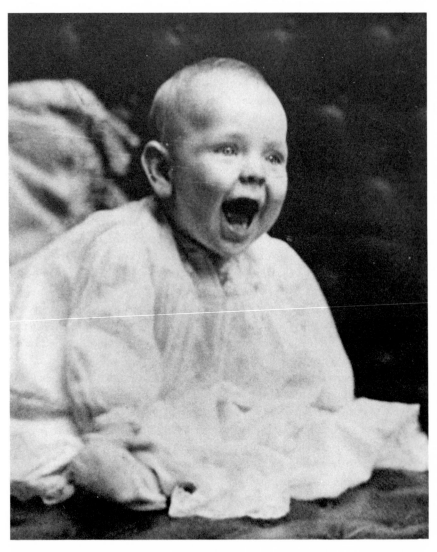

"Billy" Inge, six months old. Courtesy of the William Inge Collection (hereafter WIC), Independence Community College (hereafter ICC), Independence, Kansas

The Inge house at 514 North Fourth Street in Independence. Courtesy of WIC/ICC

engaged to marry Joseph Mahan, a wealthy young man from Garden City whom she had probably met while visiting Maude's parents. "She believed only in the world of manners and social graces, which could always be manipulated to accommodate her," says Inge; "the world of deep and vulnerable feelings was not real to her then" (*Driver*, p. 88).

Luther Boy, on the other hand, was not given to the same social airs as Lucy. He considered himself the man of the family in his father's absence. Having learned to drive the car skillfully, he could run errands for Maude, who never learned to drive, or take her wherever she wanted to go in town. With his peers, Luther Boy liked to hunt, drive fast, smoke cigarettes, and chase women. Maude, for all her overprotectiveness, had somehow not influenced Luther Boy away from some of his father's inclinations or from those of his peers in town. Describing Julian, the fictional Luther Boy in *Driver*, Inge writes, "But whatever Jule's behavior away from home, he was always angelic with Mother, tenderly considerate of her most childish and unreasonable fears, and with a talent for persuading her out of them" (p. 9).

Clashes between Lucy and Luther Boy were inevitable. Lucy, to whose judgment Maude acceded in matters of dress or home decor, complained about Luther Boy's smoking, his clothing when there were guests for dinner,

The four Inge children in about 1918. Lucy stands behind Billy, then about five, and Helene stands beside Luther Boy. Courtesy of WIC/ICC

his friends, and his disdainful attitude toward her tastes. Luther Boy complained about Lucy's pervasive influence, her social airs, and her flirtations after she had become engaged. The two argued over using the car. They even argued over Luther Boy's refusal to put the seat down after standing to use the toilet.[12]

But just as Lucy and Luther Boy were often combative and generally extroverted, Helene and Billy seldom fought with each other and were generally quiet. Helene recalls that Maude often said she felt she had raised two different families because of the differences, both in age and behavior, between the two older and the two younger children.[13] Helene was so shy and quiet that when she was about ten, Maude arranged elocution lessons for her. Helene would practice the short pieces, many of which were in dialect, that were popular at the time. Billy would be in the same room, Helene remembers, and would often learn the pieces faster than she would. Frequently, he recited pieces with more expressive vigor than she would muster, and the adults within earshot would be highly entertained. In fact, it was this ability to recite that caused Billy to discover early his knack for performing and his appreciation for having an audience.

"Billy was a handsome youngster," Helene recalls; "rather plump, towheaded, freckles across his nose, big blue eyes, and a decided 'lisp' that was quite irresistible." One neighbor in particular so enjoyed hearing Billy "speak a piece" that he would give him a nickel to hear:

> Mother calls me William,
> Daddy calls me Will,
> Sister calls me Willie,
> But the boys all call me Bill.[14]

Billy also liked to imitate the older children as they went off to school: he would pick up a book and head out the door with them each morning— only to be sent back into the house before he could leave the yard. Such precocious behavior had to please Maude, even though it meant to her that Billy should start school early and thus leave her alone in the house. She enrolled him in kindergarten at nearby Washington School a year before the usual age.[15]

WHEN BILLY Inge began school, Independence was enjoying the greatest economic boom of its history. Oil and gas had been discovered in the area, and fortunes were being made. According to some accounts, until the Great Depression, Independence had the largest per capita bank deposits of any city in the nation.[16]

Chief among the newly oil wealthy was Harry Sinclair, founder of Sinclair Oil Company (later Atlantic-Richfield, or ARCO, and its subsidiaries), one of the nation's largest oil companies. Local Independence lore has it that Sinclair launched his fortune by shooting himself in the foot and then investing the insurance proceeds in oil exploration. There is no proof of such a tale, but it was so widespread that many years later, a reference to the story in Inge's *The Dark at the Top of the Stairs* brought knowing laughter among Independence people who saw or read the play.[17] Landowners on whose property oil and gas were discovered, various petroleum investors, and owners of smaller oil companies all became wealthy; and the vibrant oil industry naturally had positive economic effects on banking and retail businesses. The social structure of Independence became more tightly drawn along economic lines, relegating the already rich and the newly rich to the councils of power best symbolized by membership in the new country club south of town. Short of wealth based on ownership, the next-best position was to be an employee of Sinclair Oil or Prairie Pipeline, preferably in management.[18] Luther Inge himself was not a part of this socioeconomic scene, but his sisters had married men who became powerful community figures, thus allowing his younger children to grow up as cousins to wealth and influence.

Also, at about the time Billy began school, the older Inge children were now adults, ready to leave home. Lucy, whose appreciation of wealth and social status had always been strong, wed the well-to-do Joseph Mahan. Luther Boy, who never cared much about wealth or society, had his own job and had his eye on a young neighbor girl, Marguerite Leppelman. Maude would have preferred that her older son continue to show interest in Marguerite's older sister, whom he dated first. But Luther Boy and Marguerite eloped on February 29, 1920, to begin a tragically short life together. Not quite nine months later, Luther Boy nicked himself while shaving hurriedly at work, contracting a powerful blood poisoning that took his life on November 12, 1920. His son, Luther Claude, was born about five months later, on April 5, 1921.[19] The death of Luther Boy was a shocking loss for the whole family, but especially for Maude, who still counted on him to drive her on errands and be a male presence in Luther's absence. Billy, then only seven, also lost his only brother, one who might have had a decisive influence on Billy as he grew to adolescence.

Maude's grief over Luther Boy was strong and lasting, even though she surely felt some relief when Holman Charles Banks married Marguerite. Banks provided a lasting marriage and a home for Marguerite and Luther Claude in the same neighborhood as the Inges and the Leppelmans. Thus, Luther Claude was to grow up near all his grandparents and his Uncle Billy, though of course Maude had to share him too much to be very influential. Maude still had Helene and Billy at home to care for. With two extra bedrooms in the house now, Maude decided to take in roomers. She rented the rooms to unmarried women schoolteachers, who usually stayed only during the school months. The succession of female teachers rooming at the Inge home gave Billy an even larger live-in audience, who "made" over him, much as Maude did. And female teacher-roomers would become some of the most significant characters he ever created.

Meanwhile, Independence continued its economic boom. Such wealth, along with its being a key railroad stop between Kansas City and Tulsa, helped to make Independence a lively center for entertainments. Road shows stopped to perform at the Beldorf Theatre and Memorial Hall. Summer Chautauqua programs for the area were held under a big tent on a lot at Eighth and Pine streets. The Beldorf brought Hollywood's latest film features, and young Billy Inge, who loved to attend all sorts of performances, became especially fond of the silver screen. Although Luther and Maude were not sharing in the great wealth that made some of Luther's relatives important figures at the new country club, they benefited from the thriving ambience of prosperity. Business in general was good, so Luther's sales were good – good enough to finance vacations to Colorado, one of which plays a significant role in *Driver*, and one memorable vacation to California, where the star-struck Billy, who for some time had been collecting autographed pictures of movie stars, hoped to see some of his idols in person.

The California trip was a group expedition, taken with members of the Sewell and Wagstaff families. The Sewells were Luther's sister and brother-in-law; the Wagstaffs were neighbors. The tourists divided their time between swimming at the beach and lingering near the movie lots in Hollywood, where they were fortunate enough to be at the Paramount studio on a payday, enabling them to see several stars come for their checks.[20] Helene recalls Billy's excitement at seeing Douglas Fairbanks on this trip and his disappointment at missing Rudolph Valentino when others claimed to have spotted him at the beach. This fascination with the famous affected all these Kansas tourists that summer of 1922, but none so profoundly as Billy, who

Billy Inge at about seven years of age. Courtesy of WIC/ICC

spent hours doting over his growing picture collection after the family's return to Independence. Among his most cherished were photographs of John Gilbert, Thomas Meighan, Gloria Swanson, and Norma Shearer.[21]

As he continued in school, Billy's precociousness grew, undoubtedly to Maude's approval. When his third-grade teacher at Washington school asked, during a free period, if any of the children wished to share a song or a recitation, Billy rose and delivered a dialect piece that delighted his teacher and his classmates: "Hi-yo Peter Johnson, come inside that fence; I done told yo' yesterday yo' ain't got no sense." The success of this delivery deeply impressed Billy, who basked in the approval of a new audience. Soon after this incident, he was in local demand for similar recitations at gatherings of Kiwanis, Rotary, Elks, and ladies' clubs. It was the beginning of his long pursuit of an acting career, and it was also the beginning of his reputation as a sissy and a "momma's boy."[22]

It's easy to imagine the impression Billy Inge made upon other boys in his class. He didn't play football, basketball, or baseball, and he was easily intimidated by any sort of roughhousing. Maude dressed him for his recitations in a Norfolk jacket and knickerbockers. She fussed and fretted over him so much that, as he was to tell interviewer Gilbert Millstein many years and several psychiatrists later: "I thought at times Mother made me a physical coward, because she was quite a highstrung woman and whenever anything went wrong, she would get quite beside herself." Going on to say he felt guilty even if he had a cold because it would upset Maude, Inge recalled: "Every time I got hurt, Mother would be more hurt than I was. If I went swimming, she would be terribly worried; she would worry if I went on a hike" (Millstein, p. 63). Such obvious overprotectiveness at home, coupled with a public image as a prissy deliverer of recitations and the inevitable status of "teacher's pet," cast Billy Inge early in the role of a sissy, a precious momma's boy who was quite different from the other boys in his class. Warm approval from Maude, his teachers, and other adults, however, was a specific antidote for the poisonous taunts of his peers. As long as most grownups liked him and paid attention to him, Billy could cope.

In this coping he was imaginatively resourceful and talented. So that he could always vary his performances, he sent off to Kansas City and Chicago for new recitation material (Millstein, p. 63). He practiced mannerisms, and he delighted in costumes. One day he stunned Maude and Helene when, as they approached the house, they were greeted by a little old lady with a monocle, bent over and hobbling toward them with the aid of a cane. Billy had so ingeniously decked himself out that they had been completely de-

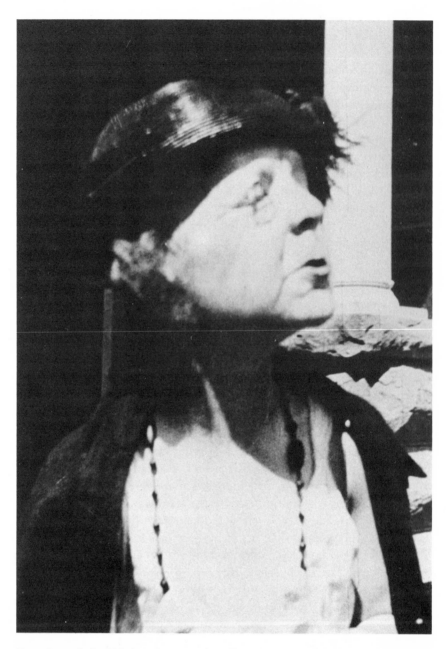

Dressed as a little old lady with a monocle, Billy completely fooled his mother and sister. Courtesy of WIC/ICC

ceived.[23] In addition to the performing models he saw on screen at the Bel-dorf or on stage at Memorial Hall, Billy occasionally was treated to road-show performances in Wichita and Kansas City with his Uncle John Gib-son, Maude's brother. A frustrated actor who had settled for a career in the harness business in Wichita with Maude's other brother Mack, John Gibson took considerable interest in the acting talents of his nephew.[24]

Not so Luther. "My father was indifferent," Inge was to recall many years later, when giving the last interview of his life; "except he considered [acting] a little unmanly."[25] If the youthful Inge was ever deeply bothered by his father's indifference, it was not readily apparent to those who knew him in those days. Two childhood next-door neighbors, Nora and Stella Stein-berger, remember Billy as a slightly older, frequently manipulative, and al-ways interesting boy. They do not recall him as enigmatic or troubled.

Billy was about eleven when the Steinbergers moved in one door south, on the corner, in 1924. By this time, there were several children in the neighborhood, all a little younger than Billy, and he frequently gathered them together and organized their play. Although there were occasional mar-ble, croquet, or hide-and-seek games, more often Billy's love of performing dominated the activities. There was a barn on the lot behind the Inge house, and Billy converted one room in it into a theater, complete with a "curtain" rigged with an old sheet on a wire. Although he often featured himself, he was always careful to include other children from the neighborhood, usually rotating their participation to guarantee a more willing audience as children awaited their turns. The Steinberger sisters remember these little plays and performances as highly entertaining—well worth the penny apiece that was the usual admission for those children not performing on any particular day. As for Billy, the benefits of being a youthful theatrical entrepreneur were considerable: not only did he enjoy performing, but he also used the pen-nies toward the cost of his own admission to the movies. His management was nothing if not practical; when the sheet "curtain" needed new pins, he simply substituted a pin as the price of admission.[26]

Playing with the younger children suited Billy much of the time before his teens, for there were few other boys his own age with whom he often played. He had cousins roughly the same age—Al Sewell, for one, who was in his class at school. But Al was later to recall that "Bill was a little bit dif-ferent from the rest of the people in our gang; his interests weren't quite the same; he was somewhat of a mother's boy."[27] Those are the carefully chosen words of an adult relative many years later. Another adolescent ac-quaintance, John Clement, expressed the contemporary feeling more suc-

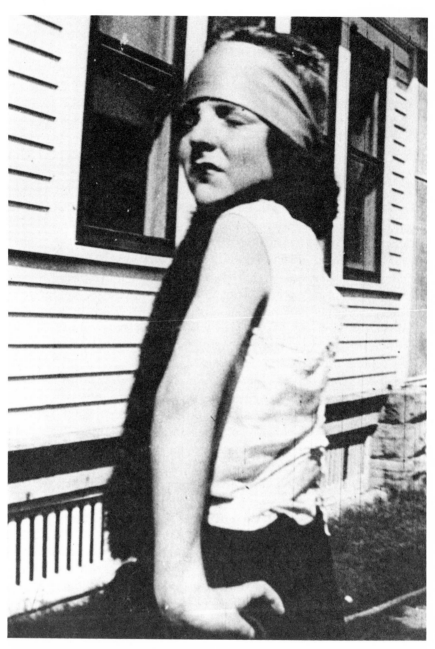

Billy Inge, about ten, costumed as a young girl. Courtesy of WIC/ICC

cinctly: "You know he was a sissy."[28] Such attitudes can be sharply exclu-
sionary in early adolescence, and as he grew older, there were doubtless
times when Billy felt the sting of being left out. Later, in high school, he
found ways to win greater acceptance among his peers. But for the time being, on the brink of his teenage years, Billy mostly played with the slightly
younger neighborhood children—or by himself.

Helene by now was finishing high school, and she planned to go away
to college. She had never overcome her shyness to the extent that she dated
often, and Maude was sure that college and possibly a subsequent teaching
career were good plans for her younger daughter. More than ever, Maude
was conscious that time was taking her children from her. She frequently
visited Mrs. Steinberger next door and lamented the losses of little Irene and
Luther Boy and complained about the "blues" she felt knowing that Lucy
was married and living far away and that Helene would soon be leaving home.[29]
Maude's only nearby grandchild, Luther Claude, had to be shared with the
Leppelmans and his adoptive grandparents. More than ever, Billy became
the center of Maude's attentions, ambitions, and fears. She knew he was
special, different; she knew he suffered the taunts of his peers; and she tried
to soothe him when this happened. Many years later, in the first of his plays
to be produced, *Farther off from Heaven*, a very similar mother soothes a very
similar son in language that must have been very familiar to Billy Inge:
"You're just . . . not like the other boys. You're a speckled egg and the old
hen that laid you can't help wonderin' what you're going to hatch into." Prophetically, she adds: "You'll find people somewhere you'll get along with.
You'll find other speckled eggs. But somehow I just can't see you spending
your life in this little burg."[30]

IN THE FALL of 1926, Billy entered Independence High School. By now he
was thirteen, a difficult age for anyone, but harder for Billy because he was
physically becoming a man while being surrounded by doting older females.
With his only brother dead and his father so often gone (and unassertive
while at home), Billy had no pronounced male presence in his life. Because
he was not an athlete, he was seldom around a male coach, and virtually
all of his other teachers were female. Thus he had no real prospects of ac-
quiring a significant male role model. Though this experience doubtless
helped forge his later great sensitivity in understanding and creating female
characters, it was at the time a social handicap with which he had to cope.

He was, however, resourceful and talented, keen to sense the characteristics of the various social situations in which he found himself. Academically, he was easily bright enough to excel but did not tax himself, thus making good marks without attracting additional "egghead" or "brain" labels. He had a ready wit and sense of humor that generally served him well with his schoolmates. He knew how to be congenial with the right people, and he participated actively enough in such extracurricular activities as vocal-music ensembles, pep club, and yearbook that no one considered him a serious "loner." For a time, he was a cheerleader, as was his friend Fred Sheldon.[31] Although cheerleading has never been considered the most manly endeavor, it was more common among male students in those days, and it has always been the province of popular students. "Sissy" he may have been, but he was not disliked. Although he showed artistic ability in drawing—for a time he had taken art lessons along with Helene—he put most of his interest and effort into drama, a natural extension for one smitten so early with performing and performers. At Independence High School he and his fellow drama students were particularly blessed with a dedicated, first-rate teacher, Anna Ingleman.

Many Independence residents today remember Anna Ingleman with the nostalgic warmth most people feel for the influential teachers in their lives. "She was an inspiration," says Margaret Goheen, retired drama teacher at Independence Community College.[32] Ingleman liked Inge's enthusiasm for acting, and he earned a role in most of her productions. "That boy was a genius in some ways and I knew it," Ingleman recollected many years later, though she considered Vivian Jones (later Vivian Vance) the most versatile of her former students. Inge displayed a special talent for satiric comedy involving female impersonation. "He gave some of the cleverest take-offs on women I have ever seen," recalled Ingleman.[33] "Especially society women. He was a scream in that," said Ingleman, citing a particular monologue called "At the Bathing Beach."[34] Inge's female impersonation, then, was something more than the kind of skylarking visible in a 1929 "Spring Festival" photo in the William Inge Collection, in which all members of the boys' chorus—including football player John Clement—are dressed as females. Inge had a knack for performing as a female, if not in fact a nascent impulse toward transvestism. This, too, doubtless contributed to Inge's affinity with the female characters he was to create. But it cannot be said to what degree it indicates early signs of his homosexuality.

It seems certain that Inge's high-school years were in part a personal battle ground over his sexuality. For one thing, he was good-looking. He had a handsome face, with fine features, including striking blue eyes. Trim and tall,

Billy Inge, extreme left, and the Independence High School boys' chorus, dressed as chorines for the 1929 "Spring Festival." Among Billy's friends in the chorus are John Clement, Fred Wilhelm, and Fred Sheldon, fourth, fifth, and sixth from the left respectively. Courtesy of WIC/ICC

he always kept his blond hair neatly combed in the part-and-pompadour style that was very popular among men of the time. Women thought him attractive, and surely as he grew older, some of them let him know it. But no one who knew Billy Inge in those days remembers him "going with" any one girl for any length of time; rather, their impression is that he very seldom dated. To be sure, he had to contend with one young man's handicap of his socioeconomic class: he did not own a car; if he wanted to use one, he had to borrow the family car, available only when Luther was home. But unlike Luther Boy before him, Billy did not relish driving after he learned to, and he was not one to socialize at length with other young men in town who often drove and discussed cars. Also unlike Luther Boy, he did not learn to hunt or fish, and he was therefore seldom in the company of young men who did. Rather, he seemed content on the periphery of several groups, not really belonging to any.

Of course, Maude's cautions, sharpened after the death of Luther Boy, undoubtedly contributed to Billy's social behavior. But acquaintances detected a reticence that was Billy's own as well, a reticence that made him different without really being reclusive. In fact, although he had many ac-

quaintances, few of whom he saw often enough to be called friends, he apparently had no truly close friend, male or female, with whom he shared
daily experience in any enduring relationship.[35]

Sex in the Inge home then was the greatest of taboos, never frankly discussed, only occasionally hinted at in negative euphemisms. The absence of
frank and unprejudiced talk about sex is a common condition in many
American families even today, but it was especially acute during Inge's youth.
The result had to be confusion at best, fear at worst, and some measure of
both. In his youth, Inge writes in *Driver*, "Sex was as fearful as black magic
to all of us. Even a married woman could not honorably claim that she had
any desire for her husband, and the male was forced to look upon his own
desires as something ignoble. In retrospect, we all seem thwarted people"
(p. 16). Maude's influence resonates in those words.

Helene once mentioned to an interviewer that Billy was given a beating
by one of his grade-school teachers for kissing a girl.[36] If such an experience
did occur, accompanied by a stern lecture about what is "nice" and "proper,"
it could certainly have fueled the confusion and fear of a growing boy who
already had reason to think that sexual expression was always wrong or
"dirty." In *Driver*, Joey Hansen (Inge) says that it was while in sixth grade
that he "first learned about copulation—from a precocious boy . . . who told
me about it . . . in a way that made the act of love seem prurient and degrading" (p. 149). And if heterosexual expression was always wrong, what
about homosexual expression? Elsewhere in *Driver* lies the answer. Inge tells
of a man and wife in the small town who are discovered to be a pederast
and a lesbian. When she hears about this, Bess Hansen (Maude) calls them
"*degenerates* . . . too *disgraceful* to talk about" (Inge's italics, p. 98). Any sexual
urge, then, of any kind, for young William Inge was a bad thing.

It is difficult now to pinpoint a particular time, incident, individual, or
specific sequence of experiences that confirmed Billy as a homosexual. Years
of his own secrecy and the understandable reticence of the few survivors
who were closest to him make such precision not only difficult but also,
finally, of dubious importance. His homosexuality was a signal cause of unhappiness in a life that was predominantly unhappy, and the years of perplexing inward struggle about his sexuality almost surely began during high
school, where many people remember Billy as being popular but not especially close to anyone.

A talented and resourceful youth such as Billy Inge, however troubled,
nonetheless had reason to believe in a liberating dream, a promise of escape

in the future to a better place, a better life. For Billy, that promise was in acting. He knew that he would someday leave Independence, first to go to the University of Kansas in Lawrence to study drama. Thereafter he would pursue a performing career and take his best shot at New York, or Hollywood, or both. Such a dream might well have been punctured for many of high-school age, but Billy had the encouragement of Maude and the reinforcement of near-constant performing in Ingleman's productions. People who saw him perform from his earliest grade-school days told him he was good. He had ambition and reason to believe in his talent, and in these lay considerable compensation for whatever confusion and pain his young life brought him. Moreover, on the silver screen then he could see others with southeastern Kansas backgrounds who were proving the dream was possible: Louise Brooks of Cherryvale, Buster Keaton of Piqua, and ZaSu Pitts of Parsons.

During his high-school years, Inge also developed a vital interest in reading. His interest in literature went well beyond whatever study was necessary for good grades in his English classes. He writes in *Driver* that from his early teens he had "discovered the world of poetry and literature. . . . And my mind was always full of what I'd read" (p. 118). A particular favorite was William Wordsworth, whose poetry would later lend both themes and titles to Inge's own work. Perhaps then the reading was purely a matter of personal escape; already he was aware that Maude's clinging was costly to him, although he could hardly have realized how much. And he could not have known that the love of reading, with its concomitant intellectual growth and appreciation of writing styles, would one day serve him long after his acting ambitions had died. Billy Inge was different, then—a "speckled egg," no doubt at times bewildered by his hormones and his environment—but he found equilibrium in acting and reading, and he thus avoided the reclusive path that might well have led to a much-earlier suicidal despair. He was, in the phrase often reserved for young people of high promise, "going somewhere."

Margaret Clement of Independence has one memory of Billy Inge in high school that in retrospect seems symbolic. She lived on the same side of town the Inges did, and each school day she would walk to and from school twice because she, like Billy, went home for lunch. Always, it seemed, Billy wordlessly passed her on the sidewalk, striding with rapid, solemn purpose. He wasn't unfriendly, she recalls; he was just intent, preoccupied.[37] Nora Steinberger remembers that as Inge progressed in high school, he paid less attention to the nearby slightly younger people who had once been so important to his neighborhood plays. He sat on the front porch of the Inge house with a big glass of lemonade and a book or movie magazine; he could not be persuaded to enter into any other activity.[38] Perhaps Billy's preoccupation was not extraordinary, but it contributed to his image at the time as one who was somehow different, one who, in retrospect, was "going somewhere."

The high-school years brought Billy a bit closer socially to his wealthy cousin Al Sewell.[39] Perhaps it was Sewell's membership in the country club that made it possible for Billy to learn to play tennis, the one sport in which he developed a brief interest. The appeal of tennis, however, may have been secondary to the appeal of the country club, a realm of privilege, a social milieu that Billy had not previously experienced. Perhaps his family was not wealthy, but in tennis whites at the country club, the handsome young Billy Inge could not be immediately distinguished from the real thing. Perhaps he didn't have a car, but his country-club tennis associates did. Of course, Billy didn't really "fit" here, any more than he did anywhere else in Independence, and the country-club set would eventually gain its share of criticism in his writing. It must have pleased Billy at the time, however, to be able to move in these circles and taste some of the elegance he hoped one day he might earn on his own. Other tennis friends were Fred Sheldon and Freddie Wilhelm. Wilhelm, who spent the summer of 1929 at Culver Military Academy in Indiana, received some letters from Billy that provide an interesting picture of Inge that summer.

One letter in particular, dated only July, 1929, offers several small pages of gossipy chitchat about several matters, including tennis, who was dating whom, and the like: Luther has had an operation for piles (p. 1); Freddie's family has a new LaSalle (p. 2); one particular girl is "built like a Packard" (p. 3); "Rosemary is out there vamping all the tennis players" (p. 4). The fourth page also confides to Freddie that Billy is smoking in the house when his parents are gone, and offers an illustration of a stick figure puffing away. The fifth page announces that an exciting new toy, the yo-yo, is a big hit in Independence and provides a stick figure operating a yo-yo: "Everyone here is working them. Young and old." (In fact, Donald F. Duncan, Sr., introduced the yo-yo in the United States that year.) Regarding Wilhelm's girl friend, Jeanne, Billy tells Wilhelm that there's no cause for jealousy: "Really there's nothing thick between us" (p. 8).[40] Such a breezy, rather lengthy letter would have been extraordinary for most young men to write, but because Maude was a frequent letter writer who kept a card table covered with post cards, stationery, and stamps set up in the living room, it probably seemed natural to Billy.[41]

Inge apparently enjoyed writing to Wilhelm and others who also were away that summer, but other letters make it clear that his efforts as a faithful correspondent were not often rewarded by return mail. "I'm very sorry you're not satisfied with my letters," begins a letter to Wilhelm dated July 16; "Although I've written you two letters instead of one, and the last letter I wrote, I sat here an hour just wracking [*sic*] my brain for everything I could think of to say." He concludes the brief letter with self-deprecation ("I know this is a tacky letter like the rest of mine") and a plea for a return letter with a "promise to answer all your letters with everything I know or ever heard of. Love, Bill."[42] A third letter, written on August 14, begins with a whine and another disclaimer of any romantic interest in Jeanne: "What's wrong? I haven't heard from you for 2 weeks. Why don't you write? Jack & Al quit long ago. I had one letter from Jack & two from Al, but I thought you'd not go back on me. Do you think I'm dating Jeanne? Well I'm not."[43]

What became of the other letters Inge wrote that summer or the few that were written to him is not known. But the picture afforded by these available letters is of a lively, willing writer, eager to please his reader, as well as of a young man who both misses and wants to keep his tennis friends, even if it makes him seem a little desperate. Possibly, Wilhelm, Jack, and Al (Sewell?) didn't write often—or finally at all—because, like many young people, they found it too much of a chore. But it is also possible they didn't write because Billy so obviously and so pleadingly wanted them to. If Wilhelm seldom wrote because he was jealous, then it seems likely that he had little reason for such jealousy. In any case, these letters again show that Billy Inge was different from his peers, even though he shared with them such common interests as gossip, tennis, yo-yos, and clandestine smoking.

Smoking wasn't the only secret Billy tried to keep from Maude. His nephew, Luther Claude, remembers that Billy kept copies of *Cornet* magazine—considered "racy" at the time—hidden in his room. Luther Claude doesn't think Maude ever found them, because "she never snooped."[44] But he may overestimate her virtue; Maude apparently never caught Luther Claude peeking at Billy's *Cornets*. That summer of letters, secret smoking, and stashed *Cornets* was 1929, when Billy was sixteen, with one year of high school remaining.

During the 1929/30 school year, Billy continued to perform in Anna Ingleman's productions, and he remained involved in vocal music, the yearbook, and other extracurricular activities. He enjoyed getting after-school soft drinks with other students at the New York Candy Kitchen downtown. His long-time Independence friend Loretta Watts, who was then another of Ingleman's students and a cheerleading partner of Billy's, recalls that they

Billy Inge, center stage, in one of Anna Ingleman's plays at Independence High School. Courtesy of WIC/ICC

often talked about drama as they sipped their sodas. "When Bill was young, when I first knew him, he was an extrovert," remembers Watts, who was later a Chautauqua performer herself and who many years after that portrayed Rosemary Sydney in a local production of *Picnic*. "But as he grew older and better educated, and he went into therapy himself, and as he probed himself, he became an introvert and you couldn't pull anything out of Bill."[45] Although her understanding of psychology may be a bit more sophisticated, Watts is typical of Independence contemporaries who saw Billy Inge frequently in the days of their youth, then kept at least a distant acquaintance alive throughout the years. Always, they liked him; always, he struck them as somehow different from them in ways that could not be completely accounted for by his obvious talent or his later successes as a writer.

The stock-market crash of late 1929 staggered Independence more than most small towns because much of its oil-money prosperity had become tied to speculation in other areas of the market. Significant parts of local fortunes were "on paper," paper that became less and less valuable. The fullest effects would not be felt during Billy's senior year of 1929/30, but eventually Luther would share in the general decline enough to affect Billy's college years. Meanwhile, as Billy neared graduation in the spring of 1930, he and Maude planned for his move to Lawrence and his enrollment at the University of Kansas. Helene, who had by now studied art in college and earned a teaching certificate, was teaching art in a junior high school in Lawrence. Al Sewell and Freddie Wilhelm were also going to KU, and Dick Peck, a slightly older friend from Ingleman's classes, was already there. Billy would be near family and friends, although that didn't begin to compensate Maude for the loss she was going to feel. Nor was Maude alone in her apprehension: for Billy, this was a massive change that he both dreaded and welcomed.

Accounts differ regarding Inge's actual departure for Lawrence. Inge, the source of all available accounts at this writing, told Gilbert Millstein in 1958 that Maude insisted on spending the first week of school at KU with Inge and that "with some difficulty he persuaded her to go by bus while he went by train" (Millstein, p. 63). The version Inge gives in *My Son Is a Splendid Driver* is more dramatic, making the initial separation abrupt rather than gradual. As Joey (Billy) stands in the living room, waiting for his father to back the car out of the garage, Bess (Maude) suddenly cries, "'I'm alone now,' Her voice shook me. 'You're the last of my children, and now you're going, too. You've *all* left me, one by one. And what is there left for me but to live on with a man who doesn't love me, and grow old and feeble alone, without any of the people I love to help me?'" (pp. 132–133). Joey asks if he should stay, but Bess tells him he must go in spite of her admitted selfishness; the mistake is hers for living only for her children. She then shoos him out of the house, explaining that she cannot bear to go to the depot to say goodbye. "I kissed her hurriedly and picked up my bags and ran as though it was my last chance for survival," writes Inge. Later, on the train, Joey reflects, "How easy it would have been to stay. How deeply I felt my love for my mother. . . . I had taken her love for granted, and her presence at home. Now I had left a love that had nourished me all my years." (p. 133).

Years later, Inge wrote an unpublished, unproduced one-act play named "Departure." In it, an eighteen-year-old son with strong Oedipal ties returns home after a short while away at the university, unable to adjust to the changes, hoping he won't have to go back. His parents argue, and the mother says to the father: "You know what it was like for him *here* in school. He was terribly shy. He couldn't mix with others. He kept to himself most of the time."[46] "Well," the father replies, "I've paid a full year's tuition . . . and I won't get one red cent of it back, whether he stays in school or not. And

Inge as a seventeen-year-old high-school senior, 1930. Courtesy of WIC/ICC

what kind of future would there be for him in this town . . . without a college education? None. Absolutely none" (p. 3). The mother realizes there is
truth in what the father says; she also worries that she's harmed her son
with overprotectiveness. She says to her husband: "I guess he was the part
of you I always wanted, so I possessed him and made him my own. . . . And
I feel guilty now with his sense of failure" (pp. 6–7). The very brief play concludes with the mother's encouraging her son to return to school, and he
realizes that he must go.

There is no evidence that Inge actually made such a return to Independence as described in "Departure." In all likelihood, this undated manuscript was written while he was in psychotherapy. But it is more evidence
that his enrollment at the University of Kansas was a major—perhaps *the*
major—turning point in his young life. However the separation took place,
it was clearly difficult for both mother and son, and both knew the time
had come for the "speckled egg" to hatch and become aware of the world
beyond the nest.

WILLIAM INGE left Independence in September, 1930, carrying with him much
more than his bags and his misgivings about leaving Maude. Substantive
material for all five of his best-known major works also went with him, even
though it would be better than twenty years before he and others from
Independence—and the rest of the country—would know it.

Already he knew the blessings and curses of small-town life; already he
knew the degrees of desperation that can haunt young and old alike who
must live in tension between individual impulse and family or community
expectations. Already he sensed the human need for love, although he may
have sensed it better in aging maiden schoolteachers, neglected wives, and
other emotional isolates than he yet did in himself. Already he had observed
innumerable characteristics of life in Independence of the teens and twenties
that would one day furnish detail for the settings of his work: Neewollah,
Labor Day picnics, country-club prosperity, summer Chautauquas; farmers
coming in to the county seat on lazy Saturdays; neighbors gossiping over
clotheslines; harness salesmen watching their markets shrink as automobiles
and tractors replaced horses and mules; housewives surreptitiously drinking
vanilla extract in their kitchens; youths defying good sense and swimming
in rain-swollen rivers.[47] Already he had seen both the ugliness and the potential humor in the sort of simple vocal prejudice of people such as Maude's
sister Helen from Wichita, who often railed about "the Catholics" or the

"Communist threat."[48] Already he knew the sharp social and economic lines that were drawn in the small town, lines that might be crossed for an afternoon of tennis but never really erased. All these, and much more, were part of William Inge's experience in September, 1930, as he took his leave from Independence at the age of seventeen.

2 · Lawrence

The University of Kansas lies in the western part of Lawrence, a small, verdant city by the Kansas River, about 40 miles west of Kansas City and 150 miles north of Independence. In 1930, KU's five thousand students attended classes in buildings clustered on top and on the western slope of a large hill known as Mount Oread. Shortly after their arrival in Lawrence, William Inge and his cousin Al Sewell went through fraternity rush week; Al pledged Sigma Chi, and William pledged Sigma Nu. Sewell recalls: "If you weren't a fraternity man, you just weren't one of the boys. You had to belong to a fraternity to be in with things."[1] Pledging a fraternity was expensive, but Maude and Luther must have thought it would be socially important to their son. William roomed at the fraternity house, where he covered part of his expenses by waiting tables and washing dishes.[2]

Frequently he visited Helene, who was still unmarried and seldom dated. They would talk about his schoolwork—he was struggling a bit in all courses except English—and their mutual interest in art. William had briefly taken art lessons with Helene back in Independence, and although he did not continue them, he had continued to enjoy drawing, particularly sketches of his favorite film stars. Their residence in Lawrence enabled them to share time and combat whatever homesickness they may have felt, especially William, who, unlike Helene, was not yet used to being away.

Inge's interest in drama did not fade in the relative campus obscurity of his freshman year. Because he was a freshman taking basic courses, he was not yet eligible to declare a major or participate in campus dramatic productions. At KU then there was no drama major, so most students primarily interested in drama majored in English. Inge did very well in his introductory English courses, and he attended all dramatic productions. Occasion-

Sketches of movie actresses and an actor, drawn by Inge in the 1930s: Bette Davis, Basil Rathbone, Tallulah Bankhead, Marlene Dietrich, Joan Crawford, and Agnes Morehead. Sketches on display at WIC/ICC; photographs from wall display at ICC by Barbara Hardy

ally he took weekend trips into Kansas City to see such road-show performances as *The Barretts of Wimpole Street*, *Cyrano de Bergerac*, and the *Ziegfeld
Follies*. He planned to declare a major in English and to participate in the
classes and productions of KU's best-known drama teacher, Allen Crafton,
as soon as he could.

I could not find any accounts of Inge's years at KU beyond the taped
fragmentary recollections in the Inge Collection by a few associates and the
brief biographical pieces that appeared in magazines and newspapers of the
1950s. But much of significance can be interpreted from *My Son Is a Splendid
Driver*, which, as a novel, cannot be said to be literal autobiography but
which is without doubt Inge's artistic conception of his own early life, projected into the central character of Joey Hansen.

What *Driver* suggests about Inge's first year in Lawrence is that as the
weeks and months passed, he was more successful at academic adjustment
than he was at social adjustment. Although he was not distressingly lone-
some and was able to keep his homesickness in reasonable check, his attempts to blend in comfortably at the fraternity house were none too successful. "I was a member of my fraternity without being a part of it," Joey
says in *Driver* (p. 134). For one thing, most of his fraternity brothers were
wealthy country-club types, like Inge's erstwhile tennis friends at Independence, only worse. Their values and behavior seemed both careless and callous, as though their social class were the only one of possible merit. For
another, he was increasingly aware of what he saw as the hypocrisies of fraternity life. Drinking bootleg whiskey, for example, was routine, even though
the house rules forbade it and specified a fine for it. "It was a rule we exer-
cised only when one of the men got embarrassingly drunk" (*Driver*, p. 135).
Fraternity men would take their sorority-girl dates home by one o'clock on
weekend nights and then go in search of a prostitute or an "easy lay" (p. 135).

In *Driver*, Inge gives an account of a late-night "gang bang" in the basement of the fraternity house during the spring of Joey's freshman year, an affair in which Joey reluctantly participated. "I felt that to have refused would
have cast doubts upon my masculinity, an uncertain thing at best, I feared,
that daren't hide from any challenge" (p. 136). Waiting naked in the line, he
wanted to run, but pride and a sense that he must endure the experience
as a "painful initiation" made him stay. "When it came my turn, I had to
overcome revulsion to achieve a numb orgasm," he writes (p. 137):

For weeks afterwards, I was sure I had contracted syphilis, and I felt
a sick guilt, as if I had betrayed myself. I had pretended to my brothers

to enjoy an experience that had repelled me. I was a hypocrite. Actually, I had felt sorry for the girl I had aided in mistreating. I had wanted to go to her the next day and apologize, and ask her forgiveness. I couldn't bear to think of the humiliation we had subjected her to. (P. 137)

These were his feelings, even though the girl had loudly proclaimed that such treatment was what she wanted from the "snob sonsabitches" and even though the fraternity brother who instigated the affair claimed that she had "been on parties like that in every fraternity on campus" (p. 137). The degree of absolute fact—whether this experience actually occurred or not—is less important than what it reveals of William Inge's youthful feelings about such experiences. Joey says, in *Driver*, that this was the first sexual experience of his life (p. 138). If that was true for Inge, then it must have been traumatic indeed for the seventeen year old, further alienating him from the possibility of discovering anything good in sexual experience. Now, he had more than just Maude's assurances that sex was wrong, degrading, and repulsive; he had his own initial heterosexual encounter to cement the impression.

According to *Driver*, it was also at KU during his freshman year that Inge had his first homosexual experience. "There were tentative, groping, unfulfilled experiences with Bob Luther, from Colorado, that I never had the courage to classify with any name," says Joey (p. 138). Bob Luther is, of course, a fictional name. Whether he represents one actual person or a composite is impossible to tell. Inge describes him as good-looking, quite masculine, and shy, a fellow first-year fraternity member. First-year members had to share beds, and Bob was his bedmate. Joey describes two incidents of Bob's sexual advances under the guise of sleep, the second of which is quite intense:

> . . . I awoke in the early, still-black morning with Bob's mouth on mine, his breath panting, hugging me as if I were saving him from drowning, and one of his hands grabbing one of mine and holding it on his roused genitals. Instinct made me tactful enough to whisper, "Bob, what's goin' on? Are you having another wild dream?" Again, he rolled back to his side of the bed and gave no sign that he was awake. But it occurred to me that he was. (P. 139)

"Homosexuality was anathema in our society then," says Joey, so neither referred to the incidents again, and Bob's advances stopped. And because Bob did not conform to the effeminate stereotype that Joey had of homosexual men at the time, it was hard for him to believe that Bob was gay.

He writes that he avoided effeminate men then, "perhaps fearing an effeminate element in myself that might classify me as one of them" (p. 140). But he did try to let Bob know that they were still friends and that he would not hold those "nighttime misjudgments" against him. "I felt I had to rescue his threatened pride, perhaps because I felt a love of him" (p. 140). "Perhaps" Joey feared some effeminacy in himself (a natural fear for one who has long been called a sissy?). "Perhaps" Joey felt a love for Bob Luther. Those "perhaps" admissions in Inge's first-person narration in *Driver* are as close as he ever came in public print to admissions of his own homosexuality, although late in his life he created homosexual characters who clearly seemed to speak for him, such as Pinky in *Where's Daddy?* Inge's first year in Lawrence, then, continued his education in far more than the academic sense. Although he occasionally had to struggle in some classes, he managed to earn his freshman credits, and he did very well in English. He experienced life without the constant presence of Maude, although she occasionally had Luther bring her to Lawrence for short visits with Helene and Bill, as he increasingly wished to be called.³ The inner turmoil about sex heightened, rather than diminished, as he made his day-to-day way through life along Jayhawk Boulevard, the main campus thoroughfare. And his awareness that he was somehow different, not just in the sexual sense but also in his perceptions, ambitions, and attitudes, also surely grew. William Inge, now in Lawrence, was still "going somewhere." But as he turned eighteen and the school year ended, the Great Depression tightened its grip on the nation's economy, and business in Luther's sales district began to wane. Where William Inge was going, at least for a while, was back to Independence. Luther and Maude told him that they would not be able to afford to send him back to KU in the fall of 1931.

LITTLE IS known about Inge's year back in Independence beyond what can be interpreted from *Driver*. Academically he made sophomore-year progress toward his degree by taking some basic courses transferrable from Independence Junior College (now Community College) to KU, but overall a desire to avoid math—strictly required in the junior college's premajor transfer curriculum but not required of English majors at KU—set him far enough behind that he could not enroll as a junior when he returned to Lawrence.⁴ During the year at the junior college, Inge was again in school with several of his high-school classmates, and the high-school atmosphere was strengthened because then the college and the high school were adjacent. "The year at home attending the small junior college was like a period in purgatory,"

Inge at eighteen. Courtesy of the Kansas State Historical Society

Joey says in *Driver*; "school days lacked the excitement they had had at the university" (p. 170). Still, he was managing to stay in school at a time when the financial ability to do so was lost for many. And he lent his drawing talents to the production of the 1931/32 college yearbook.[5] Whatever seemed most purgatorial about that year likely had little to do with schoolwork, if the chapters dealing with this period in *Driver* are largely factual.

Deep problems rooted in sex again plagued the eighteen year old. Joey tells us that when he returned from his first year away at the university, he immediately learned that his traveling-salesman father had infected his mother with a venereal disease that he had contracted on the road. "Your father has given me a disease that I don't have the courage to name," says Bess Hansen to Joey (p. 145). She is consumed both by contempt for her husband and by deep shame, not only for having the disease but also for its proof that, at her age, she had had sexual union with her husband. Moreover, it was proof of what she had long suspected but what her husband had always denied: that he had sex with other women when he was gone. "Father was now a villain she could justifiably hate," says Joey (p. 151). The painful medical treatment his parents had to endure was also expensive. "That's the real reason we can't afford to send you back to school next year," Bess tells Joey (p. 145). There was also the social expense of her fear of discovery; many people in the small town (transparently and ironically named Freedom, rather than Independence) were bound to find out. And find out many did, although Joey reports that there was no perceptible change in the way neighbors and townspeople behaved toward his mother (p. 148). What loomed largest were his mother's humiliation and anger, and his father's anguished guilt.

I uncovered no proof that venereal disease had afflicted Luther and Maude Inge. But the account of Bess and Brian Hansen's affliction with it rings poignantly again, as it does so many times in *Driver*, of the complexity and pain that can proceed from the heterosexual expression of love. Sex again is seen here as wrong, even sinful; its wages are humiliation and suffering. Not even the vows of matrimony and the approved institution of family can provide positive contexts for the physical experience of sex. Joey, as Inge's adult narrator looking back over the years to when he was eighteen, knows that such a situation is bad, and he also knows that it powerfully affected his own attitudes and feelings about love and sex. And Joey *is*, to great degree, William Inge himself.

In *Driver*, other events on the periphery of sexual experience that year are significant to an understanding of William Inge's life at the time. Joey tells about that year's friendships with Nell Ramsey and Ned Brooks, probably composites of Inge's actual acquaintances, who contributed to his isolation even though they did not mean to.

Nell was a beautiful girl whom Joey had been fond of since childhood. At first after Joey's return, they spent quite a few evenings together, going to movies or wiener roasts or to the country club, where for a small fee they could dance to a jukebox. They rolled cigarettes together and shared an occasional bottle of bootleg whiskey. But they did not share intimacy. "After my one ugly experience at college," says Joey, "I was still frightened of physical love":

> This fear of course was reinforced by the predicament I had found my parents in upon returning home. I was as frightened in Nell Ramsey's arms as I had been years before of swimming in the sea, and unable to think of the sexual act as anything but a degrading thrill that could only cheapen a girl I had respect for. Perhaps Nell was as shy as I was, for our physical relations were as cautious as one's treatment of invalids. A kiss goodnight, a warm embrace, a holding of hands were the only intimate contacts we attempted. (*Driver*, pp. 157–158)

In contrast to Joey's friendship with Nell was his friendship with the handsome Ned Brooks, a summer lifeguard at the pool in Riverside Park, who "had a reputation for sexual daring" (p. 160). Joey eagerly asked Ned about his heterosexual exploits, and Ned good-naturedly answered the questions, without a hint of guilt, remorse, or doubt that such behavior was anything but normal. "You don't believe that people really fuck, *do* ya, Joey?" asks Ned, laughingly. "It was true," Joey reflects, "I didn't" (p. 159).

> It seemed miraculous to me that one could be so lighthearted about sex when it had created such a conflagration in my own home. It never occurred to Ned that he had done anything "wicked" or "obscene." And he retained a wholesomeness of character that separated him from the boys at the pool hall who practiced sex as a vice. . . . He felt no hypocrisy at all in going to church and having sexual pleasure, too. (P. 161)

Their mutual friendship with Joey brought Nell and Ned together one night, and their romance was nearly instantaneous. Joey had suggested that the three of them go to a movie together. They took Ned's car. During an after-movie soda at the New York Candy Kitchen, Nell and Ned "could not take their eyes off each other," and Ned proposed that he drive Joey home first. Joey agreed, and Nell said nothing. At home, after kissing his mother good-night and going to his room, Joey says:

> . . . a feeling of desolation came over me. The two people who had been closer to me and more beloved than any I had ever known out-side of my family, now belonged to each other. . . . And yet it was I who had given them to each other, as though something inside me had wanted to be free of them both. I lay awake the rest of that night. I may have cried. And I know I felt frightened by my compulsion to be excluded from any personal relationship that threatened to be bind-ing. (Pp. 162–163)

The phrase "my compulsion to be excluded from any relationship that threatened to be binding" contains a significant key to understanding the adult William Inge. The "binding relationships" of his youth lay exclusively within his family, most particularly with Maude. During 1931/32, as he at-tended classes at Independence Junior College, he was aware that binding relationships were sources of pain because they slowed his progress toward the elusive freedom he sought in his adult future. He knew he couldn't stay with Maude indefinitely because he knew he would be smothered. Likewise, he couldn't attach himself to anyone else in town—male or female—because his sense of his future depended upon his leaving. Too much involvement with Nell, or a girl like Nell, could jeopardize plans to leave and seek his future independently. Too much involvement with Ned, or a man like Ned, could be plainly ruinous to the friendship at minimum and to social security at maximum. No, the safest path through such potential peril was the lonely one. It was the path William Inge was to follow all his life, with very few, and always temporary, exceptions. In *Driver*, the description of Joey Hansen's "compulsion to be excluded" reminds us of Professor Benoit in *The Strains of Triumph*, one of whose speeches provides the lengthy second epigraph for this book; of Professor Lyman in *Bus Stop*; of Professor "Pinky" Pinkerton in *Where's Daddy?*: all are male teachers who avoid "binding relationships" because of a deep awe and fear of the complexity and responsibility of love.

Driver, of course, is a product of the adult Inge, who had long since stood in the bright sunlight of fame and then in the shadows of near oblivion. It is the mature work of a man who had been thoroughly psychoanalyzed to the point of questioning the value of psychoanalysis.[6] But that late-life questioning was part of a larger despair that will be treated later in this study. The psychoanalysis undoubtedly helped Inge achieve some understanding and perspective and thus contributed to his selections of detail and shadings of emphasis for *Driver*. The "period in purgatory" back in Independence was significant because it contributed to his sense that, for him, sex was either wrong or cost too much in responsibility. For him, escape to a better, happier future depended upon his solitary progress without binding relationships, upon his innate "compulsion to be excluded" from any such relationship. The most compellingly instructive relationship at hand for him was that of his parents. If *that* relationship was the result of love, the product of passion joined to commitment, then the cost was too steep. Perhaps it is no wonder that William Inge could never bring himself into an enduring, "binding" relationship with anyone of either sex. And it appears that this solitary attitude was crystallized during his year back in Independence, 1931/32.

The year seemed to bring some benefits in perspective. Although the strong ties to Maude would never really be severed, it was now certain that she would not be a present force in Inge's future. The "speckled egg" was hatched and heavily influenced, but it was also clearly gone. The year back in Independence must have removed any lingering doubts Inge may have had about his need to press onward. Except for a brief time after his return from graduate work in Nashville, he was never to live under Maude and Luther's roof again. Moreover, that year he gained a better understanding of Luther, who, in Joey's words, "had seemed no more related to me than a school principal or a boss" (p. 165). Luther, Inge realized, had sensed his son's need to get away to get the education at KU that was so expensive to provide. That need prompted arrangements for Inge's return to Lawrence in the fall of 1932.

According to *Driver*, Joey was able to return to KU because of an inheritance bequeathed when his Uncle Jay, a Wichita dentist, died. Inge had an Uncle Earl Mooney, who was a dentist in Wichita, but I do not know whether Inge received such an inheritance. There was also a scholarship made available through the KU English Department. And perhaps, the expensive treatment for Luther and Maude had been completed. In any case, Inge was able to return to KU, a return that had to seem fortuitous indeed to the nineteen year old.

BACK IN Lawrence, Inge quickly plunged into studies and activities with more relish than previously. His long-time ambition to be an actor was still alive, and soon he began to mesh his study with his love of performing. KU was to be the forge for his acting career; he would go to New York upon graduation to pursue his dream. If it ever struck him between the fall of 1932 and the spring of 1934 before his senior year that his goal was impossible or at best unrealistic, he gave no indication of this. It was a sustaining ambition, and if anyone tried to dissuade him then, the attempt failed. As soon as he was eligible, he declared his major in English and began to take drama classes with Allen Crafton, who also directed most of the campus theater productions.

Working with Allen Crafton was an ideal extension of Inge's earlier experience working with Anna Ingleman. Crafton, like Ingleman, was an enthusiastic, talented teacher who genuinely loved both the theater and the long hours spent with students in bringing productions to fruition. Crafton's students learned much more than acting techniques. He created an atmosphere conducive to understanding the theater as a social, cooperative medium. Students learned production details of staging, sets, lighting, and make-up. Besides emphasizing all aspects of production and teamwork, Crafton was a proponent of such well-made play fundamentals as unity between characterization, motivation, and plot and between conventional exposition, meaningful stage business, and traditional sets, lighting, and character-to-audience orientation. Nor was Crafton fond of experimental theater, or whatever had recently been "hot" on Broadway. As Inge was to recall many years later, Crafton "seemed unaware of Broadway . . . under his direction students got a reliable background in the plays of Shakespeare, Moliere, Shaw, and O'Casey."[7] Inge, who appeared in many of Crafton's productions, including George Bernard Shaw's *Androcles and the Lion* and Sean O'Casey's *Juno and the Paycock*, absorbed Crafton's fundamental teaching very well. In fact, all of those fundamentals later became characteristic of Inge's own play direction when he was a teacher, and later still they marked his work as a playwright. Inge was never dramatically innovative. What he consistently displayed, especially at the height of his success, was a mastery of convention.

Although performing and studying under Crafton's tutelage were Inge's central activities by the time he had achieved junior academic standing, these fortunately did not command all his scholastic attention. His love of reading and his facility in writing ensured his continuing success as an English major, and therefore he maintained his scholarship and progressed toward his degree. Perhaps an innate conservatism or caution prompted Inge, even though he was clearly bent on an acting career, to make certain that his ambition did not foster neglect for his other studies. Or perhaps Maude and Luther, or Professor Crafton, had lectured him on the vital importance of finishing his degree. In any case, he resisted any temptation to abandon his other studies in favor of his acting.

Although he was again living in the fraternity house, he was less and less active in fraternity matters. When he wasn't working on a play for Crafton or his other studies, he often visited Helene and Hazel Lee Simmons, with whom Helene shared a house. Simmons recalls that Bill was a frequent supper guest on Sunday evenings and that he also dropped by for brief visits during the week. She especially appreciated his willingness to read poetry to her while she endured the drudgery of ironing. He was an excellent reader, his voice skillfully blending sound and sense. Occasionally, Luther would bring Maude to Lawrence for a visit, and she would happily cook meals for the household, recapturing, however briefly, something of their lost home life.[8]

Around the campus, Inge was primarily known as an actor, one of Crafton's crowd. Franklin Murphy, a fellow student who many years later served as the university's chancellor, remembers becoming acquainted with Inge by attending plays. To Murphy, Inge seemed a bit shy, actively participating in conversation only if the subject—usually drama or film—really interested him. Ferrel Strawn, a fraternity brother who frequently worked with Inge while waiting tables or washing dishes at the fraternity house, knew Inge better than Murphy did. While they worked, Inge displayed a "boundless sense of humor" that Strawn genuinely enjoyed. Neither had much money and thus could not afford to participate in many fraternity activities, but Inge didn't seem to mind. Strawn doesn't say whether Inge spoke any of the reservations about fraternity life that are evident in *Driver*. At any rate, the memories of some of his acquaintances at the time seem to present Inge, after his return to KU, as reasonably happy and successful in pursuing his dramatic and academic interests.[9]

Not all of Inge's theatrical experience after his return to KU was directly guided by Crafton. Campus tradition called for annual student productions of original musical comedy–variety shows, and Inge lent his abilities to each of these shows during the 1932/33, 1933/34, and 1934/35 school years.[10] He also drew cartoons for the *Sour Owl*, the campus humor magazine, in 1932.[11] During the summer of 1933, rather than return to Independence, Inge acted in the summer theater sponsored by the Culver Military Academy in Indiana. Culver was the school that Inge's wealthy Independence tennis friends had attended during the summer of 1929, but I do not know whether he secured the summer-theater work there through their influence or through Crafton's. During the summer of 1934, before his last year at KU, Inge was employed to play juvenile roles in a touring "Toby" show, probably through Crafton's influence.[12] Toby shows were light-hearted comedies featuring the adventures of Toby, a popular clown figure of the day. "A Toby comedian was a kind of a classic figure in American drama," Inge told Lloyd Steele. "He always wore a red wig with bangs and always outwitted the city slickers. I was the juvenile. I played the romantic interests."[13]

Although Inge undertook his share of serious roles during his acting tutelage, comedy seemed to be his strength all during the Ingleman-Crafton-Toby experiences. Whether or not that was a disappointment to him is a mystery, but it seems likely that performing of almost any sort, and subsequent audience appreciation, were what Inge most desired from his acting-career ambitions. To be admired and appreciated in an exciting, romantic way—just as he admired and appreciated famous performers when he was a boy—these were the goals behind his goal of becoming an actor. He wanted to be famous. He wanted to be admired. Performing had brought him his greatest personal rewards and had been the most glamorous aspect of his life. It is little wonder that he clung to it.

But the summer work, especially the touring Toby experience, must have been instructive in some sobering ways. "We actors considered ourselves fortunate if we earned five dollars a week," he remembered many years later. "Sometimes the farmers . . . would bring in flour and meat as barter for admission to Saturday matinees."[14] A young beginning actor could easily see such financial struggling as part of his "dues," the cost of getting started in his chosen craft. But many of the Toby performers were neither beginners nor especially young. They were not paying dues while they waited for the "big break" that would take them to fame and wealth; they were scraping together a livelihood, most of them in the only way they knew how. They weren't going to New York or Hollywood; they were going to Hutchinson or Salina. It was the time of the Great Depression, but economic hard times for the country meant only that a tough career had become even tougher. Such experience had to plant some seeds of doubt in Inge's mind, or at least a sense, probably for the first time, of what odds he faced. He could see that acting carried the chance—even the probability—that while he could find work, he might well find little else: no real fortune, no real fame, just a taxing, itinerant life style.

As his senior year at KU got under way, Inge continued to work as a student actor, but he also continued to take stock of his situation. Crafton's influence was of course helpful, but it did not reach to New York. And Inge knew no one in the worlds of New York theater or Hollywood film. Young people with his talent and ambition were expected to go to New York and pound the pavement, doing whatever they could find until opportunity smiled. Actually to do such a thing took at least a small "stake" of money and a great deal of self-confident nerve. As graduation in the spring of 1935 approached, Inge found that he completely lacked the former and held diminishing reserves of the latter.

He had set his course and had always had the support and encouragement of family members, teachers, and fellow students. He had benefited from the label of being "promising," but now the time to begin to fulfill that promise was at hand. An accounting of dreams against what is needed for personal survival required a new and daunting bookkeeping. Inge began to think of at least temporary alternatives to acting, and although it would yet be some time before he realized it, that was the beginning of the end for his acting career.

An alternative that loomed large was teaching. Helene was not prosperous in her teaching job at Lawrence, but she was surviving and reasonably happy with what she was doing. Moreover, she had plans to continue in teaching and to improve her qualifications by working on a master's degree at the highly respected George Peabody College in Nashville, Tennessee. Inge contemplated joining Helene in graduate study at Peabody to bolster his own teaching credentials and thus strengthen the possibility of an alternative career in teaching. He was not fond of this idea, but to settle for rejoining a Toby troupe was equally unappealing: where did one go from there? And to return to Independence was out of the question for strong reasons, both economic and personal. Teaching was steady work, with regular, if small, pay checks that, managed carefully, could see him through the summers (most teachers were paid on a nine-month basis then; they did not receive summer checks). Going to graduate school and then teaching did not *have* to mean the end of acting; he could still perform in school-sponsored productions, and he could study to gain better credentials in teaching drama. It was a drastic compromise, nonetheless, to go to Nashville, and Inge knew it. He wanted to go to New York, but he was afraid to. He applied to Peabody with great misgivings, and when he was accepted and offered a scholarship, he decided to go when his days at KU were over.[15]

WHAT, IF any, other major changes Inge experienced after his return to Lawrence are conjectural. In *Driver*, Joey says he returned to the university "sorry to discover that Bob Luther had not returned but had transferred to a school of mines in Colorado" (p. 171). If that means that Inge had begun to yield to his homosexual nature, it is not elaborated upon. And indicative of the inner sexual struggle that seems to have haunted Inge all his life, Joey Hansen relates in *Driver* his first (and apparently only) positive heterosexual experience after his return to the university. The woman in this experience is Betsy Parsons.

Joey had met Betsy during their freshman year, before he had to return to Freedom temporarily. She was attractive, bright, and already very popular, usually dating only athletes and wealthy fraternity members. Joey felt lucky to be her friend and classmate; he was "too awed" to consider anything else (p. 134). Betsy loved acting, and by the time of Joey's return, she had become a campus celebrity for her performances. His own interest in drama, along with fortuitous course choices, kept Joey close to Betsy, who began to rely on him to help her cover up her academic laziness. "I honestly did not realize I was in love with her," says Joey; "I did not know I was allowed to be" (p. 174). While Betsy's acting bloomed, her social life became tumultuous. She was expelled from her sorority for sexual indiscretion, but she refused to drop out of school. Joey admired her all the more for this; it squared with his romantic notions of what a great, independent-minded actress would do: "Bernhardt or Duse would have done the same thing." He saw in Betsy's case the classic conflict between "the artist and society" (p. 177).

Because of Betsy and his own growing estrangement from the fraternity, Joey found himself among campus "intellectual bohemians" who were liberal in their views about art and politics. He was not really one of these bohemians himself—naturally, for there was always the "compulsion to be excluded"—but he was more at ease with them than with the fraternity crowd (pp. 178–179). And this social group accepted Betsy wholeheartedly. Moreover, they accepted Betsy's defiant affair with a black athlete, an affair that cemented Betsy's role as a campus pariah. This affair ended with Betsy's pregnancy and subsequent abortion. Throughout all this travail, Joey remained her loyal friend: "I had watched her life on campus as I would watch a great performance on stage, never criticizing Betsy for her behavior any more than I would have criticized Madame X or Sadie Thompson. Everything Betsy did, I converted in my own mind to drama" (p. 185).

Joey tells of one spring afternoon with Betsy in her room, cheers from the nearby track meet—where her erstwhile lover is performing—audible through her window. She tells him she is grateful for his loyal friendship and embraces him, then giggles, "It's almost as if I were the boy making love to the shy girl":

Then, for the first time, I dared assert myself. Some unrecognized urge took over and commanded me, and without even knowing what was happening, I accepted my maleness. Betsy had given it to me, easily and without fuss, and it was the greatest gift that I had ever received. I dared to become a man that afternoon, and to love her with all the careful tenderness that she had been unconsciously wanting all this time, with the tenderness I had been unconsciously wanting to give. (Pp. 185-186)

In all likelihood, Betsy Parsons never existed. Perhaps Inge did have a positive heterosexual experience before his college days at Lawrence were over, but it seems just as likely that if he did, it had few of the dramatically ideal trappings he gives it in *Driver*. His choice of language is as suggestive of fanciful wishing as it is genuine consummation: "I dared assert myself"; "I accepted my maleness"; "It was the greatest gift"; "I dared to become a man." References to tenderness and unconscious desire reinforce this impression. While it is realistic to imagine that a handsome and talented man like William Inge had heterosexual experience during his college years, and while it is true that he had at least one heterosexual love relationship many years later with the actress Barbara Baxley, the net effect of the Betsy Parsons episode in *Driver*, especially when juxtaposed with the earlier remarks about Bob Luther, is contradiction.

This contradiction conveys the genuine confusion about his sexuality that Inge must have endured in poignant ways by the time of his college years. A positive heterosexual experience may have helped at least temporarily to quell his sexual fears, but if it was reassuring, it was not very forceful beyond that reassurance. Although Joey claims the profound discovery of his "maleness" through his love-making with Betsy and although the two were "together constantly" after that idyllic afternoon, marriage was never discussed. Both took it "for granted that it would be a hindrance as we began our careers" (p. 186). In fact, after a rather lengthy and elaborate build-up to that afternoon in her apartment, the romantic Betsy Parsons episode in *Driver* ends in little over a page. Joey and Betsy go to their separate homes after graduation—he to return for graduate work in the fall; she to head for New York to pursue an acting career. They correspond for a while, but eventually her letters from New York stop, and his are returned as undeliverable (pp. 186-187).

Although Inge may have known a woman much like Betsy Parsons at KU, or women who serve to make her a composite character, her function in *Driver* seems primarily to be for the projections of Inge's sexual, career, and philosophical confusions. First, he projects an idealized heterosexual experience with her, probably because he so often wanted to believe that happiness or at least a kind of secure equilibrium lay in heterosexual love relationships. That is a prevailing theme in much of his drama. Second, he projects her going to New York to become an actress, then seeming to be swallowed up and lost—exactly his fears for his own fate had he opted to do that after graduating from college. Finally, he brings Betsy back into *Driver* near the end of the book via a chance encounter, many years later, in a Kansas City bookstore. Here he projects to her much of the sum of his own experience.

In this encounter, we learn that Betsy's time in New York was indeed traumatic. She had won a small part in a flop; then she had drifted through a series of increasingly brutal lovers while she herself became an alcoholic. Her talent had meant little in the sordid, high-pressure world she found in New York. After numerous beatings, drinking bouts, and drying-out stints in Bellevue, she had somehow rescued herself through Alcoholics Anonymous, faith in God, and eventual marriage to another A.A. member. She claims to be serene and adjusted and accepting of her life. "We never learn what life is all about until we fail," she tells Joey; "then you have to surrender to a real life, Joey. The life that's really yours. And make the very best you can out of the life that you have to lead" (pp. 213–214).

By the time William Inge wrote *Driver*, he considered himself largely a failure whose genuine talent had meant little in the harsh glare of New York and Hollywood. He had been a drunk who had found at least temporary respite in A.A. He had spent hours in psychoanalysis to learn that he had to accept himself and his "real life." He had produced numerous works whose message is to accept life and make the "very best" of it, and for a time those works were very well received. All these had been sustaining considerations that had prolonged his life and his will to write. But his dominant tone in *Driver* is regret.

Joey reflects that he both derides and envies the "normal" world that Betsy seems now to have found. He derides it because he senses that its solidarity is false or at best far too fragile; he envies it because most of those who live in that world are blissfully unaware of its falsity and fragility. Joey thinks that the world in which Betsy now lives—the world of acceptance, adjustment, "normal" life—is

a world I often curse, like Lucifer the heaven from which he had been expelled, knowing that I am *not* Lucifer and that it is a false heaven

I long at times to return to, wishing to God I could still find comfort in its solidarity and mirage of warmth, feeling at times I would be willing to hate Negroes, or condemn Jews, and pretend to worship God while I worship Mammon, if I could feel once again the assurance of belonging to the great mass of people who live their lives without conscience or reflection, and subscribe to mass opinion as my father subscribed to *Time* magazine, never challenging its precepts. (P. 214)

He concludes that he cannot claim that Betsy and her husband are hypocrites because they are happy, but sometimes happiness itself seems hypocritical. Thus, Joey finds himself a "stranger" to Betsy's happiness. "It was a happiness that made me feel more alone" (p. 215). By the time Inge wrote *Driver*, he had been essentially alone all his adult life. All happiness was suspect, all formulas for its achievement tenuous and temporary, like so many over-the-counter bromides that treat symptoms but cannot effect a cure. *Driver* was the last work that Inge published during his lifetime. About two years later, he killed himself.

But when he graduated from KU in June of 1935, Inge was only twenty-two years old, still about fifteen years away from beginning his own New York experience. He did not yet aspire to be a writer, and he had not yet wholly abandoned his desire to be an actor. He was a frightened young soul, confused about his sexuality and daunted by the challenges that going to New York to be an actor presented. He saw in graduate school at Peabody a chance to postpone commitment to those harsh challenges, all while seeming to progress toward a secure career alternative in teaching English and drama. He was not happy with his choice at the time, but he was still a long way from becoming the totally disillusioned and nearly burned-out fifty-eight year old who published *Driver*. Joey says, when he loses track of Betsy in New York, that "something now was missing from my life for which, again, I would have to find compensation in my work" (p. 187). Something was usually "missing" in Inge's life, but the compensation he was able to find, at least for a while, in his graduate and teaching work was ultimately to help bring significance to his unhappy existence.

3 · Nashville, Wichita, and Columbus

In 1935, George Peabody College in Nashville already had a good reputation as a training institution for teachers. When Helene and William Inge arrived in Nashville to begin the fall term that year, she was determined to improve her already established credentials in the teaching profession; he was very tentatively resigned to begin to establish his. Helene rented an apartment and enrolled to study for a master's degree in teaching art. William took a room in Peabody's East dormitory and enrolled to study for a master's degree in English.[1] Helene's presence helped Inge avoid the loneliness that would certainly have compounded his doubts about coming to Peabody, and Dick Peck, whom Inge had known in Independence and at KU, came to Peabody the following January; but despite an honest effort to become absorbed in his courses, Inge was never able to share their enthusiasm for graduate study.

Inge was reasonably successful in his course work, but as the weeks and months passed, he began to experience bouts of depression and insomnia. Central to his gathering dilemma was a near-constant self-reproach: he thought he should have had the nerve to go to New York. Even a temporary teaching career seemed now a capitulation rather than a compromise. Although she doubtless tried, Helene could do little to assuage his dissatisfaction. Even the discovery of a suitable topic for his thesis—David Belasco's contribution to realism in American theater—failed to lighten his gloom. Although he attended plays that came to Ryman Auditorium and often went to movies, he did not participate in any of Nashville's amateur theatricals. Perhaps he was already too depressed to try performance as a diversion; after all, he had already *done* such things. It was the painful beginning of the death of his acting dream that generated his dismay. "I'd sort of based my life on the

A bow-tied William Inge at George Peabody College in Nashville, 1935. Print from the WIC/ICC; courtesy of Photographic Archives, Vanderbilt University

theatre," Inge later reflected. "Having given up the theatre, I had given up the basis I'd set my life upon. I was terribly miserable and confused."[2]

As the spring term of 1936 neared its end, Inge completed a draft of his thesis that Freida Johnson, his advisor, found generally acceptable. "David Belasco and the Age of Photographic Realism in the American Theatre" would be the finishing touch on his master's degree, but it had little to do with the much larger quandary in which Inge found himself: then what? He simply did not want to teach. He should have gone to New York in the first place; now it was too late; he wasn't even sure he could act anymore. Helene, also making progress toward her degree, was so much more satisfied with her choices than he was. In fact, she had met William Bradford Connell in Nashville, the man she was to marry. At a time when most graduate students would feel a growing sense of accomplishment, Inge felt only imminent despair. He was headed for his first emotional breakdown, a breakdown that was to have a drastic effect on the next several months of his life.

According to what Inge told Gilbert Millstein many years later, the breakdown was triggered only two weeks or so before the thesis deadline for graduation. He turned his thesis over to a typist, an "excitable toiler" who called one morning to report that in her haste she had forgotten to number the thesis pages. The problem could easily be solved, but the incident, as Millstein reports, "aggravated a growing insomnia, plunged him into a depression, and made him, as he says, go 'literally to pieces.'"[3] Referring to the same time of his life when he was being interviewed by Jean Gould, Inge said that he "developed a sickness of mood and temper."[4] Any diagnosis is imprecise because it is not known whether Inge saw a doctor (if he did, it likely would have been a general physician), and moreover Inge himself is the source of the information. But the effect can be precisely reported: Inge was unable at the time to finish the work needed for the degree. He took incompletes in his last courses, left the thesis uncorrected, and had Helene drive him to Independence.

IN THE LATE spring of 1936, William Inge was again living with Maude and Luther at 514 North Fourth Street in Independence. What he had told his parents beyond the surface details of his experience in Nashville is not known. Probably, Maude and Luther had felt some relief when he had decided to go to Peabody with Helene after he graduated from KU. They knew that acting was dear to him, but they also knew that an acting career was a long shot against long odds. Helene had found her way in teaching, and it must have seemed to them a logical and viable choice for their son as well. They may not have known at first how truly difficult for him the choice had been, but by the time Helene delivered their deeply troubled son to them, they may have guessed. Like Helene, though, they could do little beyond being sympathetic and supportive.

How Inge began to collect himself back in Independence is also not known. He may have seen a medical doctor, who could have suggested mental rest through diversion; or he may have seen a local minister, who could possibly have helped him talk through his anxieties. Or he may have calmed himself in these familiar surroundings, which must also have whispered to him that he could stay awhile and catch his emotional breath but that, as he had long known, he could not remain. He was twenty-three years old, and he would have to get on with his life. There was no real career opportunity for him in Independence, although Maude may have hoped her son would return there to teach. The prospect of teaching *anywhere* had been daunting enough, let alone teaching in his hometown. At twenty-three, Inge also had to know, or strongly sense, that he was homosexual, one of those "degenerates" his mother had once pronounced disgraceful. The prospect of long, lonely years suffocating as he taught in Independence had to be out of the question.

The questions, rather, were what he *would* do, and where he *would* go; and as the summer of 1936 began, he had the time to ponder them as he waited for the anxieties of Nashville to fade away. Opportunity came disguised as physical labor. Summer is the time best suited for road construction in Kansas, when long, hot daylight hours permit work that is impossible in winter and sporadic in fall and spring. Highway crews in summer expand much as harvest crews do when the wheat is ripe: there is plenty of work to be done, and more laborers are needed to do it as soon as possible. For the first and only time in his life, Inge signed on for hard physical labor. As a road-crew member, he probably spent most of his days doing shovel work or swinging a weed cutter. Lighter duty could have included directing traffic around repair areas, but all work was from sunup to sundown, with midday temperatures soaring well over 100 degrees. He found in physical exhaustion what had eluded him in the mental fatigue of Nashville, and he began to sleep soundly each night.[5]

As fall and the end of his summer employment approached, Inge again had to think about his future. Although his appetite and ability to sleep had returned, he was not yet interested in returning to Peabody. He was also sure that he did not want to stay in Independence during the winter, where there would be nothing to do. Like many young adults in the town, he thought a city might provide the opportunity for work. He had no connections in Kansas City or Tulsa, but he still had relatives in Wichita, a city whose fledgling aircraft industry had made it more economically vigorous than other nearby depression-era cities. And so it was that sometime during the fall of 1936, Inge moved the one hundred or so miles northwest to Wichita.

Exactly what considerations prompted his move are not known. Certainly, road-gang work helped him stabilize his emotions somewhat, and it contributed toward his recognition that at least a temporary alternative to acting was still needed. It would be some time yet before he would completely abandon the idea of an acting career, but now at least he was able to see calmly that he needed to do something else and that he was still not willing to make teaching that "something else." Wichita was close enough to home that return, if needed, would be neither costly nor especially problematic; moreover, the relatives in Wichita would lend some degree of support and familiarity. Finally, Wichita was large enough to offer not only more job possibilities but also more opportunities for a certain controlled anonymity. Wichita was too big for everyone to know everyone else's business. Thus it might have appealed to Inge as a place where his sexuality might find a fuller—and safer—expression. But the word *might* must be stressed, for Inge was quite guarded about his homosexuality all his life, often preferring unfulfilled loneliness to any sort of companionship. Wichita's appeal in the fall of 1936 may have been purely for its employment opportunities.

Certainly, employment is all that Inge himself revealed about his months in Wichita. Sometime after his arrival, he went to work as an announcer for KFH, one of the city's most powerful radio stations. It is easy to imagine that his dramatic training and his rich voice—often remarked upon by his associates and clearly evident on interview tapes in the Inge Collection—served him well in that position.[6] Inge worked for KFH nearly a year—a year that is largely lost to scrutiny. Only the work at KFH is mentioned in the biographical pieces that were done after Inge achieved success and fame, and the Wichita year does not appear in *Driver*. Inge told Lloyd Steele that he got the job at KFH by winning an announcer's contest, but he provided no details.[7] So William Inge spent the end of 1936 and until August of 1937 in Wichita, announcing news and reading commercials and community items on the radio. Where he lived and what else he did are not known.

But sometime during his months on the radio, Inge began again to consider teaching as an alternative career. Perhaps the hard work on the road gang had begun to make teaching seem more appealing. And as he toiled through his second straight summer of work in 1937, this time at KFH, he might have reflected that teachers enjoyed summers off. Nothing is known about his relationship with his employers at KFH, and no remarks survive about how well he liked his radio work. Possibly, he saw no way to advance in radio, but just as possibly he found the work dull. Or perhaps he was lonely and unhappy in Wichita. Whatever his reasons, when he heard about an opening to teach English, speech, and dramatics in the high school at Columbus, Kansas—in the extreme southeastern corner of the state, about fifty miles east of Independence—he applied for the job. Shortly thereafter, he accepted an offer and signed a contract to teach there during the 1937/38 school year for $1,125.[8]

COLUMBUS, the seat of Cherokee County, is some ten miles west and fifteen miles north of the Missouri and Oklahoma lines. In 1937, Columbus had about thirty-five hundred people, and that is its approximate population now; thus it was and still is even smaller than Independence. If city size was of importance to Inge in 1937, it was outweighed by other considerations when he moved to Columbus from Wichita. He was willingly going to a very small town, apparently to absorb himself in teaching in order to give that profession an honest trial. Available information about the academic year he spent in Columbus proves that the community and the school easily got enormous value for their $1,125. Shelby Horn, who has chronicled Inge's school year in Columbus, reports that within eight months, Inge had "directed (and sometimes performed in) at least seven one-act plays, three three-act plays, several special programs, and one large-scale operetta."[9]

Such an outpouring of energy undoubtedly could not have been duplicated in successive years had Inge stayed at Columbus. He was young—only twenty-four—and this was his first teaching job, so enthusiasm naturally stemmed from his freshness and his apparent resolve to meet the challenge of teaching squarely. His students, colleagues, and other townspeople could not have known of his prior agonies about teaching, could not have known the doubts that had driven him from Peabody to road gangs and radio. Clearly, he had made up his mind to absorb himself in this job. For all his associates there knew, he had always planned to teach; and as the school year got under way, they had reason to think that they had been fortunate in their choice of a teacher to replace the departed Howard Jones, who had built an extraordinary interest in drama at the school (Horn, p. 67).

By the fall of 1937, Inge had not been directly involved in drama for more than two years. After his period of anguish, he was at last back in drama-tics—from a different perspective, to be sure, but involved again with the world of performing that he had so long loved. Of course, there was hard work new to one who had previously concentrated on acting: selecting mate-rial, coaching students, planning the details of production, taking full re-sponsibility, and all still with the knowledge of being observed and judged by a critical community audience. But in these responsibilities at Columbus, Inge fared very well.

He had many tasks, including teaching a drama class which learned ba-sics and then performed one-act plays before audiences at the school, at civic clubs, at rural schools, and at various area competitions. He selected, cast, and directed three-act plays for both the junior and senior classes. He was sponsor and director of the Masquers Honorary Dramatics Club, which also presented a three-act play and several one-act plays before various groups during the year. One "all school" group, which he selected from among his best performers, presented a one-act play on a Joplin radio station. Often, his students' productions won high ratings in area competitions (Horn, pp. 67–69). It was obvious that Mr. Inge (as his students formally called him) ably continued, or perhaps exceeded, the quality in dramatics that his pre-decessor, Mr. Jones, had established.

Inge was only six or seven years older than most of his students, but he kept, in Horn's words, "a certain distance in dealings with them," a distance that might have been seen as arrogant in someone less dedicated (p. 67). Of course, retrospect allows a new dimension to that distance: by not getting too close to his students socially, Inge could keep an effective professional balance and avoid any vulnerabilities of his private nature. It was a balance he was by now familiar with, and in different ways he struck the same sort of balance with his faculty and community friends. "There were subtle dis-tinctions between his private, public, and classroom personalities," reports Horn (p. 66). Although virtually all faculty and community people liked Inge and considered him friendly, Horn says that

a quality in his features—perhaps in his eyes—made some think he had an inner sadness. These people say he was a "loner." Others, however, tell of the many visits he made to their homes or to those of others. Perhaps the most accurate description of him during this period would be "enigmatic." Few really knew him. (P. 65)

Of course, memory is often subtly distorted among people who can claim to have known a famous person "back when," and the fame William Inge won in the 1950s must have sharpened the "enigmatic" impression Inge had left with his acquaintances in Columbus, who could then explain much of the enigma with a "little did we know" air of respect and wonder. But even their knowledge of Inge's later success cannot completely account for the truth of Horn's remark that "few really knew him."

The Inge that he allowed associates to know was, however, a pleasant, talented, and dedicated person indeed. He had amused his new colleagues early in the year when the principal, Lloyd Brown, had asked him at a faculty meeting to be the announcer during football games. Brown naturally assumed that Inge's dramatic training and radio background would ideally suit him for that job. "Not me!" Inge blurted in genuine alarm; "I don't know a punt from a forward pass!" (Horn, pp. 63–64). Inge and another young teacher of music, Paul Cumiskey, soon found that they made an entertaining team, with Inge improvising comedy routines while Cumiskey supplied impromptu background music (p. 63). Later, Inge donned blackface to participate in a minstrel show that Cumiskey directed, and the two collaborated in directing an operetta (p. 68). Inge often gave dramatic readings in "a rich, well-modulated baritone" (p. 66). Among these was a reading of "The Gift of the Magi" in the school's Christmas program.

Like other single faculty members, Inge roomed by himself. His room was in the home of Hugh Makinney, a short walk from the high school. Inge did not yet own an automobile, so the residence was convenient. He had to take his meals at restaurants or at the homes of friends or married faculty. His evenings were largely filled with grading papers, attending rehearsals or other school functions, and the usual quiet business of a small-town teacher. On weekends he often played tennis with Paul Gibson, the math teacher, who recalls Inge was a good tennis player, capable of looking neat and orderly even after a hard match. In fact, most of Inge's Columbus associates recall him as a very neat person, "immaculate" in both appearance and behavior. They also recall him as rather reserved and quiet, even among friends and co-workers. He occasionally had a date with another teacher, Lois Hunt, who "found him to be everything a gentleman should be" (Horn, pp. 64–65).

Some of Inge's Columbus colleagues may have been the first people ever to hear him say he was thinking of becoming a serious writer. Just when he began to entertain such a thought will never be precisely identified, but Paul Gibson remembers that one evening when Inge and some other faculty were dinner guests at the Gibson home, Inge mentioned this ambition. "Nobody laughed," reports Horn; "something in his manner said that this was more than just a passing fancy or a dream, and, furthermore, none of those present doubted his ability" (p. 66). The Inge they knew, of course, was only the Inge they were allowed to know, but his talent, his manner, and his hard work must have intimated that here was someone surely not destined to remain in Columbus. If they saw him as staying in teaching, they doubtless saw him as too able, too ambitious, to teach in Columbus for long. In fact, some of them correctly guessed that he was eventually headed for a college teaching job (p. 75). If they saw him as potentially a serious writer, then they also saw him as leaving Columbus. Either way, again, those around him saw William Inge as "going somewhere." This time, where he was going was back to Peabody to finish his master's degree.

Somehow, the intense year of teaching in Columbus, juggling the severe social constraints of the location with the great challenges of teaching itself, settled the last of the long internal turbulence Inge had begun to suffer at Peabody in the spring of 1936. Of course the long trail of work and adjustment had begun during the searing summer days on the road gang and had continued while he was on the air in Wichita. The decision to come to Columbus signaled his partial triumph over his disappointment: his life again had purposeful direction, and the hard-dying dream of acting no longer always haunted him, making him feel that teaching constituted a cowardly and utter capitulation. Teaching was still at best a compromise, but it was by now a compromise he seemed to be able to accept, at least for the time being. Although virtually everyone in Columbus would disagree, Inge did not feel then, nor did he ever feel, that he was a good teacher. Perhaps he believed that the really good teachers are always those who are unquestionably doing what they want to do. Whatever the reason, he was never to be satisfied with his teaching, even after the prodigiously industrious year at Columbus. But that year at least convinced him that he should finish his degree at Peabody and continue for a while elsewhere in his new alternative profession.

Another reason for leaving Columbus, probably at a subconscious level, was its size. Inge had already seen, among teachers rooming in his own home in Independence, the strict, subdued life styles that small-town teachers, especially single teachers, had no choice but to adopt. While he was in Columbus, rooming at the Makinney home, that life style necessarily became his own. As Horn observes, in Columbus, "teachers lived by a strict moral code. They were expected to be pillars of propriety, and most were" (p. 64). And so was William Inge. But probably no one then suspected what a strain that life style could create for him. To throw himself into his work and repress his innermost self for an academic year was one thing, but to consider the same absorption and repression year after year was another. Although he probably felt a sense of accomplishment and purpose, consistent with a return to finish his degree at Peabody, the same voice that once had whispered that he could not stay in Independence was whispering still in Columbus. His master's degree could take him elsewhere, perhaps to a larger city, perhaps to a less cloistered existence.

Inge was to say about teaching, many years later in an interview, that "as long as you're a teacher, you're considered someone else's property." He went on to say that all the time he taught, "My private life belonged to someone else."[10] That was his assessment fifteen years after he had left teaching to go to New York, at last, to pursue his writing, not acting, career. That assessment had to have begun even before his year in Columbus, then to have grown while he was teaching there in 1937/38. Still, he was to serve two more stints as a teacher before he abandoned his compromise alternative career. Whatever its shortcomings, teaching provided his livelihood in 1937/38, and it would continue to do so during the periods 1938 to 1943 and 1946 to 1949, even though the depression and the deep inner turbulence that had caused him to leave Nashville in 1936 would also eventually return and intensify. As the school year ended in Columbus – preceded by a deadly tornado that took ten lives and leveled part of the town – Inge directed the senior-class play, the last major production of the year. He was probably his own toughest critic, but even he had to have known that the year had been successful by any external measure. He had met the challenge; for a time, then, he would continue to meet it. But elsewhere.

INGE RETURNED to Nashville in the summer of 1938 to finish his incomplete course work and to see his thesis through to acceptance at Peabody. He stayed with Helene and her husband, William B. Connell, who had been married in Independence on June 6, 1937.[11] The work went smoothly, and he completed the degree without any difficulty. Two Inge scholars who read his thesis, "David Belasco and the Age of Photographic Realism in the American Theatre," James W. Byrd and Philip Bayard Clarkson, agree that the thesis shows little of the writing talent that was to become manifest later. Clarkson finds the thesis "repetitious, and the style is generally pedestrian"; only the interest in realism augurs something of Inge's future.[12] And when Byrd wrote to Inge in 1956 that the thesis betrayed little of Inge's talent, Inge replied, "Isn't it a basic requirement that theses be dull?"[13] Dull or not, the thesis completed Inge's master's degree, and possession of that degree opened up the possibility of teaching at the college, rather than high-school, level. The opportunity for a college job came unexpectedly later that summer, through a recent acquaintance.

While Inge was still teaching at Columbus, he occasionally spent week-ends visiting Maude and Luther in Independence. On one of those week-ends he met Harry Holtzman, who had recently moved there from New York City and married a local woman. Inge enjoyed talking with Harry about New York, and Holtzman enjoyed being viewed as a sophisticate from Manhattan. When Inge returned from Nashville for a summer visit, the Holtz-mans invited him to accompany them on a brief trip to Santa Fe, in the mountains of northern New Mexico. According to Holtzman, while the three were in Santa Fe, they encountered an old friend (whether an old friend of the Holtzmans' or of Inge's is not clear) who was working as a "field man" for Stephens College, an exclusive two-year women's school in Colum-bia, Missouri. When the friend learned that Inge had completed his master's degree (or would soon complete it), he recommended Inge to fill a vacancy in English and drama at the college.[14]

Further details of Inge's hiring at Stephens are not known. But a few weeks after both the degree and the trip to Santa Fe had been completed, William Inge moved to Columbia, Missouri, never to live in Kansas again. He began his years of college teaching at Columbia with the prospect of living, for the first time, at considerable distance from any relative. Colum-bia is by no means a large city, but it was much larger than Columbus, and at first Inge must have felt that he had found a better situation in which to work and live. It was to be his home for five years, years that were grad-ually to prove increasingly difficult, and finally desperate, for him.

Part Two • Missouri: Progressions

4 · Columbia

Columbia lies on old U.S. Highway 40 (now I-70) roughly in the middle of Missouri, somewhat closer to St. Louis than to Kansas City, the state's largest cities on its eastern and western extremities. Comparable in size and atmosphere to Lawrence, Kansas, yet more isolated because there are no nearby large cities, Columbia is the site of the University of Missouri and was the university home of Thomas Lanier (later Tennessee) Williams from 1929 to 1932.[1] In 1938, however, Columbia as yet had no claim to be a part of the past of two important playwrights. What theater excitement there was then was probably centered upon the arrival of Maude Adams at Stephens College.

Adams, a legend in American theater, had recently retired and agreed to come to Stephens to teach drama and direct plays. The prospect of working with Adams must have excited Inge, but the reality of working with her apparently proved both remote and trying. Writing about the Maude Adams Inge came to know, Joseph Kaye said: "For some reason she had turned from her past life and secluded herself in a teaching activity. It was a type of recluse existence, and she permitted few to share it with her."[2] In addition to being socially remote, Adams was difficult to work with. She had her own ideas about drama, and she had the reputation and the clout to prevail. "I don't know what it proves, exactly," Inge was to recall many years later, "except perhaps that I have a certain amount of determination; but I stayed at Stephens five years, working with Maude Adams, the famous Peter Pan actress, who was a stern taskmaster."[3] Maude Adams gave Inge his first close look at the personality of a genuine "star" performer. He may not have especially liked what he saw, but he definitely respected Adams's celebrity status, for he seldom failed to mention working with her when he recollected his years at Stephens.

Maude and Luther Inge, taken at their home on a Sunday afternoon in August, 1942.
Courtesy of Luther Claude Inge

At Stephens, Inge's teaching duties often fell in English composition, but the initial excitement over Adams's presence and the partial assignment that he had to assist in dramatics kept Inge's interest in the stage alive, even though he found himself with much less influence and control than he had had in Columbus. At twenty-five he was still young, still slender and handsome (even though his hair was beginning to thin), and ideal for male roles on a campus where males were in short supply. But there was also a sameness to acting that he began to notice, a sense of atrophy. He was, after all, doing the same sort of acting he had done four and five years earlier. In key ways he had not developed as an actor at all, and now he did not even have the compensating feelings he had experienced as a director. He became more and more self-conscious on stage, less and less instinctive and intuitive. He was very near the end of his performing career, but he did not quite realize it yet.

Meanwhile, his sleeplessness returned, and shortly thereafter the familiar dissatisfaction and depression that haunted his first stint at Peabody. A local doctor suggested that alcohol might help—a cocktail before meals and beer before bed—and Inge was soon following that suggestion all too well.[4] Of course he did not at first intend to abuse alcohol, but as time wore on at Stephens, he drank more and more, usually alone. And as he taught, acted, and drank, he found less and less satisfaction in the first two.

Inge was much later to say in several different interviews that he became too introspective and too intellectual to continue acting.[5] He identified one role as his last: "I played the choir master in an amateur production of *Our Town*," he says; "and suddenly I found I was terrified, too self-conscious to ever act again."[6] Exactly when Inge played that choir master is unclear. The 1957 *Time* magazine article, in which that information first appeared, and Robert Baird Shuman's 1965 biography both state that it occurred before Inge went to Columbia to teach, but other evidence makes that unlikely. Josephine Murphey reported in the *Nashville Tennessean* on September 20, 1953, that Inge did no acting in Nashville. Certainly he was not involved in any production during his Independence summer on the road gang. At Wichita he "performed" on the radio daily, and Shelby Horn provides ample evidence that Inge performed—including acting—frequently during his year in Columbus. Although I have not found any playbills from Stephens to confirm this, the moment when Inge's acting career truly ended was apparently in Columbia, Missouri, while his nights became sleepless and his days became disappointing, while again he saw that he had missed his best chance when he had failed to go to New York in 1935. In Columbia he began to see himself headed toward thirty, more or less trapped in a teaching career that he had always thought would be temporary but that now threatened to become permanent.

If Columbia was where Inge's dream of an acting career at last died, it was also where he began at least tentatively to write. Exactly what, how much, and why he wrote are not clear, because accounts vary. Jean Gould states that at Stephens, Inge "kept a journal, in which he recorded his reactions and ideas; he wrote short stories (none of which was published) and poetry, but only for his own pleasure and the release of inner tensions." In Gould's account, Inge did not at this time consider himself a writer, nor did he think about writing plays.[7] But Austin Faricy, another Stephens faculty member whose apartment was in the same building as Inge's, remembers that Inge wrote fragments of plays at the time. Faricy also remembers that Inge read parts of them to his associates.[8] Inge himself told Gilbert Millstein that on the advice of a Columbia medical doctor, he had begun to see a psychiatrist in Kansas City.[9] Perhaps it was the psychiatrist who suggested writing to "release inner tensions," as Gould puts it. It seems clear that Inge indeed began to write while at Stephens, although it is impossible to tell at this distance in time exactly what or why he began to write.

Thus the years in Columbia, which later were always to seem lost and rather aimless to Inge himself, were actually important in many ways. First, for whatever reason, Inge began to write with some regularity. Second, to battle disappointment and depression, he began to drink. And third, to battle the same adversaries, he turned for the first time to psychiatry. Writing eventually became his claim to endurance beyond his mortal boundaries. Drinking became a part of both his inspiration and his doom. Psychiatry, particularly the Freudian analysis most common at the time, eventually gave him insight into himself that enhanced his writing and extended his human understanding, even though it finally did not help him save himself.

AS AT COLUMBUS, Inge had faculty friends at Stephens. Many lived, as did Inge, in Ridgeway House, a large dwelling close to campus that had been partitioned into apartments. Most of Ridgeway House was occupied by humanities faculty—Inge, Austin Faricy, Helen Hafner, and Ed and Vera McGraw. These were relatively young and talented people, and they frequently gathered together for meals, local entertainments, and faculty gossip. Faricy, a one-time Rhodes Scholar, remembers Inge as a good cook, one who knew food and wine better than the rest, and who was always neatly and smartly dressed. He describes Inge at the time as "tall, slender, still very

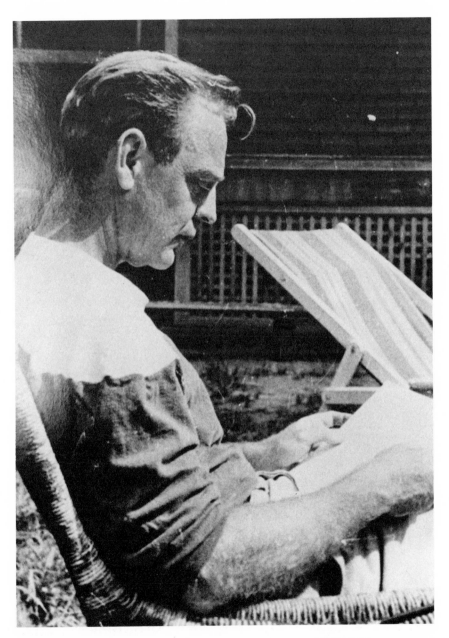

Inge relaxes while on the faculty at Stephens College. Courtesy of WIC/ICC

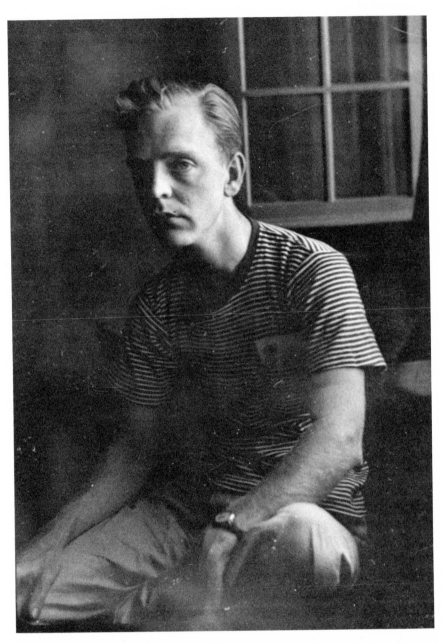

Inge, photographed by Harry Holtzman, Columbia, Missouri. Courtesy of WIC/ICC

handsome."[10] Hafner remembers hosting afternoon teas where Faricy played the harpsichord. Inge would be there, seeming to enjoy himself, but being very "quiet spoken."[11] Both Faricy and Hafner remember that at Stephens, Inge began to think of himself more and more as a writer. Both report that Inge read some of his writing to the Ridgeway group and that they all encouraged Inge to continue writing—Ed and Vera McGraw in particular (Inge dedicated his 1963 Broadway play, *Natural Affection*, "to Ed and Vera").

How much Inge's faculty friends at Stephens knew about his inner turmoil is conjectural, but it appears they didn't know much. As at Columbus, faculty friends knew him as capable, orderly, tasteful, and quiet. He was certainly part of their social group, but he was also reserved. None of them— Faricy, Hafner, or Albert and Virginia Christ-Janer (friends mentioned by Gould)—reports having knowledge of Inge's final acting trauma in *Our Town*; in fact, none of them mentions acting at all. And while all mention in some degree the presence and influence (or lack of same) of Maude Adams, they do so as a link to Inge's later career as a writer, not as a teacher. None of them says much about Inge's teaching. Did they know how deeply dissatisfied he was as a teacher? They might have known that he did not think he was very good at teaching, but probably they sensed his doubts more than he actually told them. For all his civility and social grace, he was by now a very private person. If any of his Stephens associates knew of his homosexuality, their own taste and restraint prevented them from mentioning it even many years after Inge had left Stephens, many years after he had become famous, indeed many years after his death.

Faricy, in his recollections about Inge's drinking at the time, gives some indication of how little the Ridgeway group really knew Inge: they knew he drank, and they knew he had hangovers, but they attributed the hangovers to a lack experience with drinking.[12] Inge himself, however, believed that his alcoholism began as early as his first year at Columbia.[13] Few, if any, of his Stephens associates knew the extent to which he was drinking while he lived at Ridgeway. Inge surely did not become an alcoholic with overnight suddenness, and it was to be 1948 before he was to admit his alcoholism at Alcoholics Anonymous in St. Louis. But there must have been long, solitary drunken hours, both in Columbia and in St. Louis. Again, if there were those who knew or even suspected that Inge was drinking too much while at Stephens, they chose to keep their silence about it long after that silence could have mattered much to their old friend.

How long it took Inge to decide that Columbia and Stephens were all too similar to Columbus and Cherokee County Community High School

Inge, second from right, with friends at Columbia, Missouri. Courtesy of WIC/ICC

is also conjectural. By his own account he began seeing a psychiatrist in Kansas City—a trip of about 150 miles by bus, because Inge still had no car—but in that same account he claims that seeing that psychiatrist "didn't do much good" (Millstein, p. 63). While the nature of those psychiatric visits was then and remains a private matter, Inge's frustrations about his career and his sexuality were probably at the forefront. How soon he began the weekend bus trips to escape into Kansas City or St. Louis is also not precisely known, but such forays—always by himself—became frequent well before he left Stephens.

KANSAS CITY and St. Louis had a wide variety of entertainments, most of which were completely unavailable in Columbia. Besides offering many more shows, films, concerts, and restaurants, each city was also large enough to provide a night life where anonymity and homosexuality could coalesce in ways that Inge's Columbia employment and life style would have required. Inge's movements and associations in the cities at this time are largely not known, but his work reflects, not surprisingly, a degree of shame toward them. In one of his most powerful one-act plays, *The Boy in the Basement*, the central character, Spencer Scranton, is a homosexual mortician in a small Pennsylvania town who lives with his mother and invalid father above the mortuary. Spencer, who dares not reveal his homosexuality in the town, makes frequent trips into Pittsburgh to a gay bar. His greatest fear is of being discovered, particularly by his mother. One night the gay bar is raided, and Spencer calls home for money to keep the police from jailing and charging him. Later, his mother discovers the truth, and her indictment of Spencer is Inge's indictment of himself, imagined by way of Maude:

MRS. SCRANTON: And the police raided the place because it's a meeting place for degenerates.

SPENCER *collapses over the table, his head in his arms.*

MRS. SCRANTON *now has the bearing of a tragic victor*: Dear God, my own son! My own flesh and blood! Corrupting himself in low degeneracy. Going to some disgusting saloon, where men meet other men and join together in . . . in some form of unnatural vice, in some form of . . . of lewd depravity.[14]

Spencer, of course, is crushed.

Other events push this play toward a typical Inge resolution: Spencer defiantly declares his independence and leaves, only to return, defeated by the realities of his interdependence with his parents. Mother and son are reconciled, and Spencer must accept his situation as he symbolically prepares for burial the body of a young man he had loved from afar. *The Boy in the Basement* is not an early Inge play; it was written in the early 1950s.[15] It is a play that mines his own feelings and the psychoanalysis that he was then undergoing on a regular basis. And its self-condemnation is powerful indeed for an author of about forty who, at the time, was considered a highly successful playwright.

The constraints of the closet had to be quite familiar to William Inge by the time he was on the Stephens faculty. The weekend bus trips into the city, somewhat daring as they were, doubtless held some therapeutic value, although it is impossible to tell whether they were actually recommended by his Kansas City psychiatrist or merely discovered as a natural matter of course by Inge himself. And unquestionably, they provided him with material he was eventually to use. He told interviewer Digby Diehl in 1967 that the boy-pursuing-girl idea at the center of *Bus Stop* came from a similar situation he'd seen on a bus trip to Kansas City.[16] And the drunken Professor Lyman in the same play, who aimlessly rides the bus and loathes himself, is almost certainly modeled upon Inge himself. (In fact, teachers in Inge's works tend to be a tortured lot—surely no coincidence.)

If anyone in Columbia was privy to the actual Inge, the fact has long been shrouded in silence. His niece, Jo Ann Mahan (later Kirchmaier), knew little about the company her uncle kept during the short time she was a student at Stephens. Although she became closer to him many years later, she says she didn't see him very often at all then, and she was rather hurt because he was so distant.[17] She couldn't have fully realized then his reasons for that distance; although surely by this time, members of Inge's family must have considered him a bit odd, at best. Being considered odd, or eccentric, was after all not so damning, not so shameful, given his public persona. Suspicion is only suspicion, not proof. And proof was something Inge was forever loath to provide anyone, even those who knew him well.

The great trouble with life in such a closet was that it limited most sexual relationships—if not *all* sexual relationships—to casual, anonymous (or nearly anonymous) affairs. Strong, enduring love relationships cannot be developed under such conditions; or if they are attempted, they are necessarily still quite limited. Thus, what William Inge saw for himself as the Stephens years passed by was a rather lonely and unhappy future, also a future that no longer held the dream of accomplishment, of recognition, for what he might contribute as an actor. It had to have been for him an unpleasant prospect, and nowhere in his work does he give it better expression than in the desperate speeches of the schoolteacher Rosemary Sydney in *Picnic*, as she pleads with Howard Bevans, who has just become her lover, to marry her:

ROSEMARY: Where's the preacher, Howard? Where is he?

HOWARD (*Walking away from her*): Honey, I'm forty-two years old. A person forms certain ways of livin', then one day it's too late to change.

ROSEMARY (*Grabbing his arm and holding him*): Come back here, Howard. I'm no spring chicken either. Maybe I'm a little older than you think I am. I've formed my ways too. But they can be changed. They *gotta* be changed. It's no good livin' like this, in rented rooms, meetin' a bunch of old maids for supper every night, then comin' back home alone.

HOWARD: *I* know how it is, Rosemary. My life's no bed of roses either.

ROSEMARY: Then why don't you do something about it?

HOWARD: I figure—there's some bad things about every life.

ROSEMARY: There's too much bad about mine. Each year, I keep tellin' myself, is the last. Something'll happen. Then nothing ever does—except I get a little crazier all the time. (Act III, scene 1)[18]

In the play, Rosemary is successful in pressuring Howard to marry her. She escapes her lonely life style, even though there are no guarantees that the marriage will truly be happy. She was desperate enough to try to force a radical change in her life. In his way, at Stephens, William Inge experienced a similar desperation that was to result in a radical change.

On one weekend trip to St. Louis, Inge met Reed Hynds, a critic writing for one of the city's three daily newspapers, the *Star-Times*. Hynds's beat included drama, music, art, and books—all areas of interest to his new friend; and as the friendship grew and Inge learned that Hynds was facing the wartime draft, Inge began to think that he could take Hynds's job in the interim. For reasons Inge never made clear, he was ineligible for the draft; perhaps it was because he was already over twenty-eight when the United States entered the war in 1941; perhaps it was because he was a sole surviving son. At any rate, Hynds was to be drafted, and Inge took some critical pieces he himself had written to Norman Isaacs, the managing editor of the *Star-Times*. Isaacs decided to hire Inge as a temporary replacement for Hynds.[19]

The prospect of moving to St. Louis from Columbia in 1943 and leaving teaching must have been exciting to Inge, who at thirty knew full well that he would never be an actor and would never be satisfied as a teacher. The Stephens years had been important in his coming to realize these things, even though he gives this period short shrift in *Driver*. He describes Stephens in *Driver* as "a small girls' college close to Kansas City" (p. 188). He credits the job there, in his very brief chapter 13, for helping him make his final "break from home," forcing him to become emotionally independent (p. 189). Although that assessment is not false, its simplicity masks the depth of Inge's experience from 1938 to 1943. *Driver*, however, is Inge's memoir of his formative sensibility, and it does not continue in much detail beyond his college years. Although its last two chapters (14 and 15) and the short epilogue offer some important summary material, Inge concluded the basic time setting of *Driver* well before the final years of his life. Its great value is that it shows the development of the young writer's basic sensibility and vision, and these he brought in some abundance to St. Louis.

St. Louis was a genuine city, much larger than Wichita—till then the largest city in which Inge had ever lived—and larger, too, than Kansas City. St. Louis had long been important in the family consciousness because it was the headquarters of Luther's employers, the Wheeler and Motter Drygoods Company, and Luther had made many business trips there during his younger son's early years. Now William himself would live there. He had made so many weekend trips to St. Louis that he already knew his way around the city. His job, in fact, would require him to cover the kinds of events that he would want to attend anyway. It was a major break in his life.

His long-time loves of reading, drama, and art; his more recent efforts to develop his writing; and his increasing need to wrap his drinking and his homosexuality in the anonymity of a large city—all were coalescing in an unexpected alternative career, a career that, in a modest way, would also put his name before the reading public. Becoming the all-purpose critic for the *St. Louis Star-Times*, assured of a by-line, and given entree to the cultural events of a large city, amounted to nothing short of a deliverance for William Inge in the spring of 1943. He welcomed the chance to live and work in St. Louis; he felt enough confidence to meet the challenge of daily writing for publication; he felt the necessary confidence in his judgment to meet the challenge of being a critic. When he moved to St. Louis at the close of the spring term at Stephens in 1943, he moved into the pivotal period of his life.

5 • St. Louis

Flourishing at the confluence of the Missouri and the Mississippi rivers, St. Louis has always been a city of symbolic as well as literal crossroads. The gateway city to the broad expanse of the American West after the Louisiana Purchase, St. Louis became a commercial center for trade between East and West as the country developed during the nineteenth century. By 1900, St. Louis had a well-established middle- and upper-class population, mostly based upon mercantile prosperity, and these classes helped attract the 1904 World's Fair. Subsequent cultural growth before World War II made St. Louis and Chicago America's greatest "western" cities, cities whose cultural ties were with the eastern metropolises rather than with the western villages. When William Inge came to St. Louis in 1943, it was still a vibrant, vital, and growing western city, not yet outstripped by the phenomenal postwar growth of the Pacific Coast cities. St. Louis was an exciting place to be, and it was to prove a crossroads city for Inge, as well.

Still without a car, Inge arrived with his few possessions by bus. At first he took a room at the Coronado Hotel on Lindell Boulevard, near the St. Louis University campus in the heart of the city. Charles E. Burgess, who has written the authoritative account of Inge's years in St. Louis, describes the area that was Inge's home for the next few months:

> Just east was broad Grand Boulevard in the heart of the "midtown"; its attractions included a halfdozen movie houses with considerable live theatre in those years. Lindell Boulevard led, a few blocks west, to a hotel and night-club district extending to vast Forest Park. Musical comedies with "name casts" were performed nightly during summers in the park's Municipal Opera, and in the City Art Museum in the

park the largest collection of painting and art objects in that part of the Midwest was free to view. Music and theatrical schools were nearby . . . among an array of antique shops and bohemian bars.[1]

For Inge, this was Mecca.

His nearly three years of writing for the *Star-Times* were in many ways the happiest of his life. The *Star-Times* was an afternoon paper, so Inge did not have to compose his reviews immediately after a night's performance. Rather, he often joined the cast in post-performance partying or other theater-goers who were inclined toward celebrating. Regularly he enjoyed the night life of the city, which, as long as he filed his writing in time, helped him both to indulge and to cloak his alcoholic and homosexual propensities. Burgess reports that Ray Noonan, a *Star-Times* colleague who usually arrived at 7:00 A.M., often found Inge already at his desk, "working like hell and looking like he'd been up all night." Another colleague, Mary Kimbrough, was more specific: "He always looked like he had a hangover" (p. 446).

He probably did. But he was also intent on meeting his deadlines, and he was consistent in doing so. Moreover, wartime paper shortages restricted the number of pages, but Inge fit his reviews quite well into his allotment of space. He may have been living indulgently, but he covered plays, musical events, films, exhibits, books, records, and even night-club entertainment, all while sharpening his perceptions and confidence. He also did several interviews. That Inge was a busy critic and writer is beyond debate. His most recent and thorough bibliographer, Arthur F. McClure, lists more than 400 signed Inge pieces for the *Star-Times* between June 15, 1943, and February 9, 1946. Philip Bayard Clarkson, in his Ph.D. dissertation, claims to have found 587 "signed or initialed" *Star-Times* articles by Inge.[2] However many pieces Inge actually wrote, it is easy to agree with Burgess that Inge's newspaper writing experience was valuable in his later career: "The disciplines of deadlines and writing 'tight'—both in space requirements and in physical condition—certainly were of benefit to him when he faced the overnight rewriting required for Broadway productions" (p. 455). Experience with hard-nosed editors also made him more likely to be reasonable about rewriting.

It is ironic that Inge, a playwright who could be said to have been destroyed by critics, was himself a critic before he became a playwright. Writing some years later about his St. Louis articles of criticism, Inge said, "I am embarrassed to recall those articles now. They were all written in a tone of high indignation, which I accepted as the only way one wrote about the theatre."[3] But Clarkson, who read all of Inge's *Star-Times* criticism, found him "rarely scathing" (p. 24). Classifying each piece as "favorable," "unfavorable," or "noncommittal" and trying to avoid using the last category if there was any basis at all for assigning a piece to one of the first two categories, Clarkson decided that 385 of the 587 pieces he claims to have found were favorable, 160 were unfavorable, and 42 were noncommittal (p. 33). Clarkson's totals include the many interviews Inge published, and those cannot strictly be construed as criticism; but on the whole, Charles E. Burgess's assessment that the "general tone of Inge's reviewing is genial" seems accurate (Burgess, p. 449). As might be expected, Inge's reviews were more detailed and polished when he covered plays or films, but Burgess believes the music reviews show that Inge had a good layman's knowledge of music, which grew with his experience (p. 450). His long-time love for art and literature also served him well.

However genial his written reactions to the works of others may have been, Inge nonetheless often felt when covering plays that he could have produced better work than what he was reviewing. We have already seen that Inge had done some playwriting at least as early as his years at Stephens. Jean Gould reports that in St. Louis, as he became more and more convinced that he could write as well or better than those whose work he was reviewing, Inge "began to try [to write] casually, but he still needed a final motivation to go at it in earnest."[4] That "final motivation," however, was not to come until late in 1944.

Meanwhile, Inge had moved from the Coronado Hotel to an apartment at 1213 North Seventh Avenue in Neighborhood Gardens, which Burgess describes as "one of the first high-rise, privately developed housing projects in St. Louis" (p. 445). The new apartment was close to the *Star-Times* building and was still in the area called the downtown loop, near the principal department stores, commercial buildings, and hotels. Not far away, Burgess notes, the "loop extended to the garish riverfront through sometimes dangerous blocks of sleazy 'striptease' nightclubs and burlesque houses." Bookstores, art galleries, large and ornate movie houses, and performing theaters were also nearby (p. 455). Again, Inge was well situated for his professional and private pursuits.

And again, most of his social pursuits, according to his colleagues at the *Star-Times*, were indeed private. Burgess, who interviewed a great many of Inge's colleagues, reports that "the consensus of St. Louis journalists who remember Inge is that he remained an outsider." As Mary Kimbrough described him, Inge was "not rude, but not very friendly, either." Irma Tucker conjectured that he was "the kind of person who might walk the streets all night by himself" (p. 447). Later, when Inge became better known in St. Louis's community-theater circles, some of his acquaintances were aware of his drinking and homosexuality, but they could only guess at what these problems might be costing him, as this passage from Burgess makes clear:

> Evidence abounds that his personal dilemmas included his sexual life style as well as his alcoholism. "Those things weren't talked about as much then as they are now, but we were aware of them in Bill," said Irma Tucker. Another St. Louis theatrical acquaintance, Harry Gibbs, remembers that Inge received a terrible beating at unknown hands during one night of drinking. At the time, Bill was "not quite sure which way he wanted to go" sexually, Gibbs judged. "There may have been something between him and some of the young men," guessed Kathrene Casebolt, a designer who helped Inge stage an early play in St. Louis. To hold the teaching and newspaper jobs Inge had before going to New York, any homosexual inclinations probably were severely repressed. "He didn't approve of it himself . . . in his own mind he was truly not at peace," Kathrene Casebolt added. (P. 456)

In spite of what his acquaintances may have sensed or guessed and in spite of beatings and self-doubts, Inge was later to say about his years at the *Star-Times*: "That was probably the best period of my life. . . . I felt very buoyant, very stimulated. I enjoyed life for a change. I was drinking quite a bit, but I was handling it."[5]

The liberation from teaching in a cloistered atmosphere, plus the freedom of movement in St. Louis, all while making his living by attending and writing about cultural developments and events, had to be powerfully exhilarating to Inge. Still, the pace of his life at this time makes his claim that he was "handling" things a bit dubious. How well was he "handling" things if he suffered occasional beatings? And one newspaperman acquaintance told St. Louis reporter Paul Wagman that Inge at this time could be mercurially moody:

> One evening, the acquaintance recalls he and another friend visited Inge . . . at his apartment, which was filled with books and paintings. Inge, they discovered, had made an unusual purchase; he had bought one dozen champagne glasses. At the time, "all any of us could afford was beer."

When he and the other visitor poured beer into the glasses, the newspaperman says, Inge threw them both out. He felt "we had desecrated the glasses." (Quoted by Burgess, p. 448)

Such behavior is hardly conducive to friendship, and it is not indicative that Inge was consistently "handling" the pace of his life. But while he felt the need for medical and psychiatric advice for sleeplessness, depression, and self-acceptance at Stephens, he apparently did not feel those needs during his initial years in St. Louis.

Inge bought a small black Scottie dog, which he named Lula Belle, and for a time he brought the dog on a leash with him to work (Burgess, p. 448). Lula Belle proved to be his most constant companion, even when he was cadging rides around town. Later, when he moved to the area of the Washington University campus, Inge's landlord forced him to give the dog up (p. 466). (The lost dog, of course, left a lasting impression on Inge's imagination, becoming a central symbol in *Come Back, Little Sheba*, his first play to be produced in New York.) But as 1944 began to wane, Inge, then thirty-one, and Lula Belle were living in apartment L at 1213 North Seventh Avenue in Neighborhood Gardens. He was still better than a year away from having to return to teaching, this time at Washington University, and nearly five years away from leaving St. Louis for New York. He was now about to meet Tennessee Williams, a meeting that proved to be the most important of his life.

IN NOVEMBER, 1944, Thomas Lanier ("Tennessee") Williams's mother was living in the St. Louis suburb of Clayton. Williams was known locally as a fledgling playwright who had also published a few poems. Inge heard that Williams was home briefly from New York before going to Chicago, where rehearsals for his play *The Glass Menagerie* would soon be under way for a pre-Broadway tryout run. Inge called to arrange an interview. Perhaps because of his extreme nervousness about *Menagerie* after his earlier misfortunes in Boston with his first play, *Battle of Angels*, or perhaps because he found it difficult to be at ease talking about his new play around Edwina, his mother (who is the model for Amanda Wingfield in *The Glass Menagerie*), Williams agreed to come to Inge's apartment for the interview. Inge "gave me his address and a time to come there," Williams wrote many years later. "He was living in a housing project, way downtown in a raffish part of the city, but when he opened the door I saw over his shoulder a reproduction of my favorite Picasso and knew that the interview would be as painless as it turned out to be."[6]

Donald Spoto, one of Williams's biographers, reports that "the resulting article, which appeared on November 11, was full of inaccuracies, half-truths, and Williams's typical alterations of personal history."[7] But Patton Lockwood, in his dissertation on Inge, states that whatever inaccuracies about Williams the interview presented, it "clearly reflects" Inge's admiration for Williams.[8]

That Inge might have found Williams admirable is hardly surprising. Williams was more than handsome, graceful, and possessed of a southern elegance; he was a kindred spirit in many significant ways. Both men came from father-absent, mother-dominated homes; both men loved art, music, and literature in general and theater in particular; both men were homosexuals who had experienced great ambivalence about their sexuality. Moreover, Williams had to be inspirational for Inge even before Inge saw *The Glass Menagerie*, for Williams was a bit more than two years older than Inge, yet he was still pursuing his dream of being a successful writer. Here was someone Inge could respect because at thirty-three, Williams had had many of the same reasons to give up his dreams as Inge had; but Williams had not given up, even after the *Battle of Angels* debacle nearly four years earlier. While Williams was in St. Louis, he met Inge often "at Inge's apartment, and at symphony concerts and elsewhere in the city" (Burgess, p. 451). Inge told Mike Steen, the author of *A Look at Tennessee Williams*, that the two men "enjoyed quite an intimate friendship in talking with each other about our lives, what we hoped to make of them."[9] There was clearly a strong and mutual attraction from the beginning.

Williams departed for Chicago, having found a new friend but full of fears about *The Glass Menagerie*, which he had decided was "rather dull, too nice." Moreover, Laurette Taylor, the aging star who was to play Amanda, was drinking heavily and seemed to be paying little attention to learning her lines. Additional problems of theater location, budget, and weather all seemed to be conspiring against the play's Christmas opening. But somehow, the play managed to come together with the help of stalwart favorable reviewers and an amazing transformation of Laurette Taylor, who gathered herself together for the final great role of her career.[10] When Inge went to Chicago to see the play on New Year's Eve and to support his new friend, he saw a stunning masterpiece that literally changed the course of his life.

To be sure, going to Chicago, ostensibly to report the play's opening back

to St. Louis, was a radical extension of Inge's "beat." It was the new friendship that clearly drew him as much as—if not more than—a sense of his critic's duty. Donald Spoto's report that "during his short visit to Williams the
two men had an impromptu and intense sexual affair, never resumed in their
later friendship," has no apparent substantiation. But Lyle Leverich, Williams's authorized biographer, admits that it is "probably a safe assumption"
that the two men were lovers at some point.[11] Whatever else may have occurred while Inge was in Chicago, Inge was dazzled by *The Glass Menagerie*
and thrilled that it was his friend's creation: "I realized . . . I had met a genius. It was the most beautiful play I had seen in years. Tennessee was badly
discouraged about its chances of getting to New York. I thought to myself,
Doesn't he know it's wonderful?" (Inge's italics)[12]

The two friends went to several bars after the New Year's Eve performance,
and as they made their way back to Williams's hotel, Inge confided that he,
himself, wished to be a playwright. "This confession struck me, at the time,
as being just a politeness, an effort to dispel the unreasonable gloom that
had come over me," remembered Williams.[13]

It was ever so much more than that. Seeing *The Glass Menagerie* and meeting the enormously talented person who had created it had galvanized Inge's
own creative forces. *This* was what his scattered and sputtering experience
had been progressing toward: a playwriting career of his own. Suddenly, his
love of performing and performers, his love of reading, and his long increasing hours with pen and typewriter were coalescing into a purposeful pattern
that he had not fully recognized before. With this recognition came another,
just as significant: Williams had fashioned this marvelous and wonderful
play out of the raw material of his own life, out of his own family, out of
his own emotions; and Inge knew he could do the same. That New Year's
Eve, with his gifted friend encouraging him, William Inge must have felt that
his long apprenticeship had ended with a flash of realization of just what
his trade was at last to be. After that night, he would often look back, but
he would never again go back. Inge resolved to become a serious playwright
on the night he saw convincing proof that his friend Tennessee Williams
was already a great one.

IF INGE went to Chicago to report back to St. Louis on *Menagerie*'s opening,
he forgot to do so in his new-found excitement. At any rate, no pieces by
Inge about Williams appeared in the *Star-Times* in January, 1945. In fact,
Burgess reports that nothing about Williams and *The Glass Menagerie* ap-

peared until April 3, four days after the play's successful Broadway opening (p. 452). This article mainly relays for St. Louis readers the reactions of New York critics, but it does conclude with an interesting remark. Noting that Williams was greatly skilled as a poet but that he was not able to make a living writing poetry until he put it in the form of a play, Inge said, "What better advice could he [Williams] give other poets than 'write a play'" (Burgess, p. 453). That was the advice that Inge himself had been assiduously following since his return from Chicago.

The Glass Menagerie is a memory play, recollected by Tom Wingfield about his dominating mother, his absent father, his painfully shy sister, and his tangled emotions of exhilaration and guilt for having abandoned his home and his sense of responsibility. The play awakened the nostalgia and complex emotions Inge felt for his own home. He was later to say that *Menagerie* "enabled me for the first time to see the true dynamics between life and art."[14] Since the Stephens years, he had seldom gone home, even for short visits. He had often written to Maude and Luther, crowding surface "news" onto penny post cards, but his break from home had been as complete as he could make it. In Amanda and Laura Wingfield, he had seen less dramatic but profound traces of Maude and Helene Inge. In the smiling photograph of the absent Mr. Wingfield, he had discerned reflections of Luther. In the tortured memories of the movie-escaping Tom Wingfield, he had seen elements of William Inge. The Williams family correspondences in *Menagerie*, of course, are unmistakable: Amanda is Edwina Williams; Laura is Rose Williams; Tom is Tennessee. The smiling, significantly absent father is Cornelius Williams. Inge did not set out to write his own *Glass Menagerie*, but he did write his own nostalgic family memoir. And as with so many of his later works, his title indicates his theme and comes from favorite lines of poetry: "But now't is little joy / To know I'm farther off from heaven / Than when I was a boy" ("I Remember, I Remember," Thomas Hood, 1799–1845).

Inge wrote *Farther off from Heaven* in about three months. *The Glass Menagerie* had been, in Burgess's words, "exactly the kind of family play he was ripe for to set off his own creative energies" (p. 452). Certainly, those "dynamics between life and art" were profound for Inge as he worked feverishly on this first play.

As with the Flood family in the later version, *The Dark at the Top of the Stairs*, the family in *Farther off from Heaven* undergoes a brief trauma of husband and wife being separated, which is triggered by an argument over their lack of money. Andrew Campbell, the traveling shoe-salesman father, objects strenuously when his wife, Sarah, buys an expensive dress for their painfully shy daughter, Irene, to wear to an upcoming dance. A fierce argument ensues, in which Sarah's long-time resentments are vented: Andrew is gone too often on sales trips; she suspects that he sees other women while he is on the road; he once passed up a chance to take over his father's stable shopkeeping business; he had not invested in a successful oil-venture opportunity with the now-rich Harry Shelton. Speaking of the Sheltons, Sarah says to Andrew accusingly: "Now they're living in a fine home in Wichita and driving Packard cars, and you're still driving an old Dodge all over Kansas selling shoes."[15] As in *Stairs*, the argument ends with Andrew's storming out of the house, vowing not to return.

In addition to the Kansas setting, there are numerous comparisons to Inge's family and experience in the foregoing. Maude's middle name was Sarah (in fact, on page 9 of Act II in the manuscript I examined, the mother is called Maude by another character—a slip of Inge's typewriter); Luther was a philandering traveling salesman who refused to become a shopkeeper and who drove a Dodge; Helene was extremely shy; Harry Sinclair had become a powerfully rich man, although Luther had no known opportunity to rise with him; and of course there was frequent tension between Luther and Maude. Andrew's being a shoe salesman is probably a covert acknowledgment of Tennessee Williams, whose father spent many years with a shoe company and who, both in actuality and as Tom Wingfield in *Menagerie*, also worked briefly and unhappily for the same shoe company.

The resolution of *Farther off from Heaven* is similar to the one Inge provides in *Stairs*. In Andrew's absence, Sarah turns to her sister and brother-in-law for help and finds that they are very reluctant to take her and the children in. Moreover, she learns that her sister and brother-in-law (here named Lola and Ed Delaney, very similar to the central couple in *Come Back, Little Sheba*) have a barren and unhappy marriage, devoid of the one key element that her marriage with Andrew *does* have: sex. Learning these things in Act II makes Sarah more receptive when Andrew apologetically returns in Act III, and the couple, in what was to become typical in Inge's work, reconciles, less with romance than with a simple acceptance of their relative lot (Act III, p. 18).

Their ten-year-old son, Sonny, is of principal interest in this play now, for he is clearly William Inge, and he is the one who is nostalgically "farther off from heaven" than when he was a boy. He is described as being blond, with "large blue eyes and a somewhat effeminate manner. Yet he has an intelligence and an independent spirit, manifested later, that make him likable" (Act I, p. 2). Sonny loves the movies and collects pictures of star performers. He is also a piece-speaking sissy who is taunted by the other boys at school; he doubts that such taunting is, as Sarah tries to explain, a sign of the other boys' jealousy (Act I, p. 4). Sarah is a high-strung hypochondriac who is aware that she is holding Sonny too close to her and that his difference from the other boys is significant. But in Andrew's frequent—and now threatening to be permanent—absence, her loneliness and desire for comfort draw Sarah to Sonny, whose devotion is constant and unquestioning. At the close of Act II, when Sarah knows that she cannot move in with the Delaneys, she accompanies Sonny upstairs at night, ostensibly to quell his fears of the darkness lurking there, but actually to comfort herself as well (Act II, p. 29). Later, in an effort to distance herself from Sonny, for their mutual benefit, she makes the "speckled egg" speech, which I referred to in Part One of this book (Act III, pp. 9–10).

There is little doubt that Helene Inge is the model for the shy daughter in *Heaven*, although the character's name, Irene (Reenie in *Stairs*), is actually that of the Inge daughter who died when only three years old. Irene's extreme shyness is exacerbated by a conspicuously chipped front tooth, the result of a fight with Sonny; and Helene Inge has reported that she once had such a chipped tooth as a result of a fight with Billy.[16] Trivial but heated arguments between the two children occur more in *Heaven* than in *Stairs*, and for those arguments, Inge may have been drawing more upon his memories of arguments between Luther Boy and Lucy Inge, who were much more combative than the two younger Inge children.

Lola and Ed Delaney, in *Heaven*, are the childless central couple who were later to appear as Lola and Doc Delaney in *Come Back, Little Sheba*. In *The Dark at the Top of the Stairs*, they are Lottie and Morris Lacey. In *My Son Is a Splendid Driver*, they are Joey Hansen's Aunt Patsy and Uncle Merlin of Wichita. Inge told Digby Diehl in a 1967 interview:

> I had this curious aunt and uncle. They were a childless pair, and she, my mother's sister, was really an eccentric woman. I used to think of her a lot and their relationship kind of fascinated me. The first thing I ever did with them was a little story, which had a closeness to me that nothing else I attempted did. And when I worked with it a bit, it suddenly began to grow into shape and the characters developed separate existences. They really became living people inside me who began to act on their own.[17]

The "little story" now seems to have been lost, but the recurring characters, who appear to be based upon Dr. and Mrs. Earl Mooney of Wichita, constitute a significant part of Inge's work. In each appearance, the "curious aunt and uncle" are childless. The aunt is a once-pretty, somewhat fat woman who is a slovenly housekeeper (Lola, Lottie, Patsy). The uncle is a quiet, subdued chiropractor (Ed, Doc) or dentist (Morris, Uncle Merlin), who occasionally amuses others with card tricks (Ed, Doc) or magical coin and handkerchief tricks (Uncle Merlin) but who is almost completely overshadowed by his wife.

That overshadowing is far from inadvertent. Inge was fascinated with his eccentric aunt, who was the model for some of his most memorable female characters. Inge was a playwright who, like his friend Williams, became famous for his ability to present female characters. In *Heaven*, *Stairs*, and *Driver*, the aunt often speaks coarsely, displaying prejudice and earthiness. Looking at a picture of Rudolph Valentino in *Heaven*, she says, "He looks like a nigger to me" (Act II, p. 8). In *Stairs* she completes a condemnation of actress Norma Talmadge with what she considers a withering indictment: "Besides, she's a Catholic."[18] (Recall Luther Claude Inge's memories of his grandmother Maude and her sister as they warmed to the subject of Catholicism.)

In *Heaven*, *Stairs*, and *Driver*, the aunt shocks her prim sister more than once on the subject of sex. When Cora Flood, the mother in *Stairs*, says she considers sex "only animal" and that she couldn't have sex with Rubin, her husband, if she "didn't feel he was being honorable," the aunt cries: "My God, a big handsome buck like Rubin! Who cares if he's honorable?" She follows this with a coarse phallic joke that Cora refuses to let her complete (pp. 276–277). In *Driver*, the aunt comments on a childless brother named Jay and his wife Thelma: "Thelma's so pukey pious she probably won't open her legs for him." When her sister says that isn't so, that Jay and Thelma had "prayed to God for a child," the aunt replies: "That's Jay for ya. He thinks prayin' to God brings babies."[19]

Despite such talk, the aunt also became representative of two of Inge's most frequent thematic concerns – loneliness and sexual frustration. Lola Delaney (*Heaven*, *Sheba*), Lottie Lacey (*Stairs*), and Aunt Patsy (*Driver*) are all lonely women who do not know fulfilling love with their husbands. Not only are they childless – a fact that is upsetting to all of them, for it accents their loneliness – they are also desperate for genuine affection, and they escape from their frustrations in romantic daydreams (both Lolas), movie fantasies (both Lolas and Lottie), or loud, self-defensive disclaiming (both Lottie and Patsy, for example, tell everyone that they do not want children in ways that make it clear they do). And their husbands are all seriously disillusioned, severely repressed men who try to cope with their life situations through absorption in their work, solitary walks, and in Doc's case (*Sheba*), valiant attempts to maintain tenuous sobriety by adherence to his daily alcoholic's prayer: "God grant me the serenity to accept the things I cannot change, courage to change the things I can, and wisdom always to tell the difference."[20]

The flood of inspired creativity that washed over William Inge in St. Louis during the first three months of 1945 was remarkable. Drawing from the raw material of memories, he produced, in a fusion of the "dynamics between art and life," one play that contained sizable elements of the setting, characters, and themes for two of the five works for which he will always be remembered: *Come Back, Little Sheba* and *The Dark at the Top of the Stairs.* He found in his own background and family the subjects for his artistic vision, and he found himself as a serious playwright. Although he was yet to experience some severe setbacks, from that time on he did not doubt what he wanted to do. He would have to continue as the *Star-Times* critic for another year, and he would have to retreat into teaching again, but through these, he would continue to write plays. And before his departure for New York in 1949, he would write, in embryonic forms, material that he would later rewrite to become the rest of his best known, prize-winning work: *Picnic*, *Bus Stop*, and *Splendor in the Grass*.

WHEN *Farther off from Heaven* was finished, Inge was eager to have Williams read it. But Williams was by then in New York, where *Menagerie* had opened successfully at the end of March. A face-to-face response was at least temporarily impossible. Inge shared his new enthusiasm and ambition with his St. Louis acquaintances, and he wrote of his new resolve to Maude and Luther. His old Independence neighbor, Stella Steinberger, had taken a job in St. Louis, and she occasionally met Inge for lunch and light conversation about home. She recalls both his excitement about his writing and his frequent references to manuscripts on which he was at work.[21] He was not idle while he was waiting for Williams's reaction to *Heaven*. He combed his Stephens writings for reworkable material. He also began a short play titled *The Man in Boots*, which eventually he finished but lost.[22] A longer version, a sixty-two-page three-act carbon-copy of a manuscript titled *A Man in Boots* is now in the Inge Collection. It appears to be an early sketching-out of the character who was to become the drifter Hal Carter in *Picnic*.

Meanwhile, Williams wrote or called from New York that his response to *Heaven* was favorable and that he was giving Inge's name to Audrey Wood, Williams's New York agent. If Williams saw parallels between the characteristics of *Heaven* and *Menagerie*, there is no record of it. Thrilled, Inge sent *Heaven* to Wood. He was keeping now an even faster pace of life in St. Louis than he had before meeting Williams: he covered events, produced articles, drank, and wrote. The new-found hope for a career as a playwright doubtless fueled his pace, but it did not prepare him for the blow of Wood's rejection of *Heaven*. Speaking of *Heaven* many years later, Wood said, "The first play that Bill ever gave to me I didn't feel was ready for the Broadway theatre, and being an honest person, I rejected it."[23] Wood's rejection was anything but blunt. "I truly didn't want to discourage him from continuing to write; his script showed unmistakable talent," she wrote in her memoirs. "I suggested he do another play, and hoped he'd permit me to read whatever work he did in the future."[24] But Inge was both crushed and angry. "I wrote back to the effect that my play and I could do without her," he later told Richard Gehman of *Theatre Arts* magazine.[25] Fortunately, he didn't really mean it.

And there were other blows. By September, 1945, World War II was officially over. Inge knew that Reed Hynds would soon be discharged from military service and thus would be freed to return to the *Star-Times*. That would make Inge jobless, with his best real and immediate prospect being a return to teaching. Word of the inevitable reached him before the new year began. Hynds was to return in February, 1946. Glumly, Inge began to check around to see if he could find a teaching job beginning with the new term in January. At Washington University, where an early influx of veterans was expected, he found a position as an English instructor. At least he would not have to leave St. Louis for a smaller town such as Columbus or Columbia. Still, with the hope of an eventual playwriting career temporarily stymied, the prospect of returning to teaching left him quite depressed. He was beginning a period of emotional extremes more intense than any he had previously endured.

THERE WERE, fortunately, some palliatives for Inge's distress. First, Williams's friendship and support remained strong, and the success of *The Glass Menagerie* gave Williams increasingly significant influence. Second, when William

G. B. Carson, chair of the drama department at Washington University, learned that Inge had been hired by the university, he asked Inge to help him direct productions of Thyrsus, the student drama club (Burgess, pp. 461–462). Through Carson, Inge not only got to work with young performers and writers, but he also continued his relationships with community-theater groups in St. Louis, even though his last *Star-Times* review had appeared on February 9, 1946 (Burgess, p. 458). Students and community-theater groups alike saw Inge not only as a teacher and critic but also as a budding playwright, a role he surely welcomed. Third, Williams had introduced Inge to Margo Jones when Inge had come to Chicago, and Jones, a native Texan, was an established theatrical producer and director who had a plan to begin an active regional-theater group in Dallas. At Williams's suggestion, Inge eventually sent *Heaven* to Jones.

A letter from Inge to Jones, which was probably sent with the manuscript of *Heaven*, shows his bitterness about Wood's rejection of it. He told Jones he was no longer trying to sell the play to New York. He wrote: "Well, the play is all yours and you can do whatever you like with it. I've never felt so dismally rejected . . . [Inge's ellipses] and mad as hell, too. God, the crap I've seen in the last two years and then people tell me how beautiful, honest, and real my play is and turn it down as though such things were tree-growing products."[26] Jones was having some difficulties in getting her Dallas theater started as soon as she'd hoped; both 1945 and 1946 were to pass before she was finally ready to open. But she liked *Heaven*, and with Williams's urging, she decided that she would open her theater with it in 1947. This news buoyed Inge immeasurably. Here was proof to the world—and to himself— that he was a serious playwright.

Teaching, as always, was a drain on his time and energies, but it paid his bills. After finding a home for Lula Belle, he moved to rooms on Maryland Avenue, near the university and community-theater centers (Burgess, p. 458). Many of his students were more mature and better motivated than he had found the young women at Stephens to be. Coeducational and urban, Washington University's atmosphere, particularly with veterans returning from the war, was more liberal than any that Inge had previously experienced. These factors doubtless eased Inge's painful passage back into teaching, and they helped keep his spirits high enough to continue writing. Delighted with Jones's promise to produce *Farther off from Heaven* and proud of his friendship with Williams, Inge began to work on another play, an expansion of an idea he had set down earlier, involving a group of women in a small-town neighborhood. This work, which he discussed with Carson, had at least two tentative titles—*Summer Romance* and *Women in Summer*—before eventually being called *Front Porch*; it was, actually, an early version of *Picnic* (Burgess, p. 462).

Besides his work with Carson in Thyrsus, Inge also conducted a playwriting class at the YMCA, and he joined with the local critic-playwright Jack Balch and several community actors and directors to help keep community theater active and lively. Russell A. Sharp, who led a company of players called the Experimental Group, told Burgess that he had read a version of *Front Porch* in the fall of 1946. The group had planned to do the play, Sharp claimed, but folded before it could put the play into production (Burgess, p. 463). Such local support must have been both gratifying and encouraging to Inge because Jones's inevitable delays in Dallas often subjected him to the frustrations of the impatient. And even though Sharp's experimental group failed to produce *Front Porch*, another group headed by Balch, the Morse Players, agreed to consider it.

Meanwhile, Inge kept in frequent touch with Jones. He wrote to her to let her know his willingness—in fact, his eagerness—to help in any way he could with *Heaven*. He also wrote in behalf of a former Stephens drama student, Irene Lindquist, who, in Inge's estimation, had considerable ability and the backing of Maude Adams but had not yet found any roles in New York.[27] As the production of *Heaven* at last neared and finally got under way, Inge's correspondence with Jones increased. He received a letter from Jones on April 26, 1947, detailing the plans to perform *Heaven* the following June. The letter included $150 as an advance against royalties, which, in Jones's tight budget, would be 5 percent of the gross.[28] Inge saw in Jones not only his first producer but also his great friend, advocate, and comforter. Many of the letters from Inge to Jones that are collected at the Harry Ransom Humanities Research Center at the University of Texas at Austin are characterized by complaints about New York's cold indifference, specific matters of craft within the Inge plays that Jones was reading at the time, and what amounts to requests for sympathy, encouragement, or direct help.

To her credit, Jones was consistently supportive throughout times when Inge needed such support, although her motives may have had as much to do with her feelings for Tennessee Williams as they did with her solid belief in Inge's dramatic promise. Jones was always a powerful believer in Williams; Donald Spoto reports that she once had hoped to marry Williams and, by sheer will, to change both his homosexuality and her own lesbianism.[29] By 1947, Jones may have realized that Williams had no further need of her professional help. Thus, keeping his friendship after he had become successful was a priority. Moreover, Inge was enthusiastic and attentive toward her, whereas Williams, simply by the natural demands of his success, was less so. Whatever the case, Jones's support provided a rock for Inge during his latter days in St. Louis, and American theater was the ultimate beneficiary.

While he waited for Jones to make things ready to begin the production of *Heaven*, Inge continued to develop *Front Porch*, his play about a group of small-town women in summer. He was apparently also working with the "Man in Boots" drifter character mentioned earlier but had not yet thought of moving that character into the midst of the *Front Porch* women. The coming production of *Heaven* was uppermost in his mind, and when Jones notified him that her theater would open with *Heaven* a bit earlier than originally planned, on June 3, 1947, he immediately devoted his attention to consulting with her about the script.

Most of the consulting was done by phone and mail, but as soon as the spring term at Washington ended, Inge went to Dallas to be present during rehearsals and to continue to fine tune the script with Jones and the cast. Little is known about Inge's pre-opening time in Dallas. He still didn't own a car, so he probably took a train or bus to Dallas from St. Louis. Undoubtedly he was nervous, and a person who was there during part of that time but who has asked to remain anonymous says that Inge was drinking heavily and making himself something of a nuisance for the young men involved with the production. It is not definitely known if he burned off some of this nervous energy in constant rewriting (whether it was requested or not), as he was later to do before *Front Porch* opened in St. Louis and before *Come Back, Little Sheba* opened in New York. There is some evidence to suggest that Inge did considerable rewriting, because a letter to Jones from Inge, dated Wednesday, June, 1947, goes into minute detail about whether the mother character (Sarah) should use the word *whore* twice in the play. "Once is probably enough, inasmuch as it's a word she couldn't use very easily," wrote Inge. "The first time she uses it, I feel, is right. The second time, *hussy* could easily be substituted. After all, it's a pretty hard word for an audience to take, and I don't want it to seem that Sarah is having a good time using it."[30]

Not only does that letter indicate the degree of fine tuning Inge sought for his script; it also indicates his extreme sensitivity to his Sarah character and his audience, both of whom he sees as squeamish about even moderately strong language. As *Heaven* was scheduled for only a week's run (June 3 to June 10, Tuesday through Monday), the only Wednesday on which Inge could have written the letter for it to have had any effect on Jones's production would have to have been Wednesday, June 4. Perhaps he wrote it in Dallas and mailed it there or merely left it for her before he departed to visit Independence on the way back to St. Louis. In any case, such minute attention to such minor details might have made Jones glad to see Inge leave Dallas.

Heaven, as well as Jones's entire dramatic line-up that summer in the Gulf Oil Theatre at Dallas's Fair Park, was well received. Jones called this series, which also included Williams's *Summer and Smoke*, "Theatre '47," and in subsequent summers she called each year's new line-up of plays "Theatre '48," "Theatre '49," and so on. Her pioneering efforts were perhaps treated gently by Dallas patrons and critics because they all had a healthy interest in making Dallas a cultural center so as to counter its rather boisterous image.[31] But Jones's theater and Inge's play also won notice in New York, where George Freedley of the *Morning Telegraph* praised both, and later that summer, Brooks Atkinson of the *New York Times* offered a generally complimentary summation of the Theatre '47 season.[32] Jones's success also inspired other regional-theater groups, giving a serious boost not only to America's regional theaters but also to many of America's young playwrights.

Despite whatever nuisance Inge might have been in Dallas, Jones remained his staunch supporter and friend. Inge's postscript to the letter of Wednesday, June, 1947 referred to above, indicates the level of personal interest Jones had taken, as well as Inge's gratitude: "PS: Incidentally, mother thinks you must [be] an 'awfully nice woman' and may send you a jar of strawberry preserves." In a letter from Jones to Inge, written four days after *Heaven*'s run was complete, she replied, "I'm so glad your mother feels I'm a 'nice woman' and I'll love the preserves—do tell her for me."[33]

Inge sent Jones several more letters during the summer of 1947. One, dated June 13 and written from Maude and Luther's "new" place at 205 East Sycamore (they had moved to a much-smaller house after Luther's retirement), asked Jones if she could help him get a writing job in Hollywood so that he would not have to return to teaching in St. Louis "next year" (i.e., in September). This was a request he often renewed during the next two years, but Jones, who had some Hollywood connections, was never able to help him in this regard. Another letter, dated Wednesday, June 18, returned Jones's future option on *Heaven*, signed by a most-willing Inge, who wrote, in reference to the legal language in the option: "I want you to know that I will give you any special privileges within my power to give you . . . or something [Inge's ellipses]. (Legal language and reference to parties of the first part, etc., always make me feel something of a rattlebrain)."[34]

These letters, as well as several to follow until Inge's departure for New York at last, verify the affectionate bond between Jones and Inge, but there is nothing to indicate romance. Rather, Jones's encouraging and consoling stances suggest the tenderness and concern of a mother, even though they were practically the same age. And as might be expected after the high point of *Heaven*'s production, Inge's familiar frustration returned when he realized that the fall of 1947 would find him back in front of classes at Washington University. He was still writing and hoping, but he was also still drinking and battling his familiar demons. Things were going to get worse before they would get better.

INGE'S NEXT hope for a production after *Heaven* lay with Jack Balch's Morse Players in St. Louis, who had agreed to consider *Front Porch*. By the time Balch requested the script, Inge had taken the male drifter character who had appeared in *The Man in Boots* (and in a different version of that play called *The Vermin's Will*) and had made him the instigator of dramatic action among the small-town women in *Front Porch*. It was an old dramatic convention to bring a mysterious and disturbing stranger into a settled and relatively serene environment, and it was to prove fortuitous; but Inge was apparently doubtful at the time about the quality of the result. Balch, who was also a St. Louis newspaper critic and playwright and who, according to Burgess, was both a bit of a rival and drinking buddy of Inge's, was slow to respond to the new version of *Front Porch* (pp. 463–464). Impatient as always, Inge sent the unmerged versions of *Vermin's Will* and *Front Porch* to Jones for her opinions.

Two letters from Inge to Jones, one written on August 9 and the other on August 16, 1947, indicate that Jones did not respond favorably to either play. In the first letter, Inge told Jones that Max Gordon, a friend, had liked *Vermin's Will* but had suggested "countless changes." Apparently, Jones's and Gordon's reactions had made Inge think that his reworked—that is, merged— version of *Front Porch* would appeal to Jones better than the two separate plays she had seen. The August 16 letter, which thanked Jones for a royalty check for *Heaven*, admitted that *Vermin's Will* was clumsy and artificial but declared that the new version of *Front Porch* was the best thing he had yet done. Prophetically, Inge added, "I think I've created a pretty original character in Rosemary."[35] The Rosemary Sydney who appears in *Picnic* is arguably the best of many excellent female characters that Inge created, but his decision to bring the drifter Hal Carter into *Front Porch* (and thus, later, *Picnic*) was equally important.

Balch, who found himself in the unenviable position of having to choose from among several scripts he had on hand, all by fellow writers in the St. Louis area, solved his problem by asking Kathrene Casebolt, a highly respected set designer for many community-theater productions (who did not write plays), to read the scripts and choose one for the next Morse Players production, which he would direct. Casebolt, who had not yet met Inge, picked the new version of *Front Porch* (Burgess, p. 464).

At roughly the same time (late 1947), Jones responded favorably to the new *Front Porch*, although she apparently did not want to use Inge plays in two consecutive seasons. It is likely that she agreed to try to help Inge find an interested producer, because *Front Porch* was produced as part of the twenty-fifth anniversary of the Galveston Island Little Theatre the following April, and Inge had no other regional-theater connections in Texas except for Jones. Thus, as 1947 drew to a close, Inge had the assurance that another of his plays was going to be produced.

The road to the Morse Players production in St. Louis, however, proved rocky indeed. Burgess reports that "there was considerable friction between Balch and Inge" (p. 464). According to Burgess's account, Harry Gibbs, who played the part of Hal, and Casebolt, who was the play's technical director, remember the frequent heated arguments between the two men. Inge, as with *Heaven*, was concerned with every detail; moreover, he seemed never to be sure that the general action and the resolution were the way he wanted them. Balch, according to Casebolt, was "a very powerful person" who was used to having his own way. Gibbs told Burgess: "Bill was very tentative about it. When he wanted to make cuts, Balch wouldn't permit it. Balch was a character, and he was not as talented as Inge." Casebolt remembers that Balch wanted to place tragic emphasis on Flo, the mother in the play, and "Bill would protest, 'I just wrote a little play about what happened on a front porch in the summertime.'" Casebolt says that Inge often shared his frustrations with her while they sat in the rear of the theater. Sometimes, she remembers, Inge "would get really high on scotch and work up the courage to tell off Balch" before stalking out to one of two nearby bars (p. 464).

Stalking into bars for drinks laced with his own frustration was by now routine for Inge, who was not content with regional-theater productions. He wanted to write a play that would be good enough to go to New York, but he was afraid to send Audrey Wood anything else without the prior endorsement of Williams and Jones. Margo read and responded to everything he sent her, but a response from Tennessee couldn't be counted on. When he had sent *Vermin's Will* to Jones, he had thought Williams was in Dallas, and Inge asked Jones to relay not only her opinion but also Tennessee's, because, as he told her, Tennessee had become "allergic to letter-writing."[36] But there is no record of Williams's response to that play, the manuscript of which now appears to have been lost. While the Morse Players were readying the production of *Front Porch* and Inge was arguing frequently with Balch, 1947 ended.

THE YEAR 1948 was Inge's most pivotal one in St. Louis. The new year brought what was to prove a very rocky term at Washington University as rehearsals for the February 10 opening of *Front Porch* continued. Inge was both excited and depressed. He was particularly concerned about how his acquaintances among the St. Louis critics would judge the play, and his lack of control over Balch's production made him feel powerless to influence the play's reception. In his classes he was increasingly just going through the motions, a situation that doubtless reminded him of his last years at Stephens. By his later account, Inge said that at this time he was drinking about a fifth of whiskey every day, and his relationship with his classes was "becoming blurred."[37] As always, he was generally concealing his homosexuality while he juggled his writing, his teaching, his work with Balch and the *Front Porch* production, and his ambition. The strain was enormous; eventually something would have to give.

But first there were the performances of *Front Porch*. According to Burgess, the constant friction between Inge and Balch resulted in "a rambling, somewhat unfocused play" (p. 464). Myles Standish, a usually harsh critic for the *Post-Dispatch*, said that the February 10 debut was "dull drama, one that almost dies on its feet in the first act." Standish wondered why a stronger play wasn't chosen to showcase new works by St. Louis playwrights, "or possibly a better example of Mr. Inge's own work" (Burgess, p. 465). Burgess speculates that Standish may have had *Come Back, Little Sheba* in mind when he referred to that "better example," but that isn't possible, because Inge did not write *Sheba* until the following summer. Despite Standish's review, *Front Porch* filled the one hundred seats at the Toy Theatre for each performance of its two-week run, and Kathrene Casebolt remembers that the run's $250 profit enabled the backers to give Inge nearly $100, which he later used to pay for a trip to New York to confer with Wood about the *Sheba* script (p. 465).

Although Inge could hardly have been pleased with Standish's review and was doubtless dissatisfied with Balch's treatment of *Front Porch*, the audience support in St. Louis was encouraging. Moreover, the upcoming production of *Front Porch* in Galveston would afford him another opportunity to see the play produced, this time perhaps more as he would like. Galveston Island's Little Theatre was well established, and the production of *Front Porch* there would mark the theater's twenty-fifth anniversary. Inge planned to travel to Galveston to see the play. "William Inge, midwestern playwright and professor at Washington University, will be here April 27 through May 1," announced the *Galveston Tribune* of March 24, beside a picture of Inge at his typewriter, his collar unbuttoned and his necktie hanging loose. However, an article that appeared in the *Tribune* just four days before the April 27 opening stated that Inge "will be unable to come to Galveston due to illness." Thus, Inge was not present during the Galveston production of *Front Porch*. Had he been there on opening night, wrote the *Tribune*'s reviewer Terry McLeod, "he would have been a very proud young man," for the audience was "enthralled."[38]

Inge was not in Galveston because he was a very drunk young man, and he had finally realized it. The *Tribune*'s picture and announcement of March 28, 1948, appeared just four days before Easter that year, and it was during the Easter holidays of 1948 that Inge awakened one morning and poured himself a drink, as had become his custom. "It was a nice spring day, sunny and warm," he later said to Gilbert Millstein. That morning, he realized that the drink he'd poured was *necessary*. "My drinking had passed a line. I had a need I had never had before, a physical demand. It frightened me." He realized that he was an alcoholic and had probably been one for some time but that through "an extraordinary sense of self-preservation" he had somehow been just barely getting along. A psychiatrist whom Inge called that day advised him to go to Alcoholics Anonymous, which, after getting "thoroughly drunk," he did.[39]

Inge's call to that psychiatrist and his attendance at A.A. are further evidence of the "extraordinary sense of self-preservation" that he mentioned to Millstein. The desire to recognize and blunt his self-destructive tendencies could scarcely have come at a more critical time for Inge, and the help he received was to prove important not only to his health and well-being but also to his writing itself. Not that his A.A. experience alone was sufficient to avoid disaster—Inge was too complicated for that. But at A.A., which was to become a significant part of his life for the next several years, Inge came to understand his addiction and his need to take each day at a time, bolstered by A.A.'s tenets, which are based in Christian faith and group support. He found no real solace in Christianity, but at A.A. meetings Inge learned about the alcoholic miseries of others, the pains of "drying out," and the resilient philosophy of acceptance and adjustment, as reflected in the alcoholic's daily prayer, which was eventually to find its way into the speech of Doc Delaney in *Come Back, Little Sheba*. A.A. helped Inge to help himself, and this not only became apparent in the script of *Sheba*, which he began later that year, but also in the script of *Spring Holiday*, an unpublished short play from this period, which is now in the Inge Collection.

In *Spring Holiday*, a teacher, Ida Kress, finds herself getting drunk on the first day of spring vacation. When Frances, her housekeeper, asks Ida if she is sick, Ida replies: "Yes, I'm sick. I'm sick of being . . . an old maid school marm at the university. . . . I'm sick of life in this hideous city. . . . I'm sick of the fact that I'll soon be forty." Frances, however, knows that alcohol is Ida's most serious sickness, so she suggests A.A. to Ida. In this brief play, Ida joins A.A. and overcomes her drinking problem; there are realistic speeches about the problems of alcoholics and the fact that alcoholism can overtake anyone, of any social or economic class. The shakes, Ida learns, can afflict an alcoholic, whether in a dingy alley or in an expensive asylum. Dramatically, *Spring Holiday* is a poor play. But as a surviving document of Inge's initial A.A. experiences in St. Louis, it is both revealing and poignant.[40] Part of the poignancy of *Spring Holiday* is the success that Ida has in overcoming her alcoholism; for Inge it would never be so simple. Ida's triumph is Inge's wishful, somewhat naive, hope. He needed more help than A.A. could give him, and for that he apparently turned again—but still sporadically—to psychiatry.

Perhaps the psychiatrist Inge called that spring day in 1948 was the psychiatrist in Kansas City he had earlier seen during the Stephens years. Whoever it was, there is reason to believe that Inge again came under a psychiatrist's care during the spring of 1948, at the same time as he was battling his alcoholism through A.A. The extent and timing of the psychiatric care are difficult to ascertain because accurate information is either not known or is still protected by doctor-client confidentiality. But a letter from Inge to Margo Jones, dated May 11, informed her that he was ill and had been hospitalized for a week, a circumstance he blamed on his "nervous dislike of living and working here."[41] Perhaps the hospitalization was for a painful drying out, of the sort Doc Delaney so fears in *Sheba*, but Inge's reference to his "nervous dislike" also suggests the possibility that he was under psychiatric care. Moreover, there is other evidence to suggest that Inge was hospitalized under psychiatric care at about this time.

In *My Son Is a Splendid Driver*, Inge's autobiographical narrator, the teacher Joey Hansen, refers to hospitalization in Kansas City, "having suffered a breakdown in the middle of the second semester, in the early spring. I let others attribute my illness, euphemistically, to overwork." He goes on to say he was thirty-six years old at the time (p. 198). Inge turned thirty-five on May 3, 1948. His letter to Jones does not clarify whether he was hospitalized in St. Louis or not, so it is possible that the hospitalization he refers to was elsewhere. At any rate, the hospitalization that he goes on to describe in *Driver* involved psychiatric care; Joey, feeling himself a failure, had attempted to commit suicide by taking pills and whiskey (p. 200).

Inge's description of psychiatric care in *Driver* is probably not based on only one particular instance of hospitalization. A source who requested anonymity reports that Inge was hospitalized under psychiatric care on more than one occasion at the Menninger Foundation in Topeka, Kansas, apparently the model for the institution to which Deanie Loomis is sent by her parents in *Splendor in the Grass*. Whether Inge was hospitalized at Menninger's and if so, when and how often, are all matters that Menninger's is not at liberty to verify, but Topeka's proximity to Kansas City, and the fact that Inge's one-time psychiatrist was based in Kansas City, make Inge's hospitalization at Menninger's during the spring of 1948 at least plausible. Any psychiatric help Inge may have had at this time was probably in immediate relation to his drinking and depression; at any rate, he later told Gilbert Millstein of *Esquire* that he did not begin any thorough analysis as an outpatient until he went to New York.[42]

Why Inge's drinking and depression came to a head during the spring of 1948, when the production of *Front Porch* would ordinarily seem to have been especially encouraging, might have a number of causes. He was, for instance, still in awe of New York in general and Tennessee Williams's success in particular. There seemed to be little reason why one writer's plays were accepted and successful and another's were rejected; it all seemed to be a matter of chance, connections, or both—not a matter of quality. For another, he was—in Ida Kress's word from *Spring Holiday*—"sick" of being a teacher, "sick" of life in St. Louis, and "sick" of approaching forty.

Age, in particular, was a foe of Inge's, for he had long conceived of himself not only as youthful and full of promise but also, with plenty of justification, as trim and handsome—a man possessing the refined good looks of a movie star. At thirty-five, however, his hair was rapidly thinning and his face, although still quite handsome—especially in what he often called his "Barrymore profile"—was becoming lined. It is little wonder that much of his work portrays characters (usually female) who are painfully aware of the fleeting qualities of youth and beauty. Having never been "manly" in the stereotypical, rugged sense, Inge had a consciousness of his fine features that is more akin to that of a photogenic young female, and he had a comparable concern about the erosion of those features. Attractiveness is psychologically (and sexually) important to anyone of either sex, but it was perhaps more important to Inge than to many others. His thirty-fifth birthday found him a long way from the starry dreams and ambitions of the Independence ten year old who collected pictures of movie stars and spoke elegant pieces to the delight of doting ladies. Disappointment, impatience, and depression were nearly constants in his life, constants that daily doses of whiskey could not deaden but could only aggravate, constants that would take their toll on anyone's appearance.

Going to A.A. and seeking some psychiatric treatment helped Inge through the bumpy spring of his thirty-fifth birthday. Whatever work he missed at Washington University did not jeopardize his job; Carson and other colleagues were both sympathetic and supportive. He knew he could return in the fall, but first he planned a recuperative summer, free from teaching and free to write.

AT FIRST the summer of 1948 did not go well. He was low on money, probably because of his recent medical bills, and he hoped that he might find a better job in the fall, preferably away from teaching. He had confessed earlier in a letter to Jones (February 17, 1948) that he had thought of appealing to Williams for some money, but that he was too proud to do so. Instead, he renewed his frequent request for Jones to help him find a writing job in Hollywood. In the previously mentioned letter of May 11 to Jones, Inge had asked her if she knew of a school "who would like someone to teach playwriting." He went on to ask: "Or do you think the situation has improved in Hollywood? Or do you know of a newspaper that needs a critic?"[43] Inge's hope to leave St. Louis was perhaps motivated as much by a psychological desire for a new start in new surroundings as it was by his playwriting ambitions alone. St. Louis was familiar—the acquaintances, the job, the life style—

and such familiarity might make staying dry more difficult. But Jones was unable to help him find a job somewhere else.

The writing was not going well, either. He did some rewriting on *Front Porch* but did not think that it was the play that would get him to New York. He apparently also worked on some ideas that later, in the early 1950s, found their way into some one-act plays: *People in the Wind, Glory in the Flower,* and *Bus Riley's Back in Town.* Some of these ideas were also incorporated into later major works: *People in the Wind* was eventually expanded into *Bus Stop*; elements from *Glory in the Flower* and *Bus Riley's Back in Town* were eventually added to *Splendor in the Grass.* But at the time, Inge didn't feel that he was getting much accomplished. By now he was aware that his creative method usually began with conceiving of a character or a single situation, then working with these to see if they would grow into more detailed scenes. The writing of *Front Porch* had proceeded that way and also, to a lesser extent, *Farther off from Heaven.* Nothing seemed to come together from his drafts. By August, Inge began to think about the upcoming school year, which he dreaded; and he feared that his only accomplishment of the summer would be staying relatively dry—an important accomplishment that would testify to his self-discipline but would still not be all that he had hoped for.

He later told Josephine Murphey of the *Nashville Tennessean Magazine* that at this point in the summer of 1948, he was "pretty much exhausted and let down after spending all summer on a play that didn't come off." He didn't have a new play at all, let alone one he thought good enough for New York. But then he found again the short story he had once written about his childless aunt and uncle, the couple who had served as the models for Lola and Ed Delaney in *Farther off from Heaven.* This short story, he told Murphey, he "lackadaisically" put into a one-act play. "Then I began to have ideas about developing it, and it was my first experience at the play's writing me instead of my writing the play. It just wrote itself."44 The play that "wrote itself" was *Come Back, Little Sheba.*

What probably inspired Inge was focusing more attention on the uncle, rather than the aunt, who had previously been the more interesting of the two characters to him. Why was the uncle so quiet? Why was he so seemingly disappointed? And here, again, Inge could see the "fusion between life and art" that he had first seen in his own family background after viewing *The Glass Menagerie.* Ed Delaney became Doc Delaney, a deeply frustrated and disappointed man—like his creator—who is an alcoholic and who now struggles daily to stay sober and make the best he can of his situation. Although Lola is just as important in *Sheba* as Doc is, it is Doc's frustration that gradually builds, and it is Doc who eventually gets drunk and forces the dramatic action. Indeed, Doc is one of Inge's relatively few male characters who is truly realistic and powerfully compelling. Inge's own struggle with alcoholism and his experience in attending A.A. during the spring and summer of 1948 in St. Louis so directly and sharply affected his drawing of Doc's character that many years later, after viewing a 1974 revival of *Sheba* in New York, critic John Simon said that the depiction of Doc "may ring truest" of all depictions of addicts in American drama during the previous twenty-five years.[45] That is high praise for an era in American drama that includes Don Birnam in Charles Jackson's *The Lost Weekend* and Mary Tyrone in Eugene O'Neill's *Long Day's Journey into Night*.

Inge knew he had written a good play. He later recalled: "I was kind of spellbound while I wrote this play. I couldn't believe I'd done it. Here I'd written a really good play. And, it moved me very deeply."[46] He was heartened, but he was also afraid to request the opinions of Jones and Williams; he seemed to have a sense that if *Sheba* was not the play that would go to New York, no play of his ever would. "I have written my heart out," he wrote about *Sheba* to his old mentor and friend at the University of Kansas, Allen Crafton. "If the play doesn't make it I'm through."[47] It was fall, and classes had begun at Washington University before Inge had an opportunity to share *Sheba* with Williams, who came to St. Louis for a visit.

Williams wrote in his *Memoirs* that one evening during his St. Louis stay, Inge "shyly produced" *Sheba*. "He read it to me in his beautifully quiet and expressive voice," said Williams; "I was deeply moved by the play."[48] Williams urged Inge to send the play to Audrey Wood as soon as possible, and he wired Wood in praise of the play. Inge sent *Sheba* to Wood immediately; he also sent it to Margo Jones. Reporting Williams's enthusiasm about the play to Jones, Inge wrote, "Maybe this is the one that'll take me out of this damned spot."[49] He didn't have to wait long for Wood's enthusiastic reply. "She was equally impressed," Williams states of Wood's reaction; "and Bill became her client almost at once" (*Memoirs*, p. 89). Soon, Inge also heard from Jones. It was unanimous. Now came the wait, while Wood tried to place the play with prospective New York producers. Predictably, the process of finding a producer seemed to Inge to take far too long. He desperately wanted the fall of 1948 to be the last term he would have to teach at Washington University, but by the end of the year, it was obvious that he would have to teach during the spring term of 1949.

In early 1949, Inge was again on an emotional roller coaster, alternating between optimism and despair about *Sheba*'s New York chances. Letters that Inge sent to Margo Jones during this time illustrate the highs and lows he was experiencing. "What would a struggling young (Audrey Wood tells me I am still young as playwrights go) playwright do without you?" Inge wrote to Jones on January 5. Jones apparently had offered to consider pro-ducing *Sheba* if Wood was unsuccessful in finding a New York producer. Inge goes on to say that he had reworked *Sheba* and made it better, al-though possibly not for Jones's purposes, because the revision was sexier than the original. (What was "sexier" was a javelin-posing scene involving Turk, the muscular young athlete.) "It is sexy but the sexual element is re-lieved by humor. Still, it might not do for you," Inge concludes.[50] By January 13, however, when he wrote to Jones again, Inge apologized for his earlier "squeamish" letter. No longer of the opinion that Turk's javelin scene was too obviously phallic for Dallas audiences, he had decided that Jones could do *Sheba* easily. The real issue, of course, wasn't Inge's concern about Dallas audiences; it was his concern about reactions in New York. In the January 13 letter he goes on to make that concern very clear: "I've never met Audrey Wood, and I don't know what I can expect of her in the way of finding something for me." He concludes by describing his St. Louis situation as, in one word, "stagnant."[51]

The ever-supportive Jones apparently never responded to Inge's question about the suitability of *Sheba* for her purposes, but she continued her efforts to help him escape from his "stagnant" position. On January 15 she wrote in his behalf to Laura Wilck, a Hollywood agent, to ask Wilck to read some of Inge's work and see if she could "sell him as a writer to the movies." Jones told Wilck that Inge had "tremendous talent," that his most recent play (*Sheba*) had "great, great possibilities," and that his talent was "one of the best I have encountered in these many years of reading scripts."[52] She then told Inge to send his work to Wilck right away. But in a letter from Inge to Jones on February 1, Inge says that he hasn't written to Hollywood be-cause a recent *New Republic* article on "the Hollywood situation" was "so discouraging."[53] Inge's disregard for following up on her efforts did not upset Jones, who had a great understanding of and tolerance for creative sensibili-ties. Inge's self-absorption had doubtless cost him support and friendships along the way, and it would cost him in the future; but Jones never let it become an issue between them.

Inge's letter of February 1 to Jones also indicates his disappointment that Audrey Wood's obviously persistent efforts on behalf of *Sheba* had so far been unsuccessful. Important names fall in this letter in relation to the circulating *Sheba* script:

> Gassner has it but hasn't reported yet. Cheryl Crawford turned it down, which I would have expected; Martin Ritt (whom I don't know) did likewise, saying he felt the play lacked incident. The last criticism I would never have expected. John Houseman is also reading it. Tennessee gave me such a build-up on the play that I can't help feeling pretty let-down. I'm trying to get started on another but feel too depressed most of the time to do any writing.

"Everything takes time, dear," the tireless Jones replied in a letter of February 9, "and you must work, keep right on working no matter what."[54] During these early days of February, neither Inge nor Jones knew that something very important was happening in New York. Phyllis Anderson, wife of the playwright Robert Anderson and head of the Play Reading Department of the Theatre Guild, later noted in *Theatre Arts* magazine: "*February 4, 1949: Audrey Wood has sent us a script by a new playwright, William Inge. The title is intriguing . . . 'Come Back, Little Sheba.'*"[55]

PHYLLIS ANDERSON liked *Sheba* and immediately routed it for additional readings. By February 8 she had received a positive first report. By March 15 the guild had formally optioned the play; Lawrence Langner of the guild had already suggested that Shirley Booth play Lola, a suggestion that would prove fortuitous for both Inge's and Booth's careers; and an Equity reading had been scheduled for April 5.[56] This news was dizzying to Inge back in St. Louis. Charles E. Burgess reports that Kathrene Casebolt and other St. Louis friends saw Inge off at the airport for a trip to New York to meet Wood and to confer with her about the *Sheba* script (p. 465). Inge had about $100 that he had realized from the previous year's St. Louis production of *Front Porch*, and this trip was apparently his first experience in flying.

Neither Inge nor Wood ever commented publicly about their first meeting, but it is clear that Wood then won whatever measure of confidence Inge might have been withholding from her. No record of their discussions about *Sheba* survives, but it appears that any changes they might have agreed upon were quite minor, for the early manuscript and later published version of the play differ only slightly. In retrospect, this trip was more symbolic than substantive: Inge at last "took off," figuratively as well as literally, to New York, long the goal city of his ambition. He was taking his great chance, placing his career in Audrey Wood's capable hands and his person in the airplane pilot's care. (He was, in fact, never to overcome the fear of flying that commonly afflicts many people; moreover, he suffered extreme claustrophobia when in an airplane, and his acrophobia was such that he always sought the lowest possible quarters when he moved into or stayed in highrise buildings.)[57] When he returned to St. Louis and his classes at Washington University, it was with the resolve that this would be his last term as a teacher. The April 5 Equity reading had gone well: "Everybody enthusiastic" was Phyllis Anderson's report (p. 58). Momentum toward production was clearly building, and Inge wanted to be present for everything as soon as he could be after the term ended. Meanwhile, he had to keep control: there were classes to teach and arrangements to be made, and he needed above all to stay on the wagon. He was nearing his thirty-sixth birthday, and he was full of nervous anticipation. It appears that there were times during this spring when, as he had a year earlier, he was simply unable to stay away from the bottle. At any rate, there is some evidence that he knew he would continue to need more help than A.A. could afford him.

About a year earlier, Inge had met the playwright William Gibson and his wife, Margaret, at Jessica and Allen Crafton's home in Lawrence. Some of Gibson's plays had been produced by the Civic Theater in nearby Topeka, where Margaret was a trainee on the psychiatric staff at the Menninger Foundation. The occasion was a campus production of a Gibson play, and the Craftons had hosted a postplay party. Inge remembered the Gibsons quite cordially, and he kept in touch with them when Margaret accepted a position at the Austen Riggs Center in Stockbridge, Massachusetts. Now, a year or so later, Inge wrote to Margaret at Riggs to inquire about coming there for treatment.[58] Perhaps he reasoned that at Stockbridge he could get the help he needed while still being fairly close to New York. The request indicates that he was having a rocky time of it again, possibly because nearly three months had gone by—most of April, all of May, then all of June—with no further definite word from New York about production plans after the successful Equity reading.

According to Audrey Wood, the delay was attributable to second thoughts and hesitations among members of the Theatre Guild. "Theresa Helburn and Lawrence Langner of the Guild were, to say the least, uncertain about

Inge's play and its potential with audiences," Wood later recalled in her memoirs. This, in spite of Langner's having been the first to suggest Shirley Booth to play Lola. Phyllis Anderson, however, deeply believed in the play. In Wood's recollection, if Anderson had not "hung in there, pressing and pushing to get *Sheba* into production, there might not have been a production at all." Finally, Anderson won a decision to give *Sheba* a week's tryout in Connecticut's Westport Country Playhouse, but by the time definite dates for the run were available, it was necessary to book the play after Labor Day, when the regular subscription season had ended. It was a very risky time, remembered Wood, because the regular summer audiences would be gone, and the building was neither air-conditioned nor heated, should the weather be of either extreme.[59]

Wood was careful not to share with Inge her knowledge of the guild's waffling and the riskiness of the Westport dates. Doubtless she by then knew of his worrisome bent and considered it typical, although she did not yet know about his drinking; nor was she aware of the extent of his emotional problems. She reported the Westport plan to Inge, who received it with such relief and a new surge of confidence that he immediately wrote to Margaret Gibson to cancel his request about possible admission to the Riggs Center.[60] He was going to Westport to see the play into production, and he was furthermore going to stay in the New York area.

Inge's decision to leave St. Louis in the summer of 1949 and not to return to teaching at Washington University the following fall was not wise, but it was extremely well motivated. Carson and others at the University made it clear to him that he could return if he wanted to, but as Inge was to recollect some years later, he himself did not believe he could bear to return. He left, in his words, "burning bridges behind."[61] He was thirty-six, and he believed that *Sheba* was his only real chance, doubtless his last chance, truly to achieve, to make something more of his life than it had been. He was an alcoholic, a closet homosexual, a desperate captive in a teaching career he never really wanted. He had long ago abandoned his dreams of acting fame; his good looks and fine features were part of the general erosion. He had discovered his last, best hope in writing and had fed that hope after meeting Williams and Jones, by generating two plays that had been produced in regional theaters and numerous other scripts that he might yet use; he had in *Sheba* the play on which he had staked his hope for escape. He had no idea of the stresses that awaited him in the months ahead, and it is good that he didn't have. He was going for the brass ring in an all-or-nothing grab. Had fate and audiences not smiled on his work in the years immediately to come, it is doubtful that William Inge would have lived long into the 1950s. Perhaps he had not yet actually "made a halfhearted, unsuccessful attempt" to take his own life, as had his protagonist in *Driver*, Joey Hansen (p. 200), but he knew where the abyss lay, and his drinking and depression could quickly have taken him over the edge.

Part Three • New York: The Strains of Triumph

6 · Connecticut

William Inge arrived in New York, probably by train or bus, in July, 1949. Where he first took up residence in Manhattan is not known for sure. Harry Holtzman, the New Yorker whom Inge had met in 1938 in Independence and who by 1949 had returned to Manhattan to live, recalls Inge's first New York place as being on Fifty-second Street between Fifth and Sixth avenues. That is also roughly what playwright Robert Anderson (Phyllis's husband then) recalls. However, Paul Bigelow, the Theater Guild employee who was to spend great amounts of time with Inge before *Sheba*'s Broadway opening, reports that shortly after arriving in New York, Inge sublet an apartment in the extreme east nineties.[1] It is possible that Inge lived briefly on Fifty-second Street before relocating in the east nineties. Wherever he lived first, when Inge arrived in New York, the process for the Westport production of *Sheba* was already under way. He wasn't near the production process long before he became upset. The only thing that seemed definitely established was the opening date: September 12. Questions abounded over direction and casting.

The guild had chosen Daniel Mann as director. Mann "had done some B films in Hollywood and worked in New York at the Actors Studio," remembered Audrey Wood; "but as yet he hadn't done anything important on Broadway."[2] Mann was later to become an established "name" director, but in 1949 he was still virtually unknown. The prospect of an unknown director's working with an unknown playwright's play could hardly have helped Inge's confidence. Moreover, Lawrence Langner was having trouble convincing Shirley Booth that she was right for the role of Lola. Primarily known as a comedienne for her radio role as Miss Duffy and her previous stage work in *My Sister Eileen* and *The Philadelphia Story*, Booth was wary of a major dramatic role. In fact, after keeping *Sheba*'s script for some time, she finally called Langner personally and declined it (Wood, p. 224).

But here the tenacious Wood stepped forward. Convinced that Booth would be perfect as Lola, Wood consulted with Langner, then she called Booth, who had once played ingénue roles in the stock company owned by Wood's father. "I made a long and impassioned speech on behalf of my client and his play," Wood remembered in her memoirs. She told Booth that the Westport production, and hence *Sheba*'s future as a play and Inge's future as a playwright, might well depend on her. "Miraculously," said Wood, Booth changed her mind: "Even though she had a commitment to another play for the fall, she was ready to do *Sheba*" (Wood, p. 224). The veteran character actor Sidney Blackmer was then cast as Doc, and soon other casting was completed. *Sheba* was ready to aim at the September 12 opening date. Inge now had a director and a cast for his play, and this apparently settled him enough to be whatever help he could be as rehearsals began for Westport.

Dress rehearsal was Sunday night, September 11. Because the regular season was over, the guild asked Westport business people and, in Audrey Wood's words, "other friendly locals" to the preview. It was a chilly night, and Wood and her husband, William Liebling, sat in the drafty auditorium, awaiting the audience's reaction to Doc's great drunk scene in Act II, the scene Wood considered crucial. Referring to this scene, Wood said, "If it worked for the audience, if it held them, then I was certain Inge had written a viable piece of theatre." Wood's account continues: "To my utter joy, this cold night in Westport, with an audience of complete strangers who weren't really theatregoers and had no idea whatsoever what they were going to see, when we came to that startling scene between Blackmer and Booth, you couldn't hear a sound from anywhere in the drafty theatre. We knew. *Sheba* worked!" (p. 225). Phyllis Anderson was pleased with the dress rehearsal, Mann's direction, and the play itself, but her "Diary of a Production" does not reflect the confidence that Wood felt after the dress rehearsal: "Will it get over?" she asked; "Will the Guild take it to New York?"[3]

All doubt was removed on Monday's opening night. "The shivering post-season audience was enthralled by the play," wrote Anderson. "The old barn shook with the cheers, stamping feet, and bravos that greeted the cast at the final curtain" (p. 58). Word spread quickly as the week progressed. "All sorts of theatre people had heard about Bill's play and made the trip to Westport to see it," wrote Wood (p. 225). Anderson referred to this stream of the curious as a "who's who of the theatre," many of whom offered to take *Sheba*'s production off the guild's hands. "Do they think we're simple-minded?" asked Anderson (p. 58). Now there was no doubt; *Sheba* and William Inge were going to Broadway. But *when* they were going was another question altogether.

After the Westport run, *Sheba's* momentum almost completely evaporated. Everyone now believed in the play and was eager to begin preparations to take it to New York. However, Mann and Blackmer had prior considerations that would not easily be dealt with. Worse yet, Shirley Booth was still under contract to do a new play, *Love Me Long*, scheduled for a November opening. The guild had to decide whether to wait until Mann, Blackmer, and Booth were available or to ready *Sheba* for production with a new director and principal cast. The decision was easy for the guild but hard for Inge: no one could now imagine *Sheba* without Booth and Blackmer. They would wait. Anderson resigned herself to "spend the months . . . drinking coffee with an understandably anxious Bill Inge" (p. 58).

"The months" were to stretch through the end of 1949, and the increasingly nervous Inge increasingly substituted scotch for coffee, although at first he helped to avoid any severe breakdown of equilibrium by beginning a thorough psychoanalysis. "My first six weeks of analysis were bloody hell," he later remembered, but the therapy was helpful during this early time of extreme agitation.[4] He also shared the *Sheba* script with his analyst, who reportedly, along with other psychiatrists, found it psychologically sound.[5] But Wood could see that alcohol had a powerful influence on her client. She wrote in her memoirs:

> I'd already seen what liquor did to him. A warm and shy man, under its influence he became almost mute. Thus tranquilized, Bill would look at you and you could smile at him, but he had no conversation. You could take his hand and hold it, and he'd hold yours, but you got no verbal response. It was almost like dealing with a shadow, not a man. (P. 227)

And the lengthening delay, which was accepted by Wood and members of the guild as inevitable, necessary, and not really extraordinary in the high-pressure world of Broadway theater, became finally too much for Inge, who lost control and conspicuously fell off the wagon. In retrospect, no one in New York could then have realized the extreme degree of Inge's desperate hopes for *Sheba*. No one could have realized how utterly he feared that its possible failure would change his life. He had concealed his alcoholism reasonably well at first and probably was still successfully concealing his sexuality, but under the mounting pressure that he placed upon himself, something had to give. He got drunk and stayed that way, often roaming the theater district and, in a significant deterioration of his control, often being picked up by the police.

WOOD AND members of the Theatre Guild began to fear that Inge's trouble might jeopardize the play. According to Paul Bigelow, then of the guild, Inge's contractual agreement obligated him to be involved in rehearsals and to be available for consultation and publicity. He had done these things prior to Westport, but now he was simply in no condition for any of that. When a police lieutenant from the theater district let it be known that Inge would have to be taken to Bellevue for drying out if he were picked up again, Bigelow took charge, not because he cared so much about Inge, he later explained, but because he deeply believed in the play and the guild's investment in it.[6]

As quietly as possible, Bigelow arranged for Inge to enter a sanitarium near Greenwich, Connecticut, and to come under the care of a psychiatrist who, Bigelow believes, had some theater connections, possibly an investment in *Sheba*'s production. At any rate, this doctor, who must here remain unidentified, took Inge on for a very modest fee that was paid, as Bigelow recalls, directly by the guild from *Sheba*'s budget. Inge was reluctant to go to the sanitarium, and Bigelow and another friend had a difficult time getting Inge into the car for the short trip to Greenwich. At the sanitarium, the doctor treated Inge with Antabuse, then a relatively new drug which helps keep alcoholics away from drinking because, in combination with alcohol, it makes the drinker violently ill. Inge responded to the treatment, but Bigelow and the doctor agreed that Inge should remain at the sanitarium except when Bigelow had to take him out for purposes of promoting the play.[7] Apparently, the original psychiatrist whom Inge had begun seeing in Manhattan no longer was involved with Inge's treatment.

Meanwhile, things were beginning to look good for *Sheba*. Mann and Blackmer would be available after the first of the year. Shirley Booth opened November 7 in *Love Me Long*, and although no one associated with *Sheba*'s production deliberately wished for that play to fail, it soon became apparent that it was not going to be successful. On January 2, 1950, Phyllis Anderson noted in her "Diary of a Production" that "everybody we want is at last available." Rehearsals for *Sheba* could begin again, and tryout engagements were arranged for late January in Wilmington, Delaware, and in Boston.[8]

From the sanitarium in Greenwich, the now-dry Inge began to help ease his tensions by repeatedly revising the play. "It seemed he did a new rewrite every week," recalls Audrey Wood. "I remember once I wired him, 'NOW JUST STOP. I CAN'T BEGIN TO READ YOUR PLAY EVERY WEEK'" (Wood, pp. 226–227). Daniel Mann and the cast, rehearsing daily, stayed basically with the Westport script. When matters requiring consultation with Inge arose, it was the tireless Bigelow who shuttled questions and responses back and forth, ever shielding Inge's treatment and whereabouts from the press. It was imperative to keep Inge in Greenwich, for Bigelow feared that if he brought him into the city, Inge would slip away and get drunk immediately and then become wretchedly ill because of the Antabuse. It was, all agreed—including Inge—a tough situation, especially as the January 26 Wilmington opening approached, because Inge would have to be there.

Again, it was the resourceful Bigelow who found a solution. He took Inge to a Wilmington hotel on the morning of opening day, then he sent all of the playwright's clothing to the hotel laundry to be cleaned and pressed, with strict orders that they not be returned until time to dress for the theater. No order for room service, Bigelow further instructed, should be accepted from Inge. Undressed, unable to leave the room, and unable to order anything, Inge stayed sober all day and, the hawklike Bigelow at his side, made a brief appearance at the theater, after the curtain had come down, to enthusiastic applause from the Wilmington audience.[9] "*Sheba* was even better in Wilmington than it had been that first week in Westport," wrote Wood (p. 227). "We did fairly well," was the Wilmington opinion of the more cautious Phyllis Anderson (p. 58).

On January 30, *Sheba* opened in Boston. Again, Bigelow engineered a brief appearance by Inge, this time with greater cooperation from Inge, who of course by now was realizing that whatever fate might befall *Sheba*, the wait was almost over. Reviews were mixed in Boston, it seemed to Anderson, but the play left there with the guild, Mann, and the cast confident that all would be ready for the February 15 opening at New York's Booth Theatre. "At this moment," wrote Anderson, "we have a happy company with everybody loving everybody and loving the play" (p. 58).

The night of the opening in New York, Bigelow brought Inge to midtown, but Inge could not bring himself to go to the Booth Theatre with Bigelow. (This fear of opening nights would become typical of him, even after he was established as virtually a "can't miss" playwright.) That night, Bigelow recalls, Inge was much as he had been in Wilmington and Boston: almost numb, seemingly indifferent. Bigelow thinks that perhaps the aloofness was a side effect of the Antabuse, but it is also plausible that at this point, Inge literally *was* numb with fear; he had come so far, hoped so hard, that he was nearly paralyzed. Bigelow and Inge sat in a restaurant on Forty-fifth Street, not far from the Booth Theatre, drinking countless cups of coffee. Bigelow remembers that at *Sheba's* intermission, some members of the audience came into the restaurant, and he could tell from overhearing their conversation that the play was going very well. But if Inge also heard, he gave no indication. When the play was almost over, Bigelow again tried to persuade Inge to go to the theater, but to no avail.[10] Phyllis Anderson reports that a short while later in the Booth, the audience was cheering Shirley Booth and Sidney Blackmer and calling for the author (p. 58). Eventually, Bigelow managed to escort Inge backstage, where he accepted the congratulations of those who were still gathered there.

About midnight, Inge found his way to a telephone, where he called Independence to awaken Maude with the news. The call was hampered by Maude's sleepiness and a bad connection, but she heard her son say: "The play is a success, Mom . . . I say, they liked the play tonight." "Well, Bill," the still-groggy Maude asked, "you are in New York, aren't you?" Yes, she was assured; the show was on Broadway; a letter was forthcoming.[11] Yes. He was in New York.

The reviews of February 16 were somewhat mixed about the play itself, but they were nearly unanimous in their praise of Booth and Blackmer. Typical was the comment by Richard Watts, Jr., in the *New York Post*: "There is so much that is worthy about 'Come Back, Little Sheba' that it seems a pity it isn't more skillful a drama, but Mr. Blackmer and Miss Booth are brilliant."[12] Writing in the *Daily Compass*, Arthur Pollock said that *Sheba* "is a fine play by a man who hates tripe and won't have any of it around, a moving play, true and warming, that will leave a gap in the lives of those who are careless enough not to see it."[13] Pollock predicted much of *Sheba's* eventual appeal; as Bigelow was to state, *Sheba* became "the play to see" among New York's seasoned theatergoers. That not only assured it of a modest profit for the guild but also a solid overall critical reception. Today, the words of critic and director Harold Clurman still ring true about *Sheba*: "It is a realistic portrait of small-town people cramped almost to extinction by their repressions, their shallow spiritual horizons, their mechanical Puritan prejudices, their ignorance. . . . There is in it too a certain stubborn honesty, a determination to set down the unadorned truth." Clurman goes on to align Inge's play with the works of Walt Whitman, Sherwood Anderson, Theodore Dreiser, and the painter Edward Hopper, because of the particular sense of American context evoked.[14] For Inge, as with Sherwood Anderson in particular, that context was the family in the small towns of midwestern America. It was a context he would not abandon in the work that was to become his best and his best known.

FIRST, HOWEVER, he had several entirely new matters to deal with: relative wealth, success, and celebrity. Because as the playwright, he received a percentage of *Sheba*'s gross (not net) receipts, he found himself with more money than he had ever had before.[15] Along with this comparative wealth, which was soon to be enhanced because of Wood's successful negotiations for the sale of *Sheba*'s film rights to Hollywood, came another new problem: taxes. Perhaps it was the financially astute Wood, who managed most of Inge's financial matters until the job simply became too big, who suggested that his love of modern art might be a way to ease his tax bill as well. Or perhaps it was his old friend Harry Holtzman, who was then working at a Manhattan gallery. At any rate, several sources report that very early on in New York, Inge began to buy works of modern art—mostly paintings, but some sculpture—many of which he later donated to various museums for tax write-offs. He bought only what he liked, but he had excellent fortune in often choosing what was later going to become valuable (e.g., de Kooning, Pollock, Modigliani), and as the years passed, he became increasingly knowledgeable.

There were also the matters of success and celebrity. Rather suddenly, he was in demand for interviews and various appearances. The heartening acceptance of *Sheba*, along with the Antabuse, had restored his sobriety, but he was still in need of his psychiatrist's care, and he still needed to keep his problems as secret as possible. Back in Independence, Luther and Maude were proud of him, and the town shared that pride. Inge had been gone a long time, but the values that he had brought to New York were still the values that had been forged in Independence and tempered in Columbus, Columbia, and the relative anonymity of St. Louis. Simply put, he did not want people to know that he was an alcoholic (bad) and a homosexual (worse). *Sheba* had changed his status but not himself.

During the months of *Sheba*'s run in New York, Inge shuttled as quietly as possible between rented rooms in Manhattan and rooms he had in Greenwich, either at the sanitarium or near it.[16] He no longer needed Bigelow's persistent attention, and he left important scheduling to Wood and her associates. Meanwhile, *Sheba* continued to enjoy attention. In the spring, Booth and Blackmer won Antoinette Perry (Tony) awards as the outstanding dramatic performers of the year, and they also won Donaldson Awards for the year's best performances as judged by their fellows. The New York Drama Critics Circle voted *Sheba* a narrow second to Carson McCullers's *Member of the Wedding* in their balloting for the "best new play of the year," and the same critics named Inge the "most promising" playwright of the 1949/50 season, while citing Booth and Blackmer for the outstanding performances of the same year.[17] This sort of attention, along with Wood's July sale of the movie rights to Hal B. Wallis for a reported $150,000 for Inge, certainly made Maude's "speckled egg" a decidedly hot item.[18]

Random House published *Sheba* shortly after the play closed on July 29, after having run for a quite respectable 190 performances. The publication, also arranged for by Wood, was the beginning of Inge's career as a published creative writer. He always considered the published version of his plays very important, because they represented, as he once told interviewer Roy Newquist, the "best possible piece I can write."[19] The published play, after all, was wholly his, as he wanted it recorded for posterity; it did not necessarily reflect alterations that came via the production process. This attitude about his published works was to become very significant as his career continued, but in 1950 it was just another way his name and his creative vision could come before the public.

Another way Inge's thoughts became broadly public was through published interviews, as well as articles that he himself wrote in the wake of *Sheba*'s success. Examination of these pieces now reveals that Inge shared only a very guarded picture of himself; in the interviews he spoke respectfully of his small-town Kansas background, his acting and teaching experience, and his pleasure at *Sheba*'s success. He kept everything superficial. The thoughtful pieces that he himself wrote had to do with some of the criticisms of *Sheba* and the challenges of having been named a "most promising" playwright. He recognized that there was now a public that expected to see him and hear from and about him, and he managed to meet that expectation reasonably well in those days of early television, before the proliferation of talk shows and the promotional circuitry they created. He could be heard from with some frequency in the then-dominant print media without the necessity of numerous public appearances. When the lag time between utterance and publication exists, what is lost in spontaneity is gained in considered control—a definite advantage to guarding one's responses.

In an on-camera interview, Inge could never have achieved the level of control and clarity evident in pieces such as "The Schizophrenic Wonder," in *Theatre Arts*, and "Concerning Labels," in the *New York Times*. In the former he defended *Sheba* against critics who believed, rightly or wrongly, that Doc's drunken homicidal threats are not sufficiently foreshadowed, that Doc and Lola are insufficient as tragic figures, that Lola's dream symbolism is psychologically too pat, that the play is unnecessarily depressing, that Lola and Marie are "sluts," and that the play is structurally poor because its tension builds too slowly. Despite the dubious wisdom of trying to answer critics, "The Schizophrenic Wonder" projected the gentle voice of an author, grateful for his success, who is quietly explaining what he was trying to achieve in the play, all in a very civil tone.[20] To a certain extent, this was a response in kind; even most of *Sheba*'s toughest critics donned gloves for their sharpest jabs, such as those by the *New Yorker*'s Wolcott Gibbs, who wrote of Lola's final dream: "It is doubtful whether so much elementary and perhaps slightly preposterous symbolism has ever been crowded into one dream before in the history of the theatre."[21] Noting that most critics regard dream symbolism as "phony," Inge responded that several psychiatrists had read and approved the script and that Lola's dreams had an important dramatic function whether they were scientific or not ("Schizophrenic Wonder," p. 23).

"Concerning Labels," nearly forty years after its appearance in the *New York Times*, seems a marvel of Inge's understanding of the challenge posed by being named "most promising" playwright. "Expectations, of one's self and of others, can be troubling," he wrote knowledgeably. "We are being unfair to a writer if we expect him always to equal our conception of what is his best," he continued, holding that Tennessee Williams's *Summer and Smoke* had been rejected by audiences only because it had followed *A Streetcar Named Desire*. All of *Summer and Smoke*'s "sensitive sheen" and "silky beauty were unobserved because the play was not what people expected." Such unfair standard setting, he argued, deprives a playwright of freedom of expression.[22] He goes on to deplore the lack of confidence among critics and audiences who judge plays by what they are not, and he expresses the hope that his next play, *A House with Two Doors* (yet another title for what was to become *Picnic*), already on option to the Theatre Guild, would be judged on its own merits, not by any expectations established by *Sheba*. Taken as a whole, Inge's statements in this article are so sensible, so well thought out, that it seems incredible that the person who wrote it could later allow himself to be so vulnerable to criticism. If he could have reminded himself of this perspective, if he could have convinced himself not only of its truth

Inge, photographed outside his apartment at the Dakota in New York City. Courtesy of WIC/ICC

but also of its usefulness as a counterforce to critical attack, he might have had a less bumpy time of it later. But for Inge, part of the sadness of his story is his inability to follow his own advice about critics.

Inge's reference to *A House with Two Doors* in "Concerning Labels" was premature, since *Picnic* would not open until 1953, but it helped reinforce that expectation of "What now?" that is the inescapable result of previous success. Williams knew the feeling well by now. He also knew the sting of rejection, and he undoubtedly advised his friend both to be patient and to choose his next play carefully. For Inge, *Front Porch* now loomed as his best chance to repeat his success; he had no other play that had already been tested by multiple positive readings and actual performance. But he was also sure that it needed plenty of work. To do the work properly, Inge needed to settle into a good apartment in Manhattan and establish a productive routine. It was time to stop constantly shuttling to Greenwich and to start trusting the motivation to write and the Antabuse, as well as the ongoing analysis, to keep him on keel.

He found a small apartment on a low floor of the Dakota, a distinctive old building on Seventy-second Street at Central Park West, and moved in.[23] It was an ideal location, not just because it was on a low floor, but because Inge appreciated the fact that the Dakota's residents were all successful and well-to-do, and some of them were famous. Moreover, Central Park was right across the street to the east, and the midtown theater and entertainment heart of the city was, by Inge's standards, a moderate walk to the south. Still without a car, although he was soon to buy one, Inge loved to walk about midtown for exercise and the easing of tensions that would build while he was at his writing desk.[24] He was entering the most successful and productive stage of his life, and he was staying dry most of the time. But he was also going counter to his own advice in "Concerning Labels." He was putting pressure on himself: he wanted his next play to be better than the first. He wanted to prove that *Sheba* was no fluke.

7 · The Dakota

The expansion of *Front Porch* into *Picnic* proved to be a long and arduous process. Lawrence Langner, of the Theatre Guild, and Audrey Wood liked the setting and concept of *Front Porch*, but they agreed with Inge that the characters, incidents, and dialogue all needed considerable work. Inge was still fascinated with the nostalgic images of small-town women in summer that he had first thought of when he had begun to write *Front Porch* in St. Louis, and as he was later to recall, those same images returned to him when he resumed working on that material. The images called forth "a memory of women—beautiful, bitter, harsh, loving, young, old, frustrated, happy— sitting on a front porch on a summer evening. There was something in that atmosphere, something I wanted to re-create, and that is how *Picnic* got under way."[1] In another account of the beginnings of *Picnic*, Inge remembered that the first rewriting of *Front Porch* he attempted actually did begin with a scene of women sitting on a porch. "After writing it," he said, "I was fascinated to find how protectively feminine it was, how the women seemed to have created a world of their own, a world in which they seemed to be pretending men did not exist."[2] Inge already knew that this world had to be dramatically shaken by the introduction of a handsome young male. But the details were going to take time: How many women? How would each woman respond to the man? How many complications should there be? Working out these answers would prove to be Inge's major writing task for well over a year.

Meanwhile, there were his ongoing demands of celebrity and secrecy. Now, as a recipient of frequent invitations to dinners, cocktail parties, openings, and other gatherings, he began what was to become his characteristic pattern of selective acceptances followed by brief appearances. At large gatherings he sought quiet corners in which to sip ginger ale; at the table he always declined cocktails or wine, and invariably he made gracious but early excuses and farewells. As in every other place he had lived during his adult life, he left the impression with many that he was quiet, rather shy, and a bit aloof. Robert Whitehead, who was later to be one of the producers of *Bus Stop*, recalls meeting Inge and thinking he was a very quiet man with a calm exterior, "kind of an organized gentleman," well-dressed and mannerly.[3] Doubtless, there were those, such as Audrey Wood, who by now knew why Inge was so reserved; and Tennessee Williams, for all his own flambuoyant ways, understood his friend's need to maintain that calm surface. Others who met Inge at this time saw him as intent, rather single-minded. Jo Mielziner, a set designer who happened also to live in the Dakota and who later worked on both the Broadway and film productions of *Picnic*, remembers that the first time they met, Inge spoke only about the theater.[4] Likewise, Jack Garfein, who met Inge in New York and was to become one of his closest friends during the last years in California, remembers that the first time they talked, one afternoon at Inge's Dakota apartment, Inge spoke only about his observations of people. Inge went into such detail that Garfein knew he had met a genuine student of human behavior.[5] Quietly preoccupied: this was the exterior William Inge that New York acquaintances remember from the early 1950s. The interior Inge was not nearly so placid.

For one thing, he was not enjoying his success as much as he had thought he would. In the eyes of others, he had plenty of reasons to be delighted. Old Independence acquaintances, some of them veterans of his one-time neighborhood productions, had come to see *Sheba* when they were in New York; they playfully asked him to get them tickets for pennies or pins, because he had once told them years ago that prices for his plays would never rise.[6] Although he saw the good will and humor in such requests and tried to accommodate them, he did not feel as thrilled to be an author as they felt to know one. Inge was later to recall: "Even my oldest friends, who had known me during the years when I gave myself no peace for lack of success, were baffled by me. There was absolutely no one to understand how I felt, for I didn't feel anything at all. I was in a funk." He went on to say that those who knew he was undergoing psychoanalysis at the time couldn't imagine why. "But you're a success now," he remembers them saying; "What do you want to get analyzed for?"[7] To what extent such questioners knew about Inge's alcoholism and homosexuality is not known, but it is doubtful that they would have been so puzzled if they had been aware of those matters.

For another thing, the "funk" that he says he was in made it more difficult to maintain his sobriety than he had anticipated when he took his apartment in the Dakota. How often and to what degree he fell off the wagon cannot be said; probably such bouts were wholly private, but they almost certainly occurred. He apparently still found it necessary to go to the sanitarium at Greenwich for attention. Two letters from this time, at any rate, prove that his temporary residence again was the Homestead, at 420 Field Point Road in Greenwich. One letter from the Homestead, dated January 24 (probably 1951), to Grace Crocker of Independence, a former teacher, acknowledged that Crocker's painting lessons and English classes "were a firm part" of his childhood. "I am trying to get a new play finished up here and get my health taken care of at the same time," he wrote.[8] The other letter, to Margo Jones, dated March 9, 1951, further reveals his preoccupations at this time regarding the current theater season:

> The season here has not been a good one for my money. The situation is pretty disillusioning for anyone trying to bring off a play, making him wonder if such a fickle, shallow audience is worth working for? It honestly seems to me by this time that the successful shows now are those that have come in with such an overpowering amount of publicity that no one dares to doubt them.[9]

These letters not only place Inge near his doctor's care in Greenwich; they also show his concerns for his health (although it's doubtful that Crocker knew that alcoholism was the cause of Inge's health problem) and his new play. The "funk," it would appear, was therefore also over the problem of how to follow one success with another. Even though he did not feel great pleasure or satisfaction with the success of *Sheba*, it was, after all, the most positive thing in his life. The trick now was to repeat that success, to meet that "most promising playwright" challenge.

HOW MUCH time Inge spent in treatment at Greenwich during 1951 and 1952 can only be speculation. His work on *Picnic* (still not finally named), however, continued with considerable regularity, suggesting that the doctor's treatment was both limited and generally effective. And although Inge had no official ties to the filming of *Sheba*, he did send the film's producer, Hal B. Wallis, some suggestions for scenes that Wallis had requested. "I sent him a list of about twelve scenes that I had in mind to take place outside the house," Inge recalled in an interview with Mike Steen; "and when I saw the movie I saw that all my suggestions had been used."[10]

The film version of *Sheba* became, of course, far more popular and better known than the Broadway play had been. Although Ketti Frings adapted the play for the screen, no major changes were made in the story and characterization. Inge's name as the story's originator appeared on display posters outside movie theaters everywhere, from cities such as New York and Los Angeles to villages such as Independence and Lyons in Kansas. Television had not yet closed small-town movie houses, and countless heartland Americans saw Shirley Booth bring her Broadway Lola to the screen. It was an electric performance, directed, as in New York, by Daniel Mann and inventively photographed in black and white by James Wong Howe. One of Howe's shots seems to have been taken from inside the cupboard where the recovering alcoholic Doc had stored his previously untouched bottle, the bottle he kept on hand as a constant reminder and test. From the inner darkness the door opens outward to reveal Lola's face as she peers inside; the look of abject fear that overwhelms her as she realizes that the bottle has disappeared speaks volumes.

Before long, *Sheba*'s film honors began to mount: it won "best picture" at the Cannes Film Festival, and the Motion Picture Academy of Arts and Sciences voted Booth an Academy Award—the cherished Oscar—as best film actress of 1952. In the film, Burt Lancaster had replaced Sidney Blackmer as Doc, a bit of casting purely for Lancaster's value at the marquee, to offset the relative gamble of casting Booth as Lola (several established Hollywood leading ladies had turned down the role).[11] But it was Booth who gave the triumphant performance. Her Broadway Tony and her Hollywood Oscar for Lola proved to be the highlights of her long career.

The success of the film *Sheba* added to Inge's prestige as a promising playwright, without his writing a single additional word. If he ever paused to reflect and draw any satisfaction from knowing that his story—and his name—were now well known in the land, it must have been a fleeting experience. Perhaps if there had been someone special with whom to share such feelings, he would have been happier; he might have lingered a bit in the glow. But there seems to have been no one who filled such a role in his life. Analysis had made him increasingly reluctant to maintain any but the most *pro forma* relations with Maude and Luther, which were easily handled by mail and phone. Helene was in Nashville. His niece Jo Ann was in Ohio. He met men and women who could have been better friends, but he did not cultivate many relationships.

A man named George Faricy has occasionally been mentioned by Inge associates as the one who might at this time have been closer to Inge than anyone else in New York, but Faricy was a rather mysterious figure, and the nature of the relationship is also mysterious, for little is known—or has been told—by those who have mentioned Faricy. It is not known, for example, if Faricy is still alive. It is not known if he is a relative of Austin Faricy's, with whom Inge once worked at Stephens College. Jo Ann Kirchmaier, Inge's niece, recollects that Faricy worked for her uncle as a secretary in New York, but she does not say when or for how long. Playwright Robert Anderson remembers thinking of Faricy as Inge's "companion," who would fade in and out of Inge's life at intervals of six months or so, a pleasant but odd fellow who enjoyed making hats for people he liked.[12] Perhaps Faricy was just Inge's friend and secretary; perhaps he was also a "companion." The answer seems to remain as much of a mystery as Faricy himself. Even if Faricy was a lover, it appears that he was not a constant one, the kind who would have been emotionally close enough to share Inge's deepest feelings. Thus, after the success of *Sheba*, it seems most accurate to say that Inge remained, as usual, a lone alcoholic and homosexual who tried to stay dry and closeted while he was working on *Picnic*, his next play.

No reliable evidence exists regarding Inge's initial private thoughts and ambitions for *Picnic* as he was working on it at this time. His published remarks on this subject appeared just before and after the play's Broadway debut, and they are somewhat suspect, because by that time he had been through the script battles with the director, Joshua Logan, which I will describe presently. By that time, as we shall see, he was more or less reduced to hoping for the best for his play, and its subsequent success and the possibility of awards seem to have made him reluctant to say anything negative publicly. With the appropriate grains of salt, then, we can examine his public remarks about the development of the *Picnic* script, along with those of other principals, such as Logan, who also shared their recollections after the play's success.

As Inge resumed working with the *Picnic* material, he claimed to have become convinced that whatever its theme or resolution, he wanted it to be a bright contrast to *Sheba*. Referring to Doc and Lola, he said that in *Picnic* he "felt a desire to expand beyond their dark, somewhat gloomy household and write a play that took place in the sunshine."[13] Elsewhere, he said of his time composing *Picnic*, "I began to think less in terms of writing a *play* and to think more of writing a *show*" (Inge's italics). He considered a "show" as having more entertainment value than a "play" in terms of audience reaction.[14] If that is true, then clearly Inge was going after his audience, and he wanted to create something more sprawling and lively than *Sheba* had been. Perhaps that is why at one time, still fairly early in the writing, *Picnic* called for six different sets. But the idea of distinguishing between a "play" and a "show" also sounds, in retrospect, more like Joshua Logan than like William Inge. It is impossible to tell now just where, when, and how that idea originated.

Meanwhile, Lawrence Langner continued to like *Picnic* in concept, but he saw that what Inge was creating was far too long and complicated. Perhaps sensing that Inge was pressing too hard to create a sure-fire second play, Langner, who agreed with the idea about a "show" and who knew that a strong, successful director could quickly help to tighten a script, suggested that Inge call Joshua Logan about directing the play. Logan had a highly impressive track record with such shows as *South Pacific*, *Mister Roberts*, and *Wish You Were Here*. It was a fortuitous suggestion. In his memoirs, Logan describes Inge's call, requesting that he consider the script, which was still being called *Front Porch*. "I think there's something sunny about your work," Inge told Logan; "and I'd like to have some sun on this play."[15]

Logan read the script. He found "tenderness, beauty, comedy and theatrically effective scenes in what Inge gave me," Logan says in his memoirs; but the "play sprawled so that it was hard to comprehend." Nonetheless, Logan believed it would be a good play "if Bill would organize it properly." Calling Lawrence Langner, Logan said he would do the play if Inge would cooperate with him on it (Logan, pp. 276–277). Thus began Inge's collaboration with Joshua Logan, which was even more strained than the collaboration on *Front Porch* with Jack Balch in St. Louis, but which led to a Pulitzer Prize and his most successful play.

AT ABOUT the time when he began working with Logan, Inge apparently acquired his first car. At any rate, Logan reports that as they began their collaboration, "Bill had taken a house in Old Greenwich and so could drive over to my Stamford house easily for meetings" (Logan, p. 277). In all likelihood, the house "in old Greenwich" that Logan refers to was the Homestead; Inge could thus commute between his doctor and his collaborator with ease. Probably, Inge was no more eager to drive than he ever was, especially in the New York area traffic; but the car undoubtedly saved him fares, and he was always a bit tight with his money, even when he had plenty of it. The collaboration, however, did not proceed as smoothly as the commuting.

Whatever else may be said of Joshua Logan, there can be little question that in 1952 he was a confident man, sure of his instincts and judgments and forceful in working his will on others. By his account, it had been his vision and faith alone, along with his hurried post-opening changes in the script (some 54 pages of them), that had rescued *Wish You Were Here*, the hit he was then enjoying on Broadway (Logan, pp. 271–276). And there had been many successes before *Wish You Were Here*. While Inge had to be pleased to have Logan's reputation behind his new play, he was doubtless also daunted by that reputation. As the play's author, Inge believed he had certain inviolable prerogatives, and he was not prepared for the high-powered way in which Logan felt free to question those prerogatives. What Inge believed should be at most a give-and-take relationship eventually became what seemed to him to be a give-and-give-some-more one. The novelist Thomas Heggen had experienced the same feelings about Logan when Logan had powerfully influenced the stage adaptation of *Mister Roberts*. Such power was business as usual for Logan. Only Logan's and Audrey Wood's detailed accounts of the production of *Picnic* are available, but actions and remarks that were taken and made by Inge some years later help clarify the fuller picture that follows.

In the collaboration's early going, some agreements came fairly easily. Inge, for example, suggested that the central couple – the beautiful "Neewollah Queen" Madge and the drifter Hal – should not touch each other until their climactic dancing scene in Act II. Logan saw the powerful appropriateness of that suggestion, for once Madge and Hal touch, their defiant love becomes inevitable and, hence, the play's crisis also becomes inevitable. However, the dancing scene, like many other important scenes, was buried in Inge's lengthy original script, which called for six different sets. Logan insisted that Inge rewrite the play so that all the action would take place on a single set – a highly practical suggestion in both dramatic and economic terms (Logan, p. 277). If Inge objected to Logan's plan that the set consist solely of the back (not front) porches and yards of the adjacent Owens and Potts houses, there is no record of it. This set did make it possible for Inge to unify most of the action he had written up to that point, although it obviously also meant that the play could no longer be titled *Front Porch*. Logan's idea to unify the set was the sort of strong and logical contribution Lawrence Langner had hoped Logan would bring to Inge's play. But solving the problem of the setting was effortless compared to solving the problem created by Inge's original ending of the play.

As far as Logan was concerned, Inge's original last act "consisted of complete frustration for everyone." It created nothing less than a major clash of visions, of philosophies, and of attitudes between the two. Inge, although he had wanted a play of "sunshine," originally presented a third and final act in which nothing worked out for anyone. Logan's account is a bill of specific charges:

> [Inge] even turned the beautiful Madge into the "town pump," an ending which, I was convinced, would leave the audience as unhappy as it did me. Yet each time I asked Bill to develop a more conclusive ending, he went away, worked hard and came back with the same one, only drearier. He was afraid of being slick, of pandering to the public with a "happy ending," so he kept writing this endlessly slow dimout. Everything was negative: Hal left Madge; Madge's rich suitor, Alan, left town; Howard left Rosemary; and Madge, besmirched, walked back to the dime store with local boys catcalling. (P. 277)

This "attenuated rosary of disappointments" convinced Logan that the play would fail unless drastic changes were made in it.

Inge, however, was adamant. It was *his* play, *his* characters, *his* dramatic situation, and he was not going to put his name on someone else's phony idea of reality. (Years later, in 1962, when he published *Summer Brave*, which he called "the rewritten and final version of the romantic comedy PICNIC," Inge wrote that he believed *Summer Brave* was "more humorously true than *Picnic*, and it does fulfill my original intentions." *Summer Brave* basically restores the "attenuated rosary of disappointments" to which Logan and others objected.)[16] At an impasse with Inge about Act III, Logan gave up and withdrew from the production.

But Lawrence Langner did not. He kept working with Inge, being careful not to insist on changes in Act III but proceeding with smoothing out the first two acts and other necessary preproduction details, such as ideas for casting. He called Logan to persuade him to come back, confident that when casting was completed and rehearsals began, Inge would see the problems with Act III and rewrite. So, Logan returned (Logan, p. 279).

Before casting began, Langner, other members of the guild, and Logan persuaded Inge to change the title to *Picnic*. Not only was *Front Porch* no longer an appropriate title, but also a certain irony was achieved: although a picnic is central to the play's action, no actual picnic scenes are called for. Moreover, as Logan dryly remarked, in its then-present form, *Picnic* "was no picnic" (Logan, p. 278). Logan remained convinced that unless the third act were changed—at the very least having Madge leave with Hal—*Picnic* was doomed, no matter what its title. But he cooperated with Inge and Langner in casting, and the casting went very well indeed.

Logan wrote, "The part of Hal required an uninhibited actor who could brag, pose, disguise his shabby background with golden stories and then collapse" (p. 279). Ralph Meeker, who had earlier worked with Logan on *Mister Roberts*, proved to have the rugged good looks and emotional range that the role of Hal required. Logan "saw Madge as the girl on the Art Nouveau candy box—romantic, moody, sensuous, and yet fundamentally innocent, even gullible." All agreed that finding an actress who could put across both knockout looks and gullibility—especially with vulnerability to Hal's surface braggadocio—would be hard. However, Richard Rodgers, Logan's long-time friend and frequent collaborator, sent Janice Rule to read for the part, and as Logan put it, "'Madge' walked in." Rule's "high cheekbones, long auburn hair, transparent skin and enormous eyes" made her "better than Art Nouveau. She was pre-Raphaelite" (Logan, p. 279).

As important as Hal and Madge are, *Picnic*'s ensemble cast and the Rosemary-Howard subplot made casting still vitally important even after Meeker and Rule had been signed. Inge had seen a virtual unknown, Eileen Heckart, in a television production, and he had been impressed by her. He wrote her a note, Heckart was later to recall, inviting her to come and read for the part of Rosemary. She remembers having been told upon arrival that the part was probably taken, but after she was allowed to read, she got the part.[17] Logan recalls of Heckart's audition: "This odd, roughhewn woman with a strong Middle Western accent made it clear that she was at heart a tender, yearning human being" (p. 280). To complement Heckart as Rosemary, Arthur O'Connell was chosen to play Howard. O'Connell, who, according to Logan, was "a good actor whose career had been a string of bad luck," proved to be the "Norman Rockwell type" that was needed as Rosemary's reluctant groom-to-be (p. 280).

Meeker, Rule, Heckart, and O'Connell were all to go on from *Picnic* to continue successful performing careers, but the bonanza of casting for Inge's second play did not end with them. Kim Stanley, who went on to become, in Logan's opinion, "one of our greatest actresses," won her first significant Broadway role as Millie, Madge's teen-age tomboy little sister. Logan chose Peggy Conklin to play Flo Owens, Madge's wary mother. Conklin had worked with Logan before in *The Wisteria Trees* and "still had enough glamour to suggest that Madge's mother was once as beautiful as Madge" (Logan, p. 280). The part of Alan, Madge's rich boyfriend who had known Hal in college, was the only role in the original ensemble that was miscast. Shortly after rehearsals began, Alan's role went to the understudy, who, in Logan's words, was "a handsome young man who had left the Yale Drama School and was selling encyclopedias to support his wife and three children": Paul Newman. As though enough once and future stars had not yet fallen into the cast of *Picnic*, the understudy chosen for both Rule and Stanley was Joanne Woodward (Logan, p. 280). When casting had been completed, everyone— including Logan and Inge—believed that the ensemble was first-rate.

But the dismal third act remained. When it became apparent that not only Logan and Langner but also virtually the entire cast didn't like the third act, Inge began to budge with some very grudging changes. Chief among these was his rewriting to allow Rosemary and Howard to be married after Rosemary's desperate proposal scene. That compromise, however, wasn't enough. Ultimately, Hal and Madge are the central couple; *they* are the ones about whom the audience cares most. At this point, most people associated with the production believed that unless and until Hal and Madge could be together somehow at the end of the play, *Picnic* would still be a tenuous play.

Logan's memoirs do not speculate as to why Inge clung so fiercely to his original unhappy ending, other than to note that Inge considered that Logan's proposed conclusion would be formulaic and corny. Because of his own strong background in romantic comedy and musicals, Logan simply did not realize the degree of dedication that Inge felt toward realistic theater. Inge could believe Madge's desperation; he could believe Hal's frustration; and he could believe that those two vulnerable souls might defy all manner of village and society taboos in one reckless, opportunistic evening; but he could not believe that any sort of lasting, true, or realistic relationship could possibly result from such an encounter. Inge could believe that Hal would be run out of town, and he could believe that Madge would stay behind, "besmirched," in Logan's term, and that she would have to cope with this. It was the tainted, abandoned, pathetic Madge that William Inge understood, held compassion for, and believed to be realistic. That is why he resisted changing *Picnic* for so long, and years later, he rewrote it exactly as he wanted it. There is, however, little point in faulting Logan for his accurate sense of what audiences in the early 1950s wanted to see. Logan correctly saw the way to make *Picnic* a success, and success is what everyone, including Inge, wanted.

Two different accounts exist regarding how and why Inge finally changed the Hal-Madge ending. Audrey Wood chalked it up to audience reaction once *Picnic* began its pre-Broadway run. "Audience reaction out of town was the deciding factor," says Wood. "People simply resented Inge's suggestion that Madge remained behind, and so Bill rewrote the ending."[18] But Logan says it was a more complicated business than that. After the cast had read through the revised play for the first time, Inge went to Logan's home for lunch. He asked Nedda, Logan's wife, what she thought of the play. Nedda responded that she loved it—until the end. "I hated the way those two [Hal and Madge] were separated after having my hopes encouraged. I was disappointed and frustrated." "But we can't just have a 'corny' happy ending," Inge replied. At this point, Logan ventured his opinion that such an ending, with Madge following Hal to Tulsa, would not have to be either corny or happy. Logan said:

> If Madge left with Hal, a worthless braggart with no money and no real job, it would ultimately be a disaster. Oh, they'd have a bit of sex all right, but no security and not the decent life she and her mother dreamed of. She'd obviously end up where her mother is, deserted by her man, saddled with brats and destitute. It would be grim history repeating itself. Is that happy? Is that corny? (P. 281)

There, having lunch at the Logans', Inge seemed to be convinced at last. Logan says that Inge suddenly flushed and stood up, then started to imagine a new ending out loud:

> What if Madge appeared at the door with a suitcase, wearing a flowery chiffon dress, tall six-inch heels, and a picture hat? She says, "Mom, I'm going to Tulsa." Her mother groans and begs her to stay, holding her, pleading with her, but Madge cannot be deterred. She pulls away from Flo—breaks the umbilical cord—and walks slowly and inevitably toward the bus station—while her mother collapses sobbing on the steps. (P. 281)

The Logans loved this new ending, and Inge left to write it immediately. After the lunch, Logan announced the impending change to the cast. "Everybody cheered," according to Logan.

But Inge did not appear the next day with the rewrite; nor did he appear the day after that. His absence on the third day convinced Logan that the new ending had been illusory, which indeed it had been. Back at the quiet of his desk, Inge had not been able to write the change that he had imagined so well. He produced instead a new third act in which he tried to convey more reasons why Madge doesn't accompany or follow Hal to Tulsa. Inge brought Logan the new third act four days after the lunch with Nedda. "It was virtually the same one I had seen before," wrote Logan, "only much, much longer and more turgid" (p. 281).

Unwilling to show this new version to the cast, Logan turned the rehearsal over to an assistant and confronted Inge in the lobby. He told Inge that the cast had been expecting an upbeat ending and that this new version of the old ending simply would "kill their spirit." He pleaded with Inge to write the ending he had given at the lunch; if it proved to be no good, they could always go back to the one they had. Inge was furious. But he also must have sensed that he was likely to lose Logan. "*All right*, I'll write it," he snapped at Logan, "but *I want you to know I don't approve*" (p. 282, Logan's italics). The next day, Inge brought Logan the scene he had described at lunch. "The cast leaped on it like ravenous animals," said Logan (p. 282). The debate was over, but Inge never stopped holding *Picnic*'s ending against Logan, even when the play's prodigious success might have fostered a forgive-and-forget atmosphere.

After the battle over the ending, at least in Logan's account, Inge seemed to withdraw his active interest and participation in proceedings. At the early rehearsals, he had been vocal and readily available for consultation, as he had decidedly not been during the preparations for *Sheba*. His therapy and sobriety were apparently in enough harmony to withstand the early going, in spite of Logan's powerful personality. But after the new ending, Logan reports, Inge "came in and out like a shadow at twilight. If he was unhappy, we didn't know it. Nor did we really know it when he was happy. He watched the rehearsals with the face of an impassive, blue-eyed Buddha" (p. 282). That description echoes Audrey Wood's description of Inge when, as *Sheba* went into serious rehearsals, he began to drink: "It was almost like dealing with a shadow, not a man" (Wood, p. 227). No total loss of equilibrium took place as the rehearsals for *Picnic* continued; no Paul Bigelow was needed to protect both the show and its author; but it seems clear that Inge turned over the fate of *Picnic* to Logan and then retreated to his private battlefronts.

Picnic, however, was in extremely capable hands. Logan commissioned Marshall Jamison to find an appropriate rhythmic tune for Hal and Madge to dance to. Jamison found a "play along" record of "Moonglow," which presented rhythm and harmony but no melody, an arrangement that made the dance scene a powerful highlight, exactly as it needed to be. Logan's even hand with the talented cast made the production company happy and dedicated. And it was Logan who detected the problem that was plaguing the production—a lack of audience sympathy for Hal—while the play was still on the road, a problem that was solved by a bit of change in dialogue.

The pre-Broadway tour opened in Columbus, Ohio. Criticism was mixed; it often centered on Hal, but the problem could not yet be precisely identified. Inge had come to Columbus, but in Logan's telling, he offered no ideas or suggestions. The old fear, apparently, was back. His face, Logan reports, "was puffy and almost white. He could scarcely talk when I asked him how he felt. He stuttered a bit and went to his room, and on from there to New York without seeing anyone" (Logan, p. 283). *Picnic's* author was in full retreat, but Logan apparently didn't know all the reasons why, and perhaps no one did, although Langner, other guild members, and Audrey Wood might well have had their notions. In retrospect, this retreat can be seen as Inge's way of cooperating. If he was not resisting the bottle, if he was petrified with fear and unable to make any constructive contributions, and especially if his resentment of Logan was interfering with any remaining and otherwise clear judgment, then the play was better off with him in the deep background. In New York he could see his therapist and hope for the best for his play. At any rate, he did not see another performance of *Picnic* until after it had come to New York.

If letting Logan have his way and retreating to New York can be seen as Inge's way of cooperating, it must still be said that he was not at all happy with Logan's powerful influence, and he wasn't especially quiet about it at first. Earlier, when Logan had temporarily given up on the play, Inge had shown it to Harold Clurman, a critic and director who had praised *Sheba*, in the hope that Clurman might agree to direct it. Clurman had liked the script, and he had preferred the original ending. However, Logan had returned, and the production of the play proceeded under his direction. Clurman's early knowledge of the battle over the script did not become public until after the success of *Picnic*, but it seems logical that when Inge returned to New York from Columbus, he told Clurman about Logan's changes.[19] Margo Jones, who visited Inge after his return to New York, also learned of his displeasure. Doubtless others who saw Inge (or Clurman or Jones) at this time found out about the tensions between the author and the director.

Meanwhile, the play struggled in St. Louis, where Logan had expected a warm reception because of Inge's background there. But quite the opposite occurred: the play was attacked to the point that several subscribers canceled their tickets. Logan reports, however, that his old friend and frequent co-producer Leland Hayward saw *Picnic* in St. Louis and believed it could be salvaged. In Cleveland, reviews were similarly bad. But David Merrick, who was there to see Logan, with whom he was later to collaborate, suggested the cause of the trouble: every time Hal came onstage, Merrick said, "I bristle. I can't stand the way he swaggers, brags, and poses all over the place." That night, Logan overheard two patrons complaining about Hal: "*Some hero!*" they said. Suddenly, Logan realized that most of the audience saw Hal as the play's hero and found him far too unsympathetic (p. 283).

Logan reports that he called Inge in New York to tell him about this discovery. "Josh, if you can think of anything to do, do it," Inge told Logan. "Write it down and I'll okay it. In the meantime, just put it in, if you feel it will help." Logan thought that by now Inge had figured that nothing would save the play. Perhaps that is true. Whatever the case, Langner and Logan gave Alan, who was now being played very reliably and sympathetically by Paul Newman, some new lines, which show his old friend Hal as a victim of society whose surface behavior masks many deep hurts. Over the phone, Inge changed only "a word or two" of these new lines, and once they were put in, the play took off. "We opened in Boston to out-and-out enthusiastic reviews and packed audiences," wrote Logan (p. 284). To reassure himself—and perhaps Inge—that the new ending had "artistic integrity," Logan asked the Boston critic Elliot Norton, Tennessee Williams, and the visiting English critic Kenneth Tynan to read Inge's original ending and compare it with the new ending. All three agreed that the new ending was better (p. 284). *Picnic* was on its way.

PICNIC WAS scheduled to open in New York at the Music Box Theater on February 19, 1953. Having returned to New York from Columbus, virtually leaving the play's adjustments in Logan's hands, Inge had regrouped somewhat, despite his misgivings. He published his preplay article of commentary ("'Picnic': of Women") in the February 15 issue of the *New York Times*, concluding that "what I have wanted most to do is to present the lives in 'Picnic' with all the warmth and humor and fondness and dismay that attended me when I recalled them."[20] Naturally, he was concerned about the reception of *Picnic*, but he also felt that he could do nothing more with the play. February 19 came, and although he was understandably nervous, Inge did not need the constant attention of someone to monitor or reassure him, as Paul Bigelow had done on the opening night of *Sheba*. Inge said to Josephine Murphey some seven months later: "A nice calm came over me. . . . and I thought 'what is to be will be.' I even had a nap that afternoon." After a leisurely dinner at Sardi's, said Inge, he arrived at the Music Box in time for the second act.[21] It probably wasn't that easy for Inge to overcome his opening-night fears, but he was obviously more collected before *Picnic* than he had been before *Sheba*.

How soon it became apparent to Inge that his second Broadway play was going to be successful is guesswork. But Logan's description of opening night, if it is at all accurate, must have told the tale to the author: "We opened . . . to rapt attention, tremendous laughter, suspense, tears, 'ohs' and 'ahs,' silence and even a sexual hush in the audience when Madge and Hal danced the slow jitterbug" (pp. 284–285). The obvious audience approval was ringingly seconded when the next day's reviews began to appear.

Brooks Atkinson of the *New York Times* was among the first to weigh in with accolades: "Mr. Inge knows his characters so well that you cannot distinguish them from the drama. Inge seems to have no personal point of view, but only a knowledge of people and an instinct for the truth of the world they live in." After praising Logan's direction, Jo Mielziner's set, and the superb performances of the cast, Atkinson concluded: "The promise of 'Come Back, Little Sheba' is abundantly fulfilled. 'Picnic' is an original, honest play with an awareness of people. Most of the characters in 'Picnic' do not know what is happening to them. But Mr. Inge does, for he is an artist."[22] Most reviewers shared Atkinson's high opinion, and even those few whose praise was more faint acknowledged that the play was a success. John McClain, for example, writing in the *New York Journal-American*, said that although *Picnic* did not have "the bite" of *Sheba*, it was "performed and presented with such artistry" that it measured up "to a highly satisfactory evening." Inge, he allowed, had made the characters "powerfully human," and although *Picnic* was no masterpiece, it had succeeded "wonderfully well in bringing a small theme to a high level."[23] As the play gathered momentum after opening night, the reviews in the weekly and monthly media tended more to match Atkinson's praise rather than McClain's reticence. *Picnic* was clearly a winner.

The general flush of success did not, however, prevent the story of the Inge-Logan dispute from emerging. Writing in the March 7 issue of the *Nation*, Harold Clurman revealed that he had read Inge's original script. He protested that Logan's handling had radically changed the play by cheapening its sensibility. "It is as if a good Sherwood Anderson novel were skillfully converted into a prurient popular magazine story on its way to screen adaptation," wrote Clurman, who nevertheless acknowledged that in that vein, "the play is extremely well done." He concluded: "Here at any rate is a solid success. But I am not sure whether the author should get down on his knees to thank the director for having made it one or punch him in the nose for having altered the play's values. It is a question of taste."[24]

The next day, in his column in the *New York Journal-American*, George Jean Nathan also addressed the differences between Inge's intentions and Logan's direction—even though he had not seen Inge's original script. "I should like to learn what the play was originally like before the business of converting it into the show got under way," wrote Nathan, implying that he, too, saw a difference between "a play" and "a show" and that the former was superior. He wanted to learn this, Nathan continued, because *Sheba* had convinced him that Inge "had a lot of the independent dramatic artist in him"; because Inge had told the Boston critic Elliot Norton that "all kinds" of changes had been made "following outside suggestions"; and because he had read a report that Inge had been so irritated by Logan's changes that he had walked out of later rehearsals.[25] I was not able to locate the Norton piece and the other published report to which Nathan refers, but we should remember that Logan reports that Norton preferred the Broadway version (p. 284). Moreover, there is in Nathan's piece a clear intent to criticize Logan's overall reputation as a showman. "Mr. Logan," Nathan said, "as everyone knows, is a shrewd and accomplished hand at such theatricalization and he has here again turned the trick with all his old proficiency." It is as easy to suspect that Nathan wanted to skewer Logan as it is to think that he truly wanted to strike a blow for Inge's independent artistry. Nathan essentially repeated this critique in his monthly column in the May, 1953, issue of *Theatre Arts*: "What we have got is a big Broadway show at the expense of a small but doubtless considerably superior play."[26]

Controversy, however, requires the ongoing commitment of those who are principally affected. As praise for *Picnic* mounted, Inge and Logan said nothing publicly about their differences. Margo Jones, who saw *Picnic* shortly after it became clear that it was a hit, wrote to Inge: "I preferred it when the beautiful girl did not follow the boy." But having said that, thus reaffirming her loyalty, she also said that Logan was a truly fine director because "to me he brought out what you wrote."[27] Jones's conciliatory tone perhaps did not soothe Inge's deepest feelings, but by then it may well have become clear to Inge that there was little to gain from such controversy. The play was a big success getting bigger; already there was talk of awards; already Audrey Wood was shopping its sale to Hollywood, where interest was bound to be keen. Whatever his differences with Logan, Inge once again had his name before the public as the author of a successful major play.

According to Logan, Inge did want, at least, to restore his original ending to the Random House publication of *Picnic*. But by publishing time, the play had been nominated for several prizes, including a Pulitzer and a Drama Critic's Circle Award. Logan told Inge that restoring the old ending in the published version would hurt his chances for the pending prizes. Thus, according to Logan, Inge "reluctantly stuck to our playing script" in the publication (p. 285). At the time, there was no public evidence of that reluctance. In fact, Inge dedicated the published version to Logan.

Five years later, when *Picnic* was again published along with his other three successful plays of the 1950s, Inge wrote about his experience with Logan on *Picnic*:

> We had our ups and downs with that play, which I attribute mainly to my second-play nervousness and indecision. An unstable author, who isn't sure what he wants, is a great liability to a director; so if *Picnic* did not come off entirely to please me (as rumor had it), it was my own fault. Josh only sensed my indecision and tried to compensate for it. Still, I feel *Picnic* was a good show. Josh gave it lovely picturesqueness (he is perhaps the most visual of all directors) and feeling of size. I worked on the play with him for a year and a half, during which time he gave of himself very spontaneously. I can never cease being grateful for all that I learned from him.[28]

One must indeed read those remarks closely to catch any hint by omission or innuendo of Inge's lingering displeasure.

Of course, *Picnic* did capture more prizes than any other play by Inge. The Pulitzer was awarded to *Picnic*, as was the New York Drama Critic's Circle Award. It tied with Arthur Miller's *The Crucible* for Billboard's Donaldson Award, and the Outer Circle, a group of non–New York critics, also selected *Picnic* as the best play of the year. The storm of publicity that followed these distinctions was enormous. Inge was in demand for interviews and public appearances as never before. As always, he carefully chose his spots, striking the best balance he could between the understandable demands on his time and the covert strains on his well-being. A brief feature in the *New Yorker*'s "Talk of the Town" section (April 4, 1953) is typical of the kind of "celebrity profile" pieces written about him during this time: a few remarks about *Picnic*'s success; a passing mention of *Sheba*; a bit about his Kansas, teaching, and St. Louis backgrounds; and a few comments about contemporary theater, all seasoned with brief mentions of Inge's physical

A formal portrait of Inge, 1953. Courtesy of the Kansas State Historical Society

features, his quiet and modest demeanor, and his future plans. Very light and not the least bit controversial.

And more money came his way. He moved into a larger apartment—still on a low floor—at the Dakota. He purchased more paintings, including a Modigliani.[29] Audrey Wood sold the film rights to *Picnic* to Columbia Pictures for what Inge called in a letter to Maude "a nice, big sum of money" (by one account, $350,000).[30] All of these trappings of success, however, did not make him happy. Although he may have enjoyed the idea of fame in the abstract, because public acceptance of his work was the largest of the few positives in his life, he still had his powerful negatives: alcoholism and homosexuality. His participation in A.A. appears to have been sporadic during the early 1950s, but A.A. philosophy was still strong in his life. Psychoanalysis was also helping him maintain sobriety and purposeful direction, and he was able to write regularly. In fact, he finished several one-act plays in the early 1950s, one of which, *People in the Wind*, he was soon to develop into the full-length *Bus Stop*.[31]

By now, there was ample proof that any long-term dream of fame, fostered by his youthful fascination with stage and screen performers, had been realized. But other problems, also fostered in his youth and now being clarified by analysis, were helping to inhibit his chances to enjoy that success and fame. In Independence, after Inge had won the Pulitzer Prize, an unnamed reporter interviewed Luther. Referring to his son's prize, Luther said, "I hope it doesn't spoil him, but he's pretty level-headed and it probably won't."[32] It is doubtful that Luther had any idea of what his son was going through. He certainly did not have to worry that his son might enjoy fame too much.

AT THIS time Inge found it especially difficult to deal with Maude and Luther. Calls and letters home appear to have been brief and almost perfunctory in tone. For a time, he found trips home impossible. Gilbert Millstein reports: "Three times in as many years after coming to New York, Inge boarded a train to visit his mother in Kansas. Twice, he turned around in Chicago and came back. The third time, he buckled on his armor, made the visit and returned in twenty-four hours."[33] There is no evidence, however, that such physical distancing from his parents also included financial distancing. When Luther and Maude needed a housekeeper, Inge apparently helped to pay for one. When Luther's health began to fail, Inge helped with the medical expenses. The Inge Collection in Independence includes several brief letters to Esther Latcham, who for some time was employed both to do housekeeping and light nursing work for the elder Inges. These letters are courteous but extremely short and to the point.

The perspective on Maude and Luther that analysis, especially Freudian analysis of the sort Inge was undergoing, would logically foster includes attempting to understand one's parents—their actions, motives, and attitudes—

and, if necessary or possible, attempting to forgive all deliberate or inadvertent wrongs, real or imagined. Undeniably, such understanding and forgiveness can be difficult, and it is apparent, from his actions and from the material he was then writing and would later write, that Inge found his own experience in this process difficult. Unfortunately, only one of Inge's letters to Maude is now in the Inge Collection, but it comes from this period of his life and is indicative of this difficulty:

Dear Mom,

    Just got your nice letter. Sorry not to have written sooner. No, I haven't been sick or anything. I've been busy, and maybe just careless about writing. But I think of you just the same. Yes, I sold PICNIC to the movies for a nice, big sum of money. Doesn't that make you happy? The money will be paid to me over a period of years, and I'll get a little at a time. You take care of yourself now like a good girl, and I'll be home to see you as soon as I can.

All my love
Bill[34]

A warm letter that is not.

The lower left side of this letter is oddly clipped off in such a way that it appears whoever donated the letter removed something—perhaps a postscript. It is of course impossible to know if the excision has any significance. Moreover, while it is reasonable to assume that Inge wrote several letters to his parents during these years, I do not know whether such letters still exist or whether they revealed much of Inge's turmoil about his parents. The brevity of this one letter, the suggestion of carelessness about writing, the businesslike statement about the sale of *Picnic* to a film company but without revealing the amount of the sale, and the almost *pro forma* conclusion, then, provide only a hint of Inge's analysis—induced conflict between understanding forgiveness and sense of duty where his parents are concerned. His question to Maude about selling the film rights for *Picnic*—"Doesn't that make you happy?"—seems to mock his own unhappiness at the time, and his admonition that Maude should take care of herself "like a good girl" seems resonant of his own childhood, when Maude must have made countless similar admonitions to her Billy. The surface voice of the letter is breezy and busy, while underneath is the voice of a still-loving but troubled and unhappy son.

Inge's successes came too late in their lives for Luther and Maude to attend the plays in New York. Maude's health would not permit extensive travel by 1953, and by that same year, Luther's health had already confined him to his room, where he busily collected pictures and clippings about his son.[35] Although they doubtless felt pride in his achievements, they could not see him unless he came to Independence. And whether or not they were able to express that pride during their extremely limited time together is a matter of conjecture, lost now to time. In any case, it is clear that significant communication between parents and son at this time was poor, and perhaps that was inevitable.

Working out Oedipal conflict is bound to have been a principal part of Inge's analysis process during these years. It can hardly be purely coincidental that such conflict also found its way into his writing. The resolution of Oedipal conflict is an important component of *The Boy in the Basement*, a fine one-act play that Inge wrote at this time, but did not make public until nearly ten years later. It is also central to the three consecutive major plays that appeared on Broadway after *Bus Stop*: *The Dark at the Top of the Stairs*, which began its run in 1957; *A Loss of Roses*, his first New York failure, 1959; and *Natural Affection*, his second New York failure, 1963. Moreover, his 1961 Academy Award–winning original screenplay, *Splendor in the Grass*, although not Oedipal in theme, is nonetheless heavily influenced by Freudian psychology and the need to understand – and forgive – one's parents. Analysis was clearly important in Inge's life and creativity during the early to mid 1950s, when he was establishing his name as a successful playwright and struggling with his inability to be happy about his success.

THE TOTAL impact of analysis upon Inge's creativity during the early 1950s could not be gauged at the time, but retrospect affords a much fuller view, which should prove fruitful to examine here. In 1955, Wieder David Sievers interviewed Inge regarding the extent to which Inge was affected by Freudian interpretation. Inge's reply is noteworthy: "Any writer inwardly involved with his own time cannot help but reflect the feelings and viewpoints that Freud exposed in us."[36] Sievers's inquiry was based on what he had seen of Inge's work so far – *Sheba* and *Picnic* – not on any of the one-act plays that Inge was working on at the time. Had Sievers been able to read some of these one-act plays, he might have had more questions to ask, for these plays, considered together, suggest that while Inge was undergoing analysis in the early 1950s, the analysis was also contributing to great creative ferment, the likes of which Inge had not seen since the St. Louis years immediately after he met Tennessee Williams. In St. Louis he had begun or had continued to develop, in one form or another, versions of each of his five greatest successes—*Sheba, Picnic, Bus Stop, The Dark at the Top of the Stairs*, and *Splendor in the Grass*. In New York, roughly between 1951 and 1955, he produced several one-act plays—many of them excellent—that not only show his considerable craft but also show dimensions of his innermost self.

Regarding craft, these one-act plays provide a range that testifies to Inge's ability to produce unified, well-motivated drama of brief but solid impact, as well as embryonic sketches that would later be the basis of lengthier works. *A Social Event*, for example, is a short but polished satire about the phoniness and hypocritical pretension of the "show biz" scene. *The Mall* is a complex look at love—or rather, the failures of different kinds of love among humans. Both of those plays are complete; they are rich in characterization and dialogue; and they have tightly paced plots. But the one-act-play form also served developmental purposes for Inge, as it did in St. Louis, when he combined *Front Porch* with *The Man in Boots* and took a giant step toward *Picnic*; or when, during the same New York years under discussion here, he expanded the "Man" and "Girl" roles of *People in the Wind* into the central Bo and Cherie roles of *Bus Stop*. Inge told interviewer Roy Newquist in 1964 that the efforts of writing one-act plays were often "a substitute for notetaking."[37] His comments in the Preface to the volume that contains most of his one-act plays from the early 1950s (*Summer Brave* and *Eleven Short Plays* [New York: Random House], 1962) also indicate the developmental nature of much of his short-play writing:

> *People in the Wind* may be recognized as the embryo of *Bus Stop*. *Bus Riley's Back in Town* is a play I happen to be working on now in expanded form. *The Boy in the Basement*, which may seem very sketchy in its present form, is a play I hope to do more with in the future. *The Strains of Triumph, The Tiny Closet*, and *The Mall* seem to me complete in their present form and will doubtless remain just as they are. The other pieces are fragments or sketches that I have written in exploration of characters in larger works that I may or may not develop in the future.[38]

Of course, those remarks were written roughly a decade after the composition of the one-act plays themselves. But their accuracy is proved by more than the expansion of *People in the Wind* into *Bus Stop*. The Bus Riley character so fascinated Inge that he wrote and rewrote material involving this character numerous times—as many unpublished manuscripts in the Inge Collection prove—and the film version under that title carries elements of *The Boy in the Basement.* (Although, as we shall see in Part Four of this book, Inge rejected all association with the film version of *Bus Riley's Back in Town.*) There can be little doubt that writing one-act plays was an important part of Inge's craft as he was undergoing analysis during the early 1950s.

What is most important about these one-act plays, however, is not so much their quality of craft as what they reveal about the impact that analysis was having on Inge at the time they were written. For one thing, one-act plays are not the stuff of Broadway or Hollywood success. That may have been part of their appeal to Inge at this time: no Joshua Logan is likely to bother producing, directing, or *changing* a one-act play. When a playwright publishes a one-act play, he can be reasonably certain that every character, every action, and every word, are as he wants them. There is great artistic freedom in writing one-act plays, and it is reasonable to suppose that particularly after *Picnic* on Broadway, Inge was psychologically eager to assert his artistic freedom.

For another thing, many of the one-act plays from this period advance the themes that were common to almost all his major works—the complexity of human love, loneliness, failure, frustration, and, most important of all, the need to accept life as it is—all central themes in Inge's own life, and all concerns that ordinarily become focused via analysis. There is one significant additional characteristic: many of these plays exhibit dimensions of aberrant sexuality. Such material could not have found wide public approval in the sexually reticent Eisenhower era when it was being composed, but the therapeutic value of writing it was probably very significant to Inge.

A look at some of these one-act plays lends support to the notion that their composition was at least partially therapeutic. *The Rainy Afternoon* is about children's initiation into stereotyped adult sexual roles while they play one rainy day in an "old barn in a small Midwestern town."[39] Wilma, an aggressive ten-year-old girl, directs the role playing; she does not allow the younger girl, Billie Mae, any prerogatives—including the prerogatives of quitting play and going home. When Vic, a boy of ten, joins them, Wilma decides they will "play house," with herself as the mother, Vic as the father, and Billie Mae as their little daughter. A few of what Wilma and Vic consider "grownup" lines ensue, but soon Wilma tells Vic that he must spank Billie Mae because she has been "bad." Earlier, before Vic's arrival, Wilma had directed Billie Mae to spank her doll for the same reason. When Vic only playfully pats Billie Mae, Wilma insists that he spank harder (p. 247). Wilma is not only selfish; she is also a bit sadistic.

Matters continue to escalate at Wilma's forceful urging. Vic must kiss Billie Mae goodnight and go to bed up in the hayloft with Wilma; when he balks, Wilma accuses him of being "scared" (p. 251). Eventually taking the dare, Vic goes up into the loft with Wilma, leaving Billie Mae alone below, "sleeping." There follows "a silence of several minutes" (p. 253) before Billie Mae begins to call up to Wilma and Vic. No response ever comes from the loft, despite Billie Mae's accusation that they are doing "something bad," followed by her threats to go home, to tell her mother, nevermore to play with Wilma, and so on. Finally "the feeling of rejection is too strong" for Billie Mae; and crying, "I hate you, Wilma Wadsworth," she leaves the stage, which remains empty for several more moments before the curtain falls (pp. 253–254).

This setting of the play in a barn in a small midwestern town reminds us of Billy Inge's boyhood plays with neighborhood children in the barn in the Inges' back yard. And while it is stretching things to insist that Wilma, Vic, and Billie Mae are representative of Maude, Luther, and young Billy Inge, some parallels exist there. Wilma's domination and direction of the children's play parallels Maude's rule of the Inge home. And when Vic arrives—as when Luther returned home from the road—Billie Mae's (Billy's) importance to the family is diminished. In effect, after Vic's arrival, just about everything Wilma proposes is aimed toward getting Vic up into the loft. Wilma's "script" has no important part for Billie Mae after Vic joins them, so Billie Mae naturally feels rejected, just as Billy Inge must often have felt rejected when he was temporarily supplanted in the center of Maude's attention.

Significant, too, is that although this play would clearly convey to adult audiences the idea of sex-role initiation, if not actual heterosexual experimentation, to Billie Mae's character, much of what's going on is a mystery: she doesn't like some of the things that Wilma insists upon, and she doesn't know why such things are expected of her role in the play. Above all, she instinctively feels that whatever is going on up in the loft is "something bad." During William Inge's formative years and well into his troubled adult lifetime, sex was always mysterious and always "something bad." *The Rainy Afternoon*, written as he was undergoing full psychotherapy, was very likely a part of working out understandings and insights. The ladder to the loft may well have become, in his memory, the stairway to the master bedroom in the Inge home and, later in his writing, the stairway to the master bedroom in the Flood home, in *The Dark at the Top of the Stairs*.

The Boy in the Basement has already been summarized in Part Two of this study. Contrary to Inge's remark, in his Preface to its 1962 publication, that it is "sketchy in its present form" (p. x), it is a very well unified and powerful play. It is also the first work Inge ever put before public eyes that deals openly and importantly with homosexuality. That Spencer Scranton, the mother-dominated, profoundly ashamed homosexual mortician is representative of Inge himself can scarcely be denied. Spencer is trapped in his small-town life of repression and frustration, and his mother's discovery of his secret homosexuality gives her a bleak, consuming, and triumphant power over him. Inge's striking simile describing Spencer's invalid, speech-impaired father as being "like a piece of patient wreckage" could just as well be a simile for Spencer by the end of this play (p. 179). Spencer's life is wreckage because his mother now knows his awful secret of homosexuality and will use it to hold him not only near but under control. He believes that he has no choice but to wait patiently until his mother dies—or until he dies—to be free of her. Likely, he will never be free of his sense of guilt and shame about his sexuality.

Again, it is important to note that Inge wrote *The Boy in the Basement* while he was undergoing full analysis in the early 1950s. It would be nearly a decade later before he shared the play with the public, and then it was shared through the carefully controlled medium of print, not the medium of stage production, which is so vulnerable to alterations and shadings of emphasis contributed by others who are less concerned with the author's intent. Hours and hours of therapy, it would seem, never quite served to dispel Inge's own sense of guilt and shame about his homosexuality. Like Spencer, he found it impossible to "come out" in any truly public sense, even though he was to live for about twenty more years after writing this play, twenty years during which the public tolerance of homosexuality considerably softened and sexual deviance became at least more widely understood.

Another play in this group reflects aspects of Inge's sexual life that may have been illuminated by analysis at the time. *The Tiny Closet*, set in a boarding house in a midwestern city, is about sex-role confusion and the destructive fears of the narrow-minded. Mr. Newbold, a very neat and outwardly exemplary man, has a room with a private, locked closet in Mrs. Crosby's boarding house. His constant forbidding of anyone to enter his closet naturally piques the curiosity of Mrs. Crosby, who is bound by her narrow self-righteousness to view the contents of the closet. She has "every *right*," she tells her friend Mrs. Hergesheimer; after all, she may be "harboring a *spy*, or a criminal, or a lunatic" (p. 194). What she discovers in the closet is women's hats—lovely hats, scores of them—that Mr. Newbold has made himself and that he wears in private. It is a terrible discovery for Mrs. Crosby, who reflects the early 1950s McCarthy-inspired fear of communism, as well as the era's absolute intolerance of sex-role deviancy when she states: "I'd rather be harboring a Communist than a man who makes hats" (p. 198). It is also a terrible discovery for Mr. Newbold, who, when he finds that the secret of his closet is known, becomes "a shattered man. All of his pride, his erect posture, his air of authority are gone. He has become a shy and frightened young girl" (pp. 199–200). The shame overwhelms him, and as the curtain falls, he "cries like a hopeless child" (p. 200).

The central notion of a sexual secret's being hidden in a closet is inescapably symbolic here, as Inge makes important use of the "closet" in both its literal and metaphoric applications. But equally important are Mrs. Crosby's intolerance and Mr. Newbold's shame. Sadly, Mr. Newbold's name becomes ironic during the course of this brief play: his deviancy is new neither to him nor to the society in which he lives, but the powerful taboos that generate his shame leave him anything but bold. When he wrote this play, Inge may have had in mind his youthful memories of "dressing up" in women's clothes or of his hat-making friend George Faricy, but from his own painful experience, he also knew the narrow-minded intolerance of Mrs. Crosby and the withering shame of Mr. Newbold.

Another of these short plays from the early 1950s, *The Strains of Triumph*, offers additional keys to understanding how psychotherapy might have been affecting Inge's creative life at the time. The title is an allusion to Emily Dickinson's poem "Success is counted sweetest," in which Dickinson comments that the contemplation of success is always sweetest to those who have never succeeded. Success, in other words, is not the grand thing that the unsuccessful deem it to be. Amid the depression and the disappointment that Inge experienced after the successes of *Sheba* and *Picnic*, this poem rang especially true to him; he acknowledged his appreciation of its message some years later, in 1958, after Random House published his first four successful plays: "'Success is counted sweetest by those who ne'er succeed,' according to Emily Dickinson; and her words are very meaningful to me when I compare the success I once anticipated with the success I found. They are not the same things, at all."[40]

Dickinson's assertion that "the distant strains of triumph / Break, agonized and clear" only to the defeated and the unsuccessful affords Inge a fine irony: by "strains," Dickinson is referring to the *sounds* of triumph—the exultations, for example, of a crowd of people, but the title of Inge's play

refers to the *stresses* — the anxieties, the mental anguish — that triumph, or
success, brings. All during the 1950s, Inge bore the strains of his triumph,
and after his final success with *Splendor in the Grass* in 1961, he bore the
strains of trying to achieve the standard of his *former* triumphs.

The Strains of Triumph is superficially about a love triangle set against the
background of a track meet. A young athlete, Ben, learns that Ann, the
woman he loves, is in love with Tom, his best friend on the track team. The
triangle resolves itself with Ben as the loser; but the most interesting and
significant character is an old man, Professor Benoit, who has overheard Ben's,
Ann's, and Tom's speeches. Professor Benoit tries to console the distraught
Ben with highly philosophical observations about the nature of failure and
loss and about the need to overcome bitterness while accepting life's blows
and proceeding with the business of living — all subjects in which the professor obviously has had much experience. Ben's bitterness causes him to
hate Tom and to refuse to run in the track meet, which the professor has
been watching from a hill near the stadium. Soon, and rather unconvinc-
ingly, the professor persuades Ben to quell his anger and watch the competition with him from the hill. They see Tom win his race, and Ben, now ob-
serving from the isolation of the hill, says "it all looks very different, from
a distance" (p. 299).

Ben clearly has a new perspective on things, thanks to the professor, but
it is actually the professor whose perspective is the subject of this play. Professor Benoit's longest speech, part of which provides the second epigraph
for this book, includes the commentary that competition isn't for everyone
and that life seems divided between "those who participate and those who
watch and observe" (p. 291). The professor's remarks are reinforced by his
physical location on the hill and by the role he fills in the play: without participating, he observes not only the track meet below but also the working
out of the love triangle nearby. He admits that "sometimes, in my more
melancholy moments, I wonder if I have lived life at all, if my life has not
been, rather, a period of observation on earth." He also admits, "I am very
lonely, of course," and "I sometimes become very depressed" (p. 291).

In Professor Benoit there is a considerable distillation of William Inge's
self-perception. Not only does the professor seem to hold the dominant
thematic view of most of Inge's creative work, he is also an emotional isolate
who is lonely, depressed, and struggling to see life clearly and to accept it
as it is, all while being profoundly alone. These are all matters that almost
certainly were coming into focus through Inge's psychoanalysis. We hear
resonances of Inge's past as a professor here; from *Driver*, we recall Joey Han-

sen's deliberate relinquishment of Nell Ramsey to Ned Brooks during his summer back home in Freedom (pp. 162–163), as well as his later equally deliberate relinquishment of Betsy Parsons in that same autobiographical novel (pp. 196–197). We see his reluctance or his inability to give himself wholly to anyone or anything in his life except observation, which directly leads to his writing. There is even a hint of Inge's past at the University of Kansas in this play, for Memorial Stadium on that campus is open at the south end, where a long hill rises above the field. It is part of campus tradition that track meets and football games are viewed free by people on the hill. Doubtless, the nonparticipating observer, William Inge, spent some undergraduate afternoons there, watching and hearing "the strains of triumph" for the achievements of others, never imagining that he would one day conceive of such an ironic use of the phrase.

Other short plays in this group reveal aspects of Inge's life as psychoanalysis may have been serving to illuminate them. *To Bobolink, for Her Spirit* is about a collector, like young Billy Inge, of photographs and autographs of famous actors. *Memory of Summer* is about an aging, once-beautiful woman who cannot accept the various realities that aging has brought to her life. She is more like Tennessee Williams's Blanche Dubois than like any other female character in Inge's published work. Jackie Bowen, the female love interest in *Bus Riley's Back in Town* and in another version of the same play, *Glory in the Flower*, has been to "a mental hospital in Kansas" (*Riley*, p. 234) to help her cope with the loss of love. Thus it reflects not only Inge's own psychotherapy but also that of one of his most important later female characters, Deanie Loomis in *Splendor in the Grass. The Mall* is about the complexity of human love and its almost certain failure to last if it is ever found. *An Incident at the Standish Arms* is about a sexual encounter with an anonymous person, which is followed by powerful guilt and shame.

None of these plays is a work for which Inge will be remembered, but they are all valuable for what they reveal from a very important time in his life, a time when, even in the midst of depression and psychoanalysis, he continued to write with intense imagination and soul-searching creativity. By now he knew the strains of his triumph; he knew that success alone would not make him happy. But he also knew that his writing success was his achievement, the one major positive purpose his life seemed to have. Perhaps others would not approve of him or of his life, but they did approve of his work. Their approval gave him something of himself to approve, and something for which to keep living and working.

LUTHER CLAYTON Inge died in Independence on June 13, 1954. Inge did not attend the funeral service, probably because the fear that it would cause painful memories was simply too great. In fact, there is some doubt whether Inge returned to Independence at the time of his father's death at all. A letter from Inge to Margo Jones (on which, more below) implies that he did not. His nephew Luther Claude seems to recall that Inge was in town before the funeral but did not attend the services. In the autobiographical *My Son Is a Splendid Driver*, the Inge figure, Joey Hansen, states that he could not attend his father's funeral because he was hospitalized for depression and a "halfhearted" suicide attempt.[41] There does not seem to be any evidence for a suicide attempt by Inge or a hospitalization in June, 1954, but we do know that trips home from New York had been few and quite difficult even under the best of circumstances. To return to Independence at such a sad time might have been out of the question, even if he did not plan to attend the services for his father. Whether or not Inge returned to Independence in June, Luther's death was bound to have made him feel guilty about not having come back for a visit sooner, and that guilt seems to have prompted a trip home later that year, at the end of October.

Inge had planned to meet Margo Jones, in late October, probably in Dallas. But he telegraphed a cancellation to Jones on October 31 and went to Independence to see Maude briefly instead. He was back in New York by November 4, when he explained his actions in a letter to Jones:

> I feel very terrible deserting you at the last minute, but I was in a real quandary. The cold I had when I last saw you slowly got worse until I had to go to the doctor, who pronounced it a chronic infection and kept me on anti-biotics for five days, during which I felt really dreadful. So I had to postpone my trip home, and that has been on my conscience, Margo, for five years. During my analysis, I've had a serious emotional block about making the trip, tried it twice and couldn't continue, that sort of thing. And Mother, during that time, has failed miserably in health. . . . She is senile and frail and has to be tended by nurses all the time. So when the wonder drugs finally brought me around to a reasonable state of health, I left for Kansas. . . . Well, I finally got there, after five years, and saw Mom, which took a heap off my conscience. [The trip] quite exhausted me emotionally. . . . Please understand what my personal situation was and try to forgive me.[42]

Details about that brief trip home are not known, but it does seem to have helped him overcome some of the old problems. He was to find travel back to Kansas easier in the remaining four years or so before Maude's death and easier still after her passing, even though he seldom stayed in Independence for long. *Picnic*'s success in particular made Inge a welcome visitor wherever he went in Kansas, especially in Independence and Lawrence, and he also discovered that his being from Kansas gave him a certain offbeat appeal among New Yorkers.

Years later, in 1967, Inge told interviewer Digby Diehl that for most of his life he had felt "superior" to Kansas, "that forlorn midwestern agricultural state." Feeling that he had "nothing in common" with Kansas, that it was "boring as hell," and that he "wanted out," he went on to say, however:

> It wasn't until I got to New York that I became a Kansan. Everyone there kept reminding me that they were Jewish or Irish, or whatever, so I kept reminding them that I was midwestern. Before I knew it, I actually began to *brag* about being from Kansas! I discovered I had something unique, but it was the nature of New York that forced me to claim my past.[43]

In 1954, with a Kansas-set play like *Picnic* behind him and Kansas-set *Bus Stop* growing under his hand, the notions that Inge had "nothing in common" with Kansas and that New York had "forced" him to claim his past seem radical distortions: what he had in common with Kansas was a legacy of experience, and that experience was what forced him to claim his past, via his writing. The "nature of New York" was involved only in a superficial, social way. Given the testimony of so many people who met Inge at this time that he was a quiet and modest man, it is also difficult to imagine him "bragging" about anything, let alone bragging about being from Kansas.

But it is also true that the midwestern heartland enjoyed a certain mythic appeal during the 1950s; it was seen as a bastion of good old-fashioned American values, where industry and integrity joined to produce both food and dedicated, honest people. Dwight D. Eisenhower, an army general who had been raised in Kansas, had led Americans to victory in Europe during World War II and now was leading the government. There was something seemingly wholesome about the Midwest in our popular imagination then; Kansas was just the place for a Labor Day picnic, just the place for a great leader to come from. People — even New Yorkers — probably liked *Picnic* for the same kinds of reasons they liked Ike and Dorothy and Toto.

William Inge in New York was still very much a Kansan, not only because of his nature but also because of his work. If he eventually came to feel some pride about being from an environment that seemed unique to New Yorkers, then this was in the nature of a by-product, and it was bound to be ephemeral, destined to fade when the next unique person or place caught the public fancy. If in the years immediately after *Picnic*, Inge sensed that his work's popularity would eventually fade, he did not let it blunt his will to write. His life continued to be bumpy after *Picnic*, but as we have seen, many one-act plays and *Bus Stop* resulted from this period.

One social strain occurred at about this time in his relationship with Tennessee Williams, whose *Camino Real* had opened and failed shortly after *Picnic* had opened. Williams, by this time, was by no means a stranger to failure, and indeed, he would know great success again, but the particular timing was not good when, while at lunch with Williams at the Algonquin Hotel, Inge abruptly asked, "Tennessee, don't you feel that you are blocked as a writer?"[44] The question was doubtless meant to be sympathetic, but as Williams's biographer Donald Spoto has noted, "That was all Williams had to hear from a writer he still considered an apprentice."[45] Williams replied that he would break through any block by continuing to write. But he resented the question enough that more than twenty years later, after reporting the incident in his memoirs, which were published two years after Inge's death, Williams still felt inclined to sting his friend's memory with a withering remark: "Bill's primary problem was one of pathological egocentricity: he could not take a spell of failures after his run of smash hits: so eventually he was cared for by two male nurses."[46]

Such a sharp remark would make it seem that the two men were never again friends after Inge's ill-timed question at the Algonquin, but that was not the case. The problem was essentially one of a rivalry of talents. In addition to the success of *Picnic* having been closely followed by the failure of *Camino Real*, Spoto notes that

> on March 2, 1955 (three weeks before the premiere of *Cat on a Hot Tin Roof*), Inge's *Bus Stop* opened, . . . It ran for 478 performances. Although Williams's play won the Pulitzer and Drama Critics Circle Award, the quiet contest continued. Then virtually all friendly exchange between them was severed (until Inge's illness years later) when in 1957 *Orpheus Descending* . . . opened in March and ran eight weeks, while later that year *The Dark at the Top of the Stairs* [opened and] ran for 468 performances. . . .
>
> "Williams was very jealous of Inge's success," according to [Williams's friend] Meade Roberts, . . . "He was, after all, Audrey's client, and Ten-

nessee himself had introduced Inge to Audrey. Also, he thought that Inge wrote better dialogue than he did, that Inge had a true ear for American regional speech." (P. 225)

Now that the careers of both playwrights are over, it seems amusing that a playwright of Williams's stature might ever have been jealous of William Inge, but of course, Inge did have his successes consecutively during the 1950s. At the time, Williams might have envied such a string—who would not? The well-meaning but ill-timed question that Inge posed at the Algonquin, at any rate, ushered in a time of some strain and rivalry in the friendship; but Barbara Baxley, who knew both men well and who became the closest thing to a "lady love" Inge ever had, has disputed Spoto's claim that "all friendly exchange between them was severed" after *Stairs* succeeded and *Orpheus Descending* failed. She acknowledges that there was strain and a bit of competitive feeling between them, but "when push came to shove, those two were very good friends," she said.[47]

Baxley had first met Inge at a party given by the acting teacher Lee Strasberg shortly after *Sheba* had opened in Westport, but their friendship didn't really begin until she appeared in Williams's *Camino Real* a couple of years later. She recalls that Inge liked that play and her performance in it, and at about that time she often joined Williams and Inge for dinner. She felt that she and Inge were "kindred souls" and that eventually he talked with her more openly than with anyone else, except perhaps his analyst. Still, during the time before *Bus Stop*, they were not close enough to justify Williams's assertion then that she was "Bill's girlfriend." Inge was working on *Bus Stop* while their friendship was growing, but Baxley was not yet the sounding board she would later become during Inge's composition of *The Dark at the Top of the Stairs* and *A Loss of Roses*.

In fact, it is not clear who, besides Audrey Wood, *did* read *Bus Stop* as it was going through Inge's drafts. We know that the basic idea of the play—a man pursuing an at-first-reluctant woman on a bus—is traceable to the Stephens years, when Inge frequently rode the bus to Kansas City or St. Louis and observed such a pursuit.[48] We know that the first complete form it took was the one-act play *People in the Wind*, a play with an ensemble cast that focuses on the man/woman pursuit only slightly more than on the other characters. We don't know why Inge took the "Man" and "Girl" roles in this one-act play and expanded them to make them the center of a full-length play. Even more puzzling is why, after losing the battle over a romantic ending for *Picnic*, he opted to make his next major play a true romantic comedy with an ending more implausible than the ending of *Picnic*. "*Bus Stop* is the closest thing to fantasy that I ever wrote," Inge told Digby Diehl in 1967, and that statement was still true when Inge died six years later. Why would such a realistic-minded playwright present such near-cartoon characters as Bo Decker and Cherie? And why would he conclude their story with Cherie's willingness to abandon her (admittedly unrealistic) dreams and go with Bo to his Montana ranch, there (also unrealistically) to be wed and presumably live happily thereafter?

Inge would probably not appreciate the suggestion, but the lingering influence of Joshua Logan seems relevant to the development—and the success—of *Bus Stop*. *Picnic* made it clear that mid-fifties audiences liked to see romantic resolutions. Certainly, no small amount of insight into desperate, lonely lives is present in *Picnic*, but those insights are frequently tempered by humor and the romantic ending. Similar insight is detectible in *Bus Stop*, particularly in the supporting roles. But humor and romance again carry the play. By bringing Bo and Cherie to the foreground from *People in the Wind*, Inge showed his own knack for creating a "show" (in the Logan sense) that he could be reasonably certain audiences would enjoy. The ancillary characters—Grace, the owner of the café and the bus stop; Carl, the bus driver; Elma, the young waitress; Professor Lyman, the drunken and disillusioned passenger; and Virgil Blessing, Bo's mentor and surrogate father—carry on Inge's more realistic themes in the background. Thus, *Bus Stop*, like *Picnic*, provides a rather light and entertaining central love story bordered by heavier and harsher stories or hints of stories. Both plays have ensemble casts—as indeed almost all of Inge's best work does—which creates the sense that there are other, equally interesting, stories to be told here but that the current primary interest is Hal and Madge or Bo and Cherie.

Whatever the reasons for having *Bus Stop* develop as it did with Bo and Cherie at the forefront, Inge later claimed to Digby Diehl that the play was intended as a kind of experiment in which he gave an example of several different kinds of love. In addition to the romantic—actually idealized—love of Bo and Cherie, there was also

> the earthly love, the purely physical attraction of the bus driver for the woman who runs the restaurant. There's the corrupt attraction of the old man for the young girl; there's a kind of homosexual feeling the older cowboy has for the younger, although I never thought of them

as physical lovers. They all kind of play into a pattern—the play was fun to write. (Diehl, p. 114)

That comment is noteworthy for its carefully qualified mention of homosexual attraction—which was a bit bold for the reticent Inge, even at the time of that interview in 1967—and its passing reference to the "old man," who is Professor Lyman, a traveler who has far more problems than a "corrupt attraction" to young Elma, the waitress. Professor Lyman is a drunk, a former teacher who's been fired and who now sees everything in his life—his talent, his teaching, his love of literature, his attempts at marriage—as a colossal failure. Professor Lyman of *Bus Stop* is like Professor Benoit of *The Strains of Triumph*, but minus equilibrium. He is another Inge teacher-character who represents much of Inge's self-image. And although Inge told Diehl that *Bus Stop* is a composite picture of love, the dominating emphasis on Bo and Cherie makes that a tenuous assertion. (In fact, when Joshua Logan made the film version of *Bus Stop*, he cut out the Professor Lyman character altogether—an omission that undoubtedly rankled Inge but in no way impaired the film audience's appreciation of the story line.)

When *Bus Stop* was nearing its final form, Inge and Wood took it to Robert Whitehead and Roger L. Stevens to see if they wanted to produce it. Whitehead, who had met Inge earlier and who was of course aware of his successes with *Sheba* and *Picnic*, was delighted. The play already had, it seemed to him, a finished, polished quality. "Bill always wrote very carefully," Whitehead recalls; "he didn't hand you a first draft." Inge and Whitehead quickly agreed to ask Harold Clurman to direct the play. Clurman had admired *Sheba* and, perhaps more importantly, the original ending of *Picnic*. He was both a director and a critic, and he had a fine interpretive sensibility about Inge's work. Clurman was willing and free to begin work on *Bus Stop* right away. In fact, the production of *Bus Stop* proceeded smoothly and rapidly from the very beginning. Whitehead recalls that he first read the script in October, 1954, and that the play went into production in January, 1955—a very short time by the usual New York standards.[49]

COOPERATION among author, director, and producer was excellent on *Bus Stop*. None of the great tensions that had plagued the production process of *Picnic* occurred as *Bus Stop* moved through casting and rehearsals in early 1955. The greatest difficulty in casting concerned the role of Bo Decker, which did not seem to be properly cast until Albert Salmi joined the cast in Philadelphia shortly before the New York opening on March 2. Kim Stanley, who had played Millie in *Picnic*, had the role of Cherie; Crahan Denton was Virgil Blessing, Bo's sidekick and mentor; Elaine Stritch was Grace, the proprietor of the bus stop; Patrick McVey was Carl, the bus driver; Lou Polan was Will Masters, the sheriff; Phyllis Love was Elma Duckworth, the young waitress; and Anthony Ross was Professor Lyman.

During the tryout run in Philadelphia, Inge recalled, the play "was still finding itself." In addition to the acting of the Bo character before Salmi joined the cast, the principal problem seems to have been in the balance of comedy and seriousness. "There were some serious elements in the play and the audience was a bit reluctant to laugh," said Inge; the Philadelphia audiences "didn't know how to react."[50] Whitehead recalls that Inge was amenable to whatever adjustments were necessary; Inge and Clurman worked amicably with the cast and with each other.[51] When Salmi joined the cast, only four Philadelphia performances remained, and Inge told Roy Newquist that he never believed the play crystallized out of town. (p. 362). But opening night on March 2 at New York's Music Box theater made it clear that Inge had written a third consecutive successful play.

Less is known about Inge's behavior on the opening night of *Bus Stop* than about his behavior on some of his other opening nights during the 1950s. Undoubtedly he had his fears: after all, he hadn't believed the play was as finely tuned in Philadelphia as it should have been, and any opening night is stressful for a playwright. But it appears that he overcame any worries enough to attend; he probably slipped into the back of the darkened theater after the play had begun, as he had done at *Picnic*'s opening and would later do on other opening nights. And as he recollected to Roy Newquist nearly ten years later, he was pleased with what he saw: "All our dreams materialized. It was a brilliant opening night. The response was marvelous" (p. 362).

On the next day, most of the critics agreed. Walter Kerr in the *New York Herald-Tribune* raved about Kim Stanley and pronounced *Bus Stop* "the best play we've had all season."[52] Richard Watts, Jr., in the *New York Post* claimed that in *Bus Stop*, Inge "has written a romantic comedy about ordinary people that is at once humorous, simple, steadily entertaining and vastly endearing."[53] "Having written a wonderful play two years ago, William Inge has written a better [one]," said Brooks Atkinson in the *New York Times*; "the performance is glorious."[54] None of the New York newspaper critics on the next day and none of the critics whose pieces appeared a bit later in magazines claimed that Inge had discovered anything new; many noted the well-used plot device of having travelers stranded, and there was never any doubt that Cherie and Bo would eventually work out their differences. For all its predictability, *Bus Stop*, almost all agreed, was a triumph of craft: it was a well-written play with first-rate directing and acting, all taking place on Boris Aronson's set, which Wolcott Gibbs in the *New Yorker* called "a frowsy masterpiece."[55] Robert Hatch's remarks in the *Nation* seem most typical:

> This is William Inge's third Broadway play . . . and his third Broadway success. He is probably not a great playwright (at least, I doubt that anything that he has done thus far will be included in the archives of our century), but he is an acute, compassionate, and amused observer who has trained himself to write approximately perfect theater.[56]

By any yardstick, *Bus Stop* was a hit. It would run for 478 performances, one more than *Picnic* had run. Perhaps because it was so well crafted and predictable, it won no major awards. In fact, Inge's writing was to win only one more big prize—an Academy Award for *Splendor in the Grass* as best original screenplay of 1961. But the great popularity of *Bus Stop* helped to solidify Inge's reputation as a "can't miss" playwright, and its sale to Hollywood was inevitable. The quiet Kansan in the Dakota was the hottest playwright in America as 1955 progressed, and the publicity surrounding the filming of *Picnic* did nothing to cool his reputation.

COLUMBIA Pictures planned from the beginning for *Picnic* to be a major film, a technicolor Cinemascope blockbuster with all the right box-office ingredients. The studio's choices did much to assure the film's success: in directing the movie, Joshua Logan would use his showmanship and experience with the play. The cast would feature one of Hollywood's most popular leading men, William Holden, as Hal. Rosalind Russell would bring the role of Rosemary to the screen. Columbia's newest starlet in the by-now-established Marilyn Monroe mold, Kim Novak, would play Madge. Another starlet, the famous New York acting teacher Lee Strasberg's daughter Susan, would play Millie. Both Logan and Fred Kohlmar, the film's producer, insisted that *Picnic* be shot in Kansas, despite the expense this would incur. The Academy-Award-winning cinematographer James Wong Howe, who had shot the film version of *Come Back, Little Sheba* so brilliantly, was chosen to do the pho-tography.[57] Clearly, Columbia was aiming high, and Harry Cohn, the studio's boss, made sure that there was plenty of advance publicity.

The fact that Joshua Logan was in charge of the filming of *Picnic* for Columbia is doubtless why Inge had so little to do with the enterprise. Early on, Inge had suggested possible sites in Kansas for the film, suggestions that apparently reached Logan through Jo Mielziner, Inge's neighbor in the Dakota, who had designed the Broadway set and who also designed the film for Logan.[58] Probably, Inge would have liked to help on the film—his fascination with Hollywood had never really dimmed much—but the rights had been sold, and of course his memories of working with Logan were not golden. Daniel Taradash was chosen as the screenwriter for *Picnic*, most of which was indeed shot on location in Kansas, although not in, or even especially near, Independence. Salina, Hutchinson, Halstead, Sterling, and Nickerson, all central Kansas communities, were the chosen sites.

Filming on location in May, 1955, was occasionally plagued by storms more violent than those that typically come to the prairie in the spring, but Logan and Howe were able to shoot some interiors and close-ups on those occasions, and Logan— ever the showman who knew that free publicity is always a bargain—managed to convey to the press the image of a dedicated director and a troupe willing to risk the elements for the sake of a good show.[59] Once, he recalled to interviewer Michael Wood, a tornado warning siren split the air, but Logan was so intent on filming that he didn't hear it. While he wondered why the cast, crew, and extras were scattering, Logan heard Rosalind Russell warn him, "You better get down in this ditch."[60] No twister struck, but there was ample cause for concern: on May 25, during the time that *Picnic* was being filmed in Kansas, the tiny town of Udall near Wichita was flattened in the worst killer tornado in the history of the state. Kansas had been inordinately notorious for tornadoes since *The Wizard of Oz*, and the spring storms of 1955 did little to help that perception, even though they played their part in advance publicity for the movie.

Inge was in Independence for another brief stay in April, 1955, before the filming of *Picnic* began. He was on an extended trip, begun after it had become clear that *Bus Stop* was a hit, that had already taken him to Florida, where he probably made a brief stop to visit Tennessee Williams in Key West; New Orleans; Houston; and Dallas, where he probably saw Margo Jones for the last time before her death the following July. Audrey Wood had already sold the film rights to *Bus Stop* to Twentieth Century–Fox, and Inge's trip was to culminate in Hollywood, where he planned to consult with officials of the studio about the film version. In Independence, most of the questions he answered had to do with the filming of *Picnic*. Logan and Mielziner had already been to Kansas to check sites, and the announcement of their choices had been in the news. People in Independence were naturally disappointed.

Inge told local reporter Keith Noll that he "deeply regretted" Columbia's choice to film *Picnic* elsewhere, but that "actually, I have nothing whatsoever to do with the movie version." He went on to say—to no one's belief—that any similarities the setting and characters of *Picnic* bore to Independence and some of its townspeople were "purely coincidental." He said he had been invited to spend "a day or so" on location while *Picnic* was being filmed and that he intended to do so; but there is no evidence that he actually did.[61]

Because the filming of *Picnic* did not begin until about a month later, it is probable that Inge never really intended to visit the on-site shooting. Moreover, the notion of Inge's spending a month in Kansas, especially in Independence, while waiting to visit Joshua Logan on location is hard to imagine. Finally, Hollywood continued to exert its lure. A couple of weeks before Inge's arrival in Independence, he had written from Florida to John Gassner, saying he might go on to California in May to work on the movie of *Bus Stop*. Regarding the movie work, he told Gassner: "I'm not enthused about it, wishing rather that I would get immediately involved in something new. However, I've never worked in Hollywood and I'll feel like a poor sport if I don't at least give it a try."[62] Perhaps Inge thought that Gassner regarded him as too serious and too dedicated a playwright to become willingly involved with movies, and thus those professions of no enthusiasm and the need to be a good "sport." Whatever his motives for implying to Gassner that he wasn't really enthusiastic about working in Hollywood, it is far more likely that Inge was actually eager to do so. The silver screen was far too powerful a factor in his life to make helping to film one of his plays an unappealing prospect.

Inge did, in fact, wind up his trip in Hollywood to consult with Twentieth Century–Fox about filming *Bus Stop*, but the result had to be somewhat disappointing, because, again, he wound up having nothing to do with the film that eventually resulted. Fox had Marilyn Monroe in mind for Cherie, and—probably to Inge's chagrin—Joshua Logan in mind to direct. Logan was to begin filming *Bus Stop* as soon as he could after completing *Picnic* for Columbia. At this point it must have seemed to Inge that part of the cost of having things go so smoothly with Harold Clurman in bringing *Bus Stop* to Broadway was running into Joshua Logan again and again, although such was never the design of either man. And to compound the bittersweet irony, Logan's two films of Inge's plays were to be great successes, both with the critics and with audiences.

Back in New York, Inge returned to his desk and his routine of writing. He was much in demand for interviews and gatherings as *Bus Stop*'s run at the Music Box continued and as road-show productions of both *Picnic* and *Bus Stop* fanned out across the country. Columbia released Logan's film of *Picnic* with a final burst of hoopla that would help pack the nation's movie houses in the face of the continuing threat of television, and again Inge's story, characters, and name flickered on screens that had recently been widened to accommodate Cinemascope. Random House published *Bus Stop*. Inge had accomplished much in a half-decade in New York, but characteristically, he saw no reason to desert his writing desk; indeed, there seemed nothing to desert it for: he was never one who could bask in the light of his accomplishments, never one who could enjoy the many social fruits of celebrity. Besides, he had more that he wanted to write about.

BARBARA Baxley spent more and more time with Inge as *Bus Stop*'s Broadway run continued. Inge knew that Kim Stanley, who had played Cherie since the show's opening, did not like to stay in one role for too long, so he told Baxley to get ready to assume Stanley's role. Baxley liked the Cherie character and was pleased to join the cast after Stanley left. Now in a major role in one of Inge's plays, Baxley grew even closer to him. She knew he was homosexual, but she also knew that was not his choice, and she believes that his sexuality was the greatest single reason for his long-time unhappiness. Unlike what some women might have done, Baxley did not attempt to change Inge's sexuality. Their understanding of and concern for each other was much deeper and more complex than that, although there were a few times, Baxley says, when Inge did express his love for her physically.[63] What they chiefly shared was a great sympathy and friendship. And although they did often discuss marriage, they both sensed that a marriage simply would not work, for a number of reasons besides his sexual orientation.

For one thing, Baxley says, they were both very committed to their careers, and their respect for the idea of marriage would have made them also deeply committed to their union, a commitment that both of them were afraid to make. Inge was "very guarded" about his life and work, Baxley says; he "couldn't go 100% in caring about others because that would mean an involvement, a give-and-take thing." Without a trace of resentment in her voice, Baxley recalls that Inge was selfish; he had achieved a way of living

Inge at work in his apartment in the Dakota in the mid 1950s. Courtesy of the Kansas State Historical Society

and working that he was deeply reluctant to change; and to a certain extent she felt the same way at the time. That is why, although they discussed marriage, they never even considered living together.

Inge could not write when someone else was in his apartment. He was not willing to share his space, and he had his own particular way he wanted to do things. He had to be in control of every aspect of his life, and that included with whom he would spend time and for how long. Baxley knew these things, and although she became the person closest to him, especially from roughly 1955 to 1959, she never fully shared his life. No one ever did.

For the most part, Inge continued during this period to stay away from drinking. Still, there were times he slipped and had to pay some eventual price. Baxley says she very seldom saw him drink; and she very seldom saw him seeming really to enjoy himself unless he *did* drink. Unlike Audrey Wood, whose few encounters with Inge when he had been drinking were apparently times when he was under great pressure and had been drinking for some time, Baxley saw Inge on a few occasions when he *began* drinking in relatively quiet, less tense situations. On these occasions, at least at first, Baxley reports that Inge "had a lot of fun; he was very witty . . . but he had to have booze with it."[64] At such times, the result probably involved painful withdrawal, but at least he had not begun his round of drinking alone, and he had been able to enjoy himself during the early going. It is not clear whether or not he was still attending A.A. very often during this time. Charles Jackson, the author of *The Lost Weekend*, who was Inge's neighbor at the Dakota, accompanied Inge to A.A. meetings somewhat later, according to composer Ned Rorem's *New York Diary*, but it is not clear just when Inge's attendance at those meetings began.[65]

If A.A. continued to play a part in Inge's equilibrium at this time, psychoanalysis must surely have been equally important. Baxley was also in analysis during this period—another thing they had in common—and she believes the analysis not only helped him focus his creative vision, especially when he began reworking *Farther off from Heaven* into *The Dark at the Top of the Stairs*, but also helped him keep his unhappiness, frustration, and anger under control. Very seldom did anger emerge from below the surface of his calm, but when it did it was memorable, and it was usually triggered by something trivial.

Harold Clurman, the director of *Bus Stop*, remembers having lunch with Inge one day in a New York delicatessen. Inge had put his hat on a chair, and a waitress had moved it to a wall hook. Turning a deep red, glaring at the waitress, and speaking in a choked voice, Inge had said, "I want that hat on the chair." Clurman had "the uneasy sensation that he was in the presence of a raging volcano within, as well as a cold glaze without."[66] Barbara Baxley also used the metaphor of a volcano in recalling times when Inge's anger erupted. Once, she remembers, he was fixing pancakes, and they kept sticking to the pan. She watched until she knew he was about to blow up, then she went out of the kitchen. Moments later he called her back. His calm had returned, but the pan was bent beyond repair. She says he often broke things, but those destructive bursts of anger were never directed toward Baxley or, indeed, any other person. It was as though he knew his inner violence was powerful and thus he directed it toward objects, not people. But Baxley never wondered how Inge could conceive of the drunken rage of Doc Delaney in *Sheba*'s most climactic scene or of Donnie Barker's vicious murder of a stranger at the end of *Natural Affection*.[67]

Audrey Wood remembers when Inge became angry on one occasion while seated at a table. He hit the table hard, and a jar of catsup splattered all over the table. Despite that memory, Wood said: "Actually Bill had enormous control of his anger. He rarely showed it. Maybe it would have been good for him to have gotten it out more often, but he was really a controlled man in terms of his work in the theater. He'd get very angry, but he'd control it."[68] Elia Kazan, who directed *Stairs* on Broadway and *Splendor in the Grass* on the screen, also commented on how Inge seemed to be able to control his anger: "It's as though you heard the psychoanalyst saying to him, 'Now wait, calm down; don't get panicky; let's look at this thing, examine it, wait for it to blow over.'"[69] Few people ever had any reason to think of Inge as being anything but a gentle man. And despite his occasional flare-ups, a kind of serene acceptance of all matters great and small seems to have been a steady purpose. Certainly that is the ideal expressed by Joey Hansen in *My Son Is a Splendid Driver*, the autobiographical novel of Inge's creative sensibility.[70] Just as certainly, acceptance is a dominant theme in most of his works. It is not too much to say it was the dominant theme of his life.

WHILE INGE's mid-1950s celebrity glowed, Barbara Baxley was his most frequent companion in public, often going with him to parties and other gatherings, where they were usually the first to leave. Not only did Inge wish to avoid drinking in such situations, but he and Baxley also shared a dislike of crowds. Occasionally, they would take the floor to dance, where Inge proved himself to be an excellent and graceful dancer; but more frequently they spent quiet evenings together, going on long walks in midtown or reading. Baxley claims that Inge taught her a great deal by reading to her from diverse works—Shakespeare, Molière, Byron, Shelley, and Proust—and that he communicated his own beautiful sense of language so well that later she was able to tackle roles whose language had previously daunted her.[71] Inge was a good cook, and he would occasionally host a small group for dinner. His niece, Jo Ann Kirchmaier, remembers that he never owned more than eight plates of fine china because he was never willing to have more than seven guests.[72] He enjoyed eating well, and that enjoyment began to show more as he moved further into his forties and began to gain weight.

As 1955 moved well into summer, the film of *Picnic* was doing a great box-office business. Morris Stoloff's sound-track version, of "Moonglow," the movie's theme song, was heard constantly on radios. Soon Joshua Logan would begin filming Marilyn Monroe and Don Murray as Cherie and Bo

Kim Novak (as Madge) and William Holden (as Hal) dance in a key scene from the film of Picnic. *Print from WIC/ICC. © 1955, Renewed 1983 Columbia Pictures Industries, Inc. All rights reserved. Courtesy of Columbia Pictures*

in the movie version of *Bus Stop*. Inge participated in some advance publicity for the film, probably as part of the contract for the sale of rights that Wood had negotiated, but George Axelrod was in charge of the screenplay. Inge and Monroe met at this time and enjoyed a rapport that was probably based upon their mutual intelligence and his ability to sense the frustrations of a bright and spectacularly beautiful woman like Monroe and upon her realization that his interest and concern were genuine and not motivated by sexual desire. In years to come, their names were occasionally linked by the media as if they were romantically involved, but their relationship was no more than a friendship.[73]

On July 15, Margo Jones was hospitalized in Dallas. She had accidentally inhaled fumes from a poisonous cleaning fluid while some rugs were being cleaned in her apartment, and her condition steadily worsened because the poison caused kidney failure. She died on July 24.[74] Her death at the age of forty-two (the same age as Inge) was a great blow, not only to Inge but also to Tennessee Williams, Jerome Lawrence, Robert E. Lee, and countless other writers and theater people whose lives and careers she had enriched. Perhaps it was Inge's reflection upon the untimely death of Jones, who had returned to her native Texas and had successfully continued to build her career and interests while based there, that first caused him to consider buying property near Lawrence and living there at least part time.

Whatever caused the impulse – and it proved to be only an impulse, albeit a recurring one – to establish a part-time residence in Lawrence, Inge accepted an invitation to visit Lawrence in September, when drama professor Lewin Goff was going to begin casting for a campus production of *Picnic*. Franklin Murphy, Inge's former associate from undergraduate days at KU, was then the school's chancellor. Murphy, Goff, and Inge's old mentor, Allen Crafton, all asked Inge to consider returning to KU to teach as a writer in residence, and the idea appealed to him enough that he shared the possibility with various reporters who sought him out for interviews when he arrived in late September to assist Goff. "Inge May Join Faculty at K.U." was the bold-print title of one resulting story by Dana Leibengood in the *Lawrence Journal-World* on September 22. On the same day, in an unsigned article in the university newspaper, the *Daily Kansan*, Inge was quoted as having said: "I have been toying with the idea of having a place to come and relax during a part of each year, and KU would be the ideal spot. Of course the details on that would have to be worked out later. But this possibility cannot be considered for about a year."[75] Inge did not elaborate on why any major delay in this prospect was necessary, but in all likelihood it was because he didn't really think he wanted to, or could, do it. It was the first of several flirtations with moving to Lawrence that were to follow until the mid 1960s.

Inge helped Goff cast the play and promised to return in October to be on hand for the last week of rehearsals and the three-day run. He did return for the rehearsals, but according to an item in the Lawrence paper of October 25, he developed a "severe cold" and decided to return to New York just before the opening.[76] There is no evidence that Inge did not have a bad cold on this particular occasion, but the frequency with which he claimed to have had colds in letters in collections (to Esther Latcham and Margo Jones, for example), when the problem was actually more complicated than that, makes it possible that more than a cold prompted his return to New York. Lawrence had great significance in his life, because it was the first place he lived after leaving Independence, his first "home" that wasn't really home. Being in Lawrence seemed to trigger bittersweet memories that alternately attracted and repelled him. As Franklin Murphy observed in an undated taped interview (WIC) Inge liked the idea of coming to Lawrence "in the abstract"; actually doing so was an altogether different matter. Allen Crafton had planned a reception to honor Inge after the first performance of *Picnic* on campus, and the university had planned to award him a distinguished service citation after the last performance. It could be that the prospect of such attention on home ground made Inge anxious and eager to retreat.

The paradoxical impulse toward and away from Lawrence not only has classic psychological approach-avoidance characteristics, but it also squares with the impressions of many who knew him that Inge spent a good part of his adult life looking for a home in the richest connotational sense: a place of familiar location that is also where loved ones dwell, an ideal place of ease and refuge and comfort, devoid of pretense. Such a place would be a blessing for anyone to have; for Inge it might have been salvation. Jo Ann Kirchmaier, his niece, put it this way: "He wanted so much to be a part of a family."[77] Although it is ironic for a member of his own family to have said that, she was referring to his visits to her and her family in Toledo, times at the zenith of his celebrity when he would stop by with gifts.

William Gibson recalls that when Inge began his frequent visits for therapy at the Austen Riggs Center in Stockbridge, Massachusetts (more on this later), he often called to visit the Gibsons; he never stayed long, but he seemed to enjoy the pleasant family atmosphere there. Remembering Inge's many flirtations with buying a house in or near Lawrence, his frequent shuttling between New York and California during the late 1950s and early 1960s, as well as his frequent shuttling between Manhattan and Stockbridge during that same time period, Gibson remarked that Inge seemed to be looking for a home but never finding one.[78]

John Connolly, who served as Inge's secretary in New York for six years, remembers that Inge often had him make appointments with Stockbridge realtors to look at houses that Inge loved to see but had no real intention of buying.[79] It is as though Inge vicariously took some comfort in seeing the home lives of others who seemed to him to be happy, as though seeing houses could cause him to imagine happy families living there. Such a family situation and such a home were never in the cards for Inge, but a recurring emphasis in his greatest writing is upon the struggles of individuals within families to achieve his idealized sense of "home."

INGE's idealized sense of "home" was to dominate his next major play, *The Dark at the Top of the Stairs*, but before he began working on it in earnest, he had to contend with some new difficulties. Logan was completing the

Inge in a pensive mood during the height of his success. Courtesy of the Kansas State Historical Society

film version of *Bus Stop*, and Twentieth Century–Fox decided to release the movie in August, 1956, some months earlier than originally planned. Early release ran counter to the rights sale agreement, which stipulated that the film could not be released until December 1, 1956, if any "first class" stage presentations of *Bus Stop* were still in progress prior to that date. Although *Bus Stop*'s run on Broadway was completed well before August, road-show engagements were scheduled through March 2, 1957. In July, Inge and *Bus Stop*'s Broadway producers, Robert Whitehead and Roger L. Stevens, asked the New York Federal District Court for an injunction barring the release of the film in August. They won the injunction, but Fox filed for a rehearing. Finally, on August 7, the two sides settled out of court. The amount of the settlement was not published, but Fox was freed to release the film in August.[80] The film, which eliminated Inge's stage characters of Professor Lyman and Sheriff Will Masters and which was set in Arizona, rather than Kansas, proved to be highly successful. Inge's name was again on the wide technicolor screen, but significant elements of his creative vision had again been changed by Joshua Logan.

During that same summer of 1956, Inge learned that he was going to have to change analysts. Who his analyst was at this time and why the change was necessary are not known, but it is clear that this analyst figured importantly in Inge's life, and the news hit Inge hard. Analysis had helped him significantly, especially since coming to New York. His Greenwich doctor had helped him control his drinking, and later his doctor in Manhattan — the one whose services ended in the summer of 1956 — had helped him understand himself and his past in ways that had allowed him to keep both emotional and creative balance. Now, for a time, those delicate balances were threatened. Locating a good New York psychiatrist who had available time for a new patient proved difficult. Finally, Inge decided that finding the right doctor was more important than finding one close by. Eventually, therefore, he selected Dr. Robert Knight at the Austen Riggs Center in Stockbridge, Massachusetts. Dr. Knight was probably recommended by William Gibson's wife, Margaret, a member of the Riggs Center's staff. Years before, in 1949, Inge had been about to go to the Riggs Center for help, but the Theatre Guild's option for *Sheba* had dramatically changed his plans. Now, because success had not proved to be the tonic that he needed, he was again going to Riggs. This time he arrived, and he began therapy in October.

Knight treated Inge primarily as an outpatient; so because the drive between Manhattan and Stockbridge took four hours one way, Inge rented a small apartment in a rooming house on Main Street, across from Alice

Brock's restaurant—the "Alice's Restaurant" that Arlo Guthrie would make famous in a comic narrative song about a decade later.[81] Inge was to divide his time between Manhattan and Stockbridge for the next several years as Knight continued to help him, and it was during the early stages of his analysis with Knight that Inge began to work seriously on his next play, *The Dark at the Top of the Stairs.*

Stairs, of course, is a reworking of the first play that Inge ever wrote, *Farther off from Heaven.* Perhaps something in his current therapy with Knight prompted Inge to take *Heaven* out and begin reworking it. Then, too, the loss of Margo Jones might have had something to do with it; Jones had believed in Inge when so few others had any reason to, and her production of *Heaven* had arguably been a lifesaver for him. Maybe Inge wanted to show Audrey Wood that this first play—which she had rejected—still had Broadway possibilities. Most likely, all these factors were involved as Inge began again to search his past for the family drama closest to his own experience.

We have seen that Freudian analysis had an influence upon Inge's earlier work, particularly in *Sheba* and some of the one-act plays. In late 1956, as he began to rework *Heaven,* he made the Oedipal connection between the young boy and the mother in the play much more explicit. It was still a play focused on the entire family, which he renamed the Floods, rather than the Campbells; and he preserved many of the essential conflicts from the earlier play—for example, Cora Flood's insistent desire that Rubin, her traveling salesman husband, quit the road and the philandering that seemed to go with it; and the extreme shyness of the daughter, Reenie. But in this new version the young boy, Sonny, is also more clearly in conflict with his feelings for his mother as he struggles to cope with his image as a sissy among his peers and to accept—if not to understand—Rubin's relationship with Cora. Inge had been in Freudian psychoanalysis far too long and he was far too intelligent a person not to have pondered his Oedipal experience before 1956, but for the first time that experience was finding representation in a highly autobiographical character in an autobiographical play.

He worked on *Stairs* in both Stockbridge and at home in the Dakota. Often he shared new installments with Baxley, who sensed the importance of this particular play to him. She recalls that she never offered criticism; they would simply talk about what he had written. She characterized her role in the process as that of an "emotional sounding board," and she remembers that once, in response to someone else's criticism while he was writing it, he ripped the play up and burned it. Calling Baxley from the scene of his frustration in Stockbridge, where the destruction had occurred, Inge told

Baxley in a "terrible voice" what he had done. Baxley told him to sit right down and write it again—which fortunately he did—and she called the critic and blasted him for being so harsh on a play in progress.[82] Thus, the reworking of *Heaven* into *Stairs* was not without its problems, but the result was soon to be a fourth consecutive Broadway success, and generally things went well for Inge while he was writing.

A letter from Inge to John Gassner, written in Stockbridge on April 28, 1957, indicates how well things seemed to be going for Inge. Gassner, who had written to express his concern for Inge, was doubtless encouraged by the reply:

> Your most thoughtful letter, which I got just this morning, has made a golden day moreso. Thank you very much for your real kindness. I really am feeling very fine, however. The trouble came last summer when I found I was going to have to change analysts. These moves can be very upsetting in a way that one never anticipates. But I finally found Dr. Robert Knight here at Riggs with couch time free, so I came up here last October. All has been going very well ever since, and I divide my time between here and NY, keeping a tiny apartment here that is ideal for writing.

Inge went on to say that he was about to finish a rewrite of the first play he ever wrote—although he was not publicly telling people that the material was that old—and he hoped that Gassner would read it when it was done. "You'll recognize much of FARTHER OFF FROM HEAVEN in it," wrote Inge, "but I hope you'll feel that I have done more with my material." He began his conclusion by using the weather as an indication of his generally upbeat mood: "This early spring, this glowing April, is the most cheering thing that's happened all year. It seems to me we've always had to wait until June to get weather like this in the past."[83]

AS 1957 and Inge's writing of *The Dark at the Top of the Stairs* progressed, the film version of *Bus Stop* was enjoying a box-office success that assured the continuing importance of Inge's name, not only with audiences, but with Hollywood producers. The film version of *Picnic* had been the economic bonanza that Columbia had envisioned, and although it won only two 1955 Academy Awards (for color art direction and set decoration, and for editing), it received several nominations, including one for best picture and one for Logan as best director. Logan was not nominated again for *Bus Stop* in 1956, nor did the film garner nominations as had *Picnic*, but Fox had no complaints, because audiences flocked to see Marilyn Monroe's Cherie. In Hollywood the word was out: whatever Inge wrote, grab it. Of course, a similar attitude prevailed among New York play producers, any of whom would have been delighted to have been approached in 1957 by William Inge or Audrey Wood to produce a new Inge play.

In this heady and desirable climate, Saint Subber and Elia Kazan must indeed have been pleased when they were chosen to have a look at *Stairs* for production on Broadway. For Inge the feeling was probably mutual in regard to Kazan, for Kazan in 1957 was more than a producer; he was also a proven director of powerful reputation, steeped in the tradition of Actors Studio method acting and wholly sympathetic to the type of stage and screen psychological realism that Inge most appreciated. Inge and Kazan were to become great friends and highly successful collaborators over the next four years, as Kazan directed the last two great successes of Inge's career.

The planning for *Stairs* went smoothly. Subber and Kazan were the co-producers, and Kazan was the director. Pat Hingle and Theresa Wright were cast as Rubin and Cora Flood. Eileen Heckart, who had played Rosemary in the Broadway version of *Picnic*, was cast as the garrulous, opinionated Lottie Lacey, Cora's sister. Charles Saari and Judith Robinson were cast as Sonny and Reenie, the Flood children. After rehearsals had gotten under way, a pre-Broadway run in Philadelphia was scheduled. The Music Box Theatre, where *Picnic* and *Bus Stop* had had their successful New York runs, was booked for the Broadway opening on December 5. Kazan and Inge worked well together, and Kazan worked well with the cast. Years later, Kazan recollected what it was like to work with Inge on both *Stairs* and *Splendor in the Grass*:

> Professionally he was perfect. He listened to suggestions openly, decided always from the core of his own intentions what he would do and what he would not do. When he didn't agree, he had good reasons. When he did agree he would always give you back a little more than you expected. I loved working with him; I esteemed him always.[84]

That praise omits the tension that developed between Inge and Kazan after *Splendor*, but it seems clear that the two were well suited for creative collaboration. "I was really most impressed with how we got along together," said Kazan of his work with Inge in readying *Stairs* for Broadway. "He had

had some disappointing reviews in Philadelphia, and that's the test of any author. He went away for a couple of days to mull them over, and then he came back and he went to work very hard." Typical of the Philadelphia critics was Max de Schauensee of the *Evening Bulletin*, who had complained that Inge had tried "to please too many people" by packing too many problems into the play and by not making Rubin and Cora sympathetic enough.[85] Although the critics in the earlier tryout cities of Boston and New Haven had liked *Stairs*, Inge worked with the script and, according to Kazan, "by the time we got to New York with the play he had covered the faults that the [Philadelphia] critics had pointed out."[86]

On December 1, Inge penned a pre-premiere article on *Stairs* for the *New York Times*. He had written an autobiographical play, and he knew it; but in this article he tried to play down the autobiographical element. Admitting that the play was "culled from my memories of childhood" and that "the characters are suggested by people I once knew, in and out of my family," Inge went on to declare, "there is not a specific portrait anywhere in the play." Perhaps in the strictest sense, this was true; but the correspondences between Maude and Luther Inge and Cora and Rubin Flood and between Helene and Billy Inge and Reenie and Sonny Flood are far too great to take Inge's disclaimer very seriously. In the article, Inge continued to write with a nostalgic fondness for the past that he had revealed; he spoke about the youthful fears of growing up and the continuing fears of adult life in the nuclear age. "In the midst of such confusion as we find ourselves today," he concluded, "where can we find sure values except in those very personal values that each man can sift from his own existence and cherish?"[87] *The Dark at the Top of the Stairs* was the most autobiographical work that William Inge put on the stage during his lifetime. Only his late-life novel, *My Son Is a Splendid Driver*, told more—much more—about his life. It is no wonder that he was especially tense as the opening night of *Stairs* approached.

Sensing Inge's powerful anxiety as the opening of this most personal play neared, Barbara Baxley and another friend decided that some distraction—a dinner on opening night—might help ease his mind. A small dinner with Baxley and a couple of other friends, they reasoned, would be better for Inge than stewing about, lurking within a block or so of the Music Box Theater, and trying to muster courage to take a peek in.

They put their plan into effect, but Baxley remembers that early in the evening she realized that it wasn't going to work. Inge began the evening by being quieter than usual, and as time passed he seemed to become more and more withdrawn, no matter how hard the others tried to engage him in conversation. Finally, when they sat down to eat, Inge picked at his food and said absolutely nothing. His hostess, in exasperation, then told him that he might as well go on to the theater, so he and Baxley got their coats and left, walking slowly toward the distant theater, as afraid of what they might find there as Sonny Flood was of the darkness upstairs. When they arrived, they quietly slipped in. Baxley claims that within moments in a darkened theater on opening night, one can tell if a play is going to be a success or not; it is, she says, a kind of sixth sense. And this night in the Music Box, she and Inge both quickly sensed that he had another winner. They hid at the intermission, then Baxley, her stomach upset in the wake of the tension and relief, took a cab home, knowing she could later share whatever joys he felt.[88] After the curtain, Inge joined the celebrants briefly.

On the next day, the critics again confirmed what had become a Broadway phenomenon: Inge seemed to write only hits. Citing the "quick and poignant glances into the privacy of hearts and souls" in *Stairs*, praising Kazan's direction and all the acting, Brooks Atkinson in the *New York Times* concluded: "Call 'The Dark at the Top of the Stairs' Mr. Inge's finest play. Although the style is unassuming, as usual, the sympathies are wider, the compassion deeper and the knowledge of adults and children more profound."[89] Walter Kerr of the *New York Herald-Tribune* also praised the direction and the acting; he said that *Stairs* was "wonderfully evocative: warm, troubled and deeply moving."[90] John McClain of the *New York Journal-American* found that *Stairs* "tells the tale of plain, decent people in a believable battle to raise a family, and it tells it with sympathy and understanding." The telling, McClain held, was the result of Inge's "thoughtful, unpretentious, and very gifted writing."[91] Most of the next-day critics considered *Stairs* Inge's best play yet.

The magazine reviews that appeared in December issues were a bit lighter in their praise, mostly because some of them noted, along with the next-day critic Richard Watts, Jr., that the play was episodic. Watts's term for this was a "diffuse quality," which he said created "a certain feeling that we were watching a series of individual plays."[92] Wolcott Gibbs of the *New Yorker*, echoing Watts and the earlier Philadelphia critics, described it as "too many people with too many diverse, or at least only imperfectly related, problems; too many abrupt shiftings from folk comedy to quite another mood."[93] Patrick Dennis of the *New Republic* decided that the episodic structure made *Stairs* a "literate soap opera," but the soap, he argued, was "of the best French-milled quality."[94] Such mild complaints amid general praise could hardly obscure the fact that *Stairs* was a hit; it was headed for a run of 468 perfor-

Inge on the stairs of the original set of The Dark at the Top of the Stairs *at New York's Music Box Theatre, 1957. Courtesy of the Kansas State Historical Society*

mances. And the film rights were quickly sold to Warner Brothers for an undisclosed amount.

In the wake of such a critical and commercial reception, Inge found himself at the end of 1957 at the height of his career. As *Time* magazine reported, "When newspaper critics greeted *The Dark* with cheers last week and daylong lines began forming at the box office, Inge could chalk up a topflight commercial and critical record on Broadway." No one before him had written four successful serious plays in sequence, each closing before the next one began, although Clifford Odets and Eugene O'Neill had had more than one successful play running simultaneously. Moreover, as *Time* noted, all four plays had been sold to the movies, and the first three had already been made into hit movies as well. Inge had, *Time* said, realized "close to a million dollars" for the film rights to the first three films.[95]

Such prosperity brought financial comfort to Inge, even if he never enjoyed emotional comfort. As one from a very modest economic background who had lived through the Great Depression, Inge appreciated his wealth very nearly to a fault: he was always reluctant to spend freely, even when he had plenty to spend. When he did spend, he spent carefully and was alert to ways to shield his income from taxes. That is why, as Gilbert Millstein has reported, he gave four paintings—including works by Willem de Kooning, which had appreciated enormously since Inge bought them—to the Nelson Gallery in Kansas City and why, when he ordered flowers for the women and champagne for the men in the cast of *Stairs*, "he adjured the florist and vintner to be sure to bill him before the first of the year for income-tax purposes."[96] However, Inge's financial affairs, like every other aspect of his life by the end of 1957, had become sufficiently complex that Inge and Audrey Wood were not able to keep up with everything very well anymore. That is why Inge hired John Connolly, whom he had met in 1952 at a gathering hosted by Glenway Wescott.

Connolly had been working for Saint Subber, one of the producers of *Stairs*, as a secretarial associate to Carson McCullers, who was working on a play for Subber to produce. His switch to work for Inge was heartily welcomed by Audrey Wood, who was herself far too busy to give Inge all the help he now so clearly needed. Inge, according to Connolly, "had no filing system whatsoever" and badly needed someone to bring order to his personal and business matters. Thus it was that Connolly took on the job, in his words, of doing "all the unimportant things in Bill's life."[97] These things included typing drafts of Inge's handwritten work; taking care of the bills, correspondence, and travel plans; driving Inge to and from Stockbridge and around New York; and relaying manuscripts, contracts, and other important papers to and from Wood, Inge's attorney, his accountant, and so on. It was also Connolly who handled the details of Inge's move when he decided to leave the Dakota for a newer, larger apartment at 45 Sutton Place South, on the extreme eastern side of Manhattan. Inge's distrust of heights had not abated, so the new apartment was, as at the Dakota, on the lowest living-quarters floor of the building. This was to be Inge's last New York apartment, his residence as his success began to decline and as the long, painful slide toward suicide got under way.

8 · Sutton Place

Inge had barely begun to settle into his Sutton Place apartment when the first tremors of what was to be a very difficult 1958 struck. He had dedicated the Random House edition of *Stairs* to Tennessee Williams, who had experienced the failure of *Orpheus Descending* in 1957 and was, in January, 1958, tense with concern for his newest play, *Garden District*, which had opened on the seventh of that month. Williams was in no mood to write the introduction to the Random House edition of *Stairs* that Audrey Wood had urged him to compose. Donald Spoto reports that Williams said to Wood: "Audrey, it is one thing to type three words—'For Tennessee Williams'—on a dedication page. It's quite another thing to write several pages of introduction." He finally agreed to do it, however, and as Spoto further reports, the resulting introduction is "one of the strangest pieces Williams ever wrote, best described as praising Inge with faint damns."[1] Crediting Inge with being an honest writer whose plays seemed at first deceptively smooth on the surface, then suddenly but subtly penetrating, Williams likened the plays to Inge himself, whose "handsome and outwardly serene face . . . looks a bit older than his forty years" (Inge was forty-four at the time). Inge's life, Williams implied, was his best drama, as yet unwritten.[2] Williams shared details of his first meeting with Inge in St. Louis, but he did not elaborate on his hints about Inge's personal "drama."

The Introduction was complimentary enough that few would consider significant the "faint damns" that Spoto astutely detects. Inge surely noticed them, but if he took any offense, he gave no indication. By then he was probably used to the little signs of Williams's jealousy and understood them. There was never any sign that Inge felt what Spoto called the "quiet contest" (p. 225) between the two men as strongly as Williams did, at least not during the mid-to-late 1950s; and after *Splendor in the Grass*, any such "contest," real or imagined, was over, for Inge was never successful again. The tremors lay in Williams's implications that Inge's successful plays had deceptive surfaces and that Inge's personal success had been deceptively smooth. Before the year was out, both implications would be publicly elaborated upon by others, leaving Inge vulnerable to pain that, given his nature, probably was inevitable.

Meanwhile, Connolly continued to shuttle Inge between Sutton Place and Stockbridge, where Inge's therapy continued to be helpful. He worked on some sculpture as part of his therapy while in Stockbridge, and he frequently visited the Gibsons. William Gibson recalls that Inge would call and ask if he could come over to the Gibsons to watch television – the Perry Como show was a favorite; but once there, he would become restless and seldom stayed for very long.[3] Inviting himself places, then either not staying long or not going at all, became a pattern for Inge, according to John Connolly, who recalls that Inge also would frequently accept invitations, then decide at the last minute not to go. It usually fell to Connolly to call Inge's regrets on such occasions.

Connolly doesn't believe such behavior was mean-spirited; rather, Inge suffered swings in mood, and he would selfishly conserve his energies and guard his feelings by choosing to be alone. It was as though he enjoyed being wanted or accepted, but once he had the assurance that people wanted to see him, he wouldn't want to give of himself enough to follow through. "He blew a lot of people's gaskets that way," says Connolly, "and he did it all the time." It is likely that he seldom realized how annoying his cancellations could be. Connolly assesses the situation thus: "it was just that he had a certain amount of talent, a certain amount of energy, and he conserved that very carefully."[4]

During roughly this same time, Inge occasionally attended A.A. meetings with Charles Jackson and the composer Ned Rorem. Jackson was an old friend from the Dakota, and as an alcoholic and the author of *The Lost Weekend*, he was completely understanding about the perils of alcohol. Rorem was an extremely good-looking young talent, a homosexual who had only recently realized that he was also an alcoholic. Rorem's *New York Diary* makes occasional references to Jackson and Inge, calling them the "star pupils" of the A.A. meetings and giving one of the very rare printed mentions of Inge's homosexuality. Speaking of Inge, Rorem notes in an undated entry: "A month ago, on finding himself alone with me, he jumped into my lap like a Saint Bernard imagining himself a Pomeranian."[5] That entry, which would have been embarrassing to Inge at any time in his life, was not published until about ten years after the incident it describes had occurred. There is perhaps no connection, but there is no correspondence in the Inge Collection between Inge and Rorem dated after 1967, the year Rorem's *New York Diary* was published. It is entirely possible that the friendship ended with that publication.

Another mention of Inge in Rorem's diary from roughly this same period involves a prophetic remark made at a dinner party Rorem gave. Some of the guests were discussing theater, and one of them, who did not know Inge was present, remarked that "Inge satisfied needs of this decade (as America's foremost uncontroversial playwright) but will go out with the sixties."[6] Such a remark had to have stung Inge, reminding him of Logan's ending to *Picnic* and perhaps making Inge more determined to write a play soon without a "happy" ending. In fact, the play he had begun to write, *A Loss of Roses*, despite having familiar complications and setting, was such a play, as was the screenplay he was also working on, *Splendor in the Grass*. At any rate, that kind of remark would be ringing in his ears before *A Loss of Roses* appeared on Broadway.

ON JUNE 20, 1958, Maude Gibson Inge died in Independence. She was eighty-six years old and had long been dependent upon Esther Latcham's care. Connolly accompanied Inge on the long train ride to Kansas, where Inge's first action upon entering the house on Sycamore was to stop a grandfather clock whose ticking he could not bear.[7] According to his nephew Luther Claude Inge, Inge did not stay for his mother's services; but in *My Son Is a Splendid Driver*, Inge describes Joey Hansen viewing his mother's body at the funeral home. Recalling that the burial of his paternal grandfather had made his father sob hopelessly and that he was "daunted" to see his father "reduced to such a childish state," Joey comments that "death makes children of us all," then he continues:

I had not expected such an eruption of feeling as had happened to my father, but it came. The hurt and grief sprung up from some forgotten well inside me, and gushed out of my eyes like sudden rain. For a few moments, I stood there, a child in the woods. And then I became a man again, humbled and a little embarrassed to realize what an infantile love I still bore her. It was this love that had made me so miserable for so many years, and made me crave some unattainable prominence that would finally raise me above Jule in her esteem. It was a love, after Jule's death, that bound us like a silent pact, and kept me from ever loving another so deeply. It was a love that had made me hate her, at times, for it was selfish. But I couldn't hate her now. . . . And so, I loved her again. Death makes us all innocent, and weaves all our private hurts and griefs and wrongs into the fabric of time, and makes them a part of eternity.[8]

While it is important to note that this touching description, fraught with understanding, was not published until 1971, thirteen years after Maude's death, it seems to capture as clearly as anything else he wrote Inge's complex feelings about his mother and his brother as well. It is not a coincidence that Inge chose, in this last deeply autobiographical memoir, to note the long-time impact on his own life that the tragic sudden death of his brother Luther Boy (Jule in *Driver*) had caused; it is not a coincidence that he chose in this memoir to write about his relationship with his mother in Oedipal terms. To what extent he could have articulated such feelings to members of his family in 1958 is impossible to guess, but it seems reasonable to suppose that he did not even try. At any rate, his failure to attend the funeral services left some of them puzzled and hurt.

It is also possible that at the time of Maude's death, Inge realized with finality that a return one day to live in Independence would always be out of the question, no matter what he might achieve as a writer, no matter what peace he might make with his past. In *Driver*, Joey recalls the pathetic story that had often been told to him about a forlorn and drunken Uncle Julian, his father's brother, who, after being forced out of the hotel where he normally stayed, would pass out by the for-sale sign on the doorstep of the empty house where he had spent his childhood, only to awaken the next day "to face again his homelessness." Joey applied the story to himself as he viewed his mother in her coffin: "Something final happened to the past. I could never go home again, not even in fantasy, without making the same pathetic mistake of Uncle Julian. The womb of the past could no longer comfort me. I had to live my life in the confounding present" (*Driver*, p. 221).

The "confounding present" was seldom pleasant for William Inge, and it was to become even less so as 1958 continued. And indeed, returns home, even in fantasy, were to become fewer: of all the many manuscripts Inge produced from 1959 until his death, only four would be set in the past in Kansas: *A Loss of Roses*, the 1959 Broadway play; *Splendor in the Grass*, the 1961 screenplay; *Good Luck, Miss Wyckoff*, the 1970 novel; and *Driver*, the 1971 memoir. Of those, only *Splendor* was both artistically and commercially successful. Everything else, whether produced or not, is set in the "confounding present," and everything else makes clear in one way or another the consternation of its creator.

RANDOM House scheduled the single-volume publication of Inge's four plays of the 1950s for August 5, 1958. Inge wrote the Foreword for this volume, in which he revealed that his successes had not brought him much happiness and that he had long been in psychoanalysis.[9] A few days before the publication of the book, he wrote a piece in the *New York Times* ("One Man's Experience in Living," July 27, sec. 2, p. 1), excerpted from the Foreword. The *Times* article also mentioned his unhappiness and psychoanalysis and referred to the Emily Dickinson poem, "Success is counted sweetest" (by those who ne'er succeed), which provides "the strains of triumph" phrase in the title of this book. For the first time, rank-and-file theatergoers and Inge's public learned, although still in surface ways, of some of his long-term problems. They were soon to learn more: in the August, 1958, issue of *Esquire*, the Gilbert Millstein piece that I cite so frequently in this study appeared. Inge's psychoanalysis was referred to in more depth in Millstein's article, and Inge's alcoholism was made public for the first time.[10] It is almost as though, now that Maude was gone, Inge felt he could reveal more of himself. Of course, what would have been his greatest revelation—his homosexuality—was still unthinkable to share. Given what critics such as Robert Brustein would soon be writing about him, Inge's careful guarding of his great secret vulnerability was wise.

As the summer of 1958 began to wane, Inge and Barbara Baxley went to State College, Pennsylvania, where some of Inge's one-act plays were to be produced on the campus of Pennsylvania State University, with Baxley appearing in them. While there, Inge was called by *Harper's* magazine to ask if he could furnish a photograph of himself to be used on the cover of an upcoming issue which was to feature a lengthy article about him and his work. No indication of the nature of the article was given.[11] Inge provided the photograph, a left-profile shot, which appeared with posters of his four successes on the cover of the November issue. Nothing on the cover indicated the nature of the article either; only the somewhat puzzling title—"The Men-Taming Women of William Inge"—and the critic's name, Robert Brustein, were given.

But the article was a calculated ambush. Brustein, then a professor at Columbia University, was described by *Harper's* as "a fast-rising young drama critic." He began his critique by saying, "Considering the modesty—one is tempted to say the mediocrity—of his work, it is clear that the excitement over Inge has been inspired by something other than the intrinsic value of his plays."[12] *Stairs*, Brustein asserted, wanders aimlessly, with dialogue that is "dry, repetitive, and monotonously folksy"; only Elia Kazan's direction, which was contrived to deliver small climaxes for a play without a plot climax, had provided any life for the Broadway production (pp. 52–53). *Picnic*, Brustein continued, is "a satyr play glorifying the phallic male"; *Bus Stop* is "a vulgar folk vaudeville with night-club acts and dirty jokes" (p. 53). *Sheba*, *Picnic*, and *Bus Stop*, said Brustein, are all "largely dominated" by the personality of Tennessee Williams, while *Stairs* "reinforces the opinion that Inge is a dramatist of considerable limitations" (p. 53).

Those scattershot salvos served as Brustein's preamble to his major point: that Inge's four successful plays are "preachy" endorsements of family life and love in which dominating females tame the freedom and spirit of the leading men through a kind of symbolic emasculation:

> Specifically, Inge's basic plot line revolves around a heroine threatened either with violence or sexual aggression by a rambunctious male. Both terrified and attracted by him, she tries to escape his influence until she learns that, despite his apparent confidence, he is riddled with doubts, loneliness, and need. Once he has confessed this, he loses his ogre quality and the woman is able to domesticate him without difficulty. (Pp. 53–54)

Such an observation enabled Brustein to state that the resultant "surface theme" of Inge's work is "that people find salvation from fear, need, and insecurity only through the fulfillment of domestic love" (p. 54).

Pressing on, Brustein likened this "domestication" of Inge's men to emasculation, creating a psychological subsurface theme

> to the effect that marriage demands, in return for its spiritual consolations, a sacrifice of the hero's image (which is the American folk image) of maleness. He must give up his aggressiveness, his promiscuity, his bravado, his contempt for soft virtues, and his narcissistic pride in his body and attainments, and admit that he is lost in the world and needs help. (P. 56)

This subsurface theme, Brustein contended, shows that Inge's hero "has been made to conform, not to his own image of maleness, but to the maternal woman's. Each of Inge's plays reads a little like *The Taming of the Shrew* in reverse" (p. 56).

The net result of Brustein's criticism was that all of Inge's plays up to that time had been safe and formulaic, pleasing to audiences' prejudices through a gross oversimplification of life: everything is tidily resolved in the matriarchal bosom of marriage and family values. That, said Brustein, was Inge's constant message; therefore, he could not be considered a developing playwright; instead, he was a "fiddle with one string" (p. 56). Having merely "endowed the commonplace with some depth," Inge was "yet another example of Broadway's reluctance or inability to deal intelligently with the American world at large" (p. 57).

Like any effective critical mugging, Brustein's piece had the rhetorical force of plausibility linked with good writing style. Certainly, Inge's four plays could be viewed as Brustein saw them. It matters little that such criticism could as easily have been leveled at the audiences and critics who had liked the plays; those targets were of course too small and scattered. The playwright was the bullseye, and Brustein scored a direct hit. It also matters little that the resolution of *Picnic* was not what Inge had wanted or that on a psychological level that Brustein could not have known, Inge may have depicted resilience in marital and family values because, as a lonely homosexual, he would have liked to have been able to believe in them. What does matter is that Brustein was "a fast-rising young drama critic" who knew how to punch, and William Inge was a vulnerable playwright who did not know how to bob and weave.

Brustein could not have known how important the widespread acceptance of his work was to Inge's fragile equilibrium; he could not have known how deeply he had wounded his mark. But he did not have to wait long to get an inkling: William Gibson recalls that Inge was in Stockbridge when he first read Brustein's article. Shattered, Inge called Brustein to protest, and he wept on the phone.[13] Now, Inge knew criticism's capacity to hurt, and he would never fully recover.

JOHN CONNOLLY believes that Brustein's article was "the beginning of the end" for Inge. That article, says Connolly, "cut a knife into Bill like you wouldn't imagine."[14] It doesn't matter that it shouldn't have, that as a Broadway heavyweight, Inge should have anticipated the inevitable rough stuff. Barbara Baxley also remembers the stinging hurt Inge experienced. She recalls that she, Elia Kazan, and Tennessee Williams all gathered at Inge's Sutton Place apartment shortly after Brustein's article appeared to discuss whether some response should be made. Williams, something of a battle-scarred veteran of critical attacks, felt that any response would unduly dignify the attack. Whatever jealousy he might have felt about Inge's successes was not evident at this meeting; he was there to be supportive and offer counsel. Baxley wanted a response made, in print, and quickly; but Kazan, Williams, and Inge decided that quiet was the best option. They reasoned that a response would give Brustein too much credit and attention.[15]

William Gibson, however, must have cheered his friend when, in the January, 1959, issue, *Harper's* printed Gibson's letter protesting Brustein's article. Gibson dryly noted that it was Inge, not Brustein, whose picture had graced their November cover; Inge, not Brustein, who had written the successful plays. Brustein's criticism, observed Gibson, had been smuggled aboard the magazine "like a flea on a moose." Why, Gibson facetiously asked, wasn't *Harper's* interested in publishing his article, written in the last two minutes, on *Brustein's* life's work?[16] And perhaps more to the point, in that same issue was the letter of *Harper's* reader Mrs. Monroe D. North, who, noting Brustein's broadsides, wondered, "How could I ever have enjoyed the four plays so much?"[17]

Given the perspective of time and the fact that Brustein's criticism encompassed the four Broadway plays that now stand as Inge's best and best known, it is appropriate to assess these plays, as well as Brustein's judgments, anew. In this later light, it would appear that Mrs. North had a better perspective on Inge's four famous plays than Brustein had. Brustein, after all, was exercising the prerogatives of a "fast-rising young drama critic," who was shrewdly building upon a few insights that he stretched for maximum effect. Surely, *Sheba, Picnic, Bus Stop,* and *Stairs* all show "tamed" men, if by "tamed" one means a willingness to seek solace or comfort in the kind of heterosexual love relationship usually associated with marriage. But it is unreasonable to imply that all drama is necessarily mediocre or trite if it portrays the human need for love or reinforces the institutions of marriage and family. If such were the case, then Eugene O'Neill and Tennessee Williams, playwrights of greater stature than Inge, also dealt mostly in mediocrities and clichés. Inge dealt with universals of human experience, as all good dramatists do.

In his four famous plays, Inge presented themes of loneliness, frustration, loss, despair, and, perhaps above all, the human need for love. Our first, our earliest, need for love is within the family, and Inge looked to the family as an imperfect but necessary institution. Never especially happy as he grew up in his own family, and both emotionally and sexually not prepared to mate and begin a family of his own, Inge nonetheless chose as his frequent text the tensions involved in family relationships. Given his orientation and the times in which he lived, this was a subject of constant concern to him. He often said, via his plays, that life is hard and that one must accept it and make the best one can of it. Family relationships can greatly help—or hinder—that process.

Brustein's thesis, on the other hand, asserts that Inge's plays show women in control of relationships, bent on domesticating otherwise unwilling men. But such a view distorts the poignant situations that Inge's women find themselves in. In *Sheba*, Lola is hardly a "man-tamer"; she needs Doc just as desperately as he needs her. To make the best of their lives, the Delaneys need to stay together out of a mutual dependence that has nothing to do with either one's dominance. Nor can their reconciliation be dismissed as a facile "happy ending," for their future tranquillity is not assured; they are simply going to do the best they can in a situation that is far from rosy.

Likewise, calling *Picnic* a "satyr play glorifying the phallic male" ignores that Hal is "tamed" because of his *need* to be taken seriously, his *need* to be loved, not just laid. It also plays down the powerful effect of the women's loneliness, frustration, and desperation. Madge, Millie, Flo, Mrs. Potts, and above all, Rosemary generate this powerful effect to such a degree that it is their play every bit as much as it is Hal's. Madge and Rosemary "get" their men by following them out of town (Madge and Hal) or pitifully begging them (Rosemary and Howard), not because Hal and Howard are glorified phallic males, but because Madge and Rosemary are just as lonely, frightened, and vulnerable as Hal and Howard. (And if Inge had had his way, Madge would not have followed Hal.) Neither couple, at the end of the play, seems to have entered into any sort of stereotypical happy marriage, and the rest of the women are still alone with their same problems.

That Bo Decker calms down, apologizes for causing so much ruckus, and thereby wins Cherie in *Bus Stop* is beyond debate. But Cherie is no "man-tamer," either. Bo learns his manners from other men, specifically Virgil Blessing and Sheriff Will Masters. Cherie isn't sexually innocent, but she *is* naive about life, and she is afraid of what the future might hold for her. The men she usually meets are not exactly interested in anything lasting; it's Bo who offers her that possibility, and when he stops his roughhousing, they both realize their needs and vulnerabilities. Focusing on Bo and Cherie, as Brustein does, also does little justice to the ensemble of characters who share the bus stop with the central couple. How does that drunken sad man Dr. Lyman fit into Brustein's thesis? Excessive booze and self-humiliation "tame" him, rather than the naive Elma; he certainly is not "domesticated" at the end of the play, any more than Carl, the bus driver, and Virgil, Bo's sidekick, are. As Grace, the owner of the bus stop, says to Virgil, some people just get "left out in the cold," especially if they don't fit a thesis. *Bus Stop* is a romantic comedy, at least as far as Bo and Cherie are concerned; but given the rest of the characters, it is hardly a play that ringingly endorses romance.

Finally, like Doc and Lola, Rubin and Cora Flood in *Stairs* need each other. They need to communicate better, and they need to try harder to understand and forgive each other, but in no way is Cora a "tamer" of Rubin. They reconcile because of their willingness to face their fears together. If Sonny seems to overcome his Oedipal tendencies a bit too easily or if Reenie seems to overcome her shyness through exaggerated trauma (the suicide of Sammy Goldenbaum), then Inge may have been guilty of facile plotting in order to have a satisfying show, but that doesn't fit well into Brustein's argument. The fact is, *Stairs* is an entertaining and durable play. All the plays that Brustein criticized are durable and have proved it for more than thirty years. All are still widely produced, both in small-town venues and in big-city revivals. Not bad for trite mediocrity.

At the time, however, no matter how hard he may have tried to ignore Brustein's remarks, Inge simply could not do so. Brustein's views fostered more self-doubt where there was already too much of it, and that self-doubt plagued Inge as he worked on the scripts of *A Loss of Roses*, the play he had decided would be his next on Broadway, and *Splendor in the Grass*, the screenplay he was doing for Kazan to direct.

The idea for *A Loss of Roses* had originated on a cross-country train trip in 1957. Inge, who had successfully heightened the Oedipal element in *Stairs*, was still fascinated with the dramatic possibilities of the Oedipus complex, and he was also interested in the Venus-Adonis story at the time. As the train rocked along, he began to draft a play that would incorporate elements of both. Inge preferred the train to any other sort of domestic travel, not only because his fear of heights made him extremely reluctant to fly but also because it afforded relatively comfortable and lengthy uninterrupted periods for thought and writing. (Connolly believes that the steady rocking motion of the train was both soothing and inspirational for Inge; Connolly claims that many excellent ideas for writing were generated as Inge spoke reflectively during such trips, ideas that are lost forever because Connolly didn't take notes or keep a tape recorder handy.)[18] The initial draft of *Roses* was put aside for a time, but while Inge was enduring the emotional blows of 1958, he began to revise it. That revising continued as 1959 progressed and as Inge tried to make the play ready for what he hoped would be a successful rejoinder to Brustein's criticism, but it is significant that he never seemed to be satisfied with it, never seemed to be sure he had it as he wanted it.

A MAJOR problem with the script of *A Loss of Roses* in its various versions was always one of focus. Essentially it is two strong stories in one, and while Inge had previously been adept at weaving together diverse story strands to make well-unified plays, he was never able to mesh the major story strands of this play. One major strand involves the tension and eventual resolution of an Oedipal bond between the widow, Helen Baird, and her twenty-one-year-old son, Kenny. The other strand involves the emotional decline of an aging, out-of-work actress named Lila Green. Inge tried to bring these stories together by presenting Lila as a former neighbor who had helped Helen care for Kenny when he was small; Lila, now an adult and down on her luck—indeed, she is one step away from making pornographic movies and "entertaining" male conventioneers—comes to stay for a brief time with Helen and Kenny. During Lila's stay, Inge brings the Helen-Kenny Oedipal conflict to its crisis, and Lila becomes a surrogate mother figure whom Kenny successfully seduces. Thus, the Oedipal conflict is resolved, but Lila—now rejected by Kenny—is left to her grim and demeaning last resort. The solution is too pat, and the seam always was evident in the revisions because each story strand was too strong on its own.

The strength of these two stories might be traced to two powerful creative motives, each of which would be enough to generate a play on its own, just as the Oedipus and Venus-Adonis stories are each self-sufficient. First, Inge seemed to want to do a play with the resolution of an Oedipus complex at its center. *Stairs* contained such a resolution between Cora and Sonny Flood, but that was on the periphery of the larger resolution of conflict between Cora and her husband, Rubin. The motive for an Oedipal play could have grown naturally from Inge's psychoanalytic experience and his still-recent loss of Maude, an extension of the impulse that had led to his portrayal of the Cora-Sonny relationship in *Stairs*. Inge's interest in Oedipal material was undeniably strong; in fact, it would also be central in his next Broadway play, *Natural Affection*.

Second, in Lila Green, Inge had again conceived of a memorable frustrated woman, a victim of the circumstances of her life, powerless, despite her good intentions, to change those circumstances. Lila's story, in particular her desperate grab for happiness and fulfillment with the handsome young Kenny, and the subsequent shattering of her last, best hope, was a fascinating subject in itself for Inge. He invested Lila with too much sympathy and too many dramatic lines to make her story a workable part of the Helen-Kenny drama. Inge's affection for Barbara Baxley was also at work in his conception of Lila, for he wrote the part with her in mind to play it, even though, as events turned out, she did not get the role.[19]

But the focus for the story was far from the only problem that plagued *A Loss of Roses*. Although with his track record, Inge would never have had trouble finding producers for *Roses*, he decided that he himself would be the play's principal backer. Why he made that decision is a mystery; certainly he did not expect it to fail and thus reap a tax break for himself. Perhaps backing the play was a symbolic attempt at self-confidence, a kind of "so there" to the Brusteins of the world, although if that was his motive, he negated its potential effectiveness by not letting it be known before the play's New York debut. The announced producers – Saint Subber and Lester Osterman – put up only $25,000 of the reported $125,000 that it took to mount the production; Inge put up the rest.[20] By being both the playwright and the principal producer, Inge found himself in the unusual position of holding the power of decision later, when most signs indicated that it would be best to cancel or at least postpone the show. As matters were to develop, holding the power to make that decision – whether symbolically motivated or not – backfired.

Finding the director he wanted also proved costly for Inge, according to Barbara Baxley. Elia Kazan was not available, so Inge hoped to get Arthur Penn; but when Penn declined, Inge was temporarily at a loss. When complaining to Baxley about losing Penn, Inge worried that he would not be able to find a proven director who would be available. Baxley – to her later regret – suggested that Inge ask Daniel Mann, who had done such a fine job directing both the stage and screen versions of *Sheba*. Mann accepted, even though he was also angling to direct Elizabeth Taylor in the film of *Butterfield 8* at the time. Then, when Inge told Mann that he wanted Baxley to play Lila, Mann flatly refused to cast her. And Inge, to the lasting damage of his relationship with Baxley, agreed with Mann. Baxley was deeply hurt and naturally disappointed; she couldn't understand why Inge hadn't insisted on her getting the role of Lila. They quarreled repeatedly, and as it became clear that Inge was going to let Mann have his way, Baxley decided to turn her affections elsewhere. Eventually, she says, she married a man who she and Inge knew was wrong for her. And although both the marriage and Inge's play failed, she and Inge never completely patched things up.[21]

Exactly why Inge did not stand up to Mann about Baxley can never be known. Perhaps his fears and self-doubts after Brustein's attack made him think that Mann's direction was the key to reestablishing his equilibrium. Perhaps he thought that because of the love Baxley felt for him, she should have been more understanding. Unquestionably, his failure to insist upon her was selfish and, finally, self-destructive. There is nothing to suggest that Mann felt anything like an equivalent obligation. Connolly reports that when *Roses* was in rehearsals and clearly in trouble, he had taken some important script changes to Mann's hotel room in New York, only to find Mann preoccupied with a script of *Butterfield 8*. Connolly told Inge about that, but by then, Inge was either too preoccupied himself or too fearful to realize its significance.[22] And he had even more problems.

At first, Inge was delighted that Shirley Booth had agreed to play Helen. Booth was by now a proven star, and the reunion of Inge with Mann and Booth seemed to augur great promise for *Roses*. But as rehearsals for the Washington tryout got under way, Booth complained—understandably— that the role of Helen was overshadowed by Lila, now being played by Carol Haney. Booth wanted more lines, more significance. Yet when Inge wrote more lines for her, she either did not like them or later asked that they be cut, or both. Moreover, the part of Kenny was being played by an unknown young actor named Warren Beatty, who was extremely nervous about his first Broadway role. A product of Lee Strasberg's Actors Studio, Beatty constantly slowed rehearsals to ask Mann questions about Kenny's motives. As Audrey Wood recalls in her memoirs, some of Beatty's discussions with Mann "became quite acrimonious," making relations between the two men increasingly tense and irritating the veteran Booth no end.[23]

Wood, who found herself in a no-win situation because she represented Inge, Mann, and Booth, tried her best to resolve matters. But in Washington for the first tryout run, while Inge was still tinkering with the script, Booth announced that if Inge didn't change Helen's role to suit her and if Mann didn't start paying more attention to her performance, rather than to Beatty's, she would not remain in the cast. Wood now found it completely impossible to satisfy Inge, Mann, and Booth all at the same time. As the tryout run switched to New Haven, Booth withdrew from the play. Betty Field, a fine actress who had played in the film versions of *Picnic* and *Bus Stop*, took over the role of Helen.[24] But Field, who was suffering from sinus problems and a slipped disc in her back, was joining the cast too late, and she was too ill to rehearse as much as she needed to in order to make up for lost ground.

Booth's departure from the cast naturally caught the attention of theater reporters. The Washington run had not gone well, largely because of the crisis atmosphere, and it was obvious in New Haven that the production overall—not just Field—was struggling. Although the reporter Maurice Zolotow found Inge reluctant to be critical of Booth, Inge did tell Zolotow, "I do feel . . . that our actors are afraid of heightened dialogue. . . . They have an unfortunate habit of wanting to collaborate with playwrights. They love rewriting speeches." In general, Inge lamented to Zolotow, "language has lost its importance in our theatre." Mann was not so reserved about Booth when he spoke to Zolotow. He blamed her for the many cuts that had, in fact, diminished her role, cuts that now the beleaguered Field was having to learn because they had been restored. Both Inge and Mann told Zolotow they believed that *Roses* would still be ready, and Inge said that with all due respect to out-of-town audiences and critics, it was the New York opening audience and critics who determined the fate of a play. He went a step farther and said, "It's the New York first-night audience that gives you your definition of yourself," a remark Robert Brustein would later cause Inge to regret.[25]

Despite what Inge and Mann said to Zolotow, Audrey Wood was increasingly certain that *Roses* could not be successful on its opening date in New York on November 28. She suggested to Subber and Osterman that the play should be closed. A profit, in fact, was still possible, even for Inge, because his Hollywood reputation was so good that the film rights for *Roses* had already been sold to Twentieth Century–Fox. (The amount of the sale was reported to be as high as $400,000 in one source, $200,000 in another.)[26] Subber and Osterman agreed with Wood, but when she told Inge that she didn't think the play should open, he thought about this overnight, then said the next day that he wanted the play to go on (Wood, p. 233).

And so *A Loss of Roses* limped into New York for its November 28 opening at the Eugene O'Neill Theater, with one of its stars not ready, its director at best distracted, most of its producers convinced it should be canceled, and its author and principal backer, who was still not sure that either the script or the time was right, apparently expecting a miracle. What Inge did on opening night is not known. Certainly Barbara Baxley was not with him. Perhaps he ventured into the darkened theater alone this time, and thus was alone, characteristically, when he sensed his first Broadway failure.

Emphatically, the miracle didn't happen. Brooks Atkinson of the *New York Times* offered what proved to be among the milder next-day criticisms when he said, "'A Loss of Roses' is a dull play."[27] John McClain, in the *New York Journal-American*, called *Roses* "a poor and purposeless play" in which "overtones of the Oedipus theme were rampant, but they were not well delineated." Recalling that Shirley Booth had left the play before Broadway, McClain concluded: "There is no doubt that Miss Booth knew what she was doing."[28] Richard Watts, Jr., in the *New York Post*, said, "William Inge, I regret to report, has finally written a very bad play." He went on to point out that "its weakness lies in its curiously plodding dullness and lack of emotional vitality."[29]

A few days later the magazine critics weighed in heavily as well, and more viciously. "The new William Inge play at the Eugene O'Neill Theatre is a mess," said the *New Yorker*'s Kenneth Tynan, who also said, "You cannot write a first-rate play about the Oedipus complex alone." In Tynan's view, Inge's script was the whole problem.[30] Harold Clurman, usually a powerful advocate for Inge, complained in the *Nation* that the audience had to have an understanding of Freud in order to understand Helen and Kenny; and like many critics, Clurman also noted the uncertainty about who the main character, or what the main story, of the play is.[31] In the *New Republic*, Robert Brustein quoted Inge's earlier remark to Maurice Zolotow that "it's the New York first night audience that gives you your definition of yourself"; then he said:

> Granted that a writer so insecure about his own identity is not going to write very cogently about the identity of others—granted also that one so hungry for approval might be tempted to take the easiest road to success—this still puts a heavy burden on the critics who are responsible now not only for judging the play but for the spiritual stability of the playwright.

Not one to shirk his heavy burden, Brustein concluded that *Roses* was simply the same old Inge stuff—"the relationship between the weak male and the comforting mother-woman."[32]

A Loss of Roses staggered to a halt after only twenty-five performances. Inge, reeling from the criticism, left town in his new convertible well before the closing on December 19. It was unlike him to leave alone and take the wheel himself, but it was also unlike him to write a failure. Before the premiere, he had agreed to an interview with Jack Balch, his old acquaintance

Inge at Peabody in Nashville in 1959, where he fled after the failure of A Loss of Roses. *Print from WIC/ICC; courtesy of Photographic Archives, Vanderbilt University*

and sometime adversary from St. Louis days. Balch, determined still to do the interview, tracked Inge down in Nashville, where he was visiting Helene. The resulting article, "Anatomy of a Failure," appeared in the February, 1960, issue of *Theatre Arts*. In it, Inge was still reluctant to blame Shirley Booth; he took most of the responsibility for the failure of the play upon himself.

He told Balch that he should at least have postponed the opening when Field joined the cast,

> but chiefly I felt I owed Betty the mathematical chance to achieve her miracle. You know the old saying, "Bad rehearsals, good performance"— real theatre gospel when it works, superstition when it doesn't. That's the chance I took, and shouldn't have. Everybody concerned conceded that if I wanted it, the show would be closed. I just couldn't say the word. It wasn't just my irrational dependence on a miracle; it was also that I couldn't face up to putting everybody out of work. "I *could* be wrong in my estimate that the play's in bad shape," I told myself. Then too, I was probably spoiled by not having had a failure. I was like the fellow who'd never been really hit on the jaw, and couldn't imagine himself ever getting knocked out.[33]

From Nashville, Inge went on to Hollywood to visit the film set of *Stairs* and to consult with Kazan about *Splendor*. Bob Thomas interviewed Inge in Hollywood, and again Inge blamed himself for the failure of *Roses*. "I have no quarrel with the critics," Inge told Thomas. But then he went on to say: "It amazes me how violent they get when a play is not a hit. They act as though it were a personal affront to them that such a presentation should be made." Concluding that he thought a serious playwright's serious attempt to do a play deserved greater respect, Inge said that he "was treated as if [he] had spit on the floor." Sometime later, Inge told an acquaintance that Thomas had misquoted him; "I didn't say spit," he claimed.[34]

Inge's remarks to Balch and Thomas contradict remarks he made in the Foreword to the Random House edition of *A Loss of Roses*. In that Foreword, dated January, 1960, Inge acknowledged that this published version was not the Broadway version; he also mentioned the many changes that were made during rehearsals. But he claimed that despite all the adjustments in the script, he had gone into production with "complete confidence." How that could have been true after Brustein's attack and all those rewrites—not to mention what he told Balch and Thomas—is highly suspect. He also said that when he realized that the play he thought he had written "was not happening on the stage," he "tried to prevent its coming into New York, but this would have brought me a greater personal financial loss than I could have handled."[35] That remark contradicts Audrey Wood's report that Inge himself decided that the play would continue and also that to close the play would not have cost him money.

In all likelihood, these contradictory remarks indicate an Inge who was in fact deeply hurt and rather confused, but determined to shake off the injuries somehow. He knew that failure was not unique—look at his resilient friend Williams—and he did have an exciting prospect in the offing: at last, his own screenplay, to be filmed with Kazan and to feature a small role for himself. All those boyhood dreams of Hollywood were becoming reality, not in the ways he once had imagined, but true nonetheless. Such a prospect probably helped to comfort Inge in early 1960, when otherwise he would have had a greater cause for alarm than critical rejection: he had lost his special personal relationship with Barbara Baxley, and he had for the first time gone seriously against the advice of his excellent agent, Audrey Wood. Those were significant changes: the former reinforced the lonely pattern of his life, the latter foreshadowed the bad business and creative judgments that were to follow.

HOLLYWOOD provided considerable balm for Inge's hurts as he began the new decade of the 1960s. The failure of *A Loss of Roses* was of no great moment in Hollywood, where the cash-value memory of the three hit films made from Inge's first three Broadway plays was still strong, and where *The Dark at the Top of the Stairs* was now being filmed. John Connolly, who accompanied Inge on his increasingly lengthy stays in the Los Angeles area, remembers that Inge found his time there pleasantly distracting. To visit with people such as David O. Selznick and Jennifer Jones thrilled Inge, who seemed at the time to have retained his childhood worship of stars and big-name producers.[36] In New York, he was the author of a resounding recent failure; in Hollywood, he was a genius whose stories were the stuff of almost sure-fire hit films.

Actress Shirley Knight recalls Inge's visit to the film set of *The Dark at the Top of the Stairs*. Although Inge had nothing to do with the production of the film (the screenplay was by Irving Ravetch and Harriet Frank, Jr.), he was received with great respect. Knight, who played the daughter, Reenie Flood, was thrilled when Inge told her that she looked just like a girl from Kansas, and she could tell him, to his delight indeed, that she was from the

Lyons, Kansas area.[37] The film of *Stairs*, which starred Knight, Robert Preston, Dorothy McGuire, and Eve Arden, was released in 1960 and quickly became the fourth consecutive successful movie made from an Inge play. Without question, Hollywood was hospitable to William Inge. Best of all, Inge was working in Hollywood with Elia Kazan, who had directed *Stairs* on Broadway (Delbert Mann directed the film) and who was proof that the worlds of New York theater and Hollywood could be successfully bridged.

Kazan had powerful faith in the story Inge had created in *Splendor in the Grass*. Essentially about young love thwarted by parental fears and prejudices, *Splendor* had evolved from a variety of Inge's previous experiences and writing. The setting is an oil-boom small Kansas town, again, unmistakably Independence; Bud Stamper and Deanie Loomis, the ill-fated young lovers, have antecedents in two earlier published one-act plays, *Bus Riley's Back in Town* and *Glory in the Flower*, as well as several unpublished variations of those two plays. The central conflict caused by the sexual inhibitions and materialistic priorities of the couple's parents was by now a familiar characteristic of Inge's work.

The excellent working relationship between Inge and Kazan was strengthened by their mutual belief in the poignancy of this story, which involves, rather improbably, Bud's and Deanie's repression and frustration to such extreme degree that he becomes physically and she mentally ill. Their separation is forced by Bud's father, who insists that Bud find a "loose" girl for the time being and wait to marry Deanie until after he has gone to Yale, and by Deanie's mother, who denounces sex as something "nice girls" neither do nor can possibly enjoy, even after marriage. Bud finds the sex object his father recommends, and Deanie attempts suicide because of what she believes is Bud's total rejection of her. She is then sent to a mental hospital, and Bud goes to Yale. Each of them winds up marrying someone else. Both are forced to accept what has happened, and they are determined somehow, as the Wordsworth poem that furnishes the title states, to "find / Strength in what remains behind" in their lives.

Work on *Splendor* had actually begun while Kazan was still directing *Stairs* in New York. Inge had shown Kazan the story, which at that time was not written specifically as a screenplay. Kazan had immediately liked it and suggested that it could be made into an excellent original film. Thus, Inge began to draft it with the screen in mind, taking advantage of the freedom of movement and setting that film would allow.[38] In late 1958, both Inge and Kazan, along with one of Kazan's assistants, visited Independence so that Kazan could get a feel for the location.[39] Eventually the film was shot, not in Kansas, but at the Filmways studio in New York City, with certain location shots on Long Island, Staten Island, and near Vassar in Poughkeepsie. But Kazan had captured the "look" of Kansas, and he was able to create it for the film.[40]

Inge described his working relationship with Kazan to interviewer Philip Bayard Clarkson as almost like having "an affair." Kazan would seek a personal insight into the psychology of each character, each line, and ask countless intricate questions to that end. Inge credited the success of *Splendor* to Kazan's vital interest in the script and his willingness to probe it and throw his personal, influential director's weight behind it.[41] Having Kazan's collaboration and support must have been reassuring for Inge after the debacles of Brustein's article and the failure of *Roses*. He was creating a major motion picture with an Academy Award–winning director and producer, and he was enjoying not only a sterling writer's reputation in the film capital but also a cameo role in the film as the Reverend Whiteman, the generally ineffectual would-be spiritual leader of the community.

Casting for *Splendor* also proved fortuitous. Natalie Wood, a beautiful young actress who was already very well established since she had been a child star, was chosen to play Wilma Dean ("Deanie") Loomis. Inge, who had been impressed by the dedication, talent, and striking good looks of Warren Beatty in *Roses*, convinced Kazan that Beatty would be excellent in his film debut as Bud Stamper. Pat Hingle, who had played Rubin Flood for Inge and Kazan in the Broadway production of *Stairs*, was cast in the important role of Ace Stamper, Bud's oppressive oil-rich father. Audrey Christie was cast as Deanie's equally oppressive, devastatingly inhibited mother. The filming generated considerable publicity, particularly because Kazan and Warner Brothers let it be known that Hollywood's censors had insisted on cutting certain scenes that involved nudity and sex play.

John Connolly, who attended a censorship screening with Inge and Kazan before the film was released, recalls two scenes in particular that had to be cut: the first was a wide-angle shot of Natalie Wood's naked backside as she was running down a half-darkened hallway; the other was a scene in which the fully clothed Beatty and Wood were wrestling playfully on the floor and, for a brief moment, Beatty was on top of Wood. Both of these scenes were excised from the film as released in America, but Connolly says the hallway shot was not cut from the European release.[42] Such cutting ironically reflected the very prudery that lies at the heart of the thematic conflict in the story, but it did not ultimately mar the effectiveness of the film. Moreover, the publicity about the censorship helped to create audience interest in the film, which opened to packed theaters in 1961.

Despite *Splendor*'s almost immediate box-office success, most critics didn't like it. *Esquire*'s Dwight Macdonald, recalling Warner Brothers' full-page ad for the film in the *New York Times* ("A Controversial New Motion Picture Has Caused an Event Unparalleled in Theatre History"), said he saw nothing of the kind in the film, whose theme seemed to be "Should a Nice Girl Sleep with Him or Go to a Mental Hospital? And: Should a Clean-Living Boy (etc.) or Go to Yale?" Likening the film to a Victorian melodrama revved up by Kazan's direction, Macdonald accused Inge of exaggeration, because it was hard to believe that Kansas parents in 1928 were "stupid to the point of villainy" and that their children were "sexually frustrated to the point of lunacy." At least, Macdonald had to admit, the film's downbeat ending was believable.[43]

Stanley Kauffmann, writing in the *New Republic*, noted that the story line of *Splendor* was similar to that of *Summer and Smoke*, a play by "Inge's master, Tennessee Williams." The effect, Kauffmann however noted, "is less like a high-school version of Williams's play than an Andy Hardy story with glands." Deciding that "Inge is preaching the dangers of [sexual] abstinence," Kauffmann declared that "a Martian who saw this film might infer that all adolescents deprived of sexual intercourse go crazy." He blasted the film's "simplistic, mechanical view of sex and life and its protracted sententiousness."[44] Brendan Gill, writing in the *New Yorker*, called *Splendor* "as phony a picture as I can remember seeing." Bud and Deanie, he asserted, "bear practically no relation to young people in real life," and though Inge and Kazan must have known this, they had "devised" the film "neither to instruct our minds or to move our hearts but to arouse a prurient interest and produce a box-office smasheroo."[45] Similar barbs appeared in other reviews, but the filmgoing public seemed to agree with *Newsweek*'s anonymous reviewer, who praised *Splendor* as "one of the richest American movies in years" and lauded the script, the acting, and most of all, Kazan's directing.[46]

Granted that Warner Brothers' hype whetted the audience's appetite, the *Newsweek* reviewer's adjective, "American," seems significant to understanding *Splendor*'s success. Dwight Macdonald had praised such contemporary foreign films as *L'Avventura*, *Hiroshima Mon Amour*, and *Breathless* while condemning *Splendor* as being neither innovative nor controversial nor very good (p. 69). But sexual frustration and the pain of inhibition were still fascinating subjects to Americans of the early 1960s, and as the *Newsweek* reviewer said, *Splendor*'s story was "as American as apple pie," even if it did seem extreme (p. 112). Film critics in 1961 did not possess the influence to "close" a movie the way New York theater critics could close a Broadway play. *Splendor* played in theaters all over America, and overwhelmingly the audiences liked it. Perhaps the Warner Brothers hype netted Inge his Academy Award nomination for best original screenplay for an American film, but it is doubtful that *Splendor*'s audiences would have objected.

INGE WAS riding a popular crest again—his last—in early 1962. His name had been emblazoned on the technicolor screen in 1960 (*Stairs*) and again in 1961 (*Splendor*). And even though some critics implied that in its final form, *Splendor* was more Elia Kazan's story than Inge's, Inge was nominated for the Academy Award. His one-act play *The Mall* had appeared in *Esquire* in January, 1959, and a shortened version of *A Loss of Roses* had appeared in its January, 1960, issue. He was revising a new play for Broadway, another Oedipal drama called *Natural Affection*. This one was set, not in Kansas in the past, but in present-day Chicago. Already he had been shopping for a producer for *Natural Affection*, having, at different times, talked with Cheryl Crawford and Robert Alan Aurthur. In fact, at one time Aurthur agreed to produce *Natural Affection*, but later he backed out because Inge kept vacillating about the script and because the details of their deal were finally not mutually agreeable.[47]

Inge also had a contract with Sol Siegel of Metro-Goldwyn-Mayer Studios to adapt James Leo Herlihy's novel *All Fall Down* for the screen. Inge had been reluctant to do such adaptations, but Herlihy was a New York friend, and Inge genuinely liked the novel, which had to do with conflict between brothers who are affected by an overprotective and dominating mother. Moreover, Siegel had made the screen-adaptation project financially attractive.[48] In addition to the *All Fall Down* project, Inge was readying eleven one-act plays (most of them the more revealing short plays he had written in the early to mid 1950s) for publication by Random House, along with *Summer Brave*, his preferred version of *Picnic*—the one that Joshua Logan had so vigorously opposed. With these various projects he was taking advantage of his recent crest of popularity to become more versatile and also to be more assertive; in the Preface to *Summer Brave and Eleven Short Plays*, he stated that he preferred *Summer Brave* to *Picnic*, despite the awards that *Picnic* had won, because he believed that *Summer Brave* was "more humorously true than *Picnic*" and that it fulfilled his "original intentions."[49] He also had to be keenly aware that some of the one-act plays treated more sensitive material than had any of his previously published work. Critics, he must have reasoned, would have a harder time stereotyping his work after some of those newer projects had appeared.

In most of these dealings, Inge had depended less and less upon the guidance and expertise of his long-time faithful agent, Audrey Wood. It was as though Audrey's having advised him to close *A Loss of Roses* had either shaken his faith in her or caused him to suspect that she no longer was always acting in his best interest. Nothing could have been further from the truth, according not only to Wood but also to John Connolly and others who were in frequent contact with Inge at about this time.[50] Nevertheless, he gradually began not to depend on Wood's advice, and his gratitude for her previous inestimable help to his career nearly disappeared altogether for a time. In fact, when he was interviewed for a mostly complimentary 1962 *Esquire* article on Wood, Inge implied that she had contributed to the failure of *A Loss of Roses* on Broadway by not having been firm enough in recommending that he close the show, a very curious fault to find, especially since Wood had very carefully and respectfully but emphatically urged that the show be closed.[51] Relating this incident in her memoirs, the puzzled but forgiving Wood remarked, "Do I have to explain any further how difficult it is to be an agent?" (p. 234).

Wood was not the only one of Inge's associates to find his behavior troubling in 1962. Connolly could see that although *Splendor* and the other pending projects had made Inge successful again, the shuttling among New York, Hollywood, and Stockbridge was creating more than geographical flux: Inge was changing his emotional and creative bearings as well. He was too dazzled by the routine praise of Hollywood contacts, whose habitual hyperbole he too desperately wanted to hear because it helped him forget criticism such as Brustein's. Intelligent and realistically discerning in most situations, Inge lost or deliberately blunted those faculties in the distracting whirl of filmdom, as otherwise mature adult men often do around younger sports heroes. The make-believe wonder of his childhood fascination with films seemed to return in the first flush of his success with *Splendor*, and it was fed by the nomination for an Academy Award. Connolly saw how this experience was distracting Inge emotionally, and he understood the reasons for it.

If all such distraction signaled was merely a brief honeymoon with Hollywood, it might not have been so costly. But Connolly also noticed changes in Inge's writing. Increasingly he was deserting the materials and the language closest to his creative vision, leaving the rural midwestern venues of the past that he had made so familiar for the modern cities (a trend that would soon become evident in such plays as *Natural Affection* and *Where's Daddy?*) and adding "hip" phraseology that tried to sound "with it" but was clearly phony. Examples of this misfiring language can be found in an unpublished manuscript from this period, *Bud Dooley's Revenge*, yet another version of the Bus Riley material. In this manuscript, Inge's pot-smoking character Dooley says to a party-minded friend: "By midnight, we'll have this room so full of chicks. . . ." Elsewhere in the same manuscript, Jackie, the female lead in the play, tells her psychiatrist that she finds the rebellious Bud attractive because he seems "to come from another kind of world, a world of bookies, and racetracks, and jazz musicians, and drag races, and, oh I don't know." Indeed, Inge didn't know if he thought Jackie's list of "worlds" was a likely combination to be found in one person.[52]

Another New York friend, Robert Whitehead, who had produced *Bus Stop*, also thought that film writing would ultimately be damaging to Inge's creativity. Film writers, he noted, had to produce material that too often was not only not respected by film makers but was also not at all close to the vision and inspiration of the writer. Hollywood, he suggested in an interview about Inge many years later, was liable to ask Inge to write about something alien to him, such as race cars. "Now you know Bill wasn't going to come up with a good story about race cars."[53] So far as I know, Inge never did any screen writing about race cars; but he was soon to learn just how little his original writing for the screen might be respected.

While these changes were under way, Inge seems to have been aware of them. He told a *Newsweek* reporter in 1962: "I'm going through a metamorphosis — just what kind I don't know. But I know I've got to change."[54] Why Inge believed he had to change undoubtedly had complex personal causes, mostly rooted in such mercurial events of 1958 through 1961 as Maude's death, Brustein's criticism, the failure of *Roses*, the success of *Splendor*, and the round of harsh criticism that followed both the play and the film. The criticism, in particular, is an important key, for acceptance and approval of his work had long been the energizing element in Inge's life. If Inge read such criticism of *Splendor* as that by Gerald Weales (and he probably did), he could not have helped being stung into thinking that perhaps his work had to change. Referring to Inge's cameo role as Reverend Whiteman, Weales wrote that Inge

reveals himself as kindly and ineffectual, moved by sympathy and cliche. No actor and with no part to act, Inge can only look out sadly from large and liquid eyes at a world in which good intentions are of no consequence and where all of us must settle for second best. The same eyes have been looking at the same world in all of Inge's plays, beginning with his first and best, *Come Back, Little Sheba*.[55]

Weales thereby reduced a decade of award-winning success to a decade of perpetual decline. The most lamentable thing about such critical excess is that William Inge was probably one of the few people who took Weales completely seriously.

But the criticism isn't the sole reason for Inge's changes during the early 1960s. Maude's death seems to have eased some inhibitions; as already noted, soon after Maude's death in 1958, Inge made public his alcoholism and psychoanalysis. He by no means would directly reveal his homosexuality, but after Maude's death, one can trace male characters in his work that increasingly show homosexual tendencies, beginning with the traveling actor Ronny Cavendish in *A Loss of Roses* and proceeding through Vince Brinkman in *Natural Affection* to the obviously homosexual Pinky Pinkerton in *Where's Daddy?* and culminating in such homosexual characters in the late, mostly unpublished, work as Archie, the gay death-row prisoner in *The Last Pad*; the suicidal writer Byron Todd in *The Love Death*, the one-act play that constitutes Inge's own suicidal note; and—though he stops just short of acknowledging his homosexuality—Joey Hansen, the autobiographical protagonist of *My Son Is a Splendid Driver*. There is more evidence that in his own tentative and tortured way, William Inge began "coming out" in his work after 1958.

Random House's 1962 publication of such one-act plays as *The Boy in the Basement* and *The Tiny Closet*, which feature the homosexual Spencer Scranton and the transvestite Mr. Newbold, is also indicative of Inge's greater frankness. Here was material that had been written nearly ten years earlier, but was only now being made public by its creator. *The Boy in the Basement* is almost surely a play Inge would not have wanted Maude to see in her lifetime. It seems an inescapable conclusion that as Inge continued to write throughout the 1960s, he increasingly was showing his own painful passage of experience as a reluctant homosexual amid his various attempts to write something that would again mesh with the tenor of the times and the tastes of popular audiences. Such 1960s manuscripts in the Inge Collection as *Caesarian Operations*, *The Last Pad*, *The Killing*, *Midwestern Manic*, and *The Love Death*, most of which remain unpublished, are all plays that feature male homosexuals in key roles. An unpublished last novel, *The Boy from the Circus*, is a jumbled, mostly angry confessional that conveys the bitter frustrations of someone who at last has come to resent having to be ashamed of his very nature.[56]

This increasing incidence of male homosexuality in Inge's work is a natural extension for a writer who always did write out of intensely felt personal experience; autobiographical characters appear, in greater or lesser roles and shadings, in almost all of his published major work: Doc Delaney in *Sheba*, Rosemary Sydney in *Picnic*, both Professor Lyman and Virgil Blessing in *Bus Stop*, Sonny Flood in *Stairs*, Ronny Cavendish and Kenny Baird in *Roses*, Vince Brinkman in *Natural Affection*, Pinky Pinkerton in *Where's Daddy?* Evelyn Wyckoff in the 1970 novel *Good Luck, Miss Wyckoff*, and Joey Hansen in *My Son Is a Splendid Driver*. The change toward presenting more homosexuality after 1958 might have been Inge's key to more success in the 1960s if he had somehow been able to present it in the more familiar context of his midwestern past. But except for the last two published novels, he deserted that time and place setting, which was so vital to his vision, and except for *Driver*, he also deserted the reticent speech—so resonant with submerged meaning—that had marked his work during the 1950s.

As John Connolly put it, Inge began to fear in the early 1960s that he might be "old-fashioned," that his careful backward glances to the rural Midwest of the 1920s and 1930s would no longer provide him with successful material.[57] Certainly, the critics were beginning to suggest this with their charges of sentimentality and cliché. Perhaps after *Splendor*, Inge began to hear such suggestions in California as well. Whatever was the case, he not only seemed to stop listening closely to his best friends and advisors, especially if they were in New York; he also seemed to stop listening closely to himself, to his inner voices, and to stop closely examining his storehouse of environmental experience. Thus, although he was to keep writing all during the 1960s and although several of his works from that decade were to appear, both on stage and in print, he was never again to experience success.

INGE OF course did not know it then, but on Academy Awards night in 1962 he was standing in the bright light of national celebrity for the last time. Connolly's recollection of that night and the events leading up to it show again the tremendous tension between fear of failure and desire for approval that coiled within Inge.

Although he was delighted with the nomination, at first Inge wasn't sure that he wanted to attend the Academy Award ceremonies, which were to be nationally televised. The pressure would be great, rather like an opening night. Moreover, the organizers of the ceremonies wanted the nominees to sit near the stage, an appalling notion to Inge, who always preferred the anonymity and quick avenue of escape of an aisle seat on the back row, even at performances with which he had absolutely nothing to do. As if that were not enough, the studio wanted him to attend the occasion with a starlet, a total stranger. In a stew, Inge finally decided to attend when the studio relented on the matter of escorting a starlet. But then he realized that he would have to attend alone—another appalling thought—unless Connolly, the only person he would feel comfortable enough with, would come.

The problem now was that Connolly, who never liked California and spent only such time as was necessary there with Inge, was in New York. Fortunately, Connolly had time to drive to California, bringing some extra things with him, before the ceremonies. A few days later, with just a couple of days to go before the ceremonies, a road-weary Connolly arrived back in California—just in time for Inge to realize that he absolutely had to wear his own tuxedo (a rental wouldn't do) and that his tuxedo was still in the Sutton Place apartment in New York. And so, Connolly again crossed the country, this time by air, and brought back the tuxedo. Despite the excitement of the occasion, it was doubtless with relief that Connolly settled into his seat near the stage on awards night.

But not Inge. The program had barely begun when, after telling Connolly "I can't stand it," Inge rose and sought the refuge of the back of the theater. Thus, when the dramatic moment arrived and Inge was named the winner of the Academy Award for the best original American screenplay, he had to make his long way from the rear, walking, it seemed to Connolly, as if in slow motion while "the music played endlessly."[58]

After the program, Inge was still clutching his Oscar, and he refused to relinquish it so that it could be put on display at the post-ceremonies party at the Beverly Wilshire Hotel, along with several others won that night. Instead, Inge insisted that it be locked in the trunk of the car. At the Beverly Wilshire, Inge moved as though in a fog, even though, as usual, he was not drinking. It was an overwhelming occasion, perhaps the actual climax of his life. Certainly, Connolly believes it was, in the precise dramatic sense of the word, for Connolly thinks that winning the Academy Award encouraged Inge in the changes that he had begun, justified those changes in Inge's mind, and ensured that he and his writing would never again be as before.[59]

In the Inge Collection there is a most curious undated note in Inge's hand. It is impossible to tell when it was written, but it was clearly written at a time of great stress. It, too, seems to corroborate the climactic effect that

Holding his Academy Award for Splendor in the Grass, *Inge poses with (left to right) Abby Mann, Lee Remick, and Jack Lemmon. Courtesy of WIC/ICC*

the Academy Award had on Inge; it also seems to augur the sad denouement his life:

> I win a most important prize for a movie I wrote, but when I see the movie I find that E.K., my director, has changed my own writing with bad super-imposed dialogue. And I find that winning the prize obligates me to be a member of a mafia group of men who have beheaded a female enemy. Several of us (men & women) are going up in an elevator when I discover my situation. I decline to accompany the group any further, knowing that my leaving the group could [Inge's correction] will make me liable to their revenge, and that I might even be beheaded myself.[60]

How much of this note is based on fact and how much of it is paranoiac allegory are as impossible to ascertain as the date it was written. But it is striking how it encapsulates both the triumph and the travail of Inge's screen-writing experience; how it suggests, however fancifully, the reasons for the cooling of Inge's relationship with Kazan (they never worked together again after *Splendor*); how it symbolizes the end of Inge's ascent; and how it even foreshadows his death.

INGE IMPLIED to *Newsweek* magazine in 1962 that he had moved to Holly-wood permanently.[61] But even though he was spending most of his time there by then, living in rented properties, he retained his Sutton Place apartment and stayed there when he had to be in New York, as when he was working out details for the coming production of *Natural Affection*. Gradually he phased therapy at Stockbridge out of his life. In fact, psychoanalysis became less and less personally important to him during the 1960s as he began to realize that, while it helped, it did not solve his emotional problems. *Where's Daddy?* his last Broadway play (1966), is criti-cal of the value of psychoanalysis; a brief 1970 "statement" about his own psychoanalysis, which rather clinically calls it a "great learning experience" that better enables one "to face the complexity of life today," pointedly avoids details.[62] At the time of his last interview, he told Lloyd Steele that psychotherapy had helped him "at the time" but that he "would never do it again."[63] And so, as New York began to fade more and more from his routine experience, so did psychotherapy. This was another important change for Inge, however gradually it took place, because psychotherapy *had* helped him in profound ways, both in informing his art and in understand-ing himself.

Psychoanalysis provided insight and understanding; it even reinforced the powerful theme of acceptance and adjustment that echoes in all his im-portant work. But it could not ultimately make his own acceptances and adjustments for him. These he had to make for himself, and as the 1960s continued and his career declined despite all his efforts, the emotional and spiritual strengths he needed to keep writing, keep trying, and keep living began to wane. What attempts he did make to restore his equilibrium were desperate, involving not only more psychotherapy but also a flirtation with the occult and, near the end, a half-hearted conversion to Catholicism. But ultimately, he could muster no more faith in these than he any longer could in psychotherapy.[64] However, in 1962, this severe emotional and spiritual erosion was just beginning, and Inge had his many follow-up projects to *Splendor* to keep that erosion from hastening.

All Fall Down, Inge's screenplay adaptation of Herlihy's novel, was a pos-itive experience for him in a number of ways. For one thing, he liked the story very much because of its strong element of family conflict rooted in a dominating mother. For another, he was working with John Frankenheimer, a director who respected him and his script. The cast included Warren Beatty, for whose rapidly rising star Inge could justifiably take some credit; and Bar-bara Baxley, with whom he had managed to make some amends for the fiasco of her not getting the part of Lila in *A Loss of Roses*. Baxley's marriage after the *Roses* business had proved to be the mistake that both she and Inge had sensed it would be, and the two enjoyed being near each other again, even though they would never again seriously consider the possibility of their own marriage.[65]

Naturally, Inge did not receive the attention for *All Fall Down* that he would have received had the story been originally his, but the film got mostly good reviews, and Inge received his fair share of credit. In the *New Yorker*, Brendan Gill called Inge's screenplay "skillful" and "in some respects more original than the original."[66] *Newsweek*'s reviewer called the movie "exciting" and praised the direction, the cast, and Inge's script, which he said "is content to suggest what novelist Herlihy sometimes harped on."[67] Still, the film didn't please all of the critics. Philip T. Hartung in *Commonweal* said he was "getting a bit fed-up with the frustrated papas and neurotic mamas whose confused kids can't tell their elbows from their ears." The Willart family in *All Fall Down*, Hartung continued, is "typical," and "since the film's script was written by William Inge . . . these Ohio people are Inged with the same stresses that strained the beset characters in his 'Picnic' and 'Splendor in the Grass.'"[68] *All Fall Down* was an entry at the Cannes festival, but ultimately it did not achieve the commercial or artistic success that its producer, John Houseman, and Frankenheimer had hoped for. For Inge, however, it was his last pleasant experience working in films.

Frankenheimer apparently made very few changes in Inge's script for *All Fall Down*. Inge placed more focus on the Warren Beatty character, Berryberry Willart, than Herlihy's novel does; but the effect is a nearly clinical study of Berry-berry's misogyny (clearly caused by his mother's smothering), which sets in more convincing relief the final independent maturity of Clinton Willart, the protagonist. At the end of the film, Clinton no longer admires and tries to emulate Berry-berry, whom he now sees as pathetic. The slight shifting of focus ultimately helps the film succeed without actually changing Herlihy's characters, theme, or resolution, a circumstance Herlihy undoubtedly appreciated.

Frankenheimer did make one interesting change. In the original script, Inge had some scenes involving a car rejoining traffic. Frankenheimer shot these scenes, but he later cut them, as Philip Bayard Clarkson reports, "because it looked as if the message was that to be well-adjusted one had to drive well."[69] That Inge could imagine skillful driving as an indicator of emotional adjustment does not seem so strange when one remembers how resentful and jealous he once had been of Maude's bragging about the driving skills of Luther Boy, a memory so strong it prompted the title of his final published novel. Moreover, he went so long without owning a car that he never became a confident, expert driver himself; ordinarily he depended upon others to drive him—usually Connolly and, later, before he left New York, Mark Minton. For Inge, automobiles seemed to be roughly symbolic of the modern age, which increasingly befuddled him.

Robert Alan Aurthur, in his *Esquire* tribute after Inge's death, recalls the day Inge called before driving over to show him the script of *Natural Affection*:

> Less than an hour later, piloting a white convertible, top down, Inge was in my driveway, and as my kids and I peered out a kitchen window he just sat there. When finally I went out he was red-faced, staring straight ahead. "I can't get out of the goddamn seat belt," he said. It took a lot of dual fumbling to release him, and given the circumstances a moment that should have been hilarious wasn't even funny.[70]

Many associates, from his New York as well as his California days, have commented on Inge's dislike of driving. The list includes Connolly, Minton, Barbara Baxley, and Jack Garfein. Inge was, simply, none too good at it; he allowed his fear, anger, and frustration to show behind the wheel. The incident in Aurthur's driveway seems typical.

All Fall Down and Inge's aversion to automobile driving offer one more interesting and ironic observation. In *All Fall Down*, Echo O'Brien, the beautiful thirtyish house guest, tells Annabelle Willart why she never married a young man she once loved: he had committed suicide by inhaling the exhaust from an automobile in his closed garage. When William Inge chose to take his own life on June 10, 1973, he did the same thing.

AFTER THE release of *All Fall Down*, Inge turned his attention to *Natural Affection*, a play that had been in various stages of revision for quite some time. Cheryl Crawford had read a version of it in 1960, as had Robert Alan Aurthur. A letter from Inge to Crawford, dated September 14, 1960, thanks her for her interest in producing it but names Aurthur as the producer.[71] Aurthur, of course, later declined to produce it, partly because he and Inge couldn't agree on rewrites. In a letter from Inge to John Gassner on October 25, 1960, Inge tells Gassner, "I'm eager for you to read my new play, *Natural*

Affection, but I keep doing little rewrites."[72] Many more rewrites were to follow, some by Inge's choice, some at the urging of potential producers. Robert Whitehead and Roger L. Stevens, who had produced *Bus Stop*, were interested in bringing *Natural Affection* to New York, but they declined to produce it because, after a production in Texas (probably in Dallas), Inge refused to make revisions that Whitehead believed were necessary. Whitehead later said that his decision not to produce *Natural Affection* did not anger Inge; they simply disagreed without impairing their friendship.[73]

Vacillating about revisions of *Natural Affection* was probably the result of Inge's fear of a second Broadway failure, mixed with his new-found desire to be more assertive about his work. Apparently, revisions he made of his own accord were all right; revisions urged by anyone else – even if they came from Broadway-wise friends such as Whitehead – were suspect. At any rate, how the eventual Broadway production differed from earlier trial productions (at the Sombrero Playhouse in Phoenix in February, 1962, and the Texas production by Whitehead and Stevens) is guesswork.[74] Inge finally found producers who apparently did not urge him to do rewrites he didn't want to make: Oliver Smith and Manuel Seff. The British director Tony Richardson was then hired to direct *Natural Affection*, which was scheduled to open in New York at the Booth Theatre on January 31, 1963.

Richardson had a good cast. Kim Stanley, who had begun her career on Broadway as Millie Owens in *Picnic* and had achieved full stardom there as Cherie in *Bus Stop*, was cast as the mother in the Oedipal relationship, Sue Barker. Gregory Rozakis won the role of Donnie, her juvenile-delinquent son. Harry Guardino was cast as Sue's generally no-good, parasitic live-in lover, Bernie Slovenk. Tom Bosley and Monica May were cast as Vince and Claire Brinkman, Sue and Bernie's neighbors in their Chicago apartment house. The rehearsals and trial performances apparently went well, although Inge was surely nervous about this follow-up to *A Loss of Roses*, which, although it also had an Oedipal theme, was not set in his familiar Kansas of the past; moreover, it featured the strongest language and the most violent stage action that he had yet written.

Essentially, *Natural Affection* is about Sue Barker's dilemma: she must choose between keeping Bernie, her lover, or Donnie, her son, whom she had borne seventeen years earlier out of wedlock and who has returned for Christmas from reform school with the news that he can stay, if Sue will take responsibility for giving him the home and the parental guidance that she had not been able to give him when he was younger. Sue had placed

Donnie in an orphanage because of her poverty after his birth; later, when she had a good job and had taken him back, he was already delinquent and unmanageable and soon got into the legal trouble that had landed him in reform school. She feels love for and considerable guilt about Donnie, who Inge takes care to show has an erotic fixation on her.

Bernie, on the other hand, satisfies Sue's need for the illusion of love through sex; and he keeps her hoping that he will marry her, although he clearly has neither reason nor plan to do so. In fact, he spends part of his sexual energy in secret assignations with Claire, the woman next door, who has no use for her husband, Vince, because he is an aging drunk with scarcely concealed homosexual designs on Bernie. Into this sordid little apartment-house neighborhood comes Donnie, who quickly becomes Bernie's rival for Sue's affection and who realizes contemptuously how Bernie is using Sue.

Events force Sue to choose, and Donnie tries to make her choice easier by telling her about Bernie and Claire. He clearly wants to be the man in his mother's life, and when Sue, who does not want to believe the truth about Bernie, rejects Donnie, Inge's most violent scene occurs. Sue has run from the apartment to find Bernie, when a drunken woman, a stranger who has been at a party at the Brinkmans', wanders in through the open door. She tries to seduce Donnie; but instead of having sex with this mother-surrogate, as Kenny does in *A Loss of Roses*, Donnie brutally murders her with a large kitchen knife. He then puts on his "twist" dance record, turns up the volume, and goes to the refrigerator to drink calmly from a milk container before he "walks out of the apartment forever, the twist music still blasting behind him."[75]

Shortly before *Natural Affection* opened on schedule on January 31, 1963, New York's newspapers went on a strike that continued until well after opening night. Thus, while immediate criticism was hampered by the strike, so were advertisements, noncritical feature stories, and other forms of newspaper publicity. This strike, in the opinion of Audrey Wood, Barbara Baxley, and others, hurt the play's launching and helped to doom it to failure.[76] But as the reviews began gradually to appear, it became clear that criticism would also play a part in the play's failure, strike or no strike. Most of the reviews were harsh, and many took direct aim at Inge.

New York's established newspaper critics, unable to share their views in their respective papers, expressed them in *First Nite* for the week of February 4. Norman Nadel of the *World-Telegram* and the *Sun* noted two errors that kept the powerful team of Richardson and Inge from presenting a great play: bad taste and bad judgment. These errors, he noted, seemed to stem from "an eagerness to produce the dirtiest play of the season," in which overt sex play and shocking language diverted attention from the conflict. If that weren't bad enough, Nadel argued, as did many other critics, that the gratuitous murder at the end destroys any compassion for Donnie that the play might otherwise engender and "shatters all previous values."[77] Robert Coleman of the *New York Mirror* called the play "as shocking as anything to come from the pen of Tennessee Williams"; it outdid Edward Albee's *Who's Afraid of Virginia Woolf?* in its "dip into the lexicon of four-letter words." Coleman lamented that the play, which was "loaded with sex, smut and shock," was unfortunately what "a vast segment of the public wants."[78]

Richard Watts, Jr., of the *New York Post* considered it "a matter of enormous importance when something goes seriously wrong" with a playwright of Inge's stature. Trying to fathom why Inge "failed so embarrassingly," particularly in the "overwrought sensationalism" of the second half of the play, Watts wondered:

Could it be that Mr. Inge, subconsciously imagining that the procession of American dramatists was threatening to pass him by, decided it was the qualities of sensationalism in the work of Williams and Albee that gave them their excellence and set out to beat them at their own game?

If this surmise is in any way correct, he made a terrible blunder, but it is one he can easily avoid in the future. For the fact proved by "Natural Affection" is that the sensationally lurid is not Mr. Inge's field. Instead of seeming an integral part of his work, it appears to be clumsily imposed, and, in the process of trying it, his splendid capacity for compassion and human understanding slowly disappear, and a kind of extravagant foolishness and ineptness is substituted.[79]

It may well be that Watts's surmise was at least partially correct. Although he may not have wanted to seem to be trying to outdo such recent plays as Williams's *Night of the Iguana* and Albee's *Who's Afraid of Virginia Woolf?* Inge had to be aware of those plays, and he must have realized that they were more risqué than anything he had presented to audiences during the 1950s. Moreover, there were the aforementioned changes that Inge was gradually undergoing, changes prompted at least in part by his fear of his work's being old-fashioned and too sentimental. The trouble was, as Watts said, "the sensationally lurid is not Mr. Inge's field."

John Chapman of the *New York Daily News* struck another note of truth when he wrote:

> In such greatly superior plays as "Come Back, Little Sheba" and "Picnic," Inge has shown natural affection for many of his characters, and touching insight into them. He just doesn't seem to like anybody, or understand anybody, in his newest play.
>
> Unless it is the character of a drunken neighbor, played by Tom Bosley. In a fit of remorse during a hangover, Bosley has an excellent scene in which he admits the whole world baffles him.[80]

Inge admitted such bafflement in his Preface to the Random House edition of *Natural Affection*. His play, he said, stemmed from "the tension I felt living in the late fifties and early sixties, when the newspapers were so full of violence that the morning headlines were an assault upon one's breakfast digestion." The times seemed to be desperate and irrational, he continued, causing people to feel rejected, unimportant, and consequently vulnerable to rage that can end in violence. "I wanted to expose some of the atmosphere in our lives that creates violence," he concluded; "I wish I could have written a comedy, but I couldn't at the time."[81]

As the magazine reviews of *Natural Affection* began to appear, Inge doubtless felt more of the anger, fostered by rejection, that he spoke about in the Preface. Edith Oliver, in the *New Yorker*, accused Inge of trying to be a "junior-varsity Tennessee Williams."[82] Inge's original critical nemesis, Robert Brustein, writing in the *New Republic*, called *Natural Affection* "a monstrous chimera proceeding from a heat-oppressed brain"; and continued:

> William Inge, formerly the sweetheart of the old ladies in the mezzanine, has climaxed his story of adultery, homosexuality, alcoholism, incest, nymphomania, and juvenile delinquency with a scene in which a boy stabs a woman he believes to be his mother, has intercourse with the corpse, and then drinks a carton of milk.[83]

Brustein's broadside rings so well that it seems a quibble to protest that Donnie clearly doesn't believe the woman he kills is Sue and that Inge presents no such intercourse in the published version of the play. (How could Brustein have omitted necrophilia from his list?)

Newsweek's reviewer called *Natural Affection* "a psychiatric skin show" that constituted "one of the uglier spectacles of the day," even though the cast was excellent and Tony Richardson had directed "as though he believed the play had something to say." All the play really said, however, according to this reviewer, was "that Tennessee Williams had a legitimate worry when he confessed that jealousy of Inge helped land him on a psychiatrist's couch."[84] What relevance that remark has is a mystery, considering that the reviewer clearly did not consider *Natural Affection* a success and therefore hardly a cause for Williams's jealousy. But it is representative of frequent critical comparisons of Inge and Williams during the early 1960s which tried to disparage the work of both men while still charging each with being either too much or not enough like the other. Inge increasingly got the worst of such comparisons, however, and that could only add to his chagrin.

Natural Affection closed after only thirty-six performances. When *Roses* failed, Inge stopped in Nashville to see Helene on his way toward refuge in California. This time, he stopped in Toledo to see his favorite niece, Jo Ann Kirchmaier. It was a typically brief stay, but this time, Inge complained more bitterly than usual about New York, especially its merciless critics. California, he reiterated, as he had before in letters and visits, was the place for him. He left Toledo in such a hurry to get to California that to his niece's astonishment, he was willing to fly. "I don't care if the plane goes down," he told her.[85] He may well have meant it.

IN EARLY 1963, California was still a warm and hospitable place in Inge's mind. He had written to Jo Ann on December 15, 1962, just before rehearsals for *Natural Affection* began: "It will be a great relief to get this play out of the way, so I can return to California. After two winters out there, I find myself very squeamish about this New England cold."[86] Weather, plus a Kansan's rather typical mistaken view that New York is in New England, wasn't all that was then on Inge's mind; New York's coldness extended to its wait-and-see attitude about his upcoming play. The collective memory, it seemed, went back only as far as *A Loss of Roses*. In New York, Inge's assertiveness was muted; even his old friends and associates such as Wood and Whitehead seemed only mildly supportive, in contrast to the general praise that he received in Hollywood. When *Natural Affection* failed, the coldness must have seemed all-encompassing.

In California, the film version of *A Loss of Roses*—*The Stripper*—was ready for release. Inge had arranged with Universal Studios and Elliott Kastner to expand the one-act play *Bus Riley's Back in Town* for the screen. He also was negotiating to do a script for television's Chrysler Theater. Flying back to Hollywood from Toledo, Inge may have thought, with some justification, *Who needs Broadway?* He had friends in California, among them Jerome ("Jerry") Lawrence and Jack Garfein, who had stopped living in New York in preference for California; another California friend, Leonard Spiegelgas, always made Inge feel welcome and important there; and Leonard introduced Inge to numerous film people. Moreover, other good friends from New York and elsewhere, such as Barbara Baxley, Ned Rorem, and Tennessee Williams, frequently visited the West Coast. Thus, Inge began seriously to consider selling his Sutton Place apartment and returning to New York only when necessary.

Although living in California must always have seemed the most logical alternative to living in New York, Inge did not abandon his flirtations with the notion of returning to Lawrence for at least temporary stays. He returned to Kansas for occasional visits in the Topeka–Lawrence–Kansas City area several times during the early 1960s. An item in the *Topeka Capital* of January 2, 1960, announced that Inge would be teaching a play-writing course at nearby KU (20 miles to the east) during that spring term.[87] Indeed, arrangements had been made, but when Elia Kazan wanted to proceed with *Splendor in the Grass* before the spring term would be over, Inge canceled. He then returned to Kansas City in April of that year to advise the producers of a local production of *A Loss of Roses*.[88] The following January – 1961 – he traveled to Topeka to be honored, along with other outstanding Kansans, on the occasion of the state's centennial.[89]

An item in the *Lawrence Journal-World* of June 21, 1963, stated that Inge "stole into town more than a week ago"; he was rumored to be "hunting for a permanent residence here."[90] The next day, the *Journal-World* reported that Inge might stay in Lawrence to polish some writing he was planning to do for television. Inge spoke about negotiations for a series of five dramas for CBS, negotiations that never culminated in a deal; he also told a group of drama students that he preferred the atmosphere of small towns. "People exist as individuals in small towns," Inge was quoted as saying; "it's not so in the cities." Commenting on New York theater, he said, "Everything's based on the 'smash hit' now. It's so expensive that you produce a play in panic, in terror. That's not how good things happen."[91] Despite such hints of returning to Lawrence to teach and write, Inge was never to do so, even though he did buy property near Lawrence.

The *Topeka Journal* of October 8, 1963, reported that Inge had bought a one-hundred-year-old stone barn and lot just northwest of Lawrence and that he planned to remodel the barn as a residence. Lewin Goff, the director of KU's theater, told the *Journal* that Inge wanted a place to rest, write, and "get away from it all."[92] A few days later, however, Inge's old mentor Allen Crafton told Pat Burnau of the *Topeka Capital* that he had his doubts that Inge would actually come to Lawrence: "Bill Inge is the strangest and most unpredictable person in the world, and I won't believe it until I see him here."[93] Crafton knew, or sensed, more about Inge than most people in the area did. The brief returns and flirtations with living in or near Lawrence were to continue, although with less frequency, until after the mid 1960s. It was again that quest for a home, a refuge. And Inge knew in 1963, after the failure of *Natural Affection*, that no such home would ever be his in New York City.

On September 19, 1963, Inge wrote to his old friend Helen Hafner: "I haven't moved yet, and still don't know where for sure I intend to move, although I did buy a nice piece of property in Kansas. Right now, I'm dividing my time between here [New York] and Stockbridge, favoring the latter."[94] Pleasant as Stockbridge was, however, Inge primarily went there for analysis and to visit the Gibsons. As a place to live and work, it was ultimately too close to New York, and the winters were long and cold. And Lawrence, Kansas, was, in the final analysis, too small, too isolated, and too full of his past, the past that had served him well but was not, he believed, a necessary key to the writing he might do in the future. The place to go was California, and as 1964 got under way, Inge decided to move there.

Such a move, after fifteen years in New York, had its complications. For one thing, John Connolly, who had served him so well for the last six years, would not make the move with him. This decision involved more than Connolly's personal dislike of California; he did not think the move was the right thing for Inge. Connolly had told Inge of his concern that the Hollywood experience would ultimately be detrimental. Inge did not resent these expressions of misgivings, according to Connolly; rather, he simply disagreed or, more probably, did not want to believe them. At any rate, when Inge decided to move to California, Connolly left his employ.

Connolly had long done so much for Inge that he, too, must be counted among those important New York friends and associates that Inge seemed to abandon by shifting first his primary attention and then his residence to California. The abandonment was not so much literal as figurative, for Inge remained friends with Connolly, Wood, Charles Jackson, Barbara Baxley, and the others; but for the most part he chose not to heed their advice or their expressions of doubt. In Inge's mind, New York was too heartless, too cold, too uncaring an atmosphere; and he was never again to think otherwise. Connolly, in particular, had been Inge's close friend, a confidant, a sounding board for ideas, an absolutely dependable person who took care of so many of the necessary details of his life. It was a major change when Connolly quit working for Inge.

Some who knew both Inge and Connolly may have thought of them as lovers, but Connolly denies having been anything more than Inge's loyal friend and employee. Given Inge's extreme reticence and shame about his homosexuality and given that he could not commit himself to married life with Barbara Baxley, it seems plausible that he also could never have lived with a man, even if he felt an attraction. Connolly always had his own apartment and always had his own circle of friends and activities apart from his work for Inge. Ultimately the question of whether or not they were ever lovers is much less important than the fact that Inge always lived alone and, by the testimony of Connolly, Baxley, and others who knew him well, was extremely discreet in whatever amorous contacts he may have had. He apparently had few promiscuous impulses by the time he reached his forties living in New York; whatever "cruising" was in his system had likely been indulged earlier, in St. Louis.

Connolly believes Inge would have been too embarrassed and too appalled to have sought experience in the sorts of bath-houses and gay hangouts described by his friend Ned Rorem in *New York Diary*; that belief, too, seems plausible. No longer especially young, tending to be overweight and balding, and above all shy, fearful, and ashamed, Inge may well have been practically celibate by this time in his life.[95] Whether or not Connolly's departure made any difference in whatever love life Inge had, it is clear that Inge soon realized that he needed to hire someone else to help him.

He was still trying to write each morning, as he had with great regularity when Connolly was his secretary, and he needed someone to come in the afternoons to type his handwritten work. There were all the daily details that Connolly had so ably handled, and now there were new details attendant to the coming move: finding a buyer for the Sutton Place apartment, deciding what to keep and what to sell from his art collection, consulting with his friend Monroe Wheeler, director of collections at the Museum of Modern Art, on how best to arrange for the shipping of the art he would take west; deciding on what to do about Stockbridge; and much more. To help him with all this, Inge offered the secretarial job to Mark Minton, a

Kansan from the Independence area who was now living in New York and whom Inge had known for several years.

MARK MINTON had met William Inge years earlier in Independence, when Inge had been back for a visit from St. Louis. After Inge had become successful, Minton occasionally had seen him in New York while visiting there; in 1960 Minton had moved to New York himself and had gone to work for an import company. He renewed his friendship with Inge shortly thereafter, and he decided to take Inge's offer of the secretarial job after Connolly quit. For the most part, Minton took over the same duties Connolly had had, but he wasn't as aware as Connolly had been of the changes Inge was going through until after he had helped with the move to California. Connolly had seen Inge's mood swings and periods of depression, and he knew that Inge would struggle back from them and continue working, as long as he stayed sober, made occasional trips to Stockbridge, and had occasional positive responses to his work. It took Minton a while to perceive this same pattern, but having no basis for comparison, he didn't know that Inge's depressions were beginning to get deeper in 1964 and that he was beginning to take more medication, usually Librium, to help fight the symptoms.

It seems reasonable to venture that by 1964, even though the decision to move provided a sense of direction and purpose, Inge was still very apprehensive about the changes in his life. As we have seen, psychiatry seemed to be losing its ability to seem helpful, and New York seemed to have dismissed him and his work. Although he had prospects for work in California, he had, after all, experienced the disappointment of Kazan's having altered his dialogue in *Splendor*, which, given the honor of the Academy Award, must have reminded Inge of his experience with Joshua Logan on *Picnic*, a disappointment that had been assuaged by a Pulitzer Prize. *All Fall Down* had gone well, but his original story of *A Loss of Roses* had not: at first, Fox had decided against making the film at all on the curious grounds that a film that was set in the Great Depression couldn't succeed, even though *Splendor* was set in exactly that era.[96] Then Fox proceeded with making the film, choosing correctly to place the primary emphasis on Lila but completely changing the ending to a happy one—a serious distortion of Inge's vision and intent in the play.[97] As much as Inge may have wanted to believe that Hollywood was the place for him, such matters could hardly have escaped his notice and concern. Box-office whimsy dictated major decisions, and the list of works by serious writers that had been gutted by film makers was too long to ignore.

Inge had made his choice, however; and when a buyer for the Sutton Place apartment was found, Inge sold it and, with Minton's help, arranged for the move to a rented house in Los Angeles. Shortly before leaving the apartment, Minton recalls, Inge made a show of symbolizing the change and meeting its challenge by gathering up his Librium and throwing it down the trash chute.[98] Perhaps Inge had begun to worry about using Librium during his periods of depression, and knowing what a dependence on alcohol could be like, perhaps he didn't want to risk another form of drug dependence. Or perhaps he felt that a fresh start, in general, meant fighting disappointment and depression entirely on his own. Whatever his reasons, his brave act was doomed to have almost no effect, and his bold move to revitalize his writing and career—in other words, his life—was also doomed to failure.

Part Four • California: Postscripts

9 · Hollywood

Inge "officially" moved from New York to Los Angeles on August 1, 1964. There apparently was no farewell or welcome gathering to mark the occasion at either end of the journey; Inge had been leaving New York and coming to California for so long, both in his plans and in his actual movements, that the move itself seems to have attracted very little attention. After helping Inge settle into the rental, the first of several places he briefly rented until buying the house at 1440 Oriole Drive, Mark Minton returned east to tie up such loose ends as closing out Inge's rented place in Stockbridge.[1]

Although Inge had two important scripts to do immediately, one for television's Chrysler Theater and the other for the film of *Bus Riley's Back in Town*, he also decided that it was time to act on a long-time desire to write prose. He had, after all, developed *Sheba* and *Splendor* in part from prose fragments, and the relative freedom of the prose writer doubtless appealed to him. He had some autobiographical prose material he had been sketching since the late 1950s, so he made working on this material part of his writing routine shortly after his move to California. This material soon grew into what became *My Son Is a Splendid Driver*, the reflective memoir of his formative sensibility. It is significant that Inge made working on this revealing book a part of his writing habits as early as the time right after the move to California, for the changes that the move seemed to formalize were permanent. He was to write much, much more drama during the California years, but very little of it reflects the vision and sensibility that *Driver* reveals. It is as though Inge sensed a need to set things down in the freedom of prose that would one day see print exactly as he wished it. And despite the press of the television script and the screenplay, Inge worked enough on *Driver* that less than ten months after his move to California, he wrote to his niece Jo Ann Kirchmaier: "Believe it or not, I have finished a novel. . . . I'm calling it MY SON IS A SPLENDID DRIVER and it has kind of an autobiographical flavor about it."[2] Undoubtedly, Inge revised the novel after that letter of May 13, 1965, but how much is not known. Driver was not published until 1971; it was the last work by Inge published while he was alive.

The Chrysler Theater script did not take Inge long because most of it had previously been done during the time when he was working on a series of dramas for CBS, the dramas to which he referred when he was visiting Lawrence in June, 1963.[3] Originally, the CBS producer David Susskind had wanted a series that explored small-town life, and Inge seemed perfect for that. However, Inge and Susskind soon disagreed over the approach Inge was using in his sketches. Inge later told interviewer Peter Bart that Susskind and CBS wanted such "stock" characters and situations that "we reached an impasse." One of the sketches, however, he had developed far enough that when the Chrysler Theater opportunity with NBC came, Inge had very little revision to do. Thus *Out on the Outskirts of Town*, produced by Dick Berg for "Bob Hope Presents the Chrysler Theatre," came into being.

The story, involving the marital problems and eventual reconciliation of Manny Garrit, former baseball star, with his wife, Faye, was not televised "live." Rather, it was shot in six days on a very low budget. "It was quite an experience," Inge recalled to Peter Bart. "If a scene was muffed for some reason, there was no time for retakes. The scene was just dropped." The result, he said, was that in the film, "character development is incomplete and the whole story structure is brutalized."[4] Starring Anne Bancroft and Jack Warden, *Out on the Outskirts of Town* was telecast on NBC November 6, 1964. If it had a wide audience, it apparently wasn't enough to encourage either NBC or Inge, for the network did not ask him for any more work, and in fact, Inge never again wrote for television. It is possible that Inge agreed with the critic Jack Gould, who wrote in the *New York Times* on the day after the telecast that *Out on the Outskirts of Town* was "pedestrian melodrama" with "cliche-ridden dialogue."[5] After all, Inge had thrown together the story rather quickly, salvaging something from his otherwise unfruitful CBS experience. And he never did think television was the right medium for serious drama. Moreover, he had the film script for *Bus Riley's Back in Town* to command his immediate attention.

"WHEN you write a play," William Inge once told the *New York Times* writer Murray Schumach: "you kind of solve an emotional problem. Then you do not want to have anything more to do with it. If you have to adapt it to another medium, it becomes tedious."[6] At the time – 1961 – Inge was explaining why he doubted that he would ever adapt his new play, *Natural Affection*, for the screen. But he must not have believed what he said, or he would surely have avoided the corrosive experience he had with adapting *Bus Riley's Back in Town*.

Perhaps Inge agreed to do a screen version of the Bus Riley material because he had never really considered it a finished work in all its many previous forms. The one-act play by that title, published with *Summer Brave* and ten other short plays in 1962, he described then as "a play I happen to be working on now in expanded form."[7] And versions of unpublished plays involving a character named Bus Riley (or Bud Dooley or Bud Dailey, who are all the same fellow) are probably more numerous than any other versions of unpublished plays in the Inge Collection. Bus Riley was a character who fascinated Inge. Like Turk in *Sheba*, Hal in *Picnic*, Bo in *Bus Stop*, and several other of Inge's male characters, Bus Riley is young and muscular, the sort of athletically trim male who is attractive both to women and to homosexual men, although this latter attractiveness is seldom emphasized in the several manuscripts. Most versions of Bus Riley's story involve his return, after some years, to a small community from which he had earlier been exiled and to a woman whom he had earlier been forbidden to love, usually because he was from a much lower socioeconomic class than she. Variations of this character and story are traceable in Inge's writing as far back as the early 1950s; in fact, John Connolly believes the person on whom the character is principally based was an acquaintance of Inge's as far back as his St. Louis days.[8] Inge's keen sensitivity to differences in social class goes all the way back to his youth in Independence. Whatever Bus Riley's origins, he was clearly an important character to William Inge, and Inge apparently never was able to tell Bus's story the way he wanted to.

The attempt to adapt Bus's story into a movie became more than merely "tedious" for Inge, even though matters did not begin that way. Elliott Kastner and Universal Studios agreed to film Inge's scenario, but of course they did not agree, as would have been routine in Broadway theater, to clear with Inge any changes in script. In Hollywood, the writer simply does not have that sort of clout, even if he does have an impressive name. At first, however, there were no strong indications that Inge's original script would not be followed closely. In Inge's script, Bus returns to a small town after serving a hitch in the navy. His old forbidden flame, Laurel, remains forbidden because she has married an older, wealthy man. Laurel's husband, however, is capable of meeting only her material desires, thus making Laurel's temptation and seduction of Bus inevitable. This much is in Inge's script, as are Bus's eventual refusal of Laurel and his discovery of love with a girl who is his sister's friend. The differences that exist between Inge's script and the script of the released film are matters of degree and emphasis as a result of casting Ann-Margret as Laurel.

Ann-Margret's career, particularly her "sexy redhead" image, was literally getting started as *Bus Riley* was being filmed. The release of *Viva Las Vegas*, in which she starred with Elvis Presley, increased her recognition significantly, as did a publicized romance with Presley. Producer Elliott Kastner and the first-time film director Harvey Hart, whose previous directing experience had been in television, decided to take advantage of Ann-Margret's having become a "name" star by expanding her role in *Bus Riley*. The problem, essentially, was that the role of Laurel needed no expanding; in fact, Inge had already allocated as much on-camera time to Laurel as his story could reasonably tolerate. The story, after all, was Bus's, not Laurel's; and Bus was being, in Inge's estimation, ably played by Michael Parks, a "James Dean type" who had recently been the motorcycle-riding protagonist of a television series called "Then Came Bronson." To complicate matters more, Ann-Margret's considerable talents of singing and dancing—easily accommodated in the Presley picture—were completely unnecessary in *Bus Riley*, which limited any expansion of her role primarily to presenting her as incredibly provocative. It wasn't long before Inge was bridling at requests for more chance meetings and intimate scenes between Bus and Laurel, scenes that were requested purely to get Ann-Margret on screen, preferably in shorts or a negligee.

The sense of losing control of his story soon engulfed Inge. After one particularly bitter confrontation, he not only left the studio but also left town. Mark Minton, who was back in New York at the time, recalls that he got a late-night phone call from Inge, who had stopped at a motel in Albuquerque. The distraught Inge told Minton all about the mounting changes in the film, his lack of control, his sense of being swallowed. Minton, who by this time had become much more aware of Inge's personality and problems, tried to soothe his distant friend, but it wasn't easy. Inge was a seriously unhappy man. "Can I come back?" Inge asked Minton, as though Minton had the answer. Assuming that Inge meant "come back" to New York, Minton replied, "Of course"; he went on to suggest that a writer of Inge's stature could do exactly what he wanted to do. Minton doubted that Inge was serious about returning to New York, but at this point the idea was to try to talk Inge out of some of his despair and into a good night's sleep. Eventually it worked. Saying that he would sleep on things, Inge hung up, leaving Minton to a fitful remainder of the night. On the next day, Inge returned to Hollywood.[9]

When the picture was finished — or at least finished as far as Inge knew — it was given a sneak preview in Long Beach, where it was generally well received. Inge's basic story was still intact, though Laurel of course was on screen out of proportion to her actual importance to that story. All things considered, Inge decided that it could be worse, so he turned most of his attention to a full-length play, *Where's Daddy?*[10]

Meanwhile, Mark Minton had returned from New York to help Inge catch up with whatever writing was new and with whatever details Inge needed help. Minton also returned to tell Inge that after things got caught up, he would be returning to New York permanently. Minton had not developed a dislike for Inge; quite the opposite, he had developed a sense of powerlessness to help him. "I felt that Bill was depressed," Minton later explained; "I felt that he was making bad decisions." Most of all, he said, "I felt that there was no way I could help him." Whether, in telling Inge about his plans, Minton also added what he added many years later — "I'm not a psychiatric nurse" — is doubtful. Minton probably knew that his quitting would hurt Inge enough; there was no need to add to the pain with such an opinion. And so, Inge was again without a secretary who also was a friend and confidant. (Minton, like John Connolly before him, claims that he never was Inge's lover.)[11] This time, Inge didn't find a replacement.

Then, through what Peter Bart of the *New York Times* calls "unofficial channels," Inge learned that Elliott Kastner and Universal Studios had ordered *Bus Riley* to be rewritten, with several scenes rephotographed. Inge had not been asked or even told about any of these changes. Inge demanded a copy of the new script, which had been reworked by several staff writers at Universal. After seeing the new script, Inge decided that now not only was Laurel's part overblown but also that this had been done at too much expense to the integrity of his story. He responded by insisting that his name be removed from the picture's credits.[12] Thus, when the picture was released, the screenplay was credited to the completely bogus "Walter Gage." And one of Inge's favorite characters and stories lay on the Hollywood cutting-room floor.

Inge's screenwriting career also lay in the darkness of that cutting-room floor, though he was not yet fully aware of this. He could have continued writing for films; after all, *Splendor* and *All Fall Down* were still to his credit. But the experience of first being essentially ignored while *Bus Riley* was being filmed and then actually ignored while it was being redone, reminded Inge that there still were better ways to get his writing before the public. Cold and cruel as New York's theater critics seemed to him, he remembered that at least in the theater the writer controlled the changes in the script. That must have been one reason for Inge's decision to work on *Where's Daddy?* for Broadway after *Bus Riley* had been released. He never again wrote exclusively for film, even though a sampling of the reviews after the release of *Bus Riley* would seem to confirm his good judgment in disassociating himself from the film. *Time's* reviewer called it "trite melodrama" that "abundantly fulfills the promise of mediocrity put forth by playwright-scenarist William Inge, who demanded that his name be deleted from the opening credits."[13] Philip T. Hartung, writing in *Commonweal*, said that the Ann-Margret character "throws the whole theme out of kilter" but that the film still was "not a total loss" because "a little of the good Inge still shows through."[14]

Whatever satisfaction such reviews may have given Inge, it was not enough to overcome his reluctance to write for films again. Thus, in less than a year after his move to California, Inge was no longer to write directly either for films or television. Almost everything he wrote thereafter was either for the stage or for the printed prose page, with the possible exception of *The Lady Gay*, a story based on Dodge City's Wild West past, which may have been conceived of as at least potentially for filming. It had not taken long for Inge to realize that his new "home" was no more artistically hospitable than New York had been.

WITH HIS experience writing for film and television essentially behind him and because of his reluctance to do either again, Inge turned his eyes back to Broadway. Not that he had completely shelved his prose; *Driver* was virtually finished, and he had ideas for at least two more novels that he would write eventually. Prose began to loom as a last resort, however; its freedom was appealing, but this advantage was also undercut by the fact that prose was not recognized as his medium. He had established his mark as a playwright, and there was evidence, despite the failures of *A Loss of Roses* and *Natural Affection*, that playwriting still afforded his best opportunity to reclaim success.

All of his four successful plays of the 1950s were still being produced throughout the country in local and regional theaters. They, with *Splendor*, were keeping his name alive. Moreover, Inge knew that several factors beyond the control of any single playwright had altered the production process so much, particularly in New York, that the failure of even the best-established writers was much more common. All of his playwright friends—Tennessee Williams, Robert Anderson, Jerome Lawrence and Robert E. Lee, William Gibson, Edward Albee (although Inge apparently no longer considered Albee a friend), and others—had experienced failures that seemed the result less of poor writing than of the whims of critics, production costs, shifting popular tastes, and the more volatile times.[15] With so many good playwrights in the same boat and with the negative experience of film writing still fresh in his memory, Inge probably reasoned that he had little to lose by taking another shot at Broadway.

In any new Broadway attempt, Inge was strongly encouraged by his friend Jerome Lawrence. Lawrence, who had lived on the West Coast for some time and had known and admired Inge and his work for years, sensed Inge's depressions and doubts. Lawrence would invite Inge out to his beach-front home and would listen as Inge read from his manuscripts in his still-impressive voice. Inge seldom asked for criticism, so Lawrence seldom offered any. When Inge read an early version of *Where's Daddy?* Lawrence recalls having suggested only that Inge change the title. "You've always had such great titles," Lawrence told Inge, as he urged something more stiking. For a time, Inge called the play *Family Things, Etc.*, but eventually he changed the title back to *Where's Daddy?* and never told Lawrence that at least one version of the play (now in the Inge Collection) had been called *The Bastard*.

Lawrence's friendship and support had to mean a great deal to Inge, especially at this time when he was truly alone, without even the secretarial assistance and encouragement of Connolly or Minton; but Inge didn't acknowledge it. With his acquaintances in California, Inge was, as in New York, given to accepting invitations or calling to invite himself, then often either not coming at all or staying only briefly before, making fidgety excuses, he would leave. Lawrence tolerated such behavior because he knew Inge was suffering. Audrey Wood, with whom at this point Inge had virtually nothing to do, often called Lawrence to inquire about Inge or to tell Lawrence that Tennessee Williams was going to be on the coast and to suggest that Williams and Inge be invited out. But Inge was erratic, as Lawrence recalls; even Tennessee couldn't persuade Inge to come over if he didn't want to.[16]

It is impossible to say to what extent Inge was able to continue to abstain from liquor or drugs at this time. Lawrence reports no signs that Inge was drinking then, but Barbara Baxley recalls an incident when she was in California, briefly renting a place while working out there. She invited Inge over for a dinner party, and he came early, joining her in the kitchen while she made preparations. She could tell he was nervous and out of sorts, and she knew something was wrong when he poured himself a drink. Baxley had been through too much with Inge, and she cared too much for him to ignore this development. "Bill, I can't be happy to see you do this," she told him. His reply acknowledged that she was right to be upset, but although he didn't pour another drink, he also made excuses and soon left without staying to meet the other guests and have dinner. This incident was Baxley's first indication that things weren't right for Inge in California, but she did not know what she or anyone else could do.[17]

If there were binges or lapses, they must have been quiet and lonely. And they must not have lasted, for Inge kept writing. While at work on *Where's Daddy?* he also took the time to write commentaries for two artists' exhibits. One was a brief introduction for a Willem de Kooning exhibit that ran from March 22 to April 30, 1965, at the Paul Kantor Gallery.[18] The other was a similar introduction for "Recent Paintings by James Gill," which ran from November 1 to 21, 1965, at the Felix Landau Gallery.[19] Both commentaries show that Inge's love of modern art and the immediacy of its experience for him had not diminished. In the abstractions and distortions of de Kooning and Gill, Inge found a truth that he admired, a reflection of the distorted times in which he felt he lived, the times he had tried to portray in *Natural Affection*. And as he wrote these commentaries, he was also at work creating Pinky Pinkerton, his professorial homosexual spokesperson, in *Where's Daddy?*

PINKY Pinkerton is the most personally revealing character that William Inge ever put on the stage. Although he had earlier created many roles that showed some powerful characteristic of his own personality and experience— for example, Doc Delaney's drunken despair, Rosemary Sydney's lonely frustration, Sonny Flood's "mama's boy" embarrassments—there had always been a creative distance that had buffered any direct identification between the author and the character, although in the case of Sonny, the distance was almost purely one of time. Such distancing exists in *Where's Daddy?* but it is quite superficial. Inge presents Pinky as "a chubby little man in his fifties" (Inge was fifty-two at the time and overweight), a homosexual professor who defends the institutions of marriage and family and the idealized notion of heterosexual love precisely because he feels that he is an outsider to these things he rather desperately wants to believe in. He says to Tom Keen, the male protagonist who is afraid of the prospects of becoming a father, settling down, and taking on the responsibilities of family: "It's [fatherhood] a terrifying step to take, Tom. Some of us never take it, but just grow up into old boys, and go to our graves without dignity or bearing. Take the step, Tom. I beg you. And take your part in this life as a man."[20]

If *Natural Affection* was an attempt to show the possible realistic consequences of the failure of familial love and responsibility, *Where's Daddy?* was an attempt to affirm the importance of marriage and family to the well-being of our culture. The central couple, Tom and Teena Keen, are present-day aspiring actors in mid Manhattan who met while taking acting lessons. Teena was fleeing a highly proper and financially comfortable middle class background that had included unhappiness profound enough to cause her to make a suicide attempt. Tom was trying to overcome an orphan bastard's background, which had included being a fifteen-year-old male prostitute until he met the benevolent but not purely intentioned Pinky. Pinky had kept and cared for Tom in the dual role of lover and father figure, but when Tom had met Teena, Tom was on his own. The romance between Tom and Teena resulted in her pregnancy; Tom married her strictly to give the child a "legitimacy" he had never known. At the beginning of the play, Tom and Teena, who are both seeing analysts, have decided to put the baby up for adoption immediately after its birth, then get a divorce.

It quickly becomes clear that Teena is not actually in agreement with Tom about the adoption and divorce, but she dutifully mouths the same rationalizations, usually couched in the jargon of analysis, that Tom gives for these actions, telling her mother that she and Tom are not "emotionally prepared for parenthood" (p. 9) and that "we *thought* we were in love, but we were both too 'emotionally immature' to know what we were doing" (p. 12, Inge's italics and quotes). Because she feels guilty for somehow having failed Teena as a parent and because she doesn't want to lose the slight contact she still has with her daughter, Teena's mother wisely does not criticize Teena when she tells her mother that in putting the baby up for adoption and by getting a divorce, Tom and Teena are "trying very earnestly to live by the highest principles of contemporary thinking and philosophy" (p. 18). But the mother naturally wonders what, exactly, the world is coming to. Pinky wonders the same thing, and shows no such restraint.

Pinky appears because Tom has written to him, asking for a place to stay and partial support after the divorce, because Tom doesn't believe he can afford to rent a place of his own. But Pinky isn't buying any of Tom's rationalizations:

PINKY (*Bluntly*): Why are you leaving your wife and child?

TOM: Because I'm not prepared to play the role of father.

PINKY: Why not?

TOM: I'm just not emotionally mature enough.

PINKY: Such nonsense.

TOM: I know it's hard for you to understand, Pinky. But after all, there's a generation or two between us, and . . .

PINKY: I think I understand perfectly.

TOM: You do?

PINKY: You're scared shitless. (P. 35)

Pinky still cares for Tom, but more as a father than as a lover, and because he believes Tom should stay married and accept fatherhood, Pinky refuses Tom's request (p. 51).

As the plot unfolds, Tom shows signs of weakness in his resolve, but he leaves anyway, just as the baby is about to be born. Helen and Razz, a neighboring black couple, get Teena a doctor and help her immediately after the birth of the baby boy. Tom then returns, sheepishly noting that he had kept the key to the apartment, a fact that his analyst had found indicative that he didn't really want to leave in the first place (p. 75). Tom has come to stay until the birth, he says, and when he learns that the baby has already been born, he once again becomes terrified and calls Pinky, telling him to come over. Then, unable to stand his panic, Tom bolts from the apartment before Pinky arrives (p. 81).

At this point, Teena decides that she will keep the baby. She tells Helen: "I'm a mother. . . . I think, now, that's probably all I ever wanted to be" (p. 83). She tells Razz to inform the adoption agency about her decision, declares to Helen that she loves Tom, and expresses joy that she was not successful when she tried to commit suicide, for she would have missed the happiness she now feels (p. 84). After Pinky's arrival, Tom appears again, this time with instructions from his analyst to see the baby, stay around for a few days, and "see if I can become adjusted." To Tom's amazement, Teena refuses to let him do so. "Not for a few days," she says; "it's got to be for good" (p. 100). Teena's ultimatum drives Tom away yet again, but not before Pinky gives him another tongue lashing and condemns his selfish behavior, which is rationalized by "a lot of Freudian mumbo-jumbo you don't even know the meaning of" (p. 103).

Tom, of course, isn't gone for long this time, either. He returns, displaying the apartment key he has again forgotten to leave behind and this time declaring that he will stay (pp. 109–110). When Teena asks him if he's staying because his analyst told him to, Tom replies: "I don't have an analyst any more. He won't even talk to me" (p. 110). Thus, the play's major conflict is resolved, and heterosexual love, marriage, and family responsibility are all resoundingly endorsed.

Inge seasoned the play with a contemporary concern about racism, primarily handled in scenes involving Razz and Mrs. Bigelow, Teena's mother; and there are a few satirical touches in such scenes as Tom's rehearsing an inane commercial for television and a rather heated argument between Tom and Teena over whose analyst is better; but the primary critical thrust of this play is carried by Pinky. As we have seen, Inge's gathering disillusionment with psychoanalysis is quite clear in *Where's Daddy?* There are many scenes in which that disillusionment is obvious; for example, when Tom tells Pinky: "Analysis has freed me. . . . I'm a bastard, but I'm no longer ashamed of it." Pinky's reply is withering: "Science is wonderful" (p. 48).

Inge indicts more than psychoanalysis in this play. He also takes a swipe at existentialistic absurdism by having Tom, as part of the "highest principles of contemporary thinking and philosophy," characterize Teena's pregnancy as "what Camus would call just an absurdity that happened" (p. 27). To Tom's highly contemporary mid-1960s claim to need to "find" himself, Inge's Pinky replies: "Why? What for? Where is everyone hiding?" (p. 37). Tom's need to "find" himself, Pinky suspects, is an outgrowth of studying "method" acting, an approach Pinky finds completely phony. It doesn't take much imagination to hear Inge himself complaining behind Pinky's voice: "In my day, actors played *parts*. They didn't play themselves. They didn't *want* to play themselves" (p. 38). When Tom dismisses Pinky's memories of fine acting and fine plays as irrelevant, Pinky delivers, for William Inge, yet another shot at the theater world which he has come to believe has deserted him: "I suppose you prefer those plays with people coming out of ashcans and urinating on the floor" (p. 39). It is as if, through Pinky, Inge were saying: "If I have to write plays like *Endgame*, then I'm not sure I want to write plays." And in a way, that's exactly what he *was* saying.

He was also saying, as Pinky declares to Mrs. Bigelow, after she ventures that she "may be old-fashioned" because she thinks fathers should be present when their children are born:

I'm a very old-fashioned man, too, Mrs. Bigelow. I still believe in God, and love, and the sanctity of the home, and all those virtues that everyone today considers terribly reactionary. To tell the truth, I seldom ex-

perience these phenomena, but I believe in them devoutly. . . . I'm a
conventional man, in my own way. . . . I have always considered marriage between a man and a woman a divinely beautiful institution. . . .
I've always been so idealistic about marriage, I've never felt I dared to
face the reality of it. (P. 95)

In that speech, there is no distance between Pinky and William Inge at all.

DESPITE the doctrinaire profamily theme of *Where's Daddy?* and despite Pinky's
often strident tone, Inge had no difficulty in finding producers to bring it
to Broadway. At first, Robert Whitehead, who had produced *Bus Stop* and
who had been a prospective producer of *Natural Affection*, agreed to produce
Where's Daddy? Michael Wager later joined as a coproducer, and Harold
Clurman, who had directed *Bus Stop* and who had always liked Inge's work,
was signed to direct. Beau Bridges and Barbara Dana were cast as Tom and
Teena, and Betty Field and Hiram Sherman were cast as Mrs. Bigelow and
Pinky. Pre-Broadway runs were set for Falmouth, Massachusetts, on Cape
Cod, then Westport.[21]

Back in New York City for necessary preliminaries to *Where's Daddy?* in
the summer of 1965, Inge quartered himself at his favorite hotel, the Algonquin, and tried to make the best of what was inevitably a nervous situation:
here he was, in the town he hated, trying again to be successful with a new
play on Broadway. Before things got cracking on rehearsals, he decided to
test the waters regarding another version of the Bus Riley story that he had,
called *Bud Dooley*. Inge discussed *Bud Dooley* with Robert Anderson and
Audrey Wood. Earlier, he had discussed the play with Jerome Lawrence's
writing partner, Robert E. Lee. Lawrence, Lee, Anderson, and some other
artists at the time had formed a production group called simply the American Playwrights. In a letter to Lawrence, written at the Algonquin, Inge said
that he wanted the American Playwrights to produce *Bud Dooley*, although
it needed considerable rewriting and a new title. *Almost a Love Song* is the
title that he was toying with and the one that he eventually gave to the
manuscript. Although nothing actually came of this play or the idea to produce it, Inge's remarks to Lawrence in this letter reveal much about his state
of mind during the summer of 1965, in New York.

For one thing, there is an echo of the old mistrust of Joshua Logan. "Incidentally, this play was never read by Josh, or offered to him," Inge told

Lawrence. "So regardless of what he told you, he has not seen it, and I would not offer it to him." Inge went on to say that an earlier version had been seen by Oliver Smith, but that after the failure of *Natural Affection*, Inge had "hid in Stockbridge," while "feeling very depressed" and liking "nothing I'd ever written." Now, however, Inge thought the play could be very good, but he also saw potential problems. The letter continued:

> I can get a NY production, if I wish, very easily. But if I do, I'll not be able to get the play produced as I see it, with the tangential continuity of the many diversified scenes. It will be a costly production and require a big, very modern theatre. It would also require stars, probably, and I detest them all.
>
> So, if you still think your group will be interested, I'll get to work as soon as possible to get the script into final shape.

No wonder nothing came of the play, given the "produce this if you dare" tone of Inge's letter. But such was his frame of mind when he wrote from New York to his good friend Lawrence in California. He concluded with the by-now-expected complaint about New York City: "FAMILY THINGS, ETC. goes into rehearsal two weeks from today. I dread having to remain here all that time. Already, it's hot, sticky, and miserable. I'll never again subject myself to a long stay in this ghastly town."[22]

As things were to develop, the production of *Where's Daddy?* ran into some difficulties that caused delays, chief among which was the loss of Robert Whitehead's close supervision as producer. Whitehead's wife died after the rehearsals had started, and he was not able to bring his full attention back to the production. Finally, he turned the production over entirely to Michael Wager, who was able to get matters back on track, although the opening by then had been pushed back to March 2, 1966, at the Billy Rose Theatre in New York.[23] Thus, Inge's stay in the "ghastly town" was extended, as were his agitation and nervous apprehension, even though his working relationship with Clurman and the cast seemed to go well. As opening night finally began to approach, Inge wrote from the Algonquin to Ned Rorem in Nantucket: "I am still in this mean, ugly city, wishing every day that I could go home." But going home, he continued, would have to wait until his new play had opened. His conclusion clarifies his worries; he takes a particular jab at critic Stanley Kauffmann of the *New York Times*, who had recently observed that "three of the most successful American playwrights of the last twenty years are (reputed) homosexuals" whose plays betray a "disguised homosexual influence" that necessarily distorts their presentations of women and marriage. Inge says:

> My play is titled *Where's Daddy?* A morality half farce, half pathos.
> I like it and think we have the promise of a good production now, but
> one works here with such a feeling of combatting hostility, particularly
> from the *Times*. That Kauffman [sic] man seems out to get us at [sic]
> all. Really, it's beginning to take on the nature of a pogrom.[24]

Although Kauffmann had not named the playwrights and although he admitted that these playwrights had "no choice but to masquerade," Inge clearly felt he was one of those whom Kauffmann was referring to; moreover, in his letter to Rorem, he makes abundantly clear his fear of *any* sort of criticism.

And just as he had feared, the New York critics, including Stanley Kauffmann, did not like *Where's Daddy?* "The play simply plods and wriggles along," said Kauffmann in the *New York Times*, who liked Hiram Sherman's contribution as Pinky but virtually nothing else. Kauffmann thought that when Pinky appeared, perhaps Inge was going to raise a very serious theme, because Pinky is just as clearly likable and honorable as he is homosexual. "But that," Kauffmann decided, "is to credit Mr. Inge with more ingenuity of decision and more ambition than his play ever reveals."[25] Walter Kerr, writing in the *New York Herald-Tribune*, was even harsher: "I don't care where daddy is," said Kerr, "where's William Inge?" Noting that Inge had once written words that "bounced off the walls and rattled back down the corridors of his memory and ours, summoning up the hearsay that persistently haunts every man," Kerr laments that in *Where's Daddy?* "the words hit the wall and hang there, moist and clammy." Kerr found Pinky "relentlessly pious," a character who "seems to have swallowed *The Reader's Digest* whole" and whose "homilies on sanity, marital sanctity, and the beauties of living conventionally would be quite enough to drive us over to the side of the castigated kids, if only we liked the kids."[26]

Norman Nadel, writing in the *New York World-Telegram and Sun*, wished that he could approach Inge's new comedy with the respect that a distinguished Pulitzer Prize winner such as Inge deserved, but Nadel said that *Where's Daddy?* "warrants no respect," being a "gross and unattractive drama which restates the obvious and is burdened with stereotypes." Of Pinky, Nadel said that although Pinky isn't likely to be named "PTA man of the year," he is "honest, candid, clever, and except perhaps for the sexual abuse of young boys, a nice guy, though I am not so enlightened as to find a homo-sexual endearing."[27] Douglas Watt of the *New York Daily News* found the play an "adult soap opera," a nice attempt to make a serious statement but "disturbingly out of focus."[28] John McClain of the *New York Journal-American* concluded that *Where's Daddy?* was "really a preposterous play, but with an odd emotional impact. Let it go at that."[29] Only Richard Watts, Jr., of the *New York Post* truly liked the play. "Mr. Inge is back with a wise and winning comedy."[30] Watts's approval was far from enough.

A few days later, the magazine critics added to the consensus. John McCarten, writing in *The New Yorker*, praised the performances of Betty Field and Hiram Sherman and appreciated the irony of Pinky's being the advocate of orthodox values, but finally, McCarten found the play too pre-dictable.[31] Wilfrid Sheed, in *Commonweal*, thought it puzzling that Inge had even written the play:

Inge has always . . . simplified social and emotional issues to the point of insult. But at least he used to be writing about cornpone themes which he seemed to know about. Here he is dealing with New York hippies, concerning which he knows, or is telling, less than your favor-ite national magazine.[32]

Newsweek's anonymous reviewer said that the play "attempts to be terribly modern, *au courant* and complex, and succeeds only in being preposterous." The reviewer continued that "Inge is clearly shocked by a world rapidly in-validating the homespun pieties of his own psyche and grasp of reality."[33]

That last criticism cut very close to the bone, for it is clear that in *Where's Daddy?* Inge *was* shocked by much of what he observed in the world, and to be castigated for honestly presenting what he saw must have served to exasperate Inge all the more. *Where's Daddy?* was indeed a heartfelt attempt not only to be modern and to affirm values but also to be a "comeback" success. But it closed after only twenty-one performances. Inge went back to California shortly after the first reviews came out, more bitter than ever about critics and on the verge of a severe emotional tailspin.

10 • 1440 Oriole Drive

A short while before Inge took *Where's Daddy?* to New York in the summer of 1965, he bought a house in the hills above Sunset Boulevard. The house at 1440 Oriole Drive in Los Angeles was the only one he would ever own; buying it, rather than continuing to rent apartments or buying an apartment, as he had done in New York, was a kind of statement, a declaration that the move to California was permanent. A house afforded greater privacy and space—a yard, an attached garage—a stretching out that had been impossible on Manhattan. When Inge returned to this house after the failure of *Where's Daddy?* he was in a severe emotional depression that the spacious house and the California climate were not enough to counter.

Inge was clearly suffering from this latest rejection, wondering what in the world it was going to take to win some approval. A letter Inge wrote to George Oppenheimer shortly after returning to California reveals his state of mind. Oppenheimer had told Inge that he, for one, had liked *Where's Daddy?* Inge replied:

> I'm very proud that you liked the play. I guess all that one can hope to do anymore is please a few friends. Sorry I didn't get to see you while I was in town, but I didn't see much of anyone; the city kind of terrifies me now, and I went out hardly at all.[1]

That Inge had rarely gone out of his New York hotel except for rehearsals for *Where's Daddy?* is confirmed by the preplay article by Inge that was published in the *New York Herald-Tribune* on February 27. This article, which normally would have been about the play itself, was entitled "On New York—and a New Play," and it told only about how Inge eventually had come to write about New Yorkers, rather than Kansans, and how harried Inge felt in New York City. About the city's cold lack of humanity he wrote: "Oedipus could stab his eyes out in Macy's window and people would gather to gawk as at a psychotic exhibitionist before the police carried him off to Bellevue."[2] Inge's depression, then, had begun even before the premiere of the play. This depression he soon exacerbated at his house in California with liquor and pills, and thus he was not in very good shape when the time came, later that spring, to go to Lawrence, where he had promised to conduct a short playwriting workshop.

Upon arrival in Lawrence, either Inge or perhaps a concerned friend at K.U. decided that he needed some help. Rather than teach, he checked into the psychiatric section of the University of Kansas Medical Center in Kansas City. Why he didn't go to the Menninger Clinic at Topeka is a mystery; perhaps he felt that he would be too well known there. Another distinct possibility is that, given his recent erosion of confidence in psychiatry, Inge may have thought that starting fresh with new doctors in new surroundings would prove more fruitful than returning to a familiar setting. At any rate, he spent several weeks at the K.U. Medical Center that spring, where officials went out of their way, beyond normal doctor-client confidentiality, to keep his presence there a secret.

A professional nurse, who was training at the Medical Center then and who has requested anonymity, remembers that all the staff, especially students, were cautioned not to reveal, even to their closest friends, that Inge was under their care. The extra caution was perhaps not necessary, the nurse says, for few staffers knew that Inge was a celebrity. In the ensuing weeks, Inge was often in the care of this nurse, who found Inge's depression more nostalgic than morose. He talked often about his earlier work and his Kansas background. He seemed surprised that his background could have yielded imaginative work that people could enjoy. He made no references to recent disappointments. The nurse primarily remembered *Splendor in the Grass*, from recent personal teenage moviegoing experience, and she found it enjoyable to draw the assignment to walk with Inge and thus hear the reflections of this man who had created the story of Bud Stamper and Deanie Loomis.

The respite, counseling, and medication at the K.U. Medical Center helped to ease Inge's depression, although he apparently did not remain after his release to conduct the workshop at the university. By this time, any regained balance was always going to be a temporary condition for him. When he returned to the West Coast, he was determined to keep writing drama and prose, secretary or no secretary, critics or no critics. There can be little doubt that Inge's impulse to keep writing was his impulse to survive. Writing and its concomitant potential for recognition of worth had been for some time Inge's raisons d'être; thus, continuing to write was nothing less than an expression of his willingness to keep on living.

To what degree his many bouts with depression had included consideration of suicide is impossible to say, but there is such a high incidence of suicide or attempted suicide in his works, that there is no question that it was often on his mind, especially as time passed and his failures began to mount. After *Where's Daddy?* Inge was, like Pinky, well into his fifties, no longer trim and crowned with a thick, neat pompadour; and he was chagrined by a world in which he saw less and less room for himself. Writing was one important thing over which he had control, something wholly his own that had, on balance, served him well. Although he was to continue a spiritual and emotional search to complement his writing, the writing itself was to be his constant over the next few years.

Whether Inge himself was conscious of the pattern or not, his writing at this stage seems generally to fall into two major types for two major aims: (1) drama, for his hope to return as a figure of prominence as a writer; and (2) prose, for his hope to find continued meaningful, if not commercial, personal expression.

IN THE YEARS immediately after the failure of *Where's Daddy?* Inge spent long hours in his study at 1440 Oriole Drive, writing numerous dramas of varying lengths, almost all of them one-act plays with urban, modern settings and franker, coarser material than anything his earlier audiences had associated with his name, with the possible exception of those who had seen *Natural Affection.* Many of these short plays he intended as separate parts of a collection he called *Complex,* the idea being that each play would take place in a separate apartment of a large housing complex in a large city. The only unity among these plays, by his intention, is provided by the building and the grim subject matter. Unlike his earlier Kansans and Oklahomans, these people are neighbors only by physical proximity. They do not know and do not care about each other, and their life styles would both shock and dismay Doc and Lola Delaney, Flo Owens, or the Flood family.

In writing these plays, Inge was trying, as he had with *Natural Affection* and *Where's Daddy?* to generate something new, something that would "click" with the audiences of the time. As he said to Digby Diehl in an important 1967 interview:

> I think any creative person who is going to survive more than one decade or so has to find himself anew periodically because he has to change with the times. I know that the kind of play that was being done in the fifties has no audience now. And I know I don't have the same kind of approach to writing as I did in the fifties.[3]

Indeed he did not, at least not in his plays. From roughly 1966 to 1969, Inge created or revised from earlier forms several more plays, in addition to those intended for the *Complex* collection, only a few of which have ever been published or performed and none of which can be said to be successful in any significant way. Most of these plays can be found in manuscript in the Inge Collection at Independence; several, mostly duplicates or variant versions, are also in the Kansas Collection at the Spencer Research Library on the campus of the University of Kansas (in his later years, Inge proved especially sharp at donating manuscripts to libraries for their tax-write-off value, and after his death, his sister Helene donated manuscripts generously both to the Kansas and Inge Collections). Taken all together, these plays reflect Inge's sense of a world gone bad, in which basically good individuals can barely hope to cope. Only a couple of these, *Margaret's Bed* and *Bad Breath*, might properly be called comedies; the rest are too grim, even though occasional lines are genuinely funny.

Browsing through the late and largely unpublished plays of William Inge, one finds works dealing with a dread of urban violence (*The Power of Silence, Midwestern Manic, The Tube Boobs, The Call*); homosexuality (*The Love Death, Caesarian Operations, A Corner Room, The Killing, The Last Pad*); family failure (*Overnight, Midwestern Manic, The Last Pad, The Call, The Tube Boobs*); suicide (*The Love Death, The Killing, Bad Breath, I'm a Star, David: Where Angels Tread*); and the perils of lost or endangered celebrity (*A Corner Room, Tormented Woman, I'm a Star, Comeback*). Some characters drink, take drugs, assault, and kill; other characters merely deplore the lives they are leading. Sordid people, situations, and language appear with numbing regularity; alienation is atmospheric.

Occasionally, in glancing through these scripts, one finds a play that is especially revealing of Inge's feelings and attitudes at the time. For example, *Comeback* is a one-act play about Helen Cole, a faded stage star who is about to try, as the title implies, to revitalize her career with a new leading role on Broadway. The setting is backstage on opening night before the curtain rises. Helen has just received a "good luck" note from Nick, her costar. She tells Norma, her friend and attendant, that while Nick's note is "sweet," it is also true that "*my* success means the show's success, and a long run for Nick and the other actors. So I can't think his concern is without some selfish intent."[4] Norma responds that she ought not be so cynical. "Norma dear," Helen replies, "anyone who stays in this business as long as I have can't help becoming a little cynical about human motives. Otherwise, the person is a fool. And fools don't last in the business." Norma remarks that only the talented last, but Helen says: "It's a business that takes far more guts than talent. Talent helps, of course. But guts are essential" (p. 3). Then, to help her guts, Helen takes two phenobarbitals and one Librium (p. 4).

Soon we learn that Helen has recently spent six months in a mental hospital, recovering from a breakdown. She is terrified at the challenge that lies before her (p. 5). She is bitterly suspicious of almost everyone's motives and tells Norma that "nine out of every ten customers have bought tickets hoping to see me fail." When Norma expresses shock at this declaration, Helen explains:

> Norma, dear, I'm afraid you've led a very protected life with me. You've watched my success like a child on Christmas morning, and watched my failures without ever having to suffer them personally. . . . But *I've* had to experience it *all* [Inge's italics]. I've seen friends flock around me and invite me to parties during my successes, and seen the same friends avoid me when I suffered failure. It can be very disillusioning. It's not an experience one can go through and retain any very high ideals about the nature of humankind. We're living in a very competitive world, Norma. I suppose we have no right to expect anyone to be very interested in our welfare. (P. 6)

It doesn't take great imagination to hear William Inge's late-1960s sentiments in what Helen says and to comprehend some of the anxieties he was experiencing in his lonely room at the Algonquin before *Where's Daddy?* opened. But in this little play of fourteen manuscript pages, there is more. Helen's last preplay visitor is Jim Nye, the playwright in whose work she is about to appear. When Helen mentions that for her, this is a comeback, Jim says: "For me, too. After all, my last two plays have been failures. No one expects me to write a good one any more." When Helen tries to reassure him by mentioning how well things have gone so far, Jim says, exactly as William Inge had said many times: "But nothing means anything until opening night" (p. 11).

And not surprisingly, the reason that "nothing means anything until opening night" is the critics. As Jim and Helen both admit their fear, Jim says:

> I keep telling myself it isn't right, we should feel this sickening fear. Like culprits brought before some bigotted [sic] judge who's sure to condemn them unless he happens to be moved by some humorous whim to let them survive. Why should we feel ourselves so vulnerable? We've committed no sin. We've done our work out of love, and the desire to create some disturbing truth into a form of beauty men can accept. Even if we fail, we should feel no disgrace. We've been engaged in noble work, trying to create in a world that seeks always to destroy. Why should I feel now as if I were waiting for a sentence to the guillotine? (P. 12)

After this heartfelt speech, Jim asks Helen if she has a drink handy. She doesn't. "Sorry, Jim. I've had to give it up, you know." But Norma finds him a bottle of Scotch (p. 12). By this point, both Helen and Jim have so much in common with Inge that, for our purposes, identifying the speaker is only of secondary importance.

When Helen asks Jim if he intends to sit out front, he says: "Never. I'd be much too nervous. I'll peek in once in a while and watch it from the back of the house, and then go out for another drink." Helen tells Jim she won't be going to the party afterwards. "I'll be awfully tired. I'll feel myself tempted to drink. I don't know what the hell you can do at those parties if you don't drink, anyway. And I've been to so many of them, I hate them, sitting around waiting for the reviews." To which Jim responds, "The author is always so trapped at those damned parties. Everyone else is making merry while he's waiting for his death sentence" (p. 13). For Jim, the worst part is that either way the reviews go, he feels he's lost:

> Those awful, innocuous remarks if the reviews are bad. "Well, let me tell you, Jim, those critics are *crazy*. I always did think so. That was a *great* play, I don't care what *any*one says." And how futile it all is. . . . But it's just as bad if the reviews are good. "I told ya that play was

gonna be a hit, Jim. I can allus pick 'm 'n I said to Betsy, that play has *got* it." But of course by that time you're so numb with relief, you don't care what they say. (Pp. 13–14; [Inge's italics])

Comeback then proceeds to an indeterminate ending; we never learn how the opening goes for Helen and Jim because, as Jim's speech above makes clear, it no longer makes all that much difference. The unasked question that looms over such an attitude is, Why do it at all? Perhaps by the time he wrote *Comeback*, William Inge was already working on the answer to that question.

Few of the plays from this period are so consistently personal as *Comeback*. Yet many of them contain particular details that stand out to eyes searching for more evidence of Inge's state of mind during the late 1960s. In *I'm a Star*, a published one-act play, Julia Richards is an alcoholic actress of fifty who was once a star but hasn't worked in years and doesn't want to acknowledge her present poverty and desperation. Her friend Bea, also once an actress but not a star, urges Julia to go collect unemployment compensation. Julia doesn't want to. "Dear God, I'd rather starve than make myself an object of pity," she says.[5] She girds herself for her "appearance" with a pill and a shot of brandy (p. 736). These only make her worse. Julia says: "*No* one wants me anymore. No one wants me for *anything*. I've loused up my name in the entire industry" (Inge's italics, p. 740).

Julia then threatens to take an overdose of pills, but Bea accuses her of dramatizing herself as a "discarded woman." Bea suggests that it's not Julia's fault that work is so scarce: "Well, things are tough in the theatre now. *You* know that. All those British actors and everything, coming over here in those *avant garde* plays. They're . . . just not producing the kind of plays you and I used to do" (p. 740). Julia's reply is something Inge must have said or thought to himself many times: "Sometimes it's as if life gave us fame and fortune just to show us it can take them away" (p. 741). Thereafter, Julia gets drunker and more morose; finally she wets herself as she demands that Bea call her agent to say that Julia is coming to the office to demand work. As Julia exits, she says to tell the agent that "Miss Richards is on her way." After Julia closes the door, Bea repeats: "Yes. Miss Richards is on her way" as the curtain falls (p. 745).

Several other plays from this group have characters who have some similarity to Inge. In *The Call*, Joe, an out-of-towner from Billings, comes to visit his actress sister and brother-in-law in their "splendid apartment on a high floor on New York's east side."[6] When Terry, the brother-in-law, admits Joe, he learns that Joe has climbed twenty-two flights of stairs with his heavy trunk because he gets claustrophobic and fearful of attack in New York elevators (p. 5). Joe doesn't like to fly, and he doesn't think he can stay in the apartment because he gets "dizzy" when he is as high up as twenty-two stories (p. 7). He can't drink (p. 8); he hates crowds, and if he goes to see his sister perform at all, he will lurk alone at the back of the theater (p. 10) — all of which were Inge characteristics. It soon becomes clear that Joe's problems aren't manifest only in the city: he is an emotional isolate who has not recovered from the death of his mother several years before (p. 12). He keeps trying to call a phone number that the operator insists doesn't exist (pp. 16–17). This play, like *Comeback*, has an indeterminate ending — we never learn what becomes of Joe, but we are left with the definite impression that he will never complete *The Call*, probably because the number or the party that he is trying to reach truly does not exist; he is very near a complete mental breakdown.

In *The Killing*, Mac, a severely depressed writer, brings Huey, a bar acquaintance, home to persuade Huey to kill Mac. Huey, who originally thinks that Mac is gay and is picking him up for sex, is reluctant to cooperate and tries to get Mac to explain why he's suicidal. Mac then tells Huey about his depression, his inability to make a living anymore as a writer, and his lack of desire to go on.[7] Mac has plotted a way to make his death *look* like suicide, but he needs Huey to kill him because he's "too religious" to do it himself, although "too squeamish" would make more sense here (p. 9). Huey refuses anyway, so Mac forces the issue by pointing his gun at Huey and ordering Huey to kill him with a knife. A scuffle ensues in which Mac is shot to death (p. 20); then Huey puts the gun in Mac's hand and drops Mac's prewritten suicide note beside the body (p. 21).

A good many of these plays attempt to achieve a certain contemporary timeliness or relevance such as that suggested by Inge's presenting the black neighboring couple in *Where's Daddy?* to create dialogue about the need for racial understanding. But such relevance is usually forced and flawed because it becomes obvious that Inge himself is not comfortable using his drama to advocate social change. Nor is he confident of his ability to portray people whom he truthfully either doesn't understand or deplores. Such a play is *Caesarian Operations*.

Caesarian Operations, which is one of Inge's few unpublished late plays to be produced (in Los Angeles, in 1972), features a group of jaded New Yorkers who have gathered at the apartment of Al, a homosexual, before attending the theater. Al is not the flamboyant sort, and he seems at times to be Inge's spokesperson. At the beginning of the play, we hear Al talking to his friend Mel on the telephone. Al tells Mel that Fred and Olive, a "straight" couple, are coming over and then are going to the theater with him: "I like them, and they know the score. That's *something*. I hate having to pretend with most people, don't you? Yet, I think one should have *some* friends from the straight world."[8] And in response to something Mel presumably says about homosexuals' being called "queer," Al declares: "I'm sorry, Mel, but I *prefer* the word *queer*. It's more honest. I despise the use of the word *gay*. It's a misnomer if you ask me. I certainly don't go around all the time feeling *gay*" (Inge's italics, p. 1). But Al is not so secretive and prudish as his creator. In fact, he has been romancing an athletic young man named Ron, who is now on Al's couch, sleeping off a heavy dose of sleeping pills that he has taken carelessly.

When Fred and Olive arrive, Olive immediately shows an interest in Ron, whose nudity is barely covered. Al explains that he and Ron had been to a new club the night before, a place where guests of both sexes had to disrobe before entering. (Al prefers mixed bars; he hates "gay places.") They had smoked pot but had taken no acid: "Absolutely not!" exclaims Al; "I think that stuff is really dangerous" (p. 16). Later, Ron had spoken about a "feeling of disassociation," but Al had not interpreted that to mean anything suicidal; rather, as he tells Olive, he thought it meant "the usual complaints today. Disassociation, isolation, the absurdity of existence, and so on" (p. 19). In any case, Ron is breathing, and Al figures that if Ron had seriously and deliberately taken an overdose, Ron would be dead by now. Such cavalier diagnosis does not seem extraordinary to Al or Olive and Fred.

Eventually, Olive kisses the sleeping Ron on the lips. "It's not as though he needed mouth-to-mouth resuscitation," quips Fred (p. 30). After Olive inspects under Ron's coverlet, there follows a gamy discussion of penis size, and matters continue in this vein until the arrival of Roger Cavendish, another homosexual, whom Al has invited to use Ron's theater ticket. Roger and Olive discuss modern drama, but the conversation doesn't stay elevated for long; it moves from a series of allusions to Camus, Sartre, Durrenmatt, Ionesco, and Brecht (pp. 45–46) to attacks on critics, especially Walter Kerr. Roger says he "can not forgive Mr. Kerr for his deprecation of the theatre of involvement" (p. 49). Olive offers, "The theatre of involvement does have a glorious new vitality," to which Fred's reply brings matters down to the general level of the play: "Just pardon me. I'm just a plain, ordinary Midwestern fellow who doesn't always appreciate it when some skinny, sweaty broad comes down off the stage and sits in my lap and tries to unzip my fly" (p. 50). Thus does Fred criticize the theater of involvement, and thus does William Inge imagine what's needed for a successful play in the late 1960s.

At the beginning of the conclusion of *Caesarian Operations*, Olive and Roger both volunteer to stay at the apartment to "take care" of Ron while the others attend the theater. After an argument between Olive and Fred, which Al squelches with a childhood memory of locking himself in a closet while his parents argued, they all decide that they won't go to the theater. Ron finally awakens, mutters some Latin, which Roger translates as "My soul is sad unto death: / Stay here and watch with me," and asks where he is. He then announces that he has a date and leaves. As the curtain falls, there is a "long silence as Fred, Olive, Roger and Al just stand, each feeling somehow he's been had" (p. 84). The remarks of critic Richard Watts, Jr., about *Natural Affection* seem appropriate for *Caesarian Operations* and several other of Inge's late plays: "The sensationally lurid is not Mr. Inge's field."[9]

Scribbling away in the Hollywood Hills during the late 1960s, Inge created several more plays in the vein of *Caesarian Operations*. *Midwestern Manic* doesn't have a single character Inge likes; in this play the visitors from the Midwest are ultimately as hypocritical and reprehensible as their big-city relatives. *The Tube Boobs* is about a couple who live in the "complex" and spend their time stoned, watching television, and alternately neglecting and beating their baby until the child dies. Thereupon, they incinerate the baby and return to the television set. Some plays present such atrocities in an absurdist or surrealistic style, as in *A Murder*, and *A Meeting in a Room*. Even *Bad Breath*, one of the few true comedies from this period, which uses absurdism to satirize television commercials, manages to present a suicide attempt: Mary, a housewife, slashes her wrists because she "can't make a good cup of coffee."[10] A friend, Ernestine, tells Mary that only one product, Capo, will get those stubborn blood stains out of her sink (p. 6). Later, Mary's mother suggests what to serve when the boss comes to dinner: "an *avant garde* recipe called 'Krapp's Last Crepe'" (p. 15).

It would be misleading to say that all these mentioned plays are uniformly bad. Inge never lost his ability to produce occasionally fine dialogue and sharp characterization. But few of the late characters show the fine tension, the tightly wound repression and frustration coiled within the characters in the plays of the 1950s. It is as though the freedom to be frank in speech, character, and situation failed Inge's powers; as though the modern world he was seeking to portray in socially relevant drama was just too confounding for him to capture. As a successful dramatist, Inge was one who looked

Inge on the beach at Malibu, photographed by Jerome Lawrence, 1968. Courtesy of WIC/ICC

to the somehow manageable past of his midwestern experience, when problems could be overcome, or at least seemingly overcome, by people of good will and inner fortitude. He apparently doubted that such possibilities continued to exist in the drama of the late 1960s, even though, as we shall see, he did not entirely abandon his attempts to write hopeful drama.

ALTHOUGH he began to write prolifically when he returned to California after the hospitalization in Kansas City, Inge kept, for him, fairly active socially. He spent time with Jerome Lawrence, and he saw Christopher Isherwood, whose work he admired, with some frequency. Jack Garfein, who was heading the Actors' and Directors' Laboratory then, invited Inge to participate by teaching and advising students. Garfein was aware that Inge was upset by his recent failures, so he tried to channel Inge's creative tension away from negative feelings of rejection. Garfein found that Inge was good at working with students but that he was not willing to be very critical. And if any criticism of himself was offered, Inge was hurt. His feelings, in Garfein's words, were "totally raw, everything would affect him in a deep way."[11] Still, under Garfein's auspices, some of the plays Inge wrote at the time were used in the laboratory workshops. Among these were *The Call*, which Garfein considers very representative of Inge's loneliness and depression at the time; *The Tube Boobs*, which an incredulous Garfein says Inge thought was one of his best plays ever; *Bad Breath*; and *Don't Go Gentle*, which was an early version of what became *The Last Pad*, the last of Inge's plays to be produced during his lifetime.

Garfein did not believe these plays were especially good, but he understood that Inge was trying to work his way into a new creative vein for his drama, and he thought that Inge's sheer productivity was a positive sign. Garfein was one of the few at the time who knew that Inge had had major problems long before he had ever become famous, long before *Sheba* had appeared on Broadway. Garfein was later to reflect that it was probably a miracle that Inge lasted as long as he did. Garfein believes that Inge's success during the 1950s may have hurt Inge but that it also prolonged his life. There is little doubt that Garfein is right.[12] Inge's success as a playwright was a mark of approval that Inge was never able to find for any other aspect of his life, and he worked hard to try to regain it. Still, he sensed what would happen should the success not come again, and the forebodings of suicide were not limited to the plays and the prose he was writing.

In a letter to Ned Rorem on June 2, 1967, Inge told Rorem, who was about to publish the *New York Diary*, which mentions Rorem's and Inge's experiences with Alcoholics Anonymous:

> Probably you'd better make me anonymous in connection with A.A. I don't care personally, but it's best for the welfare of the organization, which I respect enormously. I did break anonymity once in an interview for *Esquire*, and I've regretted it. After all, should I ever die drunk or decide to kill myself, it would hurt the organization. It's a responsibility I don't want.
>
> I'm so sorry to have missed seeing you out here. In fact I feel rather cheated. Do come again and let me know in advance. After all, I've no plans for killing myself, at least very soon. I work pretty intensely and have the most quiet of pleasures.[13]

Rorem didn't honor Inge's request; he used Inge's name freely in the passages about A.A. in his book. In fact, it appears that those passages and other homosexually tinged remarks that Rorem made about Inge in the *New York Diary* ended their friendship or at least put considerable strain on it. Whatever befell the friendship, Inge's letter to Rorem betrays both loneliness and a kind of quiet desperation. But he was right about one thing: he would not kill himself "very soon."

Among the definite reasons for hope were the continued writing and the ongoing interest and support of friends such as Lawrence and Garfein. Garfein had encouraged Inge to keep developing a play that involved the conversations of death-row prison inmates and the social issue of capital punishment. Perhaps Inge originally hit on the idea for this play because of the phenomenal success Truman Capote had recently had with *In Cold Blood*, the journalistic novel about a brutal multiple murder in western Kansas and the state of Kansas' equally brutal execution of the murderers. *In Cold Blood* raised the issue of capital punishment starkly and dramatically, as well as profitably, for Capote. Inge imagined a play in which the condemned would show their own humanity even though they are to be executed. Early versions of the play were called *The Disposal*; but when Garfein used it in the laboratory workshop, it was called *Don't Go Gentle*, roughly after Dylan Thomas's famous villanelle. It eventually emerged in full length, and it was produced off Broadway in New York (1970), in Phoenix (1972), and in Los Angeles (1973) as *The Last Pad*.

The protagonist of *The Last Pad* is Jess, a one-time midwestern farm boy who killed his pregnant wife and child. The play takes place on the day Jess is to be executed. Jess has several conversations with fellow condemned inmates Luke and Archie while he awaits a visit from his father. Archie is a homosexual who is also something of an intellectual; his talk occasionally alludes to literature and is embellished with French phrases; but all three sprinkle their speech liberally with the profanity that one might expect in the setting. The point of the play is the stark and unmitigated brutality of eye-for-an-eye justice and the undeniable presence of evil, or capacity for evil, in all of us. Like Camus's Meursault in *The Stranger*, Jess rejects the message of the chaplain who comes to see him to try to persuade him to repent. "God can forgive you, if man can not," says the chaplain, "because God is good." Jess's rejoinder pinpoints the theme of the play: "What's it matter if *God* is good? *Men* aren't" (Inge's italics).[14] When his father comes to see him, Jess refuses to play along with his father's *pro forma* contention that Jess is innocent. "I *ain't* innocent," Jess declares, thus hurting his father again when he hadn't wanted to (p. 73). Jess wants to face his death bravely, but when the time comes, he does not "go gentle" (p. 81).

The Last Pad seems to be proof that during his last years, Inge no longer knew what good drama was. Or perhaps he knew but had long abandoned what he knew was good for what he hoped would be popular. It isn't that *The Last Pad* has no poignance; rather, it just doesn't ring true. What, finally, did William Inge know about murderers on death row? Perhaps only that they had been hot copy for Capote. And it should be remembered that Inge told Jack Garfein that he thought *The Tube Boobs* was one of the best plays he'd ever written. During his later years, Inge was apparently liable to call *anything* he'd written his best, as long as people paid attention to it. *The Last Pad* got enough attention to be produced in New York—although in the off-Broadway Thirteenth Street Theatre for a deliberately limited run. Of the production, which attracted little attention, Mel Gussow of the *New York Times* wrote: "What is a new William Inge play doing off Off Broadway? One thought that perhaps it was too offbeat or controversial for commercial production. The truth is that it is simply lesser Inge."[15]

Another example of "lesser Inge" to come from this period is *Overnight*, a play about a dissolved marriage. Harry Broch is a Los Angeles man who, like his creator, loves and collects modern art. Broch is visited unexpectedly one night by Muriel, his nymphomaniacal, drug-addicted, and suicidal former wife. Muriel, who is also a pathological liar, manages to deceive Harry into thinking she has overcome her many problems. She seduces him, then talks of remarriage and new happiness. However, it soon develops that on this particular night she has escaped the custody of Ray Hirsch, her attorney and lover, who had taken her out of a mental hospital for a one-night stand. Ray comes to Harry's, and a tripartite raging argument ensues. This costs Harry a valuable painting, which Muriel destroys, and ends with Muriel's near-obligatory attempt at suicide.[16] Getting Muriel calmed down, taken care of, and back to the mental hospital consumes the rest of the action.

Not all of Inge's late plays are of this hopelessly sordid sort. One script, *The Lady Gay*, was intended to be a tragic love story based on an Old West tale about Dodge City. The script, according to an article in the March 30, 1967, *Wichita Eagle*, was to be the basis of a musical motion picture. In a long-distance telephone interview, Inge told the *Eagle's* staff writer Elma Byrne that his script was "very vaguely" based on the Dodge City romance of "Dora Hand, an entertainer, and Dog Kelly, who raised Russian wolfhounds for racing." Hand, who had been brought from the East to sing in a saloon, was also loved by an "unknown cowboy." Eventually, the tensions of the love triangle resulted in Hand's death. Inge, who had traveled to Dodge City and Topeka to research the story and draft the script, told Byrne that originally he had intended *The Lady Gay* for the stage but that he had found the stage "too confining" for his story, which now would become a musical film to be produced by Edward Lewis, directed by John Frankenheimer, and released by Metro-Goldwyn-Mayer. No cast had been set, and Inge told Byrne that it was "much too early to be thinking of composers or lyricists since I haven't finished the script yet."[17] In fact, it was much too early to be saying anything about *The Lady Gay* to reporters. The film was never made, although a very melodramatic finished script by that name is among the manuscripts at the University of Kansas, and a duplicate or alternate version is also in the Inge Collection.

Why *The Lady Gay* was never filmed is not known. Perhaps the material, like much of Inge's work, was not well suited to musical accompaniment, although to make that assumption based only on Inge's prior work is a bit precarious, because the Inge Collection holds several attempts and proof of attempts, most of which are by other writers, to turn *Bus Stop* into a musical. At least one musical version of *Picnic*, called *Hot September*, nearly made it to Broadway in the mid 1960s. There was even one attempt to create a musical version of *Sheba*. Perhaps the script was rejected because it was too melodramatic or because Inge's cowboys and dance-hall girls weren't believable enough, although those hardly seem serious flaws by the standards of Hollywood musicals. All that can be concluded is that in March, 1967, Inge was excited about the prospect of *The Lady Gay*'s becoming a film, and it never became one.

It is possible that Robert Alan Aurthur provides a clue to the fate of *The Lady Gay* in the tribute to Inge that he wrote after Inge's death. Aurthur recalls that when he was working on a play in California, he saw Inge with some frequency, and that "one night, very animated," Inge "told me he was leaving on assignment the next day for the Midwest to research an original film idea and work on a treatment."[18] Three months later, however, after his return from the Midwest, Inge met with Aurthur and told him that the people who had employed him to do the research and treatment were not paying him what they had promised upon delivery of a script. Inge knew that Aurthur had also had unpleasant experiences with these people, and Inge wondered what recourse Aurthur would suggest. Aurthur advised Inge to bring a legal suit, which at the time delighted Inge; but a short while later, when they met again, Inge reported that the suit he had brought had resulted in a countersuit for the original research money, which Inge had spent in the Midwest.

Aurthur never mentioned the name of the project and was careful not to identify Inge's employers, other than referring to them as "a high-flying producer-director team I'll have to call Bert and Ernie," because in detailing his attempts to console Inge, Aurthur expressed a derogatory opinion about "Ernie's" sexual proclivities. Although the project that Aurthur refers to cannot certainly be said to be *The Lady Gay*, Aurthur's recollections nonetheless point to two harsh truths about Inge's experience in California: first, he was trying to conduct his own business affairs, often with people whom Barbara Baxley calls "barracudas," and he sorely missed Audrey Wood's guidance, even though he would probably not ever have admitted it; second, he was becoming ever more deeply vulnerable emotionally to criticism of his work. As Aurthur recalls, what hurt Inge most about the whole affair was the rejection of his script. "But why," Aurthur says the wounded Inge asked, "did they hate my treatment?"[19]

That treatment may or may not have been *The Lady Gay*. But the script by that name at the University of Kansas is of interest, not only because Inge managed to work in details of the period well—references to buffalo bones, cattle drivers, and Boot Hill—but also because in writing with the screen in mind, Inge kept the language mild, as mild as he had in his plays of the 1950s.[20] Although the story itself occasionally displays the worst sort of corny melodrama (e.g., the heroine is killed in a cross fire that her lovers intend for each other, p. 168), and although the Dora Hand character, here called Lucy Keane, is more than a shade unbelievable (she sings at the saloon *and* in the church choir, and she teaches school into the bargain), one senses an earlier, less desperate Inge in the descriptions and dialogue, quite as if he had more knowledge and understanding of the late 1860s than of the late 1960s. And in any case, he was writing again about Kansas, which Lucy's remarks to her friend Fanny make clear as the two cross the prairie on the train:

> LUCY (enraptured): Just look, Fanny, the sky covers us from one horizon to the other. Like an enormous tent. I don't think I ever noticed the sky before, Fanny. I never realized the world was so big. Oh, I love it, Fanny, being able to see so far into the distance. It makes man seem so small, doesn't it?
> FANNY (cynically): Man *is* small.

LUCY: And makes all our past misdeeds seem small, too. Oh, I'm going
to be happy here, Fanny. I can tell. (P. 8)

In Inge's screenplay, Lucy is happy in Dodge City, even though she will die
there. And elsewhere in Inge's writing, Lucy's feelings that are generated by
the expanse of sky and horizon recur, but as Inge's own sentiments.

WITH THE exception of *Comeback* and a few other works that feature characters who seem, in various ways, to speak for William Inge, most of the plays
he wrote in the late 1960s ring false because they are poorly conceived attempts to recover popularity by writing sensational "relevant" drama. But
most of the prose became the medium in which he sought primarily to express himself. Flattered to be asked in 1968 by the editors of Time-Life Books
to write the introduction to a volume entitled *The Plains States*, Inge responded with a straightforward enthusiasm that not only introduces the
plains region to a reader but also serves as a kind of testament to Inge's own
beliefs about the land and the people. His lengthy opening sentence sets
his tone and philosophy:

> The Plains States are the heart of our nation, and that heart beats
> slow and sure year after year while the cities on the coastlines, crowded,
> competitively industrial, cosmopolite and more seemingly vulnerable
> to foreign influences as well as attacks in time of war, manifest our na-
> tion's violent antagonisms.[21]

But Inge's introduction is not purely laudatory primitivism. The Plains
States and their people, he continues, show a "correlation of landscape and
character, . . . plain and level and unadorned" (p. 6). The open horizon seems
to spawn an openness and an honesty in the people, who, being people,
can be just as good or as bad as people anywhere, but they are somehow
more forthright than people elsewhere, more willing to be as level as the land
in their dealings (p. 7). This openness, Inge suggests, is a result of living
under a great wide sky which can bring, at different times, such extremes
of weather that people seem barely significant:

> A person lives in this mid-country with an inherent consciousness of
> the sky. . . . And human life on the prairie is more dependent upon
> and influenced by the sky and its constant maneuverings than in

other regions. . . . Life and prosperity depend upon that sky, which can destroy a season's crops in a few hours, by hail or blizzards or tornadoes or a relentlessly burning sun that can desiccate the land like an Old Testament curse. (P. 6)

After detailing several instances in which he personally had experienced such harshness of weather, Inge counters, "of course there is beautiful weather on the plains," and he proceeds to prove that point as well. He also echoes Lucy Keane's speech in *The Lady Gay* about the sky near Dodge City when he says:

No mountains can be as beautiful to me as the far horizon, level as a floor, 20 or 30 miles in the distance. The sight fills me with a wonderful feeling of personal freedom, and also with a sense of infinity. Man finds his solitude here and in the still atmosphere cannot help but wonder about the nature of all being. (P. 7)

The introduction to *The Plains States*, of course, is Inge prose without any disguise of being fiction. But when fiction was supposedly his intent in *My Son Is a Splendid Driver*, the result is even better written and no less truly heartfelt. Joey Hansen describes a sunset over the plains of Western Kansas:

As we looked to the west, there was nothing of man's creation between us and the horizon. Occasionally, a ramshackle farm or shed. Nothing on earth seemed of the slightest consequence; but in the sky, something important was happening. Day was being destroyed by coming night, and the burst of orange in the sky was like a final flush of blood in the body's system before a being passes away. I have seen many prairie sunsets since that time, and they have always moved me to believe that there is something going on in the sky much bigger than man himself; that man's presence upon the earth is an incidental gift that we must make the most of while it lasts, even though our strivings, our creations, our sins and our virtues are all lost in infinity.[22]

A person can't write like that about a place without betraying a love for it. ("Oh, I love it, Fanny, being able to see so far in the distance," cries Lucy Keane in *The Lady Gay*.) But like many prairie writers before him, Inge's love for the plains was somehow not strong enough to draw him back to live there. "Its native artists usually go to some other part of the country to find appreciation and encouragement," he wrote in the introduction to *The Plains States* (p. 6). He didn't offer any idea about where those native artists should go when they failed to find appreciation and encouragement elsewhere.

My Son Is a Splendid Driver, most of which was written during this same late-1960s period in California, has already been seen, in numerous ways, to be Inge's most truthful published self-expression. As he told Digby Diehl in 1967, the novel he was working on at the time (*Driver*) was "midwestern Proustian . . . very analytical."

> In this novel I find myself writing about the failure of American man-
> hood. I'm exploring the reasons for it, the estimates of it, the tragedy
> of it. I think that the American male is in a tragic position because
> he has no real mode of personal expression. I was brought up in a semi-
> primitive society—Kansas in the twenties. Culture was far away, and
> the American man was limited to being a breadwinner. It's just one
> place where the forms of life are imposed on the man.[23]

"The American male," here, is William Inge, whose youthful family and community environments provided "no real mode of personal expression" when that mode was homosexual and whose milieu provided one basic, wholly heterosexual male "form of life" to fill: the "breadwinner." Any other "form of life" was at worst unthinkable and at best alien. No wonder *Driver* teems with regret for the many things in Inge's life that were, ultimately, no one's fault, the things that seemed to have been impressed on him by the very circumstances of his life: his parents' unhappy but enduring marriage; his childhood in Maude's nervous matriarchy, intensified by Luther's frequent and willing absence; his lonely fumbling toward the realization of his own nature, sex being, as he says in *Driver*, "as fearful as black magic to all of us." Indeed, another statement that Inge makes in *Driver* seems apt for describing his entire view of his life apart from his success as a writer: "In retrospect, we all seem thwarted people" (*Driver*, both quotations from p. 16.).

My Son Is a Splendid Driver is the story of a thwarted person whose ability to write creatively made the key, although not wholly compensating, difference in his life. During the time of his greatest success, Inge's works seemed only to endorse heterosexual marriage and traditional families. Such endorsement was the crux of Robert Brustein's initial and disastrous criticism. But what if that endorsement were also a covert capitulation and a regretful self-criticism as well? What if, in showing the reconciliations of Doc and Lola, Bo and Cherie, Rubin and Cora—even Tom and Teena—Inge was sadly accepting the imperfect institutions of conventional marriage and family as *all* that society has to offer, and therefore was endorsing them by a kind of default? After all, not one of the marriages he depicts is anything like ideal, even after the conflicts in the play have been resolved. Not one of the Inge women whom Brustein found to be "men-taming" has any more choice in the role she is expected to play than the man has. Inge's dominant theme is acceptance, making the best one can of one's situation, and that's what all of Inge's couples ultimately try to do. The note of regretful self-criticism comes in the fact that in the society William Inge had known during virtually all of his adult life, certainly during the time of his greatest success, the only acceptable couples were heterosexual. By his very nature, Inge was an outsider to the only "form of life" that society could approve for him.

In the 1950s, however, critics such as Robert Brustein weren't likely to see Inge as an "outsider," even if they either suspected or knew about his homosexuality. Because the depiction of homosexuality in drama was still taboo, it could hardly have had an influence on printed criticism at the time. But playwright Robert Patrick has suggested that homosexual playwrights in the 1950s, such as Inge and Tennessee Williams, were "inside outsiders," creators of popular entertainment who *appeared* to be cultural "insiders" but who in fact were more profoundly "outsiders" than anyone who was a member of an obvious minority. In Patrick's eloquent assessment, Inge, "the outsider inside, the homosexual, watched and saw and remembered, analyzed, distilled and idealized, criticized, satirized, commemorated, blessed, and cursed the beauty, passion, pain, poetry, harmonies and contradictions of the all-encompassing heterosexual hegemony."[24] In other words, from this unique vantage point Inge was extraordinarily able to see into marriage and family while being emphatically but covertly apart. Again, the close observer, but not the participant.

Of course, Inge was not the only "American male" who couldn't help but "fail" because, as he said to Digby Diehl, he had "no real mode of self-expression." Inge himself knew many other males who had failed as "breadwinners," not the least of whom was Tennessee Williams. But self-knowledge and self-acceptance are different matters, and Inge forever had trouble with the latter. Quite simply, he would have preferred not to be gay. Barbara Baxley believes that during the 1950s, before all the criticism and self-doubt came, Inge had a good deal of self-respect. After all, he had his drinking under control. In terms of his work and his creative imagination, she says, "He knew he was good." Then, she continues, "He was only uncomfortable with himself as a homosexual."[25] She did not mean to imply that this problem was small; in fact, it was nearly always overwhelming for him. But her remark shows how much Inge had triumphed over the circumstances of his life, how much he had realized his ambitions. Yet he still could not enjoy his success, and that is very probably because he could not accept his sexuality; and stemming from that, he was in most ways profoundly alone, with no loved companion of either sex to share his life. Like Professor Benoit in Inge's one-act play, Inge had to hear—and bear—the strains of triumph alone. *My Son Is a Splendid Driver* gives Inge's fullest explanation of why that is so, and it is the best and truest work of prose that he wrote. Fittingly, it was also the last of his works to be published, even though it had been written before he published his first novel, *Good Luck Miss Wyckoff*, in 1970.

WHILE WORKING with Garfein's workshop, about the time when Inge was writing his most lurid plays and his most lucid prose, he received an offer that must have struck him as ironic: the chance to teach again, this time, not for his livelihood, but on a part-time basis for the prestige his name would bring, as a Pulitzer Prize–winning playwright, to the Department of Drama at the University of California at Irvine. The offer came in 1968, nearly twenty years after Inge had left Washington University in St. Louis, gambling that *Come Back, Little Sheba* would enable him never to have to teach again. He had always claimed not to like teaching because he didn't think he was very good at it, but the real disadvantage of teaching for Inge was that for a long time it was a necessary career alternative to what he really wanted to do. To teach without having to and only on a part-time basis is a different circumstance, however, and Inge was probably flattered by the offer, for it had been ten years since his last successful Broadway play (*Stairs*) and fifteen years since he had won the Pulitzer for *Picnic*. So, he agreed to do it.

His friends doubtless hoped that teaching at U.C.-Irvine would boost Inge's spirits and creativity, but there is no evidence to suggest that such was the case. At least one source, Charles E. Burgess, reports that Inge "found some comfort" in the teaching, but even though his schedule was not demanding, as befitted a writer/teacher of his stature, his work was intermittent. Over the two years that he taught, interruptions became more frequent; these, according to Burgess, were for "institutional treatment."[26] The pattern for Inge, which intensified as the California years passed, was a continuous one of writing, followed by frustration, followed by liquor and sedatives, followed by medical and psychological help, which would bring him around for another pass through the pattern. Where such a life was likely to lead was not much of a mystery, even for those, such as Professor Robert Cohen of U.C.-Irvine, who didn't really know Inge very well. Inge was "ripe" for suicide, Cohen was later to recall; "everybody knew it" (Burgess, p. 442).

And of course, Inge knew it too. Despite that knowledge, he kept going back to his writing desk. As long as he could bring himself back to that desk, he might still produce something of value, something that would restore his reputation as an important writer. He also knew that his more recent work and the work that he was likely to produce would not be of the same sort on which his original reputation had been built. That awareness he illustrated dramatically in October, 1968, when Neil Edds, dean of Independence Community College, and Margaret Goheen, chair of the Drama Department, wrote to Inge to tell him that the college was going to have a new campus, south of town at the site of the old country club. They asked for his personal support—both moral and monetary—for their new fine-arts building and proposed that the theater in that building be named after him. His reply reveals his knowledge that his popularity in Independence, never overwhelming, might suffer even more. He wrote to Edds and Goheen:

> You have bestowed an honor upon me I never could have expected. It is very warming to know that my hometownspeople think enough of me to want to name your theatre center after me. It is certainly an honor, but also a responsibility which I feel I must consider carefully, out of respect for you rather than for myself. I am, after all, only fifty-five years old (old enough but young for some writers) and I *may* have my most important work yet before me (and of course I may not). I can't help wondering what the civic feeling would be should I write a play or a novel that the townspeople strongly disapproved of. And what if something should happen in my personal life that would make my name an embarrassment to the college? Please understand, I'm not *planning* on any of these things happening, but one never knows. Usually, buildings are named after people after they are dead. I have always considered this custom to be a useless one, and have always argued that we as a nation should pay more honor to artists and writers when they're living. Now I see the hazard of the practice. Dead people are much safer to honor than the living.[27] (Inge's italics)

What if he were to write a shocking play? Certainly such plays as *Cae-sarian Operations* would shock Independence. What if he were to write an upsetting novel? In fact, he was soon to do so; Margaret Clement, the one-time proprietor with her husband, John, of the local bookstore, said *Good Luck, Miss Wyckoff* "shocked this little town."[28] What if the community were to find out that he was homosexual? Although many may have long sus-pected this, none as yet had proof. But in his work, Inge was, as we have seen, ever so gradually peeking out of the closet. He didn't want to think about Independence's reaction to such possibilities. But the honor was too great and his pleasure too keen for him to decline: "If you want to take a chance on me, I can only say yes. But if you want to reconsider, I'll under-stand." The community didn't exactly reconsider, but it did hesitate. The theater was not dedicated in his name until April, 1975, nearly two years after his death.

Inge's reply continued, informing Edds and Goheen that his work had "not been very lucrative" lately, so he could not "spare a donation." However, he said that he had books, magazines, and memorabilia he could give them and that he was presently at work on a play and a novel that "*might* put him" in a financial bracket to make a "good donation in a year or two."[29] The play he was referring to could have been one of several he wrote during the late 1960s. The novel was probably *Good Luck, Miss Wyckoff*, for al-though *My Son Is a Splendid Driver* was essentially finished by then, it is un-likely that Inge saw it as a potential moneymaker.

DURING THE two years that Inge taught intermittently at U.C.-Irvine, ventur-ing out on the freeway for the hour-long drive of fifty miles on Tuesdays and Thursdays, he had an experience that inspired him to write the article "The Relevance of Theatre," which he submitted to, then withdrew from, the *At-lantic Monthly*.[30] "The Relevance of Theatre" was the result of a request that Inge had from one of his "militant" students to write an article for the school paper, explaining the relevance of theater in "today's society." Inge knew that the student believed "every institution, every profession, every goal" should be reexamined in terms of its "relevance," a powerful educational "buzz word" of the late 1960s. He also knew that this "surly but provocative boy" would hardly buy any of the conventional historical rationales for art in society.[31] So Inge didn't offer any such rationales. Instead, he responded with the purely aesthetic argument that "the theatre and the other arts are certainly

not relevant to society," for if they were, they would be serving "some propa-
gandistic function" that would "cheapen" them. The arts "serve society best
when they serve themselves best," he concluded (p. 17).

Inge didn't say whether his artful reply satisfied his student, but the resultant article he submitted to Robert Manning, editor in chief of the *Atlantic Monthly*, was full of the criticisms of the theater scene that Inge had been
leveling for some time in his public comments, his plays—both published
and unpublished, both produced and not produced—and his other works.
Among those criticisms were:

1. That theater is ultimately an artistic, not a commercial, expression
   and therefore that it deserves respect on a cultural, moral, and spiritual plane.
2. That the commercial interests and star system dominate what is
   presented to the public in the largest venues, thus relegating serious
   new drama now to small venues.
3. That New York critics—and in particular the critic for the *New York
   Times*—are too powerful in determining, on very short notice, what
   is "good" in new drama.
4. And that the reputations of playwrights, as well as their will to create, can be too easily destroyed by callous, pompous, self-serving
   criticism.

Inge also included his dismay with actors and directors, who preferred "spontaneity" to structures and scripts, and his fear that the nice new theaters
being built in regional centers would be limited to featuring only those "safe"
(inoffensive) plays that had already been given the New York "seal of approval" (pp. 11–12).

In this article, Inge pinpointed problems that have been identified and
discussed by numerous theater experts during the past twenty to thirty years.
The perceptions are largely accurate, and the bitterness that Inge felt may
only occasionally be glimpsed in this article: "The *Times* is such a powerful
newspaper throughout America, its board could appoint a halfwit in the
drama critic's position, and he would retain more power and influence than
a qualified man on a smaller publication" (p. 14). Had this article been published in the *Atlantic Monthly*, it would at least have clarified his attitude
and probably would have been a useful contribution to contemporary discussion about the theater. But after sending it to Manning, Inge began to have

second thoughts. The *Atlantic Monthly* was an important national magazine. He didn't want to sound foolish, or bitter, or both, so he decided to
withdraw the article from consideration.

On July 19, 1969, Inge wrote to Manning that he could imagine that "a
caustic New York theatregoer" might conclude that the author of "The Relevance of Theatre" was a "simple-minded" individual who "should go back to
Kansas and stay there."[32] Using a lengthy example about how the painting
and sculpture of René Magritte had suddenly become "in," Inge explained
that only the avant-garde, as certified by the proper critics, was liable to be
popular in America. That fact seemed so obvious to him now that he doubted
that his argument was worth making. He had pleaded in the article ("The
Relevance of Theatre," pp. 7–9) for more reverence for the established plays
of American dramatic literature so that they would not be ignored or forgotten just because they were no longer new or avant-garde. He did not believe
that the plays of Williams, Miller, Albee, O'Neill, Odets, Sherwood, and
others were necessarily "great," but he did believe that they were worthwhile
parts of our admittedly small national dramatic literature and, as he wrote
to Manning, thus were worthy of coexisting "with classics and contemporary plays" (p. 2). But now he feared that his argument would be misunderstood, and although he did not say so in his letter to Manning, he was tired
of being misunderstood. He did not want to risk ridicule for his honest
thoughts, straightforwardly expressed.

Manning wrote back on July 21 to say that he had been very pleased to
receive "The Relevance of Theatre," then "very disappointed" to learn that
Inge didn't want to publish it after all. "That is a pity," wrote Manning, "but
of course I do not want to put you in a difficult position . . . [so] I am returning it." He went on to say that he hoped Inge would reconsider.[33] But "The
Relevance of Theatre" was never submitted again. It is Inge's clearest statement of how he viewed the institution of theater in America near the end
of his life, and it is evidence that he had an understanding of the forces at
work that affected all contemporary drama, not just his own. His second
thoughts and his reluctance to publish the article suggest the withdrawal that
was beginning to intensify within him as the 1960s were drawing to a close.

INGE'S GRADUAL withdrawal during the late 1960s seems to have been prompted
as much by the generally lukewarm interest of others as by his own growing
doubts and disappointments. In the *Los Angeles Herald-Examiner* for November 10, 1968, Winfred Blevins called Inge "America's Ignored Dramatist" and

implied that the description might be warranted because three new Inge projects (*Don't Go Gentle, Overnight,* and a musical version of *Bus Stop*) were "uneven."[34] Five days later, Sam Zolotow, in the *New York Times,* detailed Inge's collaboration with composer-lyricist Gerry Raad and producer Robert Shelley to bring *Beau,* the musical remake of *Bus Stop,* to Broadway the following September.[35] *Beau,* however, never appeared, on Broadway or anywhere else, and the same was true of *Overnight* while Inge was alive. Only *Don't Go Gentle,* reworked as *The Last Pad,* was to see production before Inge's death.

What happened to these various plans is not known, but there is no reason to doubt that Inge was experiencing his by-now familiar problems with would-be producers and directors who showed interest in his work but did not see his written words as creative choices to be treated with utmost respect. Such experience, virtually inevitable with plays, could be avoided only with prose; yet the only novel Inge had in nearly complete form at the time was *My Son Is a Splendid Driver,* hardly the sort of novel Inge could envision as becoming a successful first venture into a new genre. At some point he began to discuss the possibility of a first novel with Atlantic–Little, Brown publishers, but he was not yet ready to abandon his playwriting efforts completely. He apparently held hope as late as 1970 that *Beau* might be produced, but a letter to a woman named Helen (probably his old friend Helen Hafner) on September 17 of that year ruefully notes: "Plans for my musical have fallen through, alas! I resume teaching at Irvine in October."[36] But soon, he was no longer teaching at Irvine, and even his friends Garfein and Lawrence found him more and more reluctant to come down from his house in the hills.

The increasing seclusion, however, did not yet mean that Inge was surrendering as a writer. In fact, he finally negotiated a deal with Atlantic–Little, Brown to publish his first novel, a story that he had developed about a female high-school teacher in "Freedom, Kansas." *Good Luck, Miss Wyckoff* was a complete return to the small-town Midwest that Inge had made so familiar in his successes of the 1950s, but with the crucial differences that the freedom of the novel form and the much more permissive times allowed Inge a latitude in matters of sex and language that he had never before had, a latitude that he in fact did not manage well.

Evelyn Wyckoff, the protagonist of the brief novel (179 pages), has a powerful kinship with Rosemary Sydney, Inge's memorable schoolteacher in *Picnic*: both are unmarried women; both are attractive but troubled because they are still single when well past thirty; both are deeply frustrated and lonely, conditions exacerbated by the moral and physical confines of the villages in which they live as embodiments of rectitude. However, in Inge's third-person narration, which is limited almost exclusively to Evelyn's point of view, it soon becomes clear that Evelyn is much more intelligent than Rosemary, much more sensitive to the limitations of her situation, and, ultimately, much more vulnerable and victimized than Rosemary. Faced with premature menopause and advised to have a sexual affair by both the local doctor she admires and the Wichita psychiatrist she respects, Evelyn is cramped, nearly paralytic because of her knowledge of the reality of her situation: where can she find what she needs in the isolation of the town of Freedom?

The physical solution is also her social and professional undoing: a lonely black athlete at the local junior college, Rafe Collins, who is working after school as a janitor, first attracts her, then boldly preys upon her weakness and desperation. The first actual seduction scene strains credulity, for given the intelligence and reticence of Evelyn, it is doubtful that Rafe could so easily have guided her hand, under the guise of feeling an injury to a ligament, through his unzipped fly to his penis.[37] But sex scenes were not what Inge wanted to write about; he wanted to write about the *results* of such scenes. And although there are feints at the sort of racial "relevance" that Inge was seeking with the characters of Helen and Razz in *Where's Daddy?* the novel *Good Luck, Miss Wyckoff* is by no means a story about racial discrimination: it is a story about sexual suffering, made profoundly disturbing by the small-town setting. When Evelyn and Rafe are discovered, Evelyn loses her job and is forced to leave town. Still, Inge implies that although she will need the "good luck" that everyone wishes her, Evelyn is somehow the better for her experience: like so many other Inge characters before her, she will, in Wordsworth's clause, "find / Strength in what remains behind."[38]

Evelyn's reflections at the close of the novel, although they are ostensibly given through the mind of a woman, are as easily Inge's own: "For the first time in her life now, Evelyn realized how a human being is totally alone in the universe" (p. 174). Evelyn's/Inge's reflections continue: "She knew for a certainty now that she would always be alone, that she would never marry. She bore the smell of aloneness in her armpits" (p. 175); and: "She should feel braver now for having faced her aloneness" (p. 176). Evelyn's story is as familiar as old regret to William Inge, but often his manner of telling is alien, for sexual frankness was never his forte.

The less-than-convincing first seduction scene has already been mentioned. Elsewhere, in projecting Evelyn's thoughts, Inge seems to surround the frank words with a primness that makes neither the primness nor the frankness very believable; for example, the use of *cocks* in the following passage describing a doctor's examination of Evelyn: "He was probing apertures in her body that had never been forced into expansion by young men's excited fingers or swollen cocks, but had remained tight-fitting doors to the unentered vaults of her body" (p. 75). Such passages prompt one to agree with the critic Haskel Frankel that "when writing explicitly, Mr. Inge flounders — one can almost see him blush — between anatomical terms and their four-letter counterparts."[39]

As Inge did in many of his last plays, in his first novel to be published, he opted for language and situations that he thought would appeal to contemporary audiences; and although his character and his story seem truthful, his *storytelling* in *Good Luck, Miss Wyckoff* does not. Inge knew Evelyn Wyckoff every bit as well as he knew himself, but in his desire to make his novelistic debut impressive, he overreached into the realm of the sensational and the phony. It was not long, either, before he realized this. In fact, he was soon to add, as Joey Hansen does in the closing pages of *My Son Is a Splendid Driver*, published only a year later, that after his initial success as a writer he "never could write just for the pleasure and fulfillment of writing, could never resist the frustrating urge to compete, which gave an artifice to my writing, deprived it of truth, and filled it with pretension" (p. 218). Joey/Inge was pretty hard on himself in that judgment, but he wasn't wholly wrong, particularly where many of the late writings are concerned.

INGE HAD placed rather high hopes on *Good Luck, Miss Wyckoff*. On May 15, 1970, he wrote to Helen (again, probably Helen Hafner): "Waiting for a novel to be released is almost as full of anxiety as waiting for an opening night. I can only hope the critics will like it as much as you."[40] His publishers also had high hopes. According to James Knudsen in an article entitled "Last Words: The Novels of William Inge," Atlantic–Little, Brown promoted the book vigorously, buying a full-page ad in *Publisher's Weekly* two months before its publication, then another full-page ad in the *New York Times Book Review* the week of its release. The ads promised a "blockbuster," but after its appearance most of the reviews it received were unfavorable, and it sold only 11,677 hard-back copies, hardly a "blockbuster" figure.[41] Sales were nonetheless good enough that Atlantic–Little, Brown was willing to publish *Driver* the following year. Inge had a third novel, *The Boy*

from the Circus, under way by the time *Wyckoff* was published, but this novel
was to be rejected (by what publisher is not known) before Inge's death, and
it has still not been published.

Whether because of fatigue from near-constant differences with potential
producers of his late plays or from disappointment that *Good Luck, Miss
Wyckoff* had not been a "blockbuster" or from some general combination
of causes, Inge's withdrawal became more pronounced in late 1970. He did
not return to teaching when the winter quarter began at Irvine in early 1971,
and an associate who has requested anonymity believes that his depressions,
fueled by loneliness, liquor, and sedatives, became much more acute at this
time. There had been problems before, the associate notes, but Inge had
bounced back to write after therapy and brief hospitalizations. Now, the
writing began much more slowly. *Driver* was virtually ready for the publisher: it had been started back in the 1950s, and its substance had been finished well before now. But Inge began no new plays, and he worked, when
he worked at all, on *The Boy from the Circus*. Alone except for his maid at
1440 Oriole Drive, Inge began to spend whole days in his bedroom. The
associate claims that Inge paid his maid extra to come to work on Sundays,
just so that he would not be completely alone in the house. Clearly, Inge
needed someone to look after him. And it was into this situation that his
sister Helene came when he invited her.

Helene had lived for better than thirty years with her husband in Nashville, but the relationship had grown increasingly strained, and by late 1970
she decided to accept her brother's offer of hospitality. Whether she knew
exactly what she was getting into cannot be said. Whether Inge invited her
out of sympathy for her situation in Nashville or for his own sense of self-
preservation in Los Angeles also cannot be said. But with or without advance knowledge, Helene soon found, after her arrival in California, that
she was eventually going to be her brother's keeper. That responsibility was
to become increasingly difficult, not because she wasn't willing to love and
care for him, but because he was to become more and more unresponsive
and self-destructive as time passed and, after each brief treatment and hospitalization, he found he had less and less will to write.

The publication of *My Son Is a Splendid Driver* in 1971 was probably not
very heartening to him. Although it was a better novel in every way than
Good Luck, Miss Wyckoff, it attracted significantly less attention. James Knudsen reports that *Driver* received only eight reviews (*Wyckoff* had received
eighteen), over half of which were from review services; and although the
reviews were clearly better for the second novel, there were too few of them.

Driver sold only 7,792 hard-back copies.[42] It was clear that Inge was not going to build a great following for his novels. In a January, 1972, interview with Dennis Brown, Inge reflected on his career since the failure of *A Loss of Roses* in 1959: "I lost my audience, and I haven't been able to get it back."[43] He had just published *Driver*, the last publication of his life, and although he doubtless appreciated remarks about it such as reviewer Robert Cayton's ("It is worthy of a place on the shelf with Inge's best plays"), he seemed to know that his audience would never return.[44]

Two already-written plays—*The Last Pad* and *Caesarian Operations*—drew the interest of producers in 1972. *Pad* had been published in a collection of plays, and it caught the eye of Keith Anderson of the Southwest Theatre Ensemble in Phoenix. He produced it there on March 23, 24, 25, and 26, 1972, and a Los Angeles production, starring Nick Nolte, was in rehearsals for the Contempo Theatre when Inge died in 1973. *Caesarian Operations* was produced with another one-act play (Walt Mandelkern's *The Loft*) at Theatre West in Los Angeles from October 6 through 22, 1972. Inge was pleased about these productions, and he gave Sylvie Drake of the *Los Angeles Star-Times* one of his last interviews when he dropped in to observe a rehearsal of *Caesarian Operations*. Inge told Drake that *Caesarian Operations* was the first satire he'd written. That is not true, however, given the publication of *A Social Event* in *Summer Brave* and *Eleven Short Plays* ten years earlier. Furthermore, the presence among his unpublished manuscripts of such plays as *Bad Breath* and *Margaret's Bed* further dispute his claim. But his tone throughout the interview, at least as presented by Drake, is airy, almost mystical, beginning with her description of him:

> Inge today has an aura of mysticism about him. His manner is monastically quiet. The large and stooping frame is crowned with white and an almost baby face. Teddy-bear eyes of moist light blue, vestigially fringed with flaxen lashes, remain remote and other worldly. Inge sometimes appears not to inhabit them.[45]

During the course of the interview, Inge told Drake that his novels provided "the more personal medium" he had been seeking, and he said that *Driver* was "quite autobiographical." He also said that he had become too claustrophobic to watch plays of pure dialog, that he had been sculpting because it was now hard to write, that he would never "start" a play in New York again, that he had recently become a Roman Catholic, and that as he neared sixty, he felt "a great desire to return to my roots, to Kansas, for my last works. I think I'd like a small town life." After a pause, he added, "I find that I think now only in terms of the eternal," and then, in Drake's words, his "voice trailed off into the distance." Inge's associational remarks—many of which, like his statement of the desire for small-town life, were of dubious sincerity—and his mystical reference to the "eternal" and his voice's trailing "off into the distance" were indications of where Inge seemed to be headed as 1972 neared its close. In less than a year, he would be dead.

His conversion to Catholicism had, in fact, been certified on September 8, 1972, at Helene's urging; the document is now in the Inge Collection. As a devout convert to that faith, Helene must have hoped—rather desperately— that her brother would find some small solace in its teachings. She and Bill had both traveled long roads since their youth in the atmosphere of Maude's anti-Catholicism. As I noted earlier, acquaintances such as Mark Minton reported that during the later California years, Inge had occasionally turned to occultism in search of spiritual respite. Inge's personal library, now part of the Inge Collection, contains works ranging from the occult to Buddhism to the Bible in matters spiritual, but there is little reason to believe that Inge found anything very lasting in any specific spiritual doctrine.

Certain passages in *Driver*, such as the one cited earlier about the prairie sunset (pp. 44–45), and another one, cited below, about the sea at sunset, suggest that Inge saw a kind of infinity in the vastness of nature, a spiritual insight that in such things as the prairie and the sea, all human care is temporal and insignificant. This vision of a somehow benevolent infinity is apparently as close as Inge came to spiritual solace during his last years. *Driver* concludes with Joey/Inge recalling a solitary time at the beach at sunset:

> I sat alone until I forgot time, and gazed at the sea as if hoping to fill my eyes with a vision I'd never forget of a world so vast that human affairs would always seem small by comparison and lose their power to hurt. And once in a while, in life or in art, I still experience this same sublimity. (P. 224)

Helene's Catholicism, if nothing else, at least provided Inge with his epigraph for *Driver*. She had urged him to read *The Imitation of Christ* by Thomas à Kempis, because it had consoled her. He chose these words from that book for the epigraph: "Woe to those who do not know their own misery and woe to those who love this wretched and corruptible life."

Inge near the end of his life. Courtesy of the Kansas Collection, University of Kansas

THINGS GOT worse. The drinking, the pills, the despair. John Connolly described Helene as being "like a nurse" to Inge during the last months, as his self-destructive tendencies quickened.[46] An associate who requested anonymity states that near the end, several psychiatrists told Helene that the only way she could save her brother was to commit him for permanent supervised care, but she promised him that she would never do that. On the other hand, he either would not or could not take the short-term therapy seriously anymore; he would enter the hospital, then, claustrophobic, check himself out a few days later. Helene tried to monitor his medicine, but he had Valium hidden, and he always had free access to alcohol.[47] At some point, he apparently finished *The Boy from the Circus* and sent it off to be considered for publication, but otherwise there were no more attempts to work.

The recollections of many people who were asked to describe Inge the last time they saw him are much the same. Audrey Wood had breakfast with him in April, 1973. Inge was overweight and remote in his conversation. She had to dredge up subjects to keep any conversation going.[48] Somewhat earlier, Inge had decided to return to Wood's management, but although she had accepted his return forgivingly, there was little she or anyone else could do. "He told me he'd been going to a psychoanalyst," Wood recalled in her memoirs, "but he'd decided it was no help, and he'd left the doctor."[49] John Connolly and Mark Minton report a similar remoteness when they last saw Inge; Barbara Baxley recalls that she could tell immediately when she saw him that he was mixing alcohol and pills. Her memory of her last visit to his house in California is especially vivid and sad: he called her into his bedroom to sit on his lap, and he asked her permission to commit suicide. Helene and Jo Ann Kirchmaier were anxiously waiting in the living room, hoping that somehow Baxley could make some difference. It was the last time Baxley spoke to Inge; when she called later from New York, she spoke only to Helene; Inge wouldn't come to the phone.[50]

Inge granted his last interview to Lloyd Steele of the *Los Angeles Free Press* in May, 1973. Steele had been trying to arrange the interview since the Theater West production of *Caesarian Operations* the previous October, but Helene and a few other friends had delayed Steele in order to make sure that his intentions were serious and professional, because the *Free Press* had the reputation of being an "underground" newspaper. Inge himself answered the door at 1440 Oriole Drive after such a long wait that Steele was about to leave. "When the door finally opened," wrote Steele, "Inge stood in his underwear, squinting against the bright morning sun, absolutely pale, absolutely vulnerable."[51]

Later, clothed in a robe "that just barely stretched across his ample stomach," Inge walked to a small chair, in Steele's words, "so slowly that I began to feel anxious for him," and gave an interview that Steele considered most unsatisfactory:

> Each time I asked a question, his eyes would seem to glaze, as if he were adrift on a sea of memories and associations, then he would speak slowly, almost ponderously, waiting for some stubborn thought to leap a synapse in his mind and become an idea.
>
> His answers were, for the most part, not evasive but inadequate, so much so that, at the time, I decided to spare him any embarrassment by not publishing the interview. (P. 18)

But within a few weeks, Inge had committed suicide, and Steele published the interview because "much of what he [Inge] had to say now seems more meaningful, more revealing, and unutterably more sad."

Much of what Inge told Steele has already been referred to in this study; still, drawing some of it together here affords something of the drama Steele saw and heard unfolding before him. Asked if he found it easy to write, Inge said, "I find it impossible to write." Asked why, he said, "Everything. . . . I can't write like I used to. It's a terrible feeling to feel used up" (p. 18). Several typical questions followed about background and career. The answers made it clear that Inge still resented Joshua Logan's ending to *Picnic*, that he was still unwilling to be critical of Elia Kazan, and that he thought *A Loss of Roses* was his best play. Then Inge flared up at the critics who had so deeply hurt him: "They had no right to be so cruel. We don't need critics like John Simon or Robert Brustein. They're frustrated, unsuccessful writers and they're destructive. They destroy theatre" (p. 21).

Asked if he had any close friends, Inge said, "A few. No, not really any close ones." Not even Tennessee Williams? he was asked. "Yes, of course. And I am close to James Herlihy and Bob Anderson. But I don't see any of them very often" (p. 21). Steele then inquired if Inge regretted never having married. "Yes," Inge answered, "It can be terribly lonely. It really can." (When I asked Barbara Baxley what her greatest regret about Inge was, she didn't hesitate: "That we didn't marry.")[52] Steele asked Inge how he saw life, and Inge replied, "It's always been very ugly for me. I can't remember ever feeling otherwise. Even when I was a child." What, Steele inquired, did Inge think the "judgment of history" would be on his work. Inge replied, "Oh, Lord. I've absolutely no idea. The following generation may find some value in my work." Asked if that mattered, Inge concluded, "Very much. More than anything else, I suppose" (p. 22).

WHEN WILLIAM Inge took his exit from this world he did not leave behind a letter or a note. Parts of Steele's interview, however, might suffice for such a final statement. Or had he thought to do so on his last night, Inge might have reached into his manuscript file and pulled out a one-act play called *The Love Death* to leave in a conspicuous place. For if ever a one-act play were a suicide note, that is what *The Love Death* is.

The play has only one character, a suicidal New York City writer named Byron Todd, whom Inge describes as "effete."[53] It begins with Byron's calling his psychiatrist. Byron claims that he is writing a story about a "foolish woman" who wants to kill herself by taking an overdose of sleeping pills, and he tells the psychiatrist that he wants to make the details realistic. How many pills, Byron asks, would do the trick without making the woman vomit the overdose, thus foiling her attempt? Once the unwitting psychiatrist tells Byron exactly what he wants to know, Byron is ready for the series of final phone calls he has planned to the people who have been most influential in his unhappy life. He takes the requisite number of pills and begins to dial.

First, he calls his mother in Dalhart, Texas, who naturally becomes upset at Byron's announcement that he plans to kill himself. He says, "Mama, please, will you just *listen* for once in your life?" Byron tries to explain, even though he says he doesn't expect anyone from Dalhart to understand the enormous difference between that place and New York. Byron tells his mother that there is a conspiracy against him and his writing: "You couldn't be expected to understand the plots and intrigues that any creative person gets unwillingly involved in. . . . No, Mama, it's *not* just the bad reviews I got on my last book. It lies much deeper than that" (p. 2). "You must realize that I'm *not* like most men, in some ways. . . . Remember how you used to taunt me that I wasn't as manly as Brother Gordon? . . . Oh, I know you didn't mean any harm, Mama. We never mean any harm, none of us" (p. 3). Byron tells his mother that he's leaving all his books to the Dalhart City Library. He says: "Maybe the Library Committee there would put them in a special collection and call it the Byron Todd Collection" (p. 4). Byron concludes by saying he does not want to talk to his father, but, he says, "Tell him I forgive him for his neglect of me."

In this first phone call we can see Inge's own relationship with Maude and Luther, his awareness of his sexual difference, his hopeless comparison with his older brother, his despair at the turns that his career as a writer had taken, and his awareness that a special collection bearing his name might bring someone to study his work. But Byron Todd's suicide dialings do not end with calling his mother; he has others he wants to reach out and touch.

Byron next calls a man named Arnold to say goodbye. Arnold lives in Queens, too far away, Byron implies, to arrive in time should he think of trying to prevent Byron's death. Byron wants to tell Arnold that despite the fact that they have some very shallow mutual friends, Byron has always loved Arnold. Byron says that Tony and Gene, two of their men friends, like only to go cruising. Zelma and Rita, two female friends, are "so *butch* . . . they might as well be lumberjacks" (p. 6). In this call we can see Inge's acknowledgment of his homosexuality and something of the revulsion it had caused him to experience about himself.

Byron next calls Florence Harshbarger, his agent, to thank her for all her efforts in his behalf. Byron explains:

> I guess I never did have the real talent. I guess I'm really just a simple, old-fashioned kind of person, and I can't help it if the standards that I hold dear are not taken seriously today. I'm a writer of my time, I suppose. But then, lots of our greatest writers were. Anyway, I know that I'm emotionally and spiritually incapable of writing the lurid trash that passes today for literature. I may be old fashioned, but I still cling to the belief that literature should ennoble men. (P. 7)

There is little to add about the significance of *that* phone call's message if one sees Byron as Inge himself, except to note how easily one might substitute Audrey Wood as the agent's name.

Finally, Byron calls Dwight Parker, a critic. He wants Parker to know that it is not Parker's review of Byron's latest work that is provoking this suicide:

> It was vicious, God knows, but I've a tough enough hide to take it from a man of your caliber, Mr. Parker. . . . My death will not be related in any way to the vicious review you wrote of my book, a review in which you didn't even come to grips with the most *callow* understanding of my characters and their motives, in which you showed only a sophomoric understanding of my most sensitive profundities. . . . I'm proud that you hated my book, Mr. Parker. I'm proud. (P. 9)

Of course, to make such a call at such a time and to claim that it has no relationship at all to the suicide would be laughable were it not so pathetic. That many critics had wounded William Inge as deeply as they had wounded his barely fictional Byron Todd is all too well known. Many names could be substituted for that of Dwight Parker.

After the call to Parker, Byron, now moving slowly, relaxes by the phone. A long silence ensues. As he drifts away, we hear a banging on the locked apartment door, and a child's voice yelling "Crazy faggot!" More silence precedes the curtain.

In 1975, Barbara Loden, who had played Ginny Stamper in *Splendor in the Grass*, directed *The Love Death* and five other one-act plays that Inge had written late in his life and had turned over to Elia Kazan, Loden's husband, for consideration. Performances were at the off-Broadway Billy Munk Theatre, and they received very little attention. However, Inge's long-time admirer and friend, Harold Clurman, who had directed Inge successes (*Bus Stop*) and failures (*Where's Daddy?*), saw the performances and reviewed them sensitively in the *Nation*. "The Love Death," Clurman wrote, "is an open confession of the author's anguish."[54]

WILLIAM INGE entered the Westwood Hospital in Los Angeles for the last time shortly after the first of June, 1973. He had overdosed. Earlier attempts by Barbara Baxley and Tennessee Williams to persuade Helene to commit him for an indefinite period had been unsuccessful, not because Helene did not fear that they were right, but because she had promised not to commit him and she knew how much he dreaded such a measure.[55] She was in a very difficult situation. The downward spiral was only temporarily checked by these brief hospitalizations, and Helene knew it. The threat of overdose was nearly constant; he often stumbled and fell; when he left Westwood it would simply be more of the same.

Inge signed himself out of Westwood on June 5 "against medical advice," as the hastily signed form in the Inge Collection states. It didn't take him long to resume his pattern. His distant long-time friend William Gibson reports Inge's last half-hearted attempt to help himself. Remembering the successful therapy he had received at the Riggs Center in Stockbridge years earlier, Inge called Gibson on June 9 to ask him to see if it might be possible for Inge to return to Riggs. Gibson could tell Inge's voice was "thick with sedation," and he agreed to see what he could do, after first making sure that Inge was not alone. He even called back later that night to tell Inge he was still working on the possibility and that there seemed to be some chance it would work out.[56]

But sometime past midnight, Inge must have decided that there was no hope for him at Riggs, either. In the quiet, he stole out to the garage, made sure that all the doors were firmly closed, and seated himself behind the wheel of the Mercedes-Benz he had once been pleased to buy. Then, summoning his last courage, he rolled down the windows and turned on the ignition.

When Helene found her brother the next morning, he had made his escape from what he called in *Driver* "the confounding present" (p. 221). Alone in the Mercedes, he had again sat, as he had once done at the beach at sunset, until he had "forgot time." Perhaps his dying eyes were again filled with a "vision of a world so vast that human affairs would always seem small by comparison and lose their power to hurt" (p. 224). Elsewhere in *Driver* he had also written: "Death makes us all innocent, and weaves all our private hurts and griefs and wrongs into the fabric of time, and makes them part of eternity" (p. 220).

11 · Epilogue

> *Though nothing can bring back the hour*
> *Of splendor in the grass, of glory in the flower;*
>   *We will grieve not, rather find*
>   *Strength in what remains behind.*
>   —William Wordsworth

In the spring of 1967, William Inge wrote to a graduate student at Fort Hays State University: "The Midwest helped to form me as a person, giving me my background, my storehouse, of subject matter, helping in the creation of my viewpoints and philosophy."[1] He was never more right about himself and the best of his work, even though by the time he wrote that response to my questionnaire, his two most recent Broadway plays (*Natural Affection*, 1963, and *Where's Daddy?* 1966) had not been set in the small-town Midwest. Moreover, in the many plays that he was then writing and would write in the next two or three years, seldom would he make any obvious use of his Kansas background. But in less obvious ways, ways more suited to character and theme than to setting, Inge never did completely abandon either his "background" or his "storehouse of subject matter," for all his work, early and late, is about loneliness, frustration, the complex pain of love, and the failure of the family to ease that pain. All of his work is about loss—the loss of security, the loss of youthful innocence, the loss of promise, the loss of love. And the later plays show another great thematic loss: where the early work shows hope, found through a kind of stoical acceptance of life's circumstances (e.g., Doc's desperate reconciliation with the equally desperate Lola in *Sheba*), the later work shows loss of that hope as well (e.g., Byron Todd's pathetic phone calls before his suicide in *The Love Death*). "Inge

272

Country" was never just the state of Kansas or the midwestern prairies; it was also and almost always a troubled state of mind.

Because he so often dealt with that troubled state of mind, especially as it stemmed from or related to family roles and interactions, Inge was more than a regional writer. Ultimately the themes, characters, and conflicts that are found in his works are universal; they transcend the boundaries of place (usually the rural Midwest) and time (usually the 1920s and 1930s) that he gave them. Place and time, however, provided authentic detail, the necessary trappings for a realistic theater as imagined by a highly conventional playwright such as Inge. Like the novelists and poets of the "Revolt from the Village," who preceded him in American Literature, William Inge showed that rural midwesterners could be as vulnerable to life's upsets as the most committed of city dwellers. Even an isolated prairie village can produce a killer or an artist, a thief or a saint, a dreamer or a builder: whatever possibilities human beings have anywhere else, they have also in the midwestern village. That such an environment is uniformly wholesome and unerringly beneficent was a myth that had been well exposed by such Inge predecessors as Sinclair Lewis, Sherwood Anderson, and Edgar Lee Masters, who was also a native of southeastern Kansas. William Inge, however, was the first American writer to expose that myth in the dramatic genre.

William Inge thus widened Broadway's subject matter. There had assuredly been previous dramas in which small-town settings had played key roles; but before Inge, Broadway had not seen such a consistent portrayal of small midwestern — mostly Kansas — town settings. *Picnic* and *Bus Stop*, the two Inge plays still most widely produced, are specifically set in small Kansas towns. *The Dark at the Top of the Stairs* is set in a small Oklahoma town. *Come Back, Little Sheba* takes place "in one of those semi-respectable neighborhoods in a Midwestern city," a set so limited to that neighborhood that the story could be taking place in a village.[2] *A Loss of Roses* is set in a small Kansas town. William Inge's midwesterners, with their flat, mostly uninflected speech, were perhaps less colorful, less richly eloquent, than his friend Tennessee Williams's southerners, but they showed, as did Williams's southerners, that Sigmund Freud had as much relevance in Independence, Kansas, and Columbus, Mississippi, as he did in Manhattan or Brooklyn. "Freedom, Kansas," is provincial; loneliness and frustration and fear are not.

Inge's friend Harold Clurman, after seeing an off-Broadway production of Inge's *Overnight* in 1974, noted that it was one of a series of Inge's late plays "in a different vein from that of his accredited hits." Nearly all of these late plays, Clurman noted, "take place in a sordid atmosphere" and "reveal the sorrow, pain and protest which were always latent in Inge's spirit but which for awhile he succeeded in tempering." Declaring that for all his success and praise during the 1950s, Inge was still underestimated, Clurman concluded:

> Serious critics thought the early plays too sweet, sentimental, facile. But whatever justification there may have been in such pejorative judgments, they were rarely set in a just perspective. Fault was found with Inge for not measuring up to standards he never set himself.
>
> Inge was the dramatist of the ordinary. He plumbed no great depths, but this limitation does not negate the honesty or genuineness of his endeavor. Inge really knew and felt his people; he was kin to them. His plays provide insight into their childlike bewilderment, for their profound if largely unconscious loneliness. His touch was popular, but never "commercial." His plays reflect a perturbed spirit modestly but nonetheless authentically groping for alleviation from the burdens of our society, particularly as they affect simple or unsophisticated citizens outside our big cities or on their fringes. As such, Inge's plays are perceptive and touching. The narrowness of their scope, their American "provincialism" is in his case an asset rather than a liability. There was very little synthetic in what he had to say; his plays were born of his own distress.[3]

Clurman knew whereof he spoke.

And so, although William Inge will always be legitimately known as America's first authentic midwestern playwright (the label is traceable to Robert Brustein, who was never wrong about everything), he will also be known as a playwright of family conflict, a vein rich and deep not only in American but also in world drama. Like O'Neill, like Williams, Inge often portrayed himself and his family, often detailed how somehow the complex love and interdependent relationship of families fade and fail as youth gives way to mature age. William Inge had to leave his childhood family and his home in Independence, but he never found compensating equivalents in his adult life. As a homosexual during the Eisenhower era, he was, in Robert Patrick's phrase, "an inside outsider" who via analysis understood himself and his upbringing perfectly, and that understanding often informed his art. But that understanding seldom brought him any happiness, even when his art became distinguished and marked his life as special.

William Inge's looks at the past—both society's past and his own—were popular dramas tinged with nostalgia and occasional regret. They portrayed a need for love and a need for the acceptance of life's vicissitudes. Over and over, throughout the five major, durable works of his life, *Sheba, Picnic, Bus Stop, Stairs,* and *Splendor*—Inge said that love is a very complex emotion which takes many forms; that family love is perhaps the most complex yet absolutely necessary of all; and that we all need the courage to accept what life brings us, adapt our lives to life's realities, and proceed to find as much light and love as we can.

Most of what Inge had to say in his small-town dramas of the 1950s and in *My Son Is a Splendid Driver* is said with an eloquent restraint; his repressed characters suffer frustration without profanity, rage without graphic violence, pain without gore. They are obsessed with sex, yet seldom do they take more than a man's shirt off. Perhaps these modesties were functions both of Inge's shyness and the general prudery of the 1950s, but the result is a potent suggestiveness, a subtle power of language that is wholly missing in Inge's later, more explicit, more "liberated" work. Today his major plays, especially *Picnic* and *Bus Stop*, continue to be widely produced, most often by amateur groups in small towns where local standards still insist that a good show exhibit such restraint in language, action, and scene. *Picnic* still plays in "Freedom," and the man who plays Hal is liable to leave his shirt on.[4]

And *Picnic* still plays in New York, in Washington, in Denver, in Los Angeles—all sites of revival runs of that play in recent years. *Come Back, Little Sheba* has had revivals off Broadway in New York. The films of *Bus Stop* and *Splendor in the Grass* were both remade into successful television movies during the 1980s. And the original film versions of all five major works still flicker on late-night and afternoon television screens. Inge could hardly have foreseen the traumas of the 1960s, which would make not only his drama but also the drama of most of his contemporaries no longer popular. He could hardly have been expected to keep turning out hits anyway, any more than any other artist could, in any field. Tastes and times change. But some works establish a certain durability, and now, nearly four decades later, Inge's four successful Broadway plays enjoy productions far from a Broadway that seems no longer able to sustain anything as modest as a domestic drama. And the same is true of many of the plays of Williams,

Miller, and other of Inge's contemporaries. In his last interview, Inge told Lloyd Steele that he hoped the following generation would find "some value" in his work. Inge need not have worried. The sad thing is that by June 10, 1973, he had run out of reasons to think he was any good, and his memories to the contrary could no longer sustain him.

Notes

Acroynyms used in citations throughout the notes:

ACC   Clippings collection of Professor Thomas Fox Averill of Washburn University, Topeka, Kans.
HIC   Helene Inge Connell
HRHRC Harry Ransom Humanities Research Center, University of Texas at Austin
KC   Kansas Collection, Spencer Research Library, University of Kansas, Lawrence
LCI   Luther Claude Inge
VC   Collection of Ralph F. Voss, Tuscaloosa, Ala.
WI   William Inge
WIC   William Inge Collection, Independence Community College, Independence, Kans.

These interviews with individuals are referred to by the person's name only, except when a person gave more than one interview; then the date is added.

Baxley, Barbara, taped in New York City on June 5, 1986, VC
Bigelow, Paul, by telephone on February 4, 1987, notes in VC
Brown, Georgia, and Nora and Stella Steinberger, taped, no date, WIC
Clement, John, and Margaret Clement, taped in Independence, Kans., June 2, 1983, VC
Connell, Helene Inge, taped on August 7, 1981, by Gary Mitchell, WIC
———, taped on September 19, 1981, by Michael Wood, WIC
Connolly, John, taped on September 13, 1981, by Michael Wood, WIC
———, taped in New York City on December 7, 1986, VC
Emert, Tim, taped in Independence, Kans., on June 8, 1983, VC
Faricy, Austin, taped on September 19, 1981, by Michael Wood, WIC
Garfein, Jack, taped on September 15, 1981, by Michael Wood, WIC
Gibson, William, in Independence, Kans., on April 12, 1986, notes in VC

————, by telephone on January 13, 1987, notes in VC
Goheen, Margaret, taped on August 26, 1981, by Michael Wood, WIC
Hafner, Helen, taped on September 14, 1981, by Michael Wood, WIC
Holtzman, Harry, taped on September 15, 1981, by Michael Wood, WIC
Inge, Luther Claude, taped on October 24, 1981, WIC
Inge, William, taped in 1959 by station WYNE, New York
————, taped on April 2, 1964, by Robert Kaplan and James Durbin, in the Living
    Literature series, sponsored by the University of Southern California
Kazan, Elia, taped in 1975 by Tim Emert, WIC
Kirchmaier, Jo Ann, taped on November 2, 1981, WIC
Lawrence, Jerome, conversations with the author in 1986 and 1987
Logan, Joshua, taped on September 14, 1981, by Michael Wood, WIC
Mahan, Joseph, no date, WIC
Mielziner, Jo, taped on March 18, 1975, by Tim Emert, WIC
Minton, Mark, taped in Pittsburg, Kans., on June 7, 1983, VC
Murphy, Franklin, taped in 1975 by Tim Emert, WIC
Sewell, Al, taped on August 27, 1981, by Michael Wood, WIC
Simmons, Hazel Lee, taped on August 29, 1981, WIC
Steinberger, Nora, two interviews taped in 1975 by Tim Emert, WIC
————, taped on August 26, 1981, by Michael Wood, WIC
————, and Stella Steinberger, taped in Independence, Kans., on May 31, 1983, VC
Strawn, Ferrel, taped in 1975 by Tim Emert, WIC
Watts, Loretta, taped in 1975 by Tim Emert, WIC
————, taped on August 27, 1981, by Michael Wood, WIC
Whitehead, Robert, taped on September 16, 1981, by Michael Wood, WIC
Wood, Audrey, taped on March 11, 1975, by Tim Emert, WIC

Chapter 1. Independence

1. Much of my information about Independence and its past comes from conversations with residents and an undated brochure, "Independence Kansas," published
by the Independence Chamber of Commerce. Additional information about the
first night baseball game is from Si Burick, "Night Ball: MacPhail's Gift to Majors,"
Sporting News, July 8, 1985, pp. 11, 39.

2. Details about the births of Inge's parents are on genealogical sheets prepared
by Luther Claude Inge, the playwright's nephew, from assorted family records. Copies
of these sheets are in WIC. I should point out here that Luther Claude Inge prefers
to use his middle initial rather than his middle name; however, I use his middle name
consistently here to avoid possible confusion with his father and grandfather, both
also named Luther. Several sources mention the unsubstantiated relationship be-
teen Maude Sarah Gibson Inge and the Booth family: e.g., Jean Gould, *Modern
American Playwrights* (New York: Dodd, Mead & Co., 1966), p. 264. Gould also reports that Maude Sarah was probably named after the two great actresses Maude
Adams and Sarah Bernhardt, but that is impossible in the case of Adams, who was
born in 1872, the year after Maude Sarah Gibson was born. Gould does not give

a source; perhaps it was Inge himself. The Booth name may have been entirely coincidental, but the claim of at least a possible relationship to the famous acting family seems to have been one of long duration within the family. Helene Inge Connell, the playwright's sister, also mentions it in a taped interview with Michael Wood. For details regarding the Gibson and Inge family businesses and Luther Clayton Inge's young attitudes, I am indebted to taped interviews in WIC (with Joseph Mahan, the playwright's brother-in-law, and LCI), as well as William Inge's autobiographical novel, *My Son Is a Splendid Driver* (Boston, Mass.: Little, Brown & Co., 1971), pp. 6–7 (hereafter cited as *Driver*).

3. Physical descriptions of Luther and Maude Inge come from an interview with Nora and Stella Steinberger, long-time next-door neighbors to the Inges in Independence. Luther and Maude's wedding and Lucy Helen's and Luther, Jr.'s, birth information are from the genealogical sheets compiled by LCI that are in WIC.

4. Information about the Inge family's move from Garden City to Independence on July 4, 1899, is from a letter that LCI wrote to me on May 11, 1987.

5. *Driver* is an artistic memoir that Inge, in an author's note, claimed to be fiction. However, his sister Helene confirmed the biographical accuracy of many details in written responses to me (September 6, 1974, and June 30, 1975). Moreover, Inge's nephew Luther Claude claims that *Driver* is the "nearest" thing he's seen to an Inge autobiography. Referring to remembered family members and events, LCI says that in *Driver*, Inge "clicks 'em off down the line" (taped interview). As will be seen, copious known details of Inge's life occur in significant, formative ways in *Driver*, making it, if not his actual autobiography, then the autobiography of his sensibility.

6. Luther Clayton Inge's limited times at home are described in *Driver*, p. 5. In several interviews during his lifetime, Inge referred to his father's frequent and protracted absence. E.g., Inge told Gilbert Millstein, "I found my father a man who was never there" ("The Dark at the Top of William Inge," *Esquire*, [August, 1958], 62).

7. That the Inges stayed together primarily for the sake of their children and appearances is implicit in *Driver* and is explicit in the recollections of such contemporaries as their son-in-law, Joseph Mahan (interview). Information about Irene Inge's birth and death is from LCI's genealogical sheets, WIC. Maude's calling Luther, Jr., "Boy" to distinguish his name from his father's is told by HIC (interview, September 19, 1981). Michael Wood later used this and several other interviews now in the WIC to help compose an excellent slide/film tribute, *William Inge: From Penn Avenue to Broadway* (1982), copy in WIC.

8. Information about the births of Helene and William is from LCI's genealogical sheets, WIC.

9. That William Inge was christened "Billy" is reported by HIC, interview, September 19, 1981.

10. Ibid. These remarks are also on p. 3 of the script for Michael Wood's *William Inge: Penn Avenue to Broadway*, WIC.

11. HIC reports the incident of Billy's head being trapped in the banister in a letter to Nora Steinberger (February 2, 1974) in WIC. HIC remembers that the sawed banister was never repaired. "It may still be 'loose,'" she wrote.

12. Inge, *Driver*, pp. 16–22. The issue of a man's not putting the seat down after standing to use the toilet was apparently hotly contested in the Inge home. Years

later, in *Picnic*, Inge's second Broadway play, Flo Owens finds Hal Carter's failure to put the toilet seat down yet another indication that the handsome drifter is no good (*Picnic*, in *Four Plays by William Inge* [New York: Random House, 1958], p. 104).

13. HIC interview, September 19, 1981; also p. 1 of "Memories of Happier Times," a brief typewritten memoir by HIC, in WIC.

14. HIC, "Memories of Happier Times," p. 1.

15. Millstein, "Dark at the Top of William Inge," p. 62.

16. References to the great wealth in Independence during the two decades prior to the Great Depression abound. Numerous residents allude to this wealth, as do several newspaper articles: e.g., Bennett F. Waxse, "Kansas Youth of William Inge," *Kansas City Times*, November 19, 1955; and "William Inge: A Short Biography," *Neodesha* (Kans.) *Daily*, April 4, 1975, clippings in WIC.

17. Interview with Tim Emert, an Independence attorney who is active in community theater and Inge Festival organization. Margaret Goheen, retired chairperson of Humanities at Independence Community College and also director of the annual Inge Festival, recalls the laughter the "Sinclair story" provoked when a roadshow company performed *The Dark at the Top of the Stairs* in Independence (Margaret Goheen interview).

18. Emert interview.

19. The courtship and elopement of Luther Boy and Marguerite Leppelman are described in *Driver*, pp. 78–84. The death of Luther Boy is also described in *Driver*, pp. 107–108. HIC has confirmed that the death of Julian (Jule) Hansen in *Driver* is exactly like the death of Luther Boy Inge (letter to me, June 30, 1975). LCI's birthdate is given on the genealogical sheets that he compiled in WIC.

20. HIC interview, September 19, 1981.

21. The named photographs are now part of Inge's personal collection of photographs in WIC. Also among Inge's sketches of film and stage stars in the WIC are quite good likenesses of Bette Davis, Basil Rathbone, Sonja Henie, Joan Crawford, Marlene Dietrich, Agnes Morehead, Tallulah Bankhead, Greta Garbo, Paul Muni, and George Arliss.

22. The profound influence of this third-grade recitation is noted in several Inge biographical sources: e.g., Robert Baird Shuman, *William Inge* (New York: Twayne, 1965), pp. 18–19; and Millstein, "Dark at the Top of William Inge," p. 63.

23. HIC interview, September 19, 1981.

24. John Gibson's interest in Billy's performing capabilities is mentioned in several sources: e.g., Gould, *Modern American Playwrights*, p. 264.

25. Lloyd Steele, "William Inge: The Last Interview," *Los Angeles Free Press*, June 22, 1973, p. 19.

26. Information about Billy's barn theater and other youthful neighborhood memories comes from my interview with Nora and Stella Steinberger and three taped interviews with Nora Steinberger in WIC: two by Tim Emert (1975) and one by Michael Wood (August 26, 1981).

27. Al Sewell interview.

28. John Clement interview.

29. Nora Steinberger interview, August 26, 1981.

30. William Inge, *Farther off from Heaven*, unpublished ms., HRHRC, act 3, pp.

9–10 (each act has separate pagination). This play was produced by Margo Jones in Dallas, Tex., in 1947. Inge later reworked it into *The Dark at the Top of the Stairs.*

31. For this composite picture of Inge's high-school activities I am indebted to many sources, including John and Margaret Clement, who were one and two years behind Inge in school respectively (interview); one-time Inge neighbors Nora and Stella Steinberger (interview); Inge's long-time Independence friend Loretta Watts (interview, August 27, 1981); Independence High School yearbooks from Inge's years of attendance (WIC); and others.

32. Margaret Goheen, p. 2 of a transcript of "William Motter Inge," February 26, 1980, one of a series of programs called "Six Kansas Writers: In Place," sponsored by the Kansas Committee for the Humanities. I thank Professor Thomas Fox Averill of Washburn University, Topeka, Kans., for a copy of this transcript.

33. Wilma Schweitzer, "Anna Ingleman Could Foresee Bright Stage Futures for Such Stars as Vivian Vance and William Inge," *Independence Daily Reporter*, January 29, 1956, clipping in the WIC.

34. Bette Jane Metzler, "Hometown Kansans Feel They Are on Broadway," *Wichita* (Kans.) *Eagle*, May 28, 1953, ACC. I thank Professor Averill for providing me with a copy of his clippings collection.

35. Numerous high-school acquaintances of Inge's have remarked to various interviewers about his being good-looking and popular but not dating very often. The Steinberger sisters and the Clements (previously cited interviews) also mention individuals—Fred Sheldon, Freddie Wilhelm, and Al Sewell—who at various times seemed good friends of Billy's; but these friendships, as will be seen below, were based more upon a single shared interest, such as tennis or drama, than upon similarity of personality. Inge's lifelong lack of enthusiasm for driving may have been a result of his unwillingness in his youth to be compared to Luther Boy, who had been a skillful driver and was often praised by Maude for having been so. Comparison with Luther Boy—who lived and behaved in ways that Inge never would have—must have been significant in Inge's life, who titled his final autobiographical novel from a remark that Maude once made about Luther Boy: *My Son Is a Splendid Driver.* Passages in *Driver* that are relevant to Luther Boy's driving and Inge's reluctance to be compared to him are on pp. 43–44 and 115–119.

36. Tom Snyder, one-time administrator at Independence Community College and one of the founders of the WIC, mentions that Helene told him about this incident on a tape collected by Gary Mitchell of Independence on August 7, 1981.

37. Margaret Clement interview.

38. Nora and Stella Steinberger and Georgia Brown, interview.

39. Al Sewell interview.

40. WI to Freddie Wilhelm, July 1929, WIC. That Donald F. Duncan, Sr., introduced the Yo-Yo in the U.S. in 1929 is reported by David Owen, "Where Toys Come From," *Atlantic*, October, 1986, p. 69.

41. Loretta Watts remembers Maude's dedication to writing letters and the card-table correspondence setup in the Inge living room (interview, August 27, 1981).

42. WI to Wilhelm, July 16, 1929, WIC.

43. WI to Wilhelm, August 14, 1929, WIC.

44. LCI interview.

45. Loretta Watts interview, August 27, 1981.

46. William Inge, "Departure," unpublished ms., WIC, p. 2. Immediate subsequent references to this manuscript are given parenthetically in the text.

47. Either youthful drownings in the nearby Verdigris and Elk rivers occurred with some frequency during Inge's boyhood or Maude had a special fear of her children's drowning and constantly cautioned them, or both; in any case, several of Inge's works depict or refer to river drownings or near-drownings (e.g., *Splendor in the Grass* and *The Boy in the Basement*). When Independence celebrated its centennial in 1970, Inge read a statement for a commemorative phonograph record in which he referred to an "old wives' tale that the Indians had left a curse on the river, that it would take one life a year in vengeance on the white man for having usurped the land." This statement appears in its entirety not only on the commemorative record, which is in the WIC, but also in several transcripts, including "William Motter Inge," the transcript of "Six Kansas Writers: In Place."

48. LCI recalls his Aunt Helen Mooney's frequent condemnations of Communists and Catholics (interview). Inge used her and her dentist-husband Earl as models for Lottie and Morris Lacey in *The Dark at the Top of the Stairs* and as Aunt Patsy and Uncle Merlin in *Driver*.

Chapter 2. Lawrence

1. Al Sewell interview.

2. Ferrel Strawn, a fraternity brother of Inge's at KU, tells about having shared dishwashing chores with Inge at the fraternity house (interview).

3. Hazel Lee Simmons, who at the time shared a house in Lawrence with Helene, mentions Maude's visits in a taped interview.

4. William Inge, *My Son Is a Splendid Driver* (Boston, Mass.: Little, Brown & Co., 1971), pp. 172–173.

5. I am indebted to Margaret Clement of Independence for her discovery of Inge's art work in the 1932 Independence Junior College yearbook.

6. In 1958, in at least two places, Inge publicly credited psychoanalysis with having been very helpful to him: Gilbert Millstein, "The Dark at the Top of William Inge," *Esquire*, August, 1958, pp. 60–63; and the Foreword to his *Four Plays by William Inge* (New York: Random House, 1958), pp. v–x. Yet by the time *Where's Daddy?* appeared on Broadway in 1966, Inge's "spokesperson" character, Pinky Pinkerton, is relentlessly critical of psychoanalytic "mumbo-jumbo" (*Where's Daddy?* [New York: Random House, 1966], p. 103). And by the time of his last interview, Inge told Lloyd Steele that psychotherapy had helped him "at the time" but that he "would never do it again" ("William Inge: The Last Interview," *Los Angeles Free Press*, June 22, 1973, p. 18).

7. "Inge, William (Motter)," *Current Biography, 1953*, ed. Marjorie Dent Candee (New York: H. W. Wilson Co., 1954), pp. 292–293.

8. Hazel Lee Simmons interview.

9. Franklin Murphy interview and Ferrel Strawn interview. Another KU dramatics associate and former resident of Independence, Richard Peck, shared this same impression of Inge during his KU years with Josephine Murphey: see "Broadway's White Hope," *Nashville Tennessean Magazine*, September 20, 1953, p. 16.

10. *Current Biography, 1953*, p. 293.

11. I am indebted to Professor Gene DeGruson of Pittsburg (Kans.) State University for the information about Inge's *Sour Owl* cartoons at KU in 1932.

12. Robert Baird Shuman, *William Inge* (New York: Twayne, 1965), pp. 13, 20. Shuman's work, which is currently being updated and revised, was published with Inge's cooperation eight years before Inge committed suicide. As such, it was necessarily limited. Nonetheless, it remains the only lengthy published work before my current study and is therefore gratefully acknowledged.

13. Steele, "William Inge: The Last Interview," p. 19.

14. *Current Biography, 1953*, p. 293.

15. Lloyd Steele, "William Inge: The Last Interview," p. 19.

Chapter 3. Nashville, Wichita, and Columbus

1. Josephine Murphey, "Broadway's White Hope," *Nashville Tennessean Magazine*, September 20, 1953, p. 7.

2. Milton Bracker, "Boy Actor to Broadway Author," *New York Times*, March 22, 1953, sec. 2, pp. 1, 3.

3. Gilbert Millstein, "The Dark at the Top of William Inge," *Esquire*, August, 1958, p. 62.

4. Jean Gould, *Modern American Playwrights* (New York: Dodd, Mead & Co., 1966), p. 266.

5. Bracker, "Boy Actor to Broadway Author," p. 3.

6. Inge's resonant voice can be heard especially well on two particular taped interviews in WIC: (1) with station WYNE in New York, sponsored by the New York Board of Education, 1959; and (2) with Robert Kaplan and James Durbin, sponsored by the University of Southern California as part of a series called "Living Literature," April 2, 1964. He may also be heard reading excerpts from *Come Back, Little Sheba* and *Bus Stop* on Caedmon Records, no. TC 1772.

7. Lloyd Steele, "William Inge: The Last Interview," *Los Angeles Free Press*, June 22, 1973, p. 19.

8. Inge's $1,125 teaching contract at Cherokee County Community High School in Columbus, Kans., is in WIC.

9. Shelby Horn, "William Inge: A Year in Columbus," *Little Balkans Review* 1 (Fall, 1980): 60. I am deeply indebted to Horn for this article.

10. WI interview with Robert Kaplan and James Durbin.

11. The date and place of Helene's wedding are on the family genealogical sheets compiled by LCI, WIC.

12. Philip Bayard Clarkson, "The Evolution from Conception to Production in the Dramas of William Inge" (Ph.D. diss., Stanford University, 1963), pp. 16–17.

13. James W. Byrd and Ralph F. Voss, "Bill Inge and the Scholars," *Peabody Reflector* 41 (September–October, 1968): 268.

14. Harry Holtzman interview.

Chapter 4. Columbia

1. Donald Spoto, *The Kindness of Strangers: The Life of Tennessee Williams* (Boston, Mass.: Little, Brown & Co., 1985), pp. 30–40.

2. Joseph Kaye, "Inge of Kansas Put Home Town Characters in His Prize Play," *Kansas City Star*, May 10, 1953, ACC.

3. Webster Schott, "Devious Path to a Career Was Taken by a Mid-Western Teacher of Drama," *Kansas City Star*, November 15, 1950, ACC. Not all reports of Inge's working with Maude Adams are negative. Jean Gould, for example, reports that Inge found the relationship "deeply rewarding" (*Modern American Playwrights* [New York: Dodd, Mead & Co., 1966], p. 267). Perhaps the truth lies somewhere in-between, unless Inge was being ironic in commenting about Adams's "star" personality.

4. Gilbert Millstein, "The Dark at the Top of William Inge," *Esquire*, August, 1958, p. 63.

5. In several interviews Inge claimed to have abandoned acting altogether because he had become too self-conscious and too intellectual; see, for example, Roy Newquist, "William Inge," in *Counterpoint* (New York: Rand McNally & Co., 1964), p. 357; and the interview with Robert Kaplan and James Durbin.

6. "New Play in Manhattan," *Time*, December 16, 1957, p. 42.

7. Gould, *Modern American Playwrights*, p. 267.

8. Austin Faricy interview.

9. Millstein, "Dark at the Top of William Inge," p. 63.

10. Austin Faricy interview.

11. Helen Hafner interview.

12. Austin Faricy interview.

13. Millstein, "Dark at the Top of William Inge," p. 63.

14. William Inge, *The Boy in the Basement*, in *Summer Brave and Eleven Short Plays* (New York: Random House, 1962), p. 177.

15. William Inge, Preface to *Summer Brave and Eleven Short Plays*, p. ix.

16. Digby Diehl, "Interview with William Inge" (1967), in *Behind the Scenes: Theatre and Film Interviews from the Transatlantic Review*, ed. Joseph McCrindle (New York: Holt, Rinehart & Winston, 1971), p. 114.

17. Jo Ann Kirchmaier mentioned how little she saw her uncle at Stephens in a conversation with me at the 1986 William Inge Festival, Independence, Kans., April 14, 1986.

18. William Inge, *Picnic*, in *Four Plays by William Inge* (New York: Random House, 1958), pp. 129–130.

19. Charles E. Burgess, "An American Experience: William Inge in St. Louis, 1943–1949," *Papers in Language and Literature* 12 (Fall, 1976): 443. I am deeply indebted to Burgess for his excellent article, which illuminates this important period of Inge's life.

Chapter 5. St. Louis

1. Charles E. Burgess, "An American Experience: William Inge in St. Louis, 1943–1949," *Papers in Language and Literature* 12 (Fall, 1976): 444–445.

2. Arthur F. McClure, *William Inge: A Bibliography* (New York: Garland, 1982), pp. 14–37. The *Star-Times* pieces in McClure's book are items 109 through 526. Philip Bayard Clarkson's claim of 587 *Star-Times* pieces is on p. 33 of his Ph.D. dissertation, "The Evolution from Conception to Production in the Dramas of William Inge" (Stanford University, 1963). Burgess, following Frances Manley's 1965 Inge bibliography (*American Book Collector*, 16 [October]: 13-21), puts the number at about 425 (p. 449).

3. William Inge, "Forgotten Anger," *Theatre Arts*, February, 1958, p. 68.

4. Jean Gould, "William Inge," in *Modern American Playwrights* (New York: Dodd, Mead & Co., 1966), p. 267.

5. Gilbert Millstein, "The Dark at the Top of William Inge," *Esquire*, August, 1958, p. 63.

6. Tennessee Williams, "Introduction," in William Inge, *The Dark at the Top of the Stairs* (New York: Random House, 1958), p. ix.

7. Donald Spoto, *The Kindness of Strangers: The Life of Tennessee Williams* (Boston: Little, Brown & Co., 1985), p. 10.

8. Patton Lockwood, "The Plays of William Motter Inge: 1948–1960" (Ph.D. diss., Michigan State University, 1962), p. 11.

9. Mike Steen, *A Look at Tennessee Williams* (New York: Hawthorne Books, 1969), p. 96.

10. Spoto, *Kindness of Strangers*, pp. 110–111.

11. Spoto, *Kindness of Strangers*, p. 112. Spoto offers no documentation for his report. In a letter to me (September 30, 1986), Lyle Leverich wrote that the only time Williams "ever mentioned a sexual encounter with Inge was an occasion when Inge and a nameless companion jumped into Tennessee's and Frank Merlo's bed! A *menage a quatre . . . ?* He didn't elaborate." Leverich continued: "It is probably a safe assumption to conclude that Inge and Tennessee concluded more than an interview when they first met in St. Louis. Tennessee did not 'come out' until he was twenty-nine, and that was, he said, 'with a bang'!" Williams was 33 when he and Inge met.

12. Millstein, "Dark at the Top of William Inge," p. 63.

13. Williams, "Introduction," in Inge, *Dark at the Top of the Stairs*, p. ix.

14. Steen, *A Look at Tennessee Williams*, p. 98.

15. William Inge, *Farther off from Heaven*, unpublished ms., HRHRC, Act I, p. 11 (each act is individually paginated); all references to this play are to this manuscript version.

16. HIC, "Memories of Happier Times," brief typewritten memoir, WIC.

17. Digby Diehl, "Interview with William Inge" (1967), in *Behind the Scenes: Theatre and Film Interviews from the Transatlantic Review*, ed. Joseph McCrindle (New York: Holt, Rinehart & Winston, Inc., 1971), p. 113.

18. William Inge, *The Dark at the Top of the Stairs*, in *Four Plays by William Inge*

(New York: Random House, 1958), p. 258; the following references to *Stairs* are to the play as it appears in this volume.

19. William Inge, *My Son Is a Splendid Driver* (Boston, Mass.: Little, Brown & Co., 1971), p. 31.

20. William Inge, *Come Back, Little Sheba*, in *Four Plays by William Inge*, p. 9.

21. Stella Steinberger interview, May 31, 1983.

22. Clarkson, "Evolution from Conception to Production in the Dramas of William Inge," p. 36.

23. Audrey Wood interview.

24. Audrey Wood, with Max Wilk, *Represented by Audrey Wood* (Garden City, N.Y.: Doubleday & Co., 1981), p. 222.

25. Richard Gehman, "Guardian Agent," *Theatre Arts*, July, 1950, p. 21.

26. WI to Margo Jones, November 6 (probably 1946), HRHRC.

27. WI to Jones, November 27, 1946, HRHRC.

28. Jones to WI, April 26, 1947, WIC.

29. Spoto, *Kindness of Strangers*, p. 101.

30. WI to Jones, Wednesday, June, 1947, HRHRC.

31. Clippings in the WIC include laudatory reviews by John Rosenfield (*Dallas Morning News*, June 4, 1947), Clay Bailey (*Dallas Times-Herald*, June 4, 1947), and Nancy Philips (*Austin Statesman*, apparently the same date).

32. Freedley's piece, "Margo Jones' Experimental Theater Opens with Well-Produced Offering," appeared in the *New York Morning Telegraph*, June 6, 1947; Brooks Atkinson's piece, "Theatre in Dallas," appeared in the *New York Times*, August 10, 1947 — both clippings in WIC.

33. Jones to WI, June 14, 1947, HRHRC.

34. The June 13 and 18, 1947, letters from WI to Jones are in HRHRC.

35. The August 9 and 16, 1947, letters from Inge to Jones are in HRHRC.

36. WI to Jones, July 18, 1947, HRHRC.

37. Millstein, "Dark at the Top of William Inge," p. 63.

38. The mentioned articles from the *Galveston Tribune* are part of the extensive clippings collection in WIC. These particular clippings were gathered through the efforts of Margaret Clement of Independence.

39. Millstein, "Dark at the Top of William Inge," p. 63.

40. William Inge, "Spring Holiday," unpublished ms. of a one-act play, WIC.

41. WI to Jones, dated simply May 11, HRHRC. I assume that the letter was written in 1948 because it begins by asking Jones if she knows anything about the production of *Front Porch* in Galveston, which had taken place in late April of that year.

42. Millstein, "Dark at the Top of William Inge," p. 63.

43. The February 17 and May 11, 1948, letters from Inge to Jones are in HRHRC.

44. Josephine Murphey, "The Birth of a Playwright," *Nashville Tennessean Magazine*, September 27, 1953, p. 11.

45. John Simon, "The 'Sheba' of Queens," *New York*, September 9, 1974, p. 67.

46. WI, quoted in the filmscript of Michael Wood's *William Inge: From Penn Avenue to Broadway*, 1982, p. 10, WIC.

47. "Back in Student Role," *Kansas City Times*, September 22, 1955, ACC.

48. Tennessee Williams, *Memoirs* (Garden City, N.Y.: Doubleday & Co., 1975), p. 89.

49. WI to Jones, dated only Friday, HRHRC. This letter, accompanying the first version of *Sheba*, to Jones, was probably written in the fall of 1948.

50. WI to Jones, January 5, 1949, HRHRC.

51. WI to Jones, January 13, 1949, HRHRC.

52. Jones to Laura Wilck, January 15, 1949, WIC.

53. WI to Jones, February 1, 1949, HRHRC. This letter is also the source of the long quotation in the next paragraph.

54. Jones to WI, February 9, 1949, HRHRC.

55. Phyllis Anderson, "Diary of a Production," *Theatre Arts*, November, 1950, p. 58.

56. Ibid.

57. Inge's fears of flying, tightly enclosed places, and heights were known to many of his acquaintances, including John Connolly, his secretary in New York for six years (interview, December 7, 1986).

58. William Gibson telephone interview, January 13, 1987.

59. Wood, *Represented by Audrey Wood*, p. 223.

60. William Gibson, "For Bill Inge," *New York Times*, July 24, 1973, p. 35.

61. WI taped interview with Robert Kaplan and James Durbin, April 2, 1964.

Chapter 6. Connecticut

1. Harry Holtzman's recollections about Inge's first residence in Manhattan are on his taped interview with Michael Wood, September 15, 1981, WIC. Robert Anderson's recollection was shared with me in conversation at the William Inge Festival, Independence, Kans., April 12, 1986. Paul Bigelow's recollections on this point were given in a telephone interview, February 4, 1987. There is also some uncertainty as to whether Inge arrived in New York in June or July, 1949. July seems more likely, for Phyllis Anderson reports in "Diary of a Production" (*Theatre Arts*, November, 1950, p. 58) that the Westport engagement of *Sheba* was not established until July 11, and it is doubtful that Inge would have come to New York until that engagement was definite. Moreover, Josephine Murphey reports that Inge moved to New York in July ("The Birth of a Playwright," *Nashville Tennessean Magazine*, September 27, 1953, p. 11). Still, Inge told Gilbert Millstein ("The Dark at the Top of William Inge," *Esquire*, August, 1958, p. 63) that he made the move in June. Perhaps by 1958, nine years later, he had forgotten exactly which month it was that he moved.

2. Audrey Wood, with Max Wilk, *Represented by Audrey Wood* (Garden City, N.Y.: Doubleday & Co., 1981), pp. 223-224.

3. Anderson, "Diary of a Production," p. 58.

4. Millstein, "Dark at the Top of William Inge," p. 63.

5. Robert Baird Shuman, *William Inge* (New York: Twayne, 1965), p. 45.

6. Bigelow interview.

7. Ibid.

8. Anderson, "Diary of a Production," p. 58.

9. Bigelow interview. Audrey Wood also reports Bigelow's laundry stratagem in her memoirs, p. 227.

10. Bigelow interview.

11. Marion Boone, "Alumnus of K.U. Dramatics Hits Broadway with a Play," *Kansas City Star*, February 26, 1950, ACC.

12. Richard Watts, Jr., "The Man, the Dog, and the Bottle," *New York Post*, February 16, 1950, WIC.

13. Arthur Pollock, "'Sheba': A Kindly Look at an Unhappy Marriage," *Daily Compass*, February 16, 1950, WIC.

14. Harold Clurman, *Lies Like Truth* (New York: Macmillan & Co., 1958), pp. 59–60.

15. I am grateful to Paul Bigelow for pointing out that while the Theatre Guild's net profit on *Sheba* was rather modest, Inge did very well because his recompense came as a percentage of *Sheba*'s gross earnings (interview).

16. Inge's shuttling between Manhattan and Greenwich at this time is indicated by information in newspaper interviews of the time and the return addresses on mail he sent at the time. A letter to Grace Crocker of Independence, dated January 24, is on stationery from the Homestead (probably the name of the sanitarium in Greenwich), WIC. A *Kansas City Star* interview of February 26, 1950, places him in an apartment near Radio City Music Hall on Fifty-second Street, but another interview in the same paper on November 15, 1950, places him in a "quiet guest home in Greenwich"–both articles in WIC.

17. *Sheba*'s awards are mentioned in many sources, but they are summarized here based on Phyllis Anderson's "Diary of a Production," p. 59, and on Philip Bayard Clarkson's dissertation, "The Evolution from Conception to Production in the Dramas of William Inge" (Stanford University, 1963), p. 55.

18. The $150,000 figure for the sale of the movie rights to *Sheba* is given in a "Twenty-Five Years Ago" item in the *Independence* (Kans.) *Daily Reporter* of July 14, 1975, WIC, which cites Maude as the source of the figure.

19. Roy Newquist, "William Inge," in *Counterpoint* (New York: Rand McNally & Co., 1964), p. 361.

20. William Inge, "The Schizophrenic Wonder," *Theatre Arts*, May, 1950, pp. 22–23.

21. Wolcott Gibbs, "The Dream and the Dog," *New Yorker*, February 25, 1950, p. 67.

22. William Inge, "Concerning Labels," *New York Times*, July 23, 1950, sec. 2, p. 1.

23. Josephine Murphey, "The Birth of a Playwright," *Nashville Tennessean Magazine*, September 27, 1953, p. 11. Several other sources mention that Inge moved into a small apartment in the Dakota first, then moved into a larger apartment in the same building later, after *Picnic* had opened on Broadway.

24. Inge's love of long walks in Manhattan's midtown area was commented on in some detail in an interview with his close friend from the New York years, Barbara Baxley.

Chapter 7. The Dakota

1. William Inge, "'Picnic': Of Women," *New York Times*, February 15, 1953, sec. 2, p. 3

2. William Inge, "'Picnic': From 'Front Porch' to Broadway," *Theatre Arts*, April, 1954, p. 33.

3. Robert Whitehead interview.

4. Jo Mielziner interview.

5. Jack Garfein interview.

6. Mark Barron, "Some Kansans Attend Hit Play of William Inge for a Few Pins," *Kansas City Star*, March 22, 1950, ACC.

7. William Inge, "One Man's Experience in Living," *New York Times*, July 27, 1958, sec. 2, p. 1.

8. WI to Grace Crocker, January 24 (no year given), WIC. The reference in this letter to "a new play" suggests that the success of *Sheba* was already established. Thus the year is probably 1951, or 1952 at the latest, because *Picnic* went to Broadway in early 1953.

9. WI to Margo Jones, March 9, 1951, HRHRC.

10. Mike Steen, "William Inge," in *A Look at Tennessee Williams* (New York: Hawthorne Books, 1969), p. 102.

11. Audrey Wood, with Max Wilk, *Represented by Audrey Wood* (Garden City, N.Y.: Doubleday & Co., 1981), p. 228.

12. Jo Ann Kirchmaier mentions that George Faricy worked for her uncle at one time (interview). Robert Anderson refers to Faricy as Inge's "companion" in a letter to me (April 16, 1986), and he remembered Faricy's hat making in a conversation with me at the William Inge Festival, Independence, Kans., on April 6, 1987.

13. Inge, "'Picnic': Of Women," p. 3. This article appeared four days before *Picnic*'s premiere on Broadway.

14. Inge, "'Picnic': From 'Front Porch' to Broadway," p. 33.

15. Joshua Logan, *Josh* (New York: Delacorte Press, 1976), p. 276.

16. William Inge, Preface and title page to *Summer Brave and Eleven Short Plays* (New York: Random House, 1962), pp. 1, ix.

17. Eileen Heckart shared her recollections about reading for the part of Rosemary with a luncheon audience at the 1986 William Inge Festival at Independence, Kans., on April 14, 1986.

18. Wood, *Represented by Audrey Wood*, p. 229.

19. Harold Clurman mentions his early knowledge about the script changes in *Picnic* and criticizes Logan's manipulations of Inge's intentions in his "Theater" column in the *Nation*, March 7, 1953, p. 213.

20. Inge, "'Picnic': Of Women," p. 3.

21. Josephine Murphey, "The Birth of a Playwright," *Nashville Tennessean Magazine*, September 27, 1953, p. 12.

22. Brooks Atkinson, "At the Theatre," *New York Times*, February 20, 1953, p. 14.

23. John McClain, "A Fine Blend of Many Talents," *New York Journal-American*, February 20, 1953, in *New York Theatre Critics' Reviews*, vol. 14 (New York: Critics' Theatre Reviews, Inc., 1953), p. 348.

24. Clurman, "Theater," p. 213.

25. George Jean Nathan, "The Show and the Play," *New York Journal-American*, March 8, 1953, p. 20-L.

26. George Jean Nathan, "George Jean Nathan's Monthly Critical Review," *Theatre Arts*, May, 1953, p. 15.

27. Margo Jones to WI, March 26, 1953, HRHRC.

28. William Inge, Foreword to *Four Plays by William Inge* (New York: Random House, 1958), pp. ix-x.

29. Logan, *Josh*, p. 285.

30. WI to Maude Inge, November 14 (probably 1953 or 1954), WIC. The $350,000 figure for the film rights to *Picnic* comes from an unsigned article, "William 'Bill' Inge Completes New Play," *Independence Reporter*, December 20, 1954, WIC.

31. In his Preface to *Summer Brave and Eleven Short Plays*, p. ix, Inge states that all but one of the one-act plays in that volume were written during the early 1950s. Some of them were published separately in the late 1950s: "The Mall" in the January, 1959, issue of *Esquire*, and "The Tiny Closet" in Margaret Mayorga's edition of *The Best Short Plays: 1958–1959* (Boston, Mass.: Beacon Press, 1959).

32. "William Inge's Play Wins Pulitzer Prize," *Independence Daily Reporter*, May 5, 1953, p. 1.

33. Gilbert Millstein, "The Dark at the Top of William Inge," *Esquire*, August, 1958, p. 62. There is some discrepancy regarding the number of trips that Inge made to Independence during his first four or five years in New York. E.g., Inge implies in a letter to Margo Jones dated November 4, 1954 (in WIC), that before a very recent visit there, he had not been home for five years. This is at variance with Millstein. The only certain thing is that any such trips were few and were very difficult for him to make.

34. WI to Maude Inge, November 14 (probably 1953 or 1954), WIC.

35. Bette Jane Metzler, "Hometown Kansans Feel They Are on Broadway," *Wichita Eagle*, May 28, 1953, ACC.

36. Wieder David Sievers, *Freud on Broadway* (New York: Hermitage House, 1955), p. 256.

37. Roy Newquist, "William Inge," in *Counterpoint* (New York: Rand McNally & Co., 1964), p. 362.

38. Inge, Preface to *Summer Brave and Eleven Short Plays*, pp. ix–x.

39. William Inge, *The Rainy Afternoon*, in *Summer Brave and Eleven Short Plays*, p. 243. Subsequent references to this and other one-act plays in this volume are given parenthetically in the text.

40. Inge, "One Man's Experience in Living," *New York Times*, p. 1.

41. In a letter dated May 11, 1987, Luther Claude Inge told me about his uncertainty in regard to his uncle's attendance at Luther Clayton Inge's funeral service. The relevant passage about Joey Hansen's missing his father's funeral is in *My Son Is a Splendid Driver* (Boston, Mass.: Little, Brown & Co., 1971), pp. 198–200.

42. WI to Margo Jones, November 4, 1954, HRHRC.

43. Digby Diehl, "Interview with William Inge" (1967), in *Behind the Scenes: Theatre and Film Interviews from the Transatlantic Review*, ed. Joseph McCrindle (New York: Holt, Rinehart & Winston, Inc., 1971), p. 111.

44. Tennessee Williams, *Memoirs* (Garden City, N.Y.: Doubleday & Co., 1975), p. 165.

45. Donald Spoto, *The Kindness of Strangers: The Life of Tennessee Williams* (Boston Mass.: Little, Brown & Co., 1985), p. 225.

46. Williams, *Memoirs*, p. 225.

47. Barbara Baxley interview.

48. Diehl, "Interview with William Inge," p. 114.

49. Robert Whitehead interview.

50. Newquist, "William Inge," p. 362.

51. Whitehead interview.

52. Walter Kerr, "Theater: 'Bus Stop,'" *New York Herald-Tribune*, March 3, 1955, in *New York Theatre Critics' Reviews*, vol. 16 (New York: Critics' Theatre Reviews, Inc., 1955), p. 346.

53. Richard Watts, Jr., "William Inge Achieves It Again," *New York Post*, March 3, 1955; also in *New York Theatre Critics' Reviews*, vol. 16 (1955), p. 347.

54. Brooks Atkinson, "Theatre: 'Bus Stop,'" *New York Times*, March 3, 1955; also in *New York Theatre Critics' Reviews*, vol. 16 (1955), p. 346.

55. Wolcott Gibbs, "Inge, Ibsen, and Some Bright Children," *New Yorker*, March 12, 1955, p. 64.

56. Robert Hatch, "Theater," *Nation*, March 19, 1955, p. 245.

57. Bob Donaldson, "Stars of Film 'Picnic' Arrive in Kansas," *Wichita Eagle*, May 16, 1955, WIC.

58. Jo Mielziner interview.

59. Bob Donaldson, "Rain and Hail Rip Decorations for Scenes in Movie, 'Picnic,'" *Wichita Eagle*, May 24, 1955, WIC.

60. Joshua Logan interview.

61. Keith Noll, "Home Town Looks Very Good to Playwright William Inge," *Independence Reporter*, April 15, 1955, ACC.

62. WI to John Gassner, from Palm Beach, Fla., April 2, 1955, HRHRC.

63. Barbara Baxley interview.

64. Ibid.

65. Ned Rorem, *The New York Diary of Ned Rorem* (New York: George Braziller, 1967), p. 145.

66. Millstein, "Dark at the Top of William Inge," p. 62.

67. Baxley interview.

68. Audrey Wood interview.

69. Millstein, "Dark at the Top of William Inge," p. 62.

70. The serene acceptance of life based on understanding and forgiveness is the principal message of the two concluding chapters and the epilog of *Driver* (pp. 209–224). Not incidentally, it is also a primary theme in *Sheba*, *Stairs*, *A Loss of Roses*, *Splendor in the Grass*, and a host of other works by Inge, both published and unpublished.

71. Baxley interview.

72. Jo Ann Kirchmaier interview.

73. Inge referred to Marilyn Monroe as "an old acquaintance" in "Defector," *Newsweek*, May 14, 1962, p. 110.

74. "Margo Jones, Founder of Theatre '55 Passes," *Dallas* (Tex.) *Morning News*, July 25, 1955, p. 1.

75. "Inge Hints at Job with University," *Daily Kansan*, September 22, 1955, WIC. Former chancellor Franklin Murphy recalled the attempts to interest Inge in joining the faculty of Kansas University (interview).

76. "Inge Returns to N.Y.C. after Illness Hits Here," *Lawrence Journal-World*, October 25, 1955, ACC. The article also mentions the planned reception at the Craftons'

home and the university's distinguished-service citation, which I refer to at the end of the paragraph.

77. Kirchmaier interview.

78. William Gibson interview, April 12, 1986.

79. John Connolly interview, December 7, 1986.

80. The legal attempt to block the film release of *Bus Stop* was reported in the *New York Times*, "'Bus Stop' Halt Asked," July 18, 1956, p. 22. The settlement was reported in "'Bus Stop' Suit Settled," ibid., August 8, 1956, p. 29.

81. The location of Inge's Stockbridge apartment was given by John Connolly (interview, December 7, 1986).

82. Baxley interview.

83. WI to John Gassner, April 28, 1957, HRHRC.

84. Elia Kazan interview.

85. Max de Schauensee, "The Living Theater: New William Inge Drama Opens on Walnut Stage," *Philadelphia Evening Bulletin*, November 26, 1957, p. 24.

86. Kazan interview. That critics in the earlier tryout cities of Boston and New Haven liked *Stairs* is reported by Maurice Zolotow in "Playwright on the Eve," *New York Times*, November 22, 1959, sec. 2, p. 3.

87. William Inge, "Culled from an Author's Past," *New York Times*, December 1, 1957, sec. 2, pp. 1–3.

88. Baxley interview.

89. Brooks Atkinson, "The Theatre: Illuminations by Inge," *New York Times*, December 6, 1957, p. 38.

90. Walter Kerr, "First Night Report / Walter Kerr's Review: 'The Dark at the Top of the Stairs,'" *New York Herald-Tribune*, December 6, 1957; also in *New York Theatre Critics' Reviews*, vol. 18 (New York: Critics' Theatre Reviews, Inc., 1957), p. 161.

91. John McClain, "Inge's Best Play—With Kazan's Aid," *New York Journal-American*, December 6, 1957; also in *New York Theatre Critics' Reviews*, vol. 18 (1957), p. 160.

92. Richard Watts, Jr., "Two on the Aisle: Another Striking Drama by Inge," *New York Post*, December 6, 1957; also in *New York Theatre Critics' Reviews*, vol. 18 (1957), p. 158.

93. Wolcott Gibbs, "The Crowded Stairway," *New Yorker*, December 14, 1957, p. 83.

94. Patrick Dennis, "A Literate Soap Opera," *New Republic*, December 30, 1957, p. 21.

95. "New Play in Manhattan," *Time*, December 16, 1957, p. 42.

96. Millstein, "Dark at the Top of William Inge," p. 61.

97. Connolly interview, December 7, 1986.

Chapter 8. Sutton Place

1. Donald Spoto, *The Kindness of Strangers: The Life of Tennessee Williams* (Boston, Mass.: Little, Brown & Co., 1985), pp. 224–225.

2. Tennessee Williams, "Introduction," in William Inge, *The Dark at the Top of the Stairs* (New York: Random House, 1958), pp. viii–ix.

3. William Gibson interview, April 12, 1986.

4. John Connolly interview, December 7, 1986. Another of Inge's friends, the

playwright Jerome Lawrence, told me in conversations at the Inge Festivals in 1986 and 1987 that Inge continued this "might or might not show" behavior in California.

5. Ned Rorem, *The New York Diary of Ned Rorem* (New York: George Braziller, 1967), p. 145.

6. Ibid., p. 171.

7. Connolly interview, December 7, 1986.

8. In a letter to me dated May 11, 1987, Luther Claude Inge reported that Inge did not attend his mother's funeral services. The lengthy quotation of Joey Hansen's feelings at the funeral parlor are from *My Son Is a Splendid Driver* (Boston, Mass.: Little, Brown & Co., 1971), pp. 219–220.

9. William Inge, Foreword to *Four Plays by William Inge* (New York: Random House, 1958), p. v.

10. Gilbert Millstein, "The Dark at the Top of William Inge," *Esquire*, August, 1958, p. 62.

11. Inge's furnishing of the cover photograph for *Harper's* is mentioned by William Gibson in his tribute after Inge's death, "For Bill Inge," *New York Times*, July 24, 1973, p. 35.

12. Robert Brustein, "The Men-Taming Women of William Inge," *Harper's*, November, 1958, p. 52.

13. Gibson, "For Bill Inge," p. 35.

14. Connolly interview, December 7, 1986.

15. Barbara Baxley interview.

16. William Gibson, "Letters," *Harper's*, January, 1959, p. 4.

17. Mrs. Monroe D. North, "Letters," ibid.

18. Connolly interview, December 7, 1986. Inge also told Gilbert Millstein that the idea for *A Loss of Roses* was conceived on a transcontinental train trip: Gilbert Millstein, "Ten Playwrights Tell How It All Starts," *New York Times Magazine*, December 6, 1959, p. 63.

19. Baxley interview.

20. Jack Balch, "Anatomy of a Failure," *Theatre Arts*, February, 1960, p. 10.

21. Baxley interview.

22. Connolly interview, December 7, 1986.

23. Audrey Wood, with Max Wilk, *Represented by Audrey Wood* (Garden City, N.Y.: Doubleday & Co., 1981), p. 232.

24. Ibid., pp. 232–233.

25. Maurice Zolotow, "Playwright on the Eve," *New York Times*, November 22, 1959, sec. 2, p. 3.

26. A Louella Parsons "Hollywood Highlights" clipping in WIC states that the Fox executive Buddy Adler paid $400,000 for the film rights to *Roses*. Adler is quoted as saying, "Yes, we paid a big price, but Inge writes only hits." The clipping, subtitled "Adler Pays $400,000 for Inge's Play," is from an unidentified newspaper and is neither dated nor paginated. Jack Balch, in "Anatomy of a Failure," reports the $200,000 figure for the film rights to *Roses* (p. 10).

27. Brooks Atkinson, "Theatre: 'A Loss of Roses,'" *New York Times*, November 30, 1959, p. 27.

28. John McClain, "Inge Wilts in His Latest," *New York Journal-American*, Novem-

ber 30, 1959; in *New York Theatre Critics' Reviews*, vol. 20 (New York: Critics' Theatre Reviews, Inc., 1959), p. 213.

29. Richard Watts, Jr., "Two on the Aisle: Everything Didn't Come up Roses," *New York Post*, November 30, 1959; in *New York Theatre Critics' Reviews*, vol. 20 (1959), p. 211.

30. Kenneth Tynan, "Roses and Thorns," *New Yorker*, December 12, 1959, p. 99.

31. Harold Clurman, "Theatre," *Nation*, December 19, 1959, p. 475.

32. Robert Brustein, "Theatre: 'A Loss of Roses,'" *New Republic*, December 21, 1959, p. 23.

33. Balch, "Anatomy of a Failure," p. 10.

34. Bob Thomas, "Inge Knew Play Wasn't Right," *Toledo* (Ohio) *Blade*, February 5, 1960, WIC. Inge's claim that he didn't say *spit* was reported by Dan Sullivan, theater critic for the *Los Angeles Times*, in a presentation entitled "William Inge and the Critics," at the 1987 William Inge Festival, April 6, 1987. Misquoted or not, Inge apparently was fond of the expression; he used the more polite version again in "Defector," *Newsweek*, May 14, 1962, p. 110.

35. William Inge, Foreword to *A Loss of Roses* (New York: Random House, 1960), p. iv.

36. Connolly interview, December 7, 1986.

37. Shirley Knight shared this memory of Inge's visit to the *Stairs* movie set with a luncheon audience at the 1986 William Inge Festival.

38. Inge discussed his adjustments to writing for the screen in William Inge, "New Scenarist's Views," *New York Times*, October 8, 1961, sec. 2, p. 9.

39. "Playwright Bill Inge and Producer Kazan Here for Short Visit," *Independence Reporter*, October 8, 1958, ACC.

40. Connolly interview, December 7, 1986.

41. Philip Bayard Clarkson, "The Evolution from Conception to Production in the Dramas of William Inge" (Ph.D. diss., Stanford University, 1963), p. 173.

42. Connolly interview, December 7, 1986.

43. Dwight Macdonald, "Films: *Splendor in the Grass*," *Esquire*, December, 1961, p. 69.

44. Stanley Kauffmann, "Movies: *Splendor in the Grass*," *New Republic*, October 16, 1961, p. 21.

45. Brendan Gill, "The Current Cinema: Small Towns," *New Yorker*, October 14, 1961, p. 177.

46. "New Films: 'Tall Grass,'" *Newsweek*, October 16, 1961, p. 112.

47. Among the Inge papers in the Billy Rose Theatre Collection of the New York Public Library, Lincoln Center, is a letter from Inge to Cheryl Crawford dated September 14, 1960. He thanks her for her interest in *Natural Affection*, but he tells her that Robert Alan Aurthur will be the producer. Aurthur recalled his meetings with Inge about *Natural Affection* in the tribute that he wrote for *Esquire* after Inge's death: "Hanging Out," *Esquire*, November, 1973, pp. 42ff. He offered vivid recollections of the difficulties that he found in working with Inge on the script of that play, and he gave other detailed examples of Inge's at-times perplexed and perplexing behavior.

48. Murray Schumach, "Inge Sets Limits as Film Scenarist," *New York Times*, August 25, 1961, p. 17. Typically, Inge told Schumach that the money for the adaptation of *All Fall Down* was good, but he didn't say how much.

49. William Inge, Preface to *Summer Brave and Eleven Short Plays* (New York: Random House, 1962), p. ix.

50. Wood, *Represented by Audrey Wood*, pp. 233–235; also Connolly interview, December 7, 1986; and Mark Minton interview. Minton was Inge's secretary after Connolly.

51. D. Newman, "The Agent as Catalyst," *Esquire*, December, 1962, p. 264.

52. John Connolly mentioned that he had seen such changes in Inge's writing on several occasions: see, e.g., the December 7, 1986, interview and the taped interview with Michael Wood, September 13, 1981, now in WIC. The unpublished manuscript, *Bud Dooley's Revenge*, is also in WIC; the quoted lines are on pp. 10 and 44.

53. Whitehead interview.

54. Inge, "Defector," p. 110.

55. Gerald Weales, "In the Grass, Alas," *Reporter*, November 23, 1961, p. 43.

56. All of the mentioned manuscripts are in WIC.

57. Connolly interview, December 7, 1986; also the interview of September 13, 1981.

58. Connolly interview, September 13, 1981.

59. John Connolly's belief that the Academy Award permanently changed Inge is expressed on several occasions, including the interviews of December 7, 1986, and September 13, 1981.

60. In the summer of 1985, this strange note was in a box of as-yet-uncatalogued materials in WIC. The box also included a copy of Inge's death certificate and his hospital release form, signed by Inge himself, from his hospitalization just before his death.

61. Inge, "Defector," p. 110.

62. William Inge, "A Statement," in *Celebrities on the Couch: Personal Adventures of Famous People in Psychoanalysis*, ed. Lucy Freeman (Los Angeles: Price/Sloan/Stern Publishers and Ravenna Books, 1970), pp. 173–174. This book is full of the recollections and comments of celebrities in a variety of fields, many of whom go into great personal detail. But not Inge: he provides only a simple, undetailed, four-sentence "statement."

63. Lloyd Steele, "William Inge: The Last Interview," *Los Angeles Free Press*, June 22, 1973, p. 18.

64. Mark Minton noted Inge's transient, but apparently rather strong, interest in the occult after Inge's move to California (interview). Inge referred to his half-hearted Catholicism in both the Lloyd Steele interview and, as Joey Hansen, in *My Son Is a Splendid Driver*, p. 218.

65. Barbara Baxley interview.

66. Brendan Gill, "The Current Cinema: The Ties That Bind," *New Yorker*, April 21, 1962, p. 170.

67. "Movies: 'True Color,'" *Newsweek*, April 23, 1962, p. 97.

68. Philip T. Hartung, "The Screen: 'Coming Through the Wry,'" *Commonweal*, April 27, 1962, p. 112.

69. Clarkson, "The Evolution from Conception to Production in the Dramas of William Inge," p. 187.

70. Aurthur, "Hanging Out," p. 42.

71. WI to Cheryl Crawford, September 14, 1960, Billy Rose Theatre Collection, New York Public Library at Lincoln Center.

72. WI to John Gassner, October 25, 1960, HRHRC.

73. Robert Whitehead interview.

74. The Phoenix production of *Natural Affection* is referred to by Milton Esterow in "News of the Rialto: Inge's Plans," *New York Times*, June 17, 1962, sec. 2, p. 1. I found no other information about this or the Texas production.

75. William Inge, *Natural Affection* (New York: Random House, 1963), p. 115.

76. Wood, *Represented by Audrey Wood*, p. 234; and Baxley interview.

77. Norman Nadel, review of *Natural Affection*, reproduced from *First Nite*, in *New York Theatre Critics' Reviews*, vol. 24 (New York: Critics' Theatre Reviews, Inc., 1963), p. 383.

78. Robert Coleman, review of *Natural Affection*, reproduced from *First Nite*, also in *New York Theatre Critics' Reviews*, vol. 24 (1963), pp. 384–385.

79. Richard Watts, Jr., review of *Natural Affection*, reproduced from *First Nite*, also in *New York Theatre Critics' Reviews*, vol. 24 (1963), p. 384.

80. John Chapman, review of *Natural Affection*, reproduced from *First Nite*, also in *New York Theatre Critics' Reviews*, vol. 24 (1963), p. 384.

81. Inge, Preface to *Natural Affection*, pp. viii–ix.

82. Edith Oliver, "The Theatre," *New Yorker*, February 9, 1963, p. 66.

83. Robert Brustein, "Theatre," *New Republic*, February 23, 1963, p. 29.

84. "Theater: Natural Affliction," *Newsweek*, February 11, 1963, p. 84.

85. Jo Ann Kirchmaier interview.

86. WI to Kirchmaier, December 15, 1962, WIC.

87. "Inge Will Teach KU Drama Class," *Topeka Capital*, January 2, 1960, ACC.

88. When Inge came to Kansas City in April, 1960, to advise about the local production of *A Loss of Roses*, he was interviewed by Giles M. Fowler of the *Kansas City Star*: "Lament for a Long Chore," April 24, 1960, ACC.

89. Inge refers to his trip to Topeka for the centennial in a letter to Jo Ann Kirchmaier, January 26, 1961, WIC.

90. "Inge Keeps His Plans Very Quiet," *Lawrence Journal-World*, June 21, 1963, ACC.

91. "Inge May Polish TV Effort Here," *Lawrence Journal-World*, June 22, 1963, ACC.

92. "William Inge Buys Farm at Lawrence," *Topeka Journal*, October 8, 1963, ACC.

93. Pat Burnau, "Hinted Return of Bill Inge Revives Old Memories at KU," *Topeka Capital*, October 19, 1963, ACC.

94. WI to Helen Hafner, September 19, 1963, WIC.

95. This picture of Inge's sexual reticence is based on interviews with John Connolly, December 7, 1986; Barbara Baxley; and Mark Minton, as well as the impressions of many others who knew him at various points in his adult life.

96. Schumach, "Inge Sets Limits as Film Scenarist," p. 17.

97. This drastic distortion in *The Stripper* of Inge's original ending of *A Loss of Roses* is criticized as being a typical Hollywood formula by Lionel Godfrey in "The Private World of William Inge," *Films and Filming* 13 (October, 1966): 24.

98. Mark Minton shared the details of his employment with Inge, including Inge's discarding the Librium, in my interview with him on June 7, 1983.

Chapter 9. Hollywood

1. Mark Minton interview.

2. WI to Jo Ann Kirchmaier, May 13, 1965, WIC.

3. "Inge May Polish TV Effort Here," *Lawrence Journal-World*, June 22, 1963, ACC.

4. Peter Bart, "Inventory by Inge," *New York Times*, March 28, 1965, sec. 2, p. 11.

5. Jack Gould, "TV: Inge's 'Out On the Outskirts of Town,'" *New York Times*, November 7, 1964, p. 54. A manuscript version of this drama is in WIC.

6. Murray Schumach, "Inge Sets Limits as Film Scenarist," *New York Times*, August 25, 1961, p. 17.

7. William Inge, Preface to *Summer Brave and Eleven Short Plays* (New York: Random House, 1962), p. x.

8. John Connolly interview, December 7, 1986.

9. Mark Minton interview.

10. Bart, "Inventory by Inge," p. 11.

11. Minton interview.

12. Bart, "Inventory by Inge," p. 11.

13. "Cinema: Hard Day's Knight," *Time*, April 23, 1965, p. 103.

14. Philip T. Hartung, "The Screen," *Commonweal*, April 30, 1965, pp. 192–193.

15. That Inge no longer considered Edward Albee a friend by the mid 1960s I base on a letter that Inge wrote to Ned Rorem on September 15, 1960, in which Inge gives a brief critique of some writing that Rorem had done and encourages Rorem to continue writing. "But don't," he cautioned, "become famous all of a sudden and turn around and write nasty pieces about me like your dirty little friend Edward Albee" (WIC). Albee had apparently said some negative things about Inge in *Harper's*, which had caused Inge to add: "God, what a smug little creature he [Albee] must be, to write as though perfectly assured of his own future prestige."

16. Jerome Lawrence shared these memories of his California friendship with Inge in an informal conversation with me at the 1986 Inge Festival, Independence, Kans., April 12, 1986.

17. Barbara Baxley interview.

18. William Inge, "Introduction," Willem de Kooning Exhibition, March 22 to April 30, 1965, Paul Kantor Gallery, 348 North Camden Drive, Beverly Hills, Calif.

19. William Inge, "Glimpses of Truth: The Paintings of James Gill," for "Recent Paintings by James Gill," November 1-21, 1965, Felix Landau Gallery, 702 North La Cienega Blvd., Los Angeles, Calif.

20. William Inge, *Where's Daddy?* (New York: Random House, 1966); on p. 32, Inge describes Pinky as "a chubby little man in his fifties." Pinky's attitudes about heterosexual love and marriage, family, and his own homosexuality become evident in several of his speeches, but nowhere more significantly than in Pinky's

quoted speech from p. 43. All references to *Where's Daddy?* are to this version of the play.

21. Inge mentioned the Falmouth and Westport schedulings of *Where's Daddy?* which he then was calling *Family Things, Etc.*, in a letter to Jo Ann Kirchmaier, May 13, 1965, WIC.

22. WI to Jerome Lawrence, June 7, 1965, in the Billy Rose Theatre Collection, New York Public Library at Lincoln Center.

23. Robert Whitehead interview.

24. WI to Rorem, February 7, 1966, WIC. Stanley Kauffmann is quoted from his "Homosexual Drama and Its Disguises," *New York Times*, Jan. 23, 1966, sec. 2, p. 1.

25. Stanley Kauffmann, "The Theater: Inge's 'Where's Daddy?'" *New York Times*, March 3, 1966; in *New York Theatre Critics' Reviews*, vol. 27 (New York: Critics' Theatre Reviews, Inc., 1966), p. 348.

26. Walter Kerr, untitled review of *Where's Daddy?* from the *New York Herald-Tribune* of March 3, 1966; also in *New York Theatre Critics' Reviews*, vol. 27, p. 348.

27. Norman Nadel, "It's Hard to Care about Inge and His 'Daddy,'" *New York World-Telegram and Sun*, March 3, 1966; also in *New York Theatre Critics' Reviews*, vol. 27, p. 349.

28. Douglas Watt, "'Where's Daddy?' A Sincere but Blurred Appraisal of Our Youth," *New York Daily News*, March 3, 1966; also in *New York Theatre Critics' Reviews*, vol. 27, p. 350.

29. John McClain, "A Persuasive Inge Comedy," *New York Journal-American*, March 3, 1966; also in *New York Theatre Critics' Reviews*, vol. 27, p. 347.

30. Richard Watts, Jr., "Two on the Aisle: Happy Return of William Inge," *New York Post*, March 3, 1966; also in *New York Theatre Critics' Reviews*, vol. 27, p. 350.

31. John McCarten, "The Theatre," *New Yorker*, March 12, 1966, p. 110.

32. Wilfrid Sheed, "Two for the Hacksaw," *Commonweal*, April 8, 1966, p. 83. In this review, Sheed also pans Tennessee Williams's *Slapstick Tragedy*.

33. "Theater: Nice Kids," *Newsweek*, March 14, 1966, p. 94.

Chapter 10. 1440 Oriole Drive

1. WI to George Oppenheimer, March 8, 1966, in Inge papers at the Billy Rose Theatre Collection, New York Public Library at Lincoln Center.

2. William Inge, "On New York—and a New Play," *New York Herald-Tribune*, February 27, 1966, p. 27.

3. Digby Diehl, "Interview with William Inge" (1967), in *Behind the Scenes: Theatre and Film Interviews from the Transatlantic Review*, ed. Joseph McCrindle (New York: Holt, Rinehart & Winston, Inc., 1971), p. 108.

4. William Inge, *Comeback*, unpublished ms. of a one-act play, p. 3, KC. All subsequent references to this play are to this version.

5. William Inge, *I'm a Star*, in *This Is My Best*, ed. Whit Burnett (Garden City, N.Y.: Doubleday & Co., 1970), p. 134. All subsequent references to this play are to this version.

6. William Inge, *The Call*, in *Two Short Plays by William Inge* (New York: Drama-

tists Play Service, Inc., 1968), p. 5. All subsequent references to this play are to this version.

7. William Inge, *The Killing*, unpublished ms. of a one-act play, p. 13, WIC. All subsequent references to this play are to this version.

8. William Inge, *Caesarian Operations*, unpublished ms. of a one-act play, p. 1, WIC. All subsequent references to this play are to this version, which, at 84 pages, is uncommonly long for a one-act play.

9. Richard Watts, Jr., review of *Natural Affection*, reproduced from *First Nite*, also in *New York Theatre Critics' Reviews*, vol. 24 (New York: Critics' Theatre Reviews, Inc., 1963), p. 384.

10. William Inge, *Bad Breath*, unpublished ms. of a one-act play, p. 3, WIC. Subsequent references to this play are to this version. The other plays mentioned here, with the exception of *A Murder*, are in unpublished manuscript form in WIC. *A Murder* is published in *Two Short Plays by William Inge*. *Midwestern Manic* is published in *The Best Short Plays of 1969*, ed. Stanley Richards (Philadelphia: Chilton Book Co., 1969), pp. 37–77.

11. Jack Garfein interview.

12. Ibid.

13. WI to Ned Rorem, June 2, 1967, WIC.

14. William Inge, *The Last Pad*, unpublished ms. of a play, p. 79, KC. Subsequent references to this play are to this version.

15. Mel Gussow, "Theater: 'The Last Pad,'" *New York Times*, December 8, 1970, p. 61.

16. William Inge, *Overnight*, unpublished ms. of a play, KC. Muriel's suicide attempt occurs on p. 102.

17. Elma Byrne, "Wild and Woolly West Comes Alive in Musical," *Wichita Eagle*, March 30, 1967, p. 13.

18. Robert Alan Aurthur, "Hanging Out," *Esquire*, November, 1973, p. 48.

19. Ibid., p. 52. Barbara Baxley characterized Hollywood wheeler-dealers as "barracudas" in my interview with her.

20. William Inge, *The Lady Gay*, unpublished filmscript, KC. The references to buffalo bones and the growing scarcity of buffalo; cattle drives; and Boot Hill are on pp. 9, 13, and 14, respectively. Subsequent references to this script are to this version.

21. William Inge, Introduction to *The Plains States*, by Evan Jones and the editors of Time-Life Books (New York: Time-Life Books, 1968), p. 6. Subsequent references to this introduction are given parenthetically in the text.

22. William Inge, *My Son Is a Splendid Driver* (Boston, Mass.: Little, Brown & Co., 1971), pp. 44–45.

23. Diehl, "Interview with William Inge," p. 109.

24. Robert Patrick, "The Inside-Outsider." Patrick wrote this paper to present at the 1984 William Inge Festival. When he was unable to attend, it was read by the actress Shirley Knight. I am grateful to Mary Davidson, conference director of that year's festival, for providing me with a copy of Patrick's paper. Knight's reading was recorded and is available in WIC.

25. Baxley interview.

26. Charles E. Burgess, "An American Experience: William Inge in St. Louis, 1943–1949," *Papers in Language and Literature* 12 (Fall, 1976): 442. Burgess, in referring

to Inge's teaching interruptions for "institutional treatment," cites Paul Wagman, "William Inge: Dark at the Bottom of the Stairs," *St. Louis Post-Dispatch*, July 1, 1973. Wagman is also the source of Robert Cohen's remark that Inge was "ripe" for suicide, which follows in the same paragraph.

27. WI to Neil Edds and Margaret Goheen, October 8, 1968, WIC.

28. Margaret Clement interview.

29. WI to Edds and Goheen, October 8, 1968, WIC.

30. That Inge commuted 50 miles to the Irvine campus on Tuesdays and Thursdays is mentioned in his letter of October 8, 1968, to Edds and Goheen, WIC.

31. William Inge, "The Relevance of Theatre," ms. of an unpublished article, p. 1, KC. All subsequent references to this article are to this version.

32. William Inge, carbon copy of a letter to Robert Manning, editor in chief of the *Atlantic Monthly*, July 9, 1969, KC, p. 1. Additional references to this two-page copy appear in this paragraph.

33. Manning to WI, July 21, 1969, KC.

34. Winfred Blevins, "America's Ignored Dramatist," *Los Angeles Herald-Examiner*, November 10, 1968, WIC.

35. Sam Zolotow, "William Inge Helps Turn His Play into a Musical," *New York Times*, November 15, 1968, p. 39.

36. WI to Helen (probably Helen Hafner), September 17, 1970, WIC.

37. William Inge, *Good Luck, Miss Wyckoff* (Boston, Mass.: Little, Brown & Co., 1970), p. 145.

38. William Wordsworth, "Ode: Intimations of Immortality from Recollections of Early Childhood," 180-181, in *The Complete Poetical Works of Wordsworth* (Cambridge, Mass.: Houghton Mifflin Co., 1932), p. 356.

39. Haskel Frankel, review of *Good Luck, Miss Wyckoff*, *New York Times Book Review*, June 14, 1970, p. 24.

40. WI to "Helen" (probably Helen Hafner), May 15, 1970, WIC.

41. James Knudsen, "Last Words: The Novels of William Inge," *Kansas Quarterly* 18 (1986): 122.

42. Ibid., p. 123.

43. Dennis Brown, "Backstage Theater News," *Kansas City Star*, January 23, 1972, p. 2F.

44. Robert Cayton, review of *My Son Is a Splendid Driver*, in *Library Journal Book Review*, 1971, p. 656.

45. Sylvie Drake, "Stage: Johannes Brahms, Please Meet William Inge," *Los Angeles Times*, October 1, 1972, p. 30. Information cited earlier regarding the Phoenix production of *The Last Pad* also comes from this article. Drake's favorable but brief review of *Caesarian Operations* appeared in the *Los Angeles Times* of October 10, 1972, sec. 4, p. 14.

46. John Connolly interview, December 7, 1986.

47. That Inge was hiding Valium is reported by Jo Ann Kirchmaier in her interview.

48. Audrey Wood interview.

49. Audrey Wood, with Max Wilk, *Represented by Audrey Wood* (Garden City, N.Y.: Doubleday & Co., 1981), p. 236.

50. Baxley interview.

51. Lloyd Steele, "William Inge: The Last Interview," *Los Angeles Free Press*, June 22, 1973, p. 18.

52. Baxley interview.

53. William Inge, *The Love Death*, unpublished ms. of a one-act play, p. 1, WIC. All subsequent references to this play are to this version.

54. Harold Clurman, "Theatre," *Nation*, August 30, 1975, p. 157.

55. Tennessee Williams describes his and Barbara Baxley's attempts to persuade Helene to commit Inge in his *Memoirs* (Garden City, N.Y.: Doubleday & Co., 1975), pp. 87–89.

56. William Gibson, "For Bill Inge," *New York Times*, July 24, 1973, p. 35.

Chapter 11. Epilogue

1. WI's response to a questionnaire sent by Ralph F. Voss, April 3, 1967.

2. William Inge, *Come Back, Little Sheba*, in *Four Plays by William Inge* (New York: Random House, 1958), p. 5.

3. Harold Clurman, "Theatre," *Nation*, August 3, 1974, pp. 91–92.

4. A call that I placed on December 28, 1987, to Dramatists Play Service in New York City, the handlers of all amateur performing rights for Inge's major 1950s plays, confirmed that all four plays are frequently performed by amateur groups throughout the parts of the world covered by various relevant copyright agreements. *Picnic* is the leader, followed by *Bus Stop*.

Index